V&R

Refo500 Academic Studies

Edited by
Herman J. Selderhuis

In Co-operation with
Christopher Brown (Boston), Günter Frank (Bretten),
Bruce Gordon (New Haven), Barbara Mahlmann-Bauer (Bern),
Tarald Rasmussen (Oslo), Violet Soen (Leuven),
Zsombor Tóth (Budapest), Günther Wassilowsky (Linz),
Siegrid Westphal (Osnabrück).

Volume 33

Bo Kristian Holm / Nina J. Koefoed (ed.)

Lutheran Theology and the shaping of society: The Danish Monarchy as Example

Vandenhoeck & Ruprecht

With 3 tables, 1 figure, and 6 coloured illustrations

Bibliographic information published by the Deutsche Nationalbibliothek:
The Deutsche Nationalbibliothek lists this publication in the Deutsche Nationalbibliografie; detailed bibliographic data available online: http://dnb.de.

ISSN 2198-3089
ISBN 9783-525-55124-0

Typesetting by 3w+p, Rimpar
Printed and bound by Hubert & Co BuchPartner, Göttingen

Printed in the EU

Contents

Acknowledgments

The work that we present here began as a joint project in the interdisciplinary research group Reformation Theology and Confessional Culture at Aarhus University. All contributors to the book participated in this group either as full time faculty members or as visiting scholars. We, especially, thank our two adjunct professors, Prof. Dr. Theodor Dieter, Strasbourg, and Prof. Dr. Vítor Westhelle, Chicago. Both Prof. Dr. Thomas Kaufmann and Prof. Dr. Hans-Martin Gutmann visited our research group and we are very grateful for their cooperative attitude. We also thank PhD Candace Kohli, who visited the group for two months, both for her participation in the group's work and for her help with the language revision of the texts.

The research group grew rapidly and became an intra-facultary network called LUMEN (Lutheran Mentality and the North Nordic). We deeply appreciate the strategic pool of the rectorate at Aarhus University for generously providing substantial funding to support the network. This funding made it possible to work on the book during a two day seminar in Norsminde, Denmark. We are very pleased that our Swedish colleagues Karin Hassan Jansson, Urban Claesson, and Kajsa Brilkmann accepted our invitation to respond to preliminary versions of the chapters at the Norsminde seminar.

Aarhus University Research Foundation has generously provided financial support for the publication, for which we would like to express our sincerest thanks. PhD-students Mattias Skat Sommer and Leonora Lottrup Rasmussen helped us in the hectic weeks of completing the manuscript for the publisher. Finalizing a book manuscript in 2017 was a challenge. We are grateful to Kasper Lynge Tipsmark for making the indices, and to Dr. Bernhard Kirchmeier of Vandenhoeck & Ruprecht for supporting the finishing of the book.

Finally we would like to thank Director Prof. Dr. Herman Selderhuis and the editorial board of Refo500 Academic Studies for accepting the book in the series.

Bo Kristian Holm Nina Javette Koefoed

October 31, 2017

Acknowledgements

Bo Kristian Holm / Nina Javette Koefoed

Studying the Impact of Lutheranism on Societal Development

An Introduction

The connection between religion and social change has steadily attracted increasing interest in recent years. In some ways, the current research situation resembles the one around 1917 just prior to and following the 400th anniversary of the Reformation. It was the research interests then that formed the background for Weber's famous study on the *Protestant Ethic and the Spirit of Capitalism.*

This book aims to dive into the complex relationship of mutual dependency between confessional forces and societal development with Denmark as a case. The book seeks to offer new insights and perspectives on the difficult question of Lutheranism's impact upon society and mindset by focusing on 1) how core ideas in Lutheran theology can be seen to imply social teachings in various ways, and 2) to what extent social teachings inherent in Lutheran theology form the background for law and social institutions, especially the family household, in the formative period of Danish history between the Reformation and 1800.

By combining historical and theological perspectives, this project aims to offer important new insights into the formative potential of Lutheran theology and contemporary society's dependence on this confessional heritage using the shaping of early-modern Danish society between c. 1500 and c. 1800 as a key entry point. In doing so, the book's perspectives extend the tradition of Weber, Troeltsch, and others from the early twentieth century who began examining the then-contemporary social legacies of specific Protestant confessions. However, this project differs from Weber's approach and those in his wake, by focusing specifically on the Lutheran contribution to societal development. The perspectives garnered from new readings of Lutheran theology will form the backdrop for new detailed studies on the possible impact of the Reformation on everyday life.

The book combines theological, sociological, and historical approaches, using the social relations and obligations of the Lutheran household as a case study, the doctrine of the three orders as a general perspective, and the historical development of Denmark as a treasure chest for illuminating examples. Research into the interrelated historical development of theology and society has often been done in separate academic discourses, and the present studies are an attempt to bridge the apparent gap between disciplines.

1. The Reformation in Denmark

There is no doubt that Lutheranism found particularly fertile soil in the Nordic countries. The two monarchies of Denmark-Norway and Sweden-Finland rapidly ascribed to the Lutheran Reformation. A remarkable number of Scandinavian students sat on the benches of Wittenberg classrooms, listening to lectures by Martin Luther and Philipp Melanchthon. These students brought the new theology back to their local communities and directly implemented these new teachings in their local cultures. This relation between the northern part of Europe and Wittenberg has been subjected to intense scrutiny (See Appel/Fink: 2013; Hasselsteen: 2002; Helk: 1987; Mäkinen: 2006; Lausten: 2010). Societal development in the Scandinavian states was supported by a process of confessionalization, which made the construction of confessional identity a common element in early-modern state building (Ingesman: 2016, 14ff).

In many ways, the Reformation was a process in Denmark. In 1536, the Lutheran Reformation ended a civil war in the country. The question of Lutheranism and religion had been one of the factors defining the power struggle between the king and nobility during the civil war. In 1523, the Lutheran-friendly Christian II fled the country after a failed attempt to regain power over Sweden. Christian II's uncle was crowned as King Frederik I with support from the nobility and the Catholic clergy, but the Lutheran influence proved difficult to abate completely. Christian II continued to play a role as an alternative (Lutheran) king and, in the southern parts of Jutland, Duke Christian (who later became Christian III) attempted a Lutheran reform of the church and legislation within his duchy. Lutheran pastors spread throughout the country during the 1520s. In 1530, Danish churches practiced both Protestantism and Catholicism (Bach-Nielsen: 2012, 118; Grell: 2016a; Holze: 2011, 11–47; Lausten: 1995; Lyby/Grell: 1995).

When Frederik I died in 1533 the Council ("Rigsrådet") was not too keen to choose between the Lutheran Duke Christian and the former King Christian II as Frederik's replacement. Instead, they postponed the election of a new king for a year. In 1534, a civil war broke out between the supporters of these competing leaders. The war ended in August of 1536 when Duke Christian conquered Copenhagen with his army and supporters and became King Christian III. During the following months, Christian III consolidated power through a widespread Lutheran Reformation. The church was excluded from political power, and the Catholic bishops were blamed for postponing the election of a new king and, thereby, for causing the civil war. The new king confiscated the bishops' property and used it to build an economic base of power independent from the nobility. The nobility had been divided by political and religious struggles, both supporting different kings and confessions. As JAKOBSEN shows in his contribution to this volume, the nobility were forced to redefine their role as a new Lutheran authority after 1536, even though Luther's social teaching had not carved out an obvious place for them. Acting as a Lutheran magistrate, the nobility took on new social responsibilities such as caring for the poor and overseeing education. The nobility played a central role in the development of an educated Lutheran elite and was crucial for Wittenberg's religious influence on Denmark (Bach-Nielsen: 2012, 120f; Grell: 2016a; Holze: 2011, 11–47; Lausten: 1995; Lyby/Grell: 1995).

In 1537, a new Church Ordinance redefined and reorganized the church as a Protestant body and also the relationship between church and state. The ordinance was written with assistance from Wittenberg reformer Johannes Bugenhagen and approved by Luther himself. The church ordinance explained the two authorities, God's and the king's. The divine ordinance was governed by unchangeable rules given by God. These matters were defined as:

> The correct preaching of the law and gospel, the correct distribution of the sacraments, proper education of children in order to keep them in faith. And finally, provisions for the men of the church, the schools, and the poor (Rørdam I, 42, VI).

Every human being was required to keep this divine ordinance, which was to be ensured by the king's legislation. At the same time, the king's ordinance could regulate the practical organization of church and society, as long as the divine ordinance was retained. Through the Church Ordinance, Christian III thus positioned himself strongly as a Lutheran king, establishing the ordinance of God as the proclamation of the gospel, administration of the sacraments and pastoral care and excluding the bishops from interference in government and jurisdiction. But Christian III also legitimized himself as legislator, working to ensure that people lived according to the gospel.

The Church Ordinance also clearly defined areas now under the king's jurisdiction. As we have seen, the divine ordinance made the poor the responsibility of the king. Because marriage was no longer sacramental, its regulation became a matter of secular law while the ceremony itself remained a church matter (Rørdam I, 73–74). One result of the explanation of the king's responsibility and legislative power in the Church Ordinance was a legal consolidation of the Reformation. This led to a change in the social inheritance of Luther's theological thinking in the years immediately following 1536 and as an ongoing process over the next two centuries. ARNÓRSDÓTTIR and KOEFOED contend with parts of this legal development in relation to marriage and the household. Arnórsdóttir attaches great importance to the Church Ordinance for establishing a Lutheran legal and social practice of marriage in the Danish kingdom including Iceland.

The Church Ordinance defined Luther's *Small Catechism* as the education guidelines for children. Furthermore, it listed seven books every pastor should own. Besides the Bible, the list named Luther's postils, his *Small Catechism*, and Melanchthon's *Loci Communes* as well as his *Apology*, which included the *Augsburg Confession*. Finally, the Church Ordinance itself supplied guidelines for visitations (Rørdam I, 118–119). The Augsburg Confession functioned as the foundation for the church, but the king was not obligated to ascribe to the Augsburg Confession (cf. Lyby/Grell: 1995). This confessional situation, in which the Augsburg Confession was acknowledged without a binding commitment, allowed confessional disputes between Calvinist leanings and more orthodox Lutherans in the second half of the sixteenth century. However, THOMAS KAUFMANN points out in his essay that these disputes were never as severe in Denmark as in Germany at the time. Kaufmann highlights the role of universities in establishing a Lutheran confessional culture.

Several figures were caught up in these religious disputes with clear political implications. One such figure was a professor of theology at the University of Copenhagen, Niels Hemmingsen, the subject of MATTIAS SKAT SOMMER's and SVEND ANDERSEN's contributions to this volume. As adviser to the king, Hemmingsen played a vital role in legal developments during the late sixteenth century and exemplified the connection between theology and legislation. The two chapters on Hemmingsen in this volume argue for Hemmingsen's central contribution to the development of a confessional culture in Denmark, in which the doctrine of the three estates had a key role. Sommer argues through his reading of Hemmingsen's *Liffsens Vey* that Hemmingsen functioned as an intermediary between Luther's doctrine of the three estates, as key locations for living out the Christian life, and Melanchthon's three uses of the law. Sommer thereby sees Hemmingsen as a central figure in the development of a societal structure built on the three estates, but also for the ensuring Lutheran moral codes and Lutheran culture through law. Through a discussion of the relation between and influence of the two kingdom's doctrine, the doctrine of the three estates, and natural law, Andersen argues that Hemmingsen combined natural law theory and the doctrine of the three estates, leaving out the two kingdom's doctrine.

Another consequence of the confessional situation was that in 1561 Frederik II declined an invitation from German princes to work towards a common confessional understanding, probably in an attempt to avoid further religious disputes in the country. Instead, he urged the writing of a Danish confession, a new church ordinance. The proposal was never published, but reflected the combination of a Lutheran doctrine with Melanchthonian inspiration, which SOMMER isolates as characteristic of Hemmingsen and Danish confessional culture in the period. The fear of unwanted religious influence led to increased control over the belief systems of immigrants moving to the Danish kingdom. The result was the Twenty-five Articles against Foreigners in 1569, which outlined doctrinal standards to which foreigners were required to subscribe. In these Articles, the confession of Augsburg was officially named as the confessional standard for the first time. During the 1570s, Denmark could no longer fully avoid the doctrinal discussions in Germany. Hemmingsen moved towards Calvinism and was finally removed from his university post in 1579, probably for political reasons. When the German confessional controversy was settled in 1577, and the Book of Concord was published in 1580, Frederik II refused to sign it as a means of keeping further discussions out of Denmark. Despite this, the Book of Concord laid the foundation for Lutheran orthodoxy in the seventeenth century (Bach-Nielsen: 2012, 224–229; Lyby/Grell: 1995, 117–123; Grell: 2016b, 89–100; Lockhart: 2004, 317).

The confessional disputes more or less ended in 1615, when Christian IV appointed Hans Poulsen Resen bishop over Zealand. Christian IV reigned from 1588 until 1648. As both confessional culture and legislation show, Christian IV's choice of bishop marked the start of an orthodox development during the first half of the seventeenth century. Luther's *Small Catechism* had a central position in childhood education from the Church Ordinance going forward; Resen published a new translation of Luther's *Small Catechism*, including the table of duties (Appel: 2001, 143–148). In 1629, an ordinance mandated knowledge of Luther's *Small Catechism* as a prerequisite for receiving communion, thus establishing a type of confirmation (Appel: 2001,145). A 1643 treaty emphasized the duty of the pastor to teach the parish the content of the catechism from the pulpit as part of the sermon (Secher, V, 148 [I.1.7]) all pointing towards a strong knowledge of the *Small Catechism* and the table of duties within the Danish population.

A constitutional commitment to the Augsburg Confession came in 1665. In 1660, Lutheran influence culminated in the introduction of absolutism in Denmark and in 1665 the constitutional foundation of absolutism was given shape in the King's Code. The King's Code legitimized and defined the absolute power as the only constitution in Europe. The king was only obliged to keep the territorial unit, the line of inheritance, and finally (or actually first) to keep the Augsburg Confession and make sure the inhabitants of the kingdom did the same. Here the confessional binding and the king's role as legislator were clearly knit together. Part of the Augsburg Confession was a commitment to the Ten Commandments, and they became a central part of legislation during early absolutism in Denmark.

This development became obvious during Christian IV's reign and in some aspects even before. The Church Ordinance established the gospel as the guideline for life within the earthly regime which clearly influenced legislation on e.g. marriage and sexuality as mentioned. This culminated in a large law-codex given in 1683, the Danish Code. To a large extent, the Danish Code summed up the legal developments of the preceding period, but not exclusively. It was the first legislation covering the whole kingdom of Denmark without any distinctions based on region, social background, or gender. Equality before God was translated into equal standing before the king and, thus, the law. The Danish Code was divided into six books. The sixth book on criminal law was structured according to the Ten Commandments and thus regulated society according to them (cf. Tamm 2000). However, the structure of the three first books is interesting as well. The first book addressed the power of the king and law; the second, the clergy; and the third, the household. This indicated a social structure aligned to the Lutheran order of the three estates: government, church, and household. In 1643, a large treaty by Christian IV reflected this movement from the doctrine of the two kingdoms, represented in the Church Ordinance, to the doctrine of the three estates. The treaty was divided into two books, one on the church and one on the secular realm. This pointed towards both the doctrine of the two kingdoms or more correctly regiments and towards an early understanding of society structured by three estates because the regulating of the church and the secular were now seen as separated, but integrated into the same law book.

This development from the Two-Kingdoms-Doctrine to the doctrine of the three estates is addressed in ANDERSEN's contribution. He argues that the doctrine of the two kingdoms was abandoned first, while, as previously mentioned, Hemmingsen continued to integrate the doctrine of the three estates into his explanation of natural law. Andersen argues further for the disappearance of the doctrine of the three estates in Holberg's explanation of natural law in the early eighteenth century as a step towards modernity. Although the doctrine of the three estates disappeared from Holberg's explanation of natural law, HARSTE and KOEFOED argue in their chapters for the presence of the doctrine of the three estates in legitimizing the absolute king and in his explanation of the *Small Catechism* and, through this, in childhood education during the eighteenth century. Harste addresses the connection between the Reformation and state development across Europe and discusses the influence of Luther's doctrine of the three estates on Bodin's theory of power, sovereignty, and organization. From here, Harste shows how Bodin's theory contributed to the constitutional foundation for Danish absolutism through the King's Code in 1665. Thus, he depicts Denmark to participate in a European process of synchronization after the Wars of Religion, military development, and state-organization while also taking a specifically Danish path influenced by the translation of Lutheranism into natural law and a particular understanding of obedience and trust between the citizen, the king, and government. Absolutism and the mono-confessional situation continued until 1848 when absolutism was replaced by a constitutional monarchy. The subsequent Constitution granted freedom of religion in 1849, even though the Lutheran evangelical church remained part of the state.

2. The Framework of Confessional Culture in the Case of Denmark

Heinz Schilling, the pioneer for confessionalization theories, has examined the process of confessionalization within Scandinavia (Schilling: 2009). However, confessionalization was not just a pan-European process of synchronization between states. Despite plenty of parallel developments, state-building and cultural development occurred differently in the various states of Europe. The internal differences between European states coincide to a large degree with differences in confession.[1] In some countries, the specific confession had a more substantial impact than in others. For this reason, Schilling has highlighted Sweden as a case study for investigating specifically the Lutheran impact on society due to Sweden's centuries-long mono-confessional status (Schilling: 2009). Schilling even thinks that contemporary Swedish culture can be seen as the result of Lutheranism's particularly deep impact on Swedish culture and mindset. Through detailed empirical studies, this book will argue for an understanding of Denmark as an almost ideal Lutheran state, especially during absolutism.

Through the concept of confessional culture, Thomas Kaufmann has offered an alternative to Schilling's notion of confessionalization, leaving more room for variation in the characteristics of specific developments, both across confessions and between countries influenced by the same confession (Kaufmann: 2016, 128). The concept of confessional culture is a theory for societal development in the meeting between confession (as religious identity) and culture (as a broad framework of society). This concept allows an analysis of the interaction between the specific confession as a structural force and broad cultural tendencies. Central to the concept is a perception that societal development is not created primarily by state discipline, but by interactions with individual actors, allowing for internal variety within a confessional culture. Consequently, "Lutheran Confessional Culture" means precisely that the "essential aspects of contemporary culture were more or less intensely shaped by ideas, attitudes, and

1 Not only with regard to poor relief and social security, as Sigrun Kahl (2005) has noticed; but clearly most obvious here.

mentalities founded in the Lutheran interpretation of Christianity and could be legitimized by respective doctrinal norms." (Kaufmann: 2016, 131). The concept of confessional culture has inspired the analytical approach of the authors in this book in their search for areas and points in time when the social teaching of the confession was translated into legal, cultural, and social practice.

In his chapter, KAUFMANN addresses possible ways in which confessional culture is established. He argues for the importance of universities both during the Reformation itself, but also for the development of a far-reaching confessional culture after the Reformation. Because of the ongoing confessional competition in the Holy Roman Empire, the educated elite was important. The universities stabilized the state-building process through education of local pastors, often from a middle-class background, who then brought the Lutheran confessional culture to villages. The pastor's family also played an important role here. Moreover, the theological professors at the universities also gained importance through the development of church liturgy and regulation, not to mention their help in developing a legislative alternative to canon law. The rapid development of a confessional culture in the German region was thus dependent on a collaboration between state, church, and universities.

The situation likely looked somewhat different in the Danish kingdom.[2] Here, the confessional situation was only loosely defined throughout the first century after the reformation. This culture was not fundamentally challenged at any point, which might have left room for more confessional discussion at the university and between the learned up to the beginning of the seventeenth century. On the other hand, Denmark witnessed a strong Lutheran orthodoxy and mono-confessional situation in the seventeenth century that strongly influenced both the confessional culture and to a very large extent legislation and politics. Although the intensity of orthodoxy lessened, the mono-confessional situation continued until the end of absolutism in 1848/49. This book aims to discuss the divergent path and development of a confessional culture in Denmark under other political conditions. One concluding argument is that the nobility and political elite played a central role in the creation of a Lutheran authority who made legislation in line with the Augsburg Confession, childhood education following the *Small Catechism*, and social responsibility central elements in the Danish confessional culture.

While the period of a clear and identifiable Lutheran confessional culture is limited with regard to the German states, the historical development of Denmark and the other Scandinavian monarchies has resulted in a nearly mono-confes-

2 Denmark was part of the double monarchy Denmark-Norway and the confessional, political and legislative situation was to a large extent alike in the two kingdoms. However, the chapters in this book mainly address Denmark.

sional culture lasting for centuries. Moreover, although the Lutheran flavor of the national confessional culture has decreased and even changed to some kind of unconscious background culture, Denmark nevertheless offers a unique situation for investigating the social formation potential of a specific confession, in this case, Lutheranism. For example, it is possible to ask whether Lutheranism was a precondition for the establishment of one of the most absolutist monarchies in the Western world.

3. The Importance of the "Social Imaginary" for Both Theology and Social Studies

In order to proceed, a more direct connection is needed between the framework build by the concept of confessional culture and the thesis that Lutheran theology contains a certain social teaching as part of its core theological insights. Charles Taylor offers this link in his Weber-inspired research on the history of the Western mind. In *A Secular Age*, the concept of the "social imaginary" plays a central role. It offers a key to understanding the possible social impact of ideas that are not necessarily explicitly expressed in social doctrines and theories.

Taylor defines the "social imaginary" as "the ways in which [people] imagine their social existence, how they fit together with others, how things go on between them and their fellows, the expectations which are normally met, and the deeper normative notions and images which underlie these expectations" (Taylor: 2007, 171). For Taylor, it is important to distinguish the "social imaginary" from social theory. The former focuses on the way ordinary human beings imagine "their social surroundings, and this is often not expressed in theoretical terms, it is carried in images, stories, legends, etc" (ibid. 171 f.).

To a certain extent, Lutheranism lacked a well-formed social doctrine or theory despite its radically new and inverse understanding of the divine-human relationship. This fact complicates the search for its relation to confessional culture. Here, the concept of the "social imaginary" is helpful because it offers an interpretative tool for reading theological texts and a methodological approach to the study of historical material of various kinds. To locate the formative power of the Lutheran tradition in a society, one must look beyond explicitly formulated codes of social behavior or instruments of discipline. The change of perspective in Lutheran theology is equally important: God is active in the God-human relationship, not the human being.

From this perspective, it seems quite obvious that Reformation theology deliberately aims at altering people's understanding of their most fundamental social relations on the basis of a new understanding of the individual's relation to the divine. The new understanding of the divine-human relation formed the basis of the Lutheran doctrine of the three estates and the role of the household. The understanding of authority in all three estates and the importance of the household for a pious life governed earthly work and social order. LAURA KATRINE SKINNEBACH indicates that both concepts possess the possibility for strong "social imaginaries" by pointing to religious objects as social imaginaries and part of the development of a confessional culture. In her contribution, SASJA MATHIASEN STOPA argues that the human relationship to God in justification informs the understanding of the relationship between humans, thus generating a social imaginary. Also, VÍTOR WESTHELLE addresses the question of how theological concepts in Lutheran understanding, in this case, faith and love, are transformed into social imaginaries.

The existential-hermeneutical school of Luther research pioneered by Gerhard Ebeling (1970) has emphasized how Reformation theology altered the understanding of God, the individual, and therefore also the world. While the existential and hermeneutical readings perhaps understood the human being's interaction in society as a vital dimension of Luther's thought, the direct social implications or ground dimension received only scarce investigation. Prior to Ebeling and as an outcome of the History of Religion-School in Germany, scholars like Ernst Troeltsch in conversation with sociologists like Weber, Sombart, and Simmel focused on the social teachings of the Church. In this respect, this volume stands on the shoulders of these monumental works from a century ago. In his towering work, Troeltsch (1965) focused mainly on the social structures of the church through his distinction between Church, Sect, and Mystical types of the Christian religion. The impact of Lutheranism on the social imaginary of ordinary people seems to have been beyond his primary concern, although he emphasized the impact of Lutheran theology upon the individual (ibid., 440f.). However, to fully understand the possible impact of a confession upon society it is absolutely necessary also to include the imaginaries of ordinary people; particularly, if the aim is to substantiate claims about Lutheranism's impact on societal change. To investigate the impact of the Lutheran Reformation upon society is also to measure the dissemination of this change of perspective in all aspects of social life.

4. Theses

The foundation of the book is the discussion of a two-fold thesis: (1) that the core ideas of Lutheran theology can be seen as social teaching, implying a certain perception of sociality, explicitly expressed in the use of social metaphors, and to some extent also economic metaphors, for the understanding of the relationship between a gracious God and the sinful human being, and supported by a new understanding of emotions; (2) that a better understanding of the Lutheran household, across different levels of society and including marital law and practice and social obligations within the household, offers an unrivaled means of examining the possible impact of Reformation thought on everyday life. From this perspective, the Lutheran household is a central part of the confessional culture as it was influenced by Luther's understanding of the place and role of the household, his understanding of the obligations within its social relations, and also by the specific cultural and political situation of the country.

To argue that Lutheran theology includes social teaching is almost a truism. From a comparative perspective, however, the Lutheran tradition seems relatively sparse when it comes to social doctrines. Although we find a rather elaborate ethics in Melanchthon, Lutheranism does not possess corpus like in Roman-Catholicism or a developed Church discipline structure as in Reformed traditions. As will be argued in this volume, the Household Code and the interpretation of the Ten Commandments in Luther's *Small Catechism* function to some extent as a social doctrine, but possibly more important is the social teaching implicitly inherent in the core ideas of Lutheran theology. Troeltsch's work on the social doctrines of the Christian churches is, for obvious reasons, an important stepping stone for the present volume. Troeltsch (1965, 436f.) argued that Luther's understanding of grace was the main new idea in Luther's theology. Although he listed four characteristics in Luther's novel conceptualization, including religious individualism and the affirmation of earthly life as consequences of Luther's new doctrine of divine grace, Troeltsch's focus on Church formation resulted in the absence of important features of culture.

5. Lutheran Theology as a Social Teaching in Itself

The first part of the book deals with Lutheran theology in order to sketch out key concepts with potential for impacting societal formation and inner tensions with dynamic potentials. The doctrine of justification in Martin Luther and Philipp Melanchthon implies a specific socially-informed understanding of the relation between God and human beings. Beginning publicly with the critique of the economy of indulgences, the Lutheran Reformation reformulated key doctrines of Christian theology and rearranged key practices of Christian piety. In the first chapter Theodor Dieter shows how Luther's 95 theses on indulgences had far-reaching consequences. On the background of the medieval role of indulgence, Dieter gives a fresh interpretation of the 95 theses by focusing on Luther's attempt to overcome economic structures in church theology and practice. Dieter emphasizes the role of divine giving in the consequences of Luther's theses for human self-understanding.

The Lutheran reformers reduced the number of sacraments dramatically from seven to two. They redirected the most crucial one, the Lord's Supper, from the sacrifice of the mass to the distribution of divine self-giving, thereby giving faith a new meaning and role for the individual's relation to both God and neighbor. The rearranged relationship between faith and love, both understood as an alternative to the mundane economy, formed the background for a Lutheran shaping of social imaginaries, as shown in VÍTOR WESTHELLE's chapter. Westhelle begins by placing the understanding of the role of the "social imaginary" in its historical context between two main schools of thought, the Weber-Troeltsch tradition of seeing religion as having a constitutional role and the Hegel-Marx tradition that emphasizes the "poetic agency" of religion in society. These two schools grant religion the possibility of instituting creative capability alongside a constituting function. As a consequence, societies differ primarily according to intervening factors on a given society: a constituting kind of emphasis is given to politics and an instituting kind of emphasis to economy. Westhelle connects this distinction between economy and politics to the medieval tripartite division of society, turned from static statuses into dynamic publics in Luther's doctrine of three estates. The dynamic forces of Lutheran theology are then found in the both complex and simple relations between faith and love. These relations lay the groundwork for an ethical matrix of social life diverging from other confessional alternatives and closely connected to the distinction between justification and sanctification, between the human being's relation to God and his or her relation to the neighbor.

HANS-MARTIN GUTMANN relates Luther's social thinking to the early-modern crises of communication and individualization, rejecting the view that Luther advocated a theology of order with regard to communal life. Instead, Gutmann argues that Luther was preoccupied with the formation of intimacy in social spaces and that his conception of intimacy was idealistic rather than realistic – thereby establishing another kind of dynamic tension within a Lutheran confessional culture.

BO KRISTIAN HOLM shows in his chapter that the new understanding of the Reformation can be seen as an uncompromising critique of any notion of the divine-human relationship as a reciprocal economy. Instead, the reformers used family metaphors to safeguard the idea of justification as a reestablished relationship with God. In the use of metaphors, dynamic tensions appear in the material: Luther seems to prefer nuptial imagery, emphasizing its symmetrical, rather than hierarchical, potential, whereas Melanchthon quite clearly prefers the asymmetrical and hierarchical metaphor of father and child.

Using Luther's expositions of the fourth commandment as material and the concept of honor as her focal lens, SASJA MATHIASEN STOPA adds important insight to the understanding of Luther's view on the hierarchical relations, which sustain the order of society. She argues that the obligation of individuals to honor authorities in the God-given earthly hierarchies mirrors their obligation to honor God. Furthermore, she discusses the seemingly paradoxical relation between Luther's emphasis on hierarchical social structures upheld through exchanges of honor and his claim that all humans are equal in relation to God. The concept of honor becomes then yet another illuminating window to the duality of hierarchical and egalitarian traces in Luther's theology.

In her chapter on the gift of the indwelling Spirit, CANDACE KOHLI focuses on Luther's construction of a theological anthropology of the regenerate soul. She points towards an often overlooked dimension of Luther's anthropology, giving more room for the work of the Spirit. In sketching out a rather robust pneumatology in Luther, she argues for a more nuanced view of Luther's understanding of human obedience and neighborly love. This opens up more space for progress in sanctification than is normally allowed in Luther interpretations inspired by Kierkegaard or Kant, which through an emphasis on human passivity have struggled to relate the works of the outer human being to the human soul. Her reading makes more room for interplay between the inner person of faith and the outer person of works.

As a whole, the book argues that the existence of tensions between hierarchy and equality, symmetry and asymmetry in the metaphors and concepts the reformers used to understand the divine–human relationship provided the Lutheran confessional culture with a certain dynamic. This dynamic was observable both in the understanding and use of the doctrine of the three orders or estates and in the actual formation of social relations and life within these three orders. For this reason, the understanding of the doctrine of the three estates as a social teaching and its influence on Danish society becomes central to the book (see below). This becomes important for understanding the Reformation's impact on law and social practices, including social relations and the question of gender. The focus on the household makes it possible to substantiate claims of an intimate relationship between a specific confession and cultural development.

Luther's thoughts had far-reaching consequences for the understanding of the household and the pious life. The priesthood of all believers and the corresponding rejection of the clergy as a special link between God and human included a break with the idealized life of isolation in the abbey. This suggested that the pious life was to be lived in the social world and, most of all, in the household. The household became the center of Luther's doctrine of the three estates, but also the locus for living out a pious life according to the will of God. In her chapter, SKINNEBACH addresses the gradual confessional adjustment through everyday devotional culture within the pious household after the Reformation. She argues for a new position of the household within Lutheran social thinking and the household as a new devotional space. Through the analysis of devotional books and epitaphs, she describes the process of establishing this devotional culture and practices within the household in both text and materiality.

AGNES ARNÓRSDÓTTIR in her chapter further argues that marriage became a model for divine life on earth by borrowing central aspects of loving care attached to the church before the Reformation. Thereby, she shows how, in practice, the family took over for monastic life as a social institution. The change in the status of marriage from sacrament to social model also meant a change from the heavenly family to the earthly. This change was reflected in practices of donation and inheritance, but also in an increase in secular control within marriage and sexual life. Arnórsdóttir goes on to argue that the authority of the husband over the household increased, but so did the mutual support between the spouses. The status of the married women also increased at the expense of the unmarried virgin because the pious life of a woman was within the household context instead of in institutions attached to the church.

The question of women's positions within the Lutheran household is also addressed by SØREN FELDTFOS THOMSEN. In his chapter, Thomsen asks how Luther's concept of marriage as a partnership built on spiritual and emotional equality between husband and wife was balanced with a traditional hierarchical understanding of gender. He focuses on the description of gender roles and emotional norms in sixteenth- and seventeenth-century marriage and household handbooks. Thus, he addresses the affective dimension of household and confessional culture. He points at the emotional ideas linked to the wife's obedience to her husband in order to highlight a tendency in the literature to marginalize emotional reciprocity out of concern for maintaining the social hierarchy.

In NINA JAVETTE KOEFOED's contribution, she emphasizes Luther's *Small* and *Large Catechism*, read as a social teaching that defines the social and emotional obligations placed within the household and the resulting influence of this on legislation. She argues that the doctrine of the three estates and the fourth commandment as a model for social relations played a central role in the development of Danish confessional culture, especially in early absolutism during the late seventeenth and early eighteenth centuries. But she also draws a more gender-equal picture, underlining the shared position of authority between the married couple in relation to the rest of the household. The understanding of social relations as constituted by mutual obligations is central to the argument. Through this, she highlights the obligations of authority and the obligations to honor – crucial to Luther's anthropology (cf. STOPA's chapter).

The present volume endeavors to continue scholarly discussions on the relation between religious confessions and societal development begun by Weber and others by analyzing new kinds of material: key theological ideas in combination with daily practices. In order to reach new conclusions, it is necessary to search for "social imaginaries" in the theological texts from the formative period of the Lutheran tradition and to compare these finding with the study of the "social imaginary" in various kinds of historical material and from multiple layers of society. This goal is ambitious and demands much more than a single volume to attain. The present volume shows, however, how Reformation research can benefit from combining numerous disciplinary approaches under a common auspice to increase our understanding of the relation between theology and everyday life, religious confession and the formation of society. The authors in this volume want to develop an approach that makes it possible to draw strong conclusions about both the role of Reformation theology in the shaping of Danish society and the social dimensions of Lutheran confessional culture, in so far as it is possible to detect such a culture.

At a concrete level, this book analyzes the social dimensions of key Lutheran concepts and their translation into the doctrine of the three estates (church, household, and state). This is deepened by investigating the level of lived experience of life within these three orders, especially within the household, which is so important in forming the ideal for both church and state. Thus, the chapters in the book work to connect the social ideas inherent in the Lutheran confession with the social formation of the Danish state from the Reformation into the period of Absolutism. The focus is on basic mediums that translated Lutheran ideas into social practice: law, primarily connected to marriage and family; and the role of the household, both as primary social relations and as basic social and political model. Although the examples in this book come from Denmark, the approach has been designed to provide new and relevant research about the relation between religion and the shaping of particular societies both on the national scene and in an international comparative context.

Bibliography

Appel, Charlotte (2001), Læsning og bogmarked i 1600-tallets Danmark, Copenhagen: Museum Tusculanum Press.

Appel, Charlotte/Morten Fink-Jensen (2013), Da læreren holdt skole: Tiden før 1780 (Dansk Skolehistorie 1), Aarhus: Aarhus University Press.

Bach-Nielsen, Carsten (2012), Kirkens Historie II, 1500–1800, Copenhagen: Hans Reitzels Forlag.

Ebeling, Gerhard (1970), Luther: An Introduction to His Thought, trans. R.A. Wilson, Minneapolis, MN: Fortress Press.

Grell, Ole Peter (2016a), The Reformation in Denmark, Norway and Iceland, in: Jens E. Olesen/E. I. Kouri (ed.), The Cambridge History of Scandinavia, vol. II, Cambridge: Cambridge University Press, 44–59.

GRELL, OLE PETER (2016b), Intellecutal Currents, in: Jens E. Olesen/E. I. Kouri (ed.), The Cambridge History of Scandinavia, vol. II, Cambridge: Cambridge University Press, 60–88.

HASSELSTEEN, PERNILLE (2002), Christian IV's Ridderakademi i Sorø og den danske adels udenlandsrejser ca. 1560–1650, in: Flemming Lundgreen-Nielsen/Hanne Ruus (ed.), Svøbt i Mår: Danske folkevisekultur 1550–1700. Lærdom og overtro, vol. 4, Copenhagen: C.A. Reitzel, 375–484.

HOLZE, HEINRICH (2011), Die Kirchen des Nordens in der Neuzeit (16. bis 20. Jahrhundert), Leipzig: Evangelische Verlagsanstalt.

INGESMAN, PER (2016), Introduction, in: Per Ingesman (ed), Religion as an Agent of Change: Crusades – Reformation – Pietism (Brill's Series in Church History and Religious Culture 72), Leiden/Boston, MA: Brill, 1–30.

KAHL, SIGRUN (2005), The Religious Roots of Modern Poverty Policy: Catholic, Lutheran, and Reformed Protestant Traditions Compared, AES 46, 91–126.

KAUFMANN, THOMAS (2016), What is Lutheran Confessional Culture?, in: Per Ingesman (ed), Religion as an Agent of Change: Crusades – Reformation – Pietism (Brill's Series in Church History and Religious Culture 72), Leiden/Boston: Brill, 127–148.

HELK, VELLO (1987), Dansk-Norske studierejser fra reformationen til enevælden 1536–1660. Med en matrikel over studerende i udlandet, Odense: Odense Universitetsforlag.

LAUSTEN, MARTIN SCHWARZ (1995), The Early Reformation in Denmark and Norway 1520–1599, in: Ole Peter Grell (ed.), The Scandinavian Reformation from Evangelical Movement to Institutionalisation of Reform, Cambridge: Cambridge University Press, 12–41.

LAUSTEN, MARTIN SCHWARZ (2010), Die Heilige Stadt Wittenberg: Die Beziehungen des dänischen Königshauses zu Wittenberg in der Reformationszeit, Leipzig: Evangelische Verlagsanstalt.

LOCKHART, PAUL DOUGLAS (2004), Frederik II and the Protestant Cause: Denmark's Role in the Wars of Religion, 1559–1596 (The Northern World 10), Leiden/Boston, MA: Brill.

LYBY, THORKILD/OLE PETER GRELL (1995), The Consolidation of Lutheranism in Denmark and Norway, in Ole Peter Grell (ed.), The Scandinavian Reformation from Evangelical Movement to Institutionalisation of Reform, Cambridge: Cambridge University Press, 114–178.

MÄKINEN, VIRPI (ed.) (2006), Lutheran Reformation and the Law (SMRT 112), Leiden/Boston, MA: Brill.

SCHILLING, HEINZ (2009), The Confessionalization of European Churches and Societies – an Engine for Modernizing and for Social and Cultural Change, in Norsk Teologisk Tidsskrift 110, 3–22.

TAMM, DITLEV/JENS CHRISTIAN V. JOHANSEN/HANS EYVIND NÆSS/KENNETH JOHANSSON (2000), The Law and the Juridical System, in: Eva Österberg/Sølvi Bauge Sogner (ed.), People Meet the Law. Control and Conflict-handling in the courts, Oslo: Universitetsforlaget, 27–56.

TAYLOR, CHARLES (2012): A Secular Age, Cambridge, MA: The Belknap Press of Harvard University Press.

TROELTSCH, ERNST (1965), Die Soziallehren der christlichen Kirchen und Gruppen, 2nd ed., Aalen: Scientia Verlag.

Theodor Dieter

Martin Luther's 95 Theses on Indulgences

Overcoming Economic Thought Structures in Theology and Economic Practices of the Church

Introduction

Luther's 95 theses on indulgences triggered what we call "the Reformation." Indulgences were a widespread ecclesial practice in medieval times with broad social, legal, and economic ramifications and preconditions. Economic models played an important role in the theological understanding of indulgences, and economic interests of the Roman church were served by the practice of indulgences. Thus, it is easily understood that a different, critical understanding of indulgences had far-reaching consequences as soon as it appeared convincing to many people. In this case, a new theology had political, social, economic and, of course, ecclesial impact. In view of these circumstances, it is astonishing that the theses have not yet found a comprehensive commentary and that they are unknown to most of our contemporaries even though (or because) they have been seen as responsible for the alleged decline of the medieval church and as reflecting an attitude of coping with wrongdoings by using money. In this chapter, I will describe the medieval background for the indulgences and their theological understanding and how economic thinking influenced the theological understanding of the relationship between human beings and God (1). Secondly, Martin Luther's criticism of indulgences is analyzed. This study will not offer a comprehensive interpretation of the whole set of theses; rather it will focus on those theses that form a line of thought that dismisses this economic pattern of thinking (2). Finally, the self-understanding of human beings motivated by this theological understanding is outlined (3).

1. The Medieval Background of Indulgences

Indulgences have their theological place within the sacrament of penance. This sacrament aims at the remission of sins. Sin (*peccatum*) has two aspects: guilt (*culpa* – violation of God or a person or an order) and punishment, penalty (*poena*). Punishment is something negative that the sinner has to bear either as an inner consequence of sin (e. g. illness) or through imposition from outside (by God or by a priest). The sacrament of penance consists of three elements (from the side of the penitent): 1) Oral confession (*confessio oris*) – something external, 2) contrition of the heart (*contritio cordis*) – something internal, and 3) satisfaction by good works (*satisfactio operum*) – something external (with respect to other persons, e. g. giving alms, or with respect to one's body, e. g. fasting) or something internal (with respect to one's spirit, e. g. saying prayers). *Indulgences* only deal with the punishment and satisfaction, not with the guilt. Justification of a person has to do with the remission of guilt that takes place in the sacrament of penance. The guilt is forgiven if a person is contrite and confesses her sins, and the priest absolves her. Nevertheless, the penitent is obliged to do some of the aforementioned works of satisfaction after he has been liberated from the guilt of sin and thus has been reconciled with God. It is the priest who imposes such penalties on the penitent. Indulgences deal with this part or, more precisely, with the *temporal* punishment after the guilt of sin has been forgiven. However, after absolution, temporal punishments remain to be served. Indulgences are means to minimize or cancel temporal punishment.

The development of the institution and theology of indulgences presupposes a certain understanding of the righteousness of God: Even if God has forgiven a mortal sin (which as such separates a person from him), has thus again received the person into communion with him, and withdrawn the punishment of remaining eternally separated from God (= hell), he nevertheless imposes some temporal punishment as a consequence of his righteousness. This opinion goes back to Augustine who emphasizes the mercy of God in forgiving sins but also points to the righteousness of God that does not allow for any sin to remain unpunished. A person is called to recognize her sin and acknowledge it in judgment of herself. If a person does not execute this judgment on herself, God will become active in punishing the person.[1] In medieval times, this under-

1 With respect to Ps 50:4, Augustine notes in his *Enarrationes* (50, 7 [CChr.SL 38, 603]): "Vide enim quem inuoces; iustum inuocas: odit peccata, si iustus est; uindicat in peccata, si iustus est; non poteris auferre a Domino Deo iustitiam eius. Implora misericordiam, sed attende iustitiam: misericordia est ut ignoscat peccanti, iustitia est ut puniat peccatum. Quid ergo? Quaeris misericordiam, peccatum impunitum remanebit? Responderit Dauid, resonderint lapsi, responderint cum Dauid, ut misericordiam mereantur sicut Dauid, et dicant: Non, Domine, non erit impunitum peccatum meum; noui iustitiam eius, cuius quaero misericordiam; non im-

standing was summarized in the formula "God who does not forgive any sin unpunished."[2] Augustine also said, "Life must be turned to the better, and with respect to previous sins God has to be reconciled through alms."[3] This idea can also be found in Peter Abaelard when he reflects on the problem that a punishment imposed by a priest is lower than it should be according to the righteousness of God. He argues that God, who does not forgive any sin unpunished and punishes each sin individually, will reserve a just satisfaction according to the magnitude of the sin.[4] In his *Sentences*, the textbook for theological learning in medieval times, Peter Lombard explains the understanding of punishment for sins as follows: God is merciful and righteous. From each of these attributes follow different things: From his mercy, God forgives the person who is penitent so that there is no eternal punishment; but from his righteousness, God lets no sin be unpunished. Penitence is realizing this punishment, in which one has to distinguish between an inner and an external penitence. If the inner penitence is so strong that it is an appropriate punishment for the sin, God does not require an additional punishment. However, if this is not the case, what is missing needs to be completed by external penitence. God, who knows the kind and magnitude of the sins and the punishments, accordingly adds an additional punishment.[5] Since

---

punitum erit, sed ideo nolo ut tu me punias, quia ego peccatum meum punio; ideo peto ut ignoscas, quia ego agnosco." Regarding Ps 58:6, he states (*Enarrationes* 58, 1, 13 [CChr.SL 39, 740]): "Quia hoc in te odisti, quod et ille odit, ut incipias placere Deo, dum hoc in te punis quod displicet Deo. Nam non potest impunitum relinqui peccatum." About Ps 102:19 (*Enarrationes* 102, 26 [CChr.SL 40, 1472]), he says: "Faciat quisque quod uult in terra, non erit impunitum peccatum, non erit infructuosa iustitia; quia Dominus qui ante thronum iudicis hominis irrisus est, in caelo parauit thronum suum." In *Sermo* 19, it reads with respect to Ps 51:5 (CChr.SL 41, 252f): "Sibi non parcebat [David], et ideo ut sibi parceretur non impudenter rogabat. Peccatum enim, fratres, impunitum esse non potest. Si peccatum impunitum remaneat iniustum est, ergo sine dubitatione puniendum. Hoc tibi dicit deus tuus: 'Puniendum est peccatum aut a te, aut a me.' Punitur ergo peccatum, aut ab homine paenitente, aut a deo iudicante [...]. Quid est enim paenitentia, nisi sua in se ipsum iracundia?".

2 "Deus qui nullum peccatum impunitum remittit." (Cf. Angenendt: 1994).

3 Augustine, *Enchiridion de fide spe et caritate* (Barbel: 1960, 128f, no. 70): "In melius est quippe vita mutanda, et per eleemosynas de peccatis praeteritis est propitiandus deus; non ad hoc emendus quodammodo, ut ea semper liceat impune committere. *Nemini enim dedit laxamentum peccandi*, quamvis miserando deleat iam facta peccata, si non satisfactio congrua negligatur."

4 Abaelard, *Scito te ipsum* [*Ethica*] (Steger: 2006, 136, § 71): "Si quid tamen de pena satisfactionis minus est institutum, quam oporteat, deus, qui nullum peccatum impunitum dimittit et singula quantum debet punit, pro quantitate peccati satisfactionis equitatem seruabit, ipsos uidelicet penitentes non eternis suppliciis reseruando, set in hac uita uel in futura penis purgatoriis affligendo, si nos, inquam, in nostra satisfactione negligentes fuerimus." As confirmation, Abaelard points to 1 Cor 11:31.

5 Petrus Lombardus, Sent. IV, d. 20, cap. 2.2 (Brady: 1981, 374, 10–18): "Deus enim, cum sit misericors et iustus, ex misericordia poenitenti ignoscit, non reservans peccatum ad poenam aeternam; ex iustitia vero impunitum non dimittit delictum. Aut enim homo punit, aut Deus. Homo autem punit poenitendo. Et est poenitentia interior et exterior. Si ergo interior poe-

human life is not long enough to suffer all penalties due to divine righteousness, or because people enjoy their lives instead of working out any punishment for their sins, this understanding of the righteousness of God requires the idea of purgatory as a possibility after death for suffering the remaining part of the divinely imposed punishment (See Le Goff: 1984; Dinzelbacher: 1999, 89–118). This is a necessary consequence of this understanding.

Thomas Aquinas distinguishes between two different dimensions of satisfactory punishment – either to complete what is owed to God (as punishment) or to undergo, so to speak, a medical treatment in order not to commit the same sin again. With respect to the first meaning of punishment, someone else, it was imagined, can perform the penitential works instead of the sinner, while with respect to the second meaning, the person cannot be replaced by someone else. If someone is sick, nobody else can take the medicine instead of him or her.[6] Already the Fourth Lateran Council (1215) determined the role of the priest in the sacrament of penance to be that of a doctor and a judge. As a judge, he had to determine the penalty, and as a doctor, he aimed at healing the penitent, as the Council declares:

> The priest shall be discerning and prudent so that like a skilled doctor he may pour wine and oil over the wounds of the injured one. Let him carefully inquire about the circumstances of both the sinner and the sin, so that he may prudently discern what sort of advice he ought to give and what remedy to apply, using various means to heal the sick person. Let him take the utmost care, however, not to betray the sinner at all by word or sign or in any other way. (Fourth Lateran Council [1215], chapter 21, in: Tanner: 1990, 245.)

However, the distinction between the medicinal and the punitive aspect of penalties is not easy to grasp. Let us suppose that a punishment of forty days of fasting was imposed on a person. Now this person receives an indulgence of forty days of fasting. What would be the consequence? Would this person feel obliged to fast forty days with respect to the healing effect of this punishment since only the function of satisfaction was solved by the indulgence? One would not assume this. Thus, the dimension of satisfaction (understood as punitive or expiatory)

---

nitudo tanta fuerit, ut sit sufficiens ultio peccati, Deus qui hoc novit, ab illo qui taliter poenitet ulterius poenam non exigit. Si vero interior poenitudo non sufficit in vindictam peccati, nec exterior poenitentia impletur, Deus qui modos et mensuras peccatorum et poenarum novit, addit poenam sufficientem."

6 Aquinas (1252–1256/2011), writing in the Super Sent., lib. 4, d. 20, q. 1 a. 2 qc. 3 co: "poena satisfactoria est ad duo; scilicet ad solutionem debiti, et ad medicinam pro peccato vitando. Inquantum est ad remedium sequentis peccati, sic satisfactio unius non prodest alteri; quia ex jejunio unius caro alterius non domatur, nec ex actibus unius alius bene agere consuevit […]. Sed quantum ad satisfactionem debiti unus potest pro alio satisfacere, dummodo sit in caritate, ut opera ejus satisfactoria esse possint."

became the dominant one in medieval time, while for Luther, as we will see, it is just the opposite: The medicinal aspect of punishment is the only one on his mind. This has far-reaching consequences, and we will have to ask for the reasons for Luther's focus on this dimension.

One may ask how priests could determine which punishment divine righteousness would require from a sinner for a certain sin. In order to answer their question, countless penitential books allowed priests to identify which punishments would be appropriate for which sin committed under certain circumstances.[7] A good example of this concept of punishments can be found in Geoffrey Chaucer's *The Canterbury Tales.* At the end of the book, in "The Parson's Tale," one finds an extensive explanation of penitence as well as many examples of punishments to be imposed for the respective sins.[8] Sins were quantified and also punishments; a reification and objectification of both emerged. Punishments could be separated from the penitent as "things." This was the presupposition for an economic approach in dealing with punishments. The possibility of changing a punishment of one type into a punishment of another type but of the same "value" emerged. This was necessary since the times of fasting often increased to weeks or months or even years so that sinners could not cope with these penalties. Thus, for example, it was made possible to exchange fasting with singing psalms; one could also do it together with squats. For example, one day of fasting could be replaced with citing or singing seventy psalms or fifty psalms together with squats, or 300 psalms with squats or 420 without could replace one week of fasting (see Angenendt: 2013,149). Rich people could give alms (for ransoming prisoners, for the altar, or for people in need) instead of fasting. This was an old tradition, but the innovation is to be seen in the quantification of the works in order to commute with certain times of fasting. Depending on the wealth of a sinner, one day of fasting could be replaced by one denarius or more. Another way of dealing with the magnitude of punishments besides this *commutatio* was the *redemptio*, according to which other persons could take over the penance, a deputy of penance. Here, it is obvious that penance was no longer seen as something personal but as something that could be separated from the person; consequently, the debt could be paid by another person.[9]

---

7 See, for example, the collection of penitenial orders in Wasserschleben (1958).

8 See Coghill (2003, 485–488) (translation of *The Canterbury Tales* into modern English). The complete text is much longer, see Düring (2008, 631–726).

9 Angenendt (2013, 150) comments on this as follows: "[Diese Redemptionen = Loskäufe sind] Ausdruck einer andersartigen, im Grunde sogar nicht-christlichen Bußableistung. Denn die christliche Buße ist personal, verlangt die innere Umkehr von Herz und Geist zu Gott. Solcherart Buße versteht sich von der Gesinnung her, ist darum strikt persönlich zu leisten, kann in einem einzigen Umkehr-Moment geschehen und darf nicht von anderen übernommen werden. Genau diese Übernahme durch eine andere Person aber empfehlen die Re-

Such a person had to be reimbursed, for example, a priest who as confessor could bear part of the burden of a penitent. Special masses (*missa specialis*) became particularly important for vicarious solving of the penitential requirements. For a long time, masses had been seen as propitiatory sacrifices, but now their effects were appropriated to a special penitent with a certain quantified effect. Thus, one mass could replace seven or twelve days of fasting, ten masses four months, twenty masses seven or nine months, etc. (Angenendt: 2013, 151). The father confessor could also celebrate masses for the penitent thus taking over a part of the penitential works of the sinner. This practice changed both the penance and the masses. Two masses created the double effect while one mass intended for two people had half the effect for each person. This would lead to a multiplication of masses (Angenendt: 2013, 151, see also Werbeck: 1972). Quantification, commutation, and redemption allowed for and required introducing economic thinking into the process of penance. Actually, the concept of divine righteousness had to lead to such practices since without them the problem of the accumulation of punishments could not be solved. Otherwise, people would not have been able to come to terms with their penalties. One should keep in mind that the Fourth Lateran Council obliged all faithful to confess at least once a year, during Lent, all their sins to their local priest (Fourth Lateran Council, chapter 21, in: Tanner: 1990, 245). In the long run, this practice increased the self-awareness of what people had done wrong and thus also the expectation of penalties to bear.

Out of the practice of redemption, the practice of offering indulgences developed. If indulgences were meant to minimize penalties *and* do justice to the divine righteousness, there must be an infinite amount of merits that can be transferred to the penitents and become their own so that they are able to pay their debts to divine justice. Thus, it is obvious that something like the concept of the "treasures of the church" had to be developed. In 1343, in his bull *Unigenitus Dei Filius*, Pope Clement VI officially used for the first time the phrase "treasure," which Christ had gained for the Church Militant and to which Mary and the saints also contributed since they had done more good works than were expected from them or had suffered for Christ's sake (Denzinger/Hünermann: 1999, nos. 1025 and 1027). This concept clearly shows the influence of economic thinking. This treasure was a closed treasure. It was in the hands of the pope who alone was able to grant indulgences from it (Denzinger/Hünermann: 1999, no. 2026). This was explained by the analogy of an abbot of a monastery who had the authority and supervision over the possessions of the abbey. He was the one who was able to distribute the riches of the abbey. Thus, the whole treasure of the church – the merits of Christ and the saints – was at the disposal of the pope. He was entitled to

demptionen, dass man sich einen Stellvertreter suchen solle, der die Ableistung des Bußpensums übernehme."

offer portions of this treasure to solve portions of the satisfactory works required from a penitent. It was a happy exchange that the church offered: The penitent gave a certain amount of his money, visited certain churches, or did other spiritual exercises while in return he received something of a much higher value.[10] He himself did not need to perform the required acts of satisfaction, and, even more importantly, he could take measures to avoid the purgatory after his death. This was a great relief for most people since they were well aware that they would have to suffer a more serious punishment in purgatory than on earth if they had not fulfilled all penitential requirements in their lifetime. However, an indulgence letter promised them that in the hour of death, after confession and absolution, they would get rid of all penalties (plenary indulgence) so that they could go directly to heaven. Indulgences could be perceived as the social care of the church in the eternal life or even as a comprehensive insurance for the beyond (Laudage: 2016, 200). Thus, they were appreciated as a great grace. Nevertheless, the thought structure in this understanding of indulgences was an economic one of exchange, minimizing costs and maximizing profits, even though one should keep in mind that indulgences – for living persons – were not bought, as such; what was bought were indulgence letters that became operative after someone had gone through the sacrament of penance.

While indulgences converted the temporal goods of Christians into eternal goods, the church in offering the merits of Christ and the saints converted, so to speak, eternal goods into temporal goods or earnings. The church offered indulgence letters, and the Christians paid for them. Indulgences played an important role in the financial system of the church – for building churches, cathedrals, hospitals, and things like bridges, too. Indulgences have been characterized as something like crowdfunding of ecclesial projects in medieval times (Laudage: 2016, 200).

One should put the development of indulgences into the wider context of the development of medieval societies. From the eleventh to the thirteenth centuries, an economic development took place in Europe with an increase of population, flourishing of towns (with craftsmen and merchants), and a transition from a barter economy to exchange economy with an increasing role of money. This process was characterized, on the one hand, by intellectualization (skills like counting, measuring, calculating, planning, and accounting were needed) and, on the other hand, by materialization (constant dealing with goods, attraction to material things, realization of profit as a goal of one's life, etc.) (See Hamm: 2011 for this and what follows).

10 One should emphasize that indulgences were not necessarily acquired by offering money to an indulgence commissioner; there could also be other contributions of the penitent, which the pope or bishops had decided would open the treasure of the church.

Professional life and religious life were intimately connected so that the increased significance of economy for societies also influenced the human beings' relation to God and their self-understanding. Monastic life, for example, was understood almost literally as earning eternal life: "As many steps a person does fulfilling her vow of obedience, as many cents she puts in the hand of God in order to buy eternal life."[11] In 1501, a provost in Nuremberg comforted a sister who mourned her father, saying:

> We should not mourn if someone has merited coming home from exile [...], especially if someone has gained many good works through happy entrepreneurship. For we have all come into the pilgrimage of this world like merchants in order to conquer eternal gain and usury [!] through temporal goods. (See Hamm: 2011, 302, note 2).

One may wonder how it was possible that economic thinking was able to influence the understanding of human beings' relation to God since temporal and eternal goods are entirely different (see for the following Dieter: 2001, 183–193). In an important medieval tradition, the idea of the *pactum Dei* made it possible to establish an economic relation between human efforts and divine reaction. A model for explaining this *pactum* was an economic one: the king and the leaden coin (See Courtenay: 1972). The material value of a leaden coin may be very low, but if there is the sign of the king on it, it gains a much greater value than its material one. Thus, through the *pactum*, an act of love for God of the sinner gains the value of gaining justifying grace. "Love of God above all" is the highest act of the will possible for a human being by his natural power (i.e. *facere quod in se est*); it is rewarded according to the divine pact.

Nevertheless, one should note that the original purpose of developing the idea of the *pactum* was not an economic one. It was meant to safeguard the absolute freedom of God who cannot be necessitated by any human action and to establish a relationship of this to the freedom of human beings. Since the difference between the creator and the creatures cannot be bridged from the side of the creatures, the creator must do this, and he has done it for eternity by binding himself through the *pactum*. This *pactum* can be conceived in many ways. Since it has the structure, "if A (what the human being does), then B (what God will give as a reaction to the human action)," one can emphasize A very much and thus stress the capacity and need for human performance while simply presupposing the fact that the *pactum* exists. However, one can also emphasize that any relation between A and B is only possible by grace and that the *pactum* itself cannot be merited – thus, grace may be emphasized while the human contribution may be minimized. Heiko Oberman argues that Biel's doctrine of justification, which

11 Manuscript of the Nuremberg Dominican Monastery St. Catherine (see Hamm: 2011, 301, note 1).

shares this understanding, can be characterized by both *sola gratia* (if one looks at the relation between A and B through the *pactum*) and as *solis operibus* (if one emphasizes that B simply requires A and thus attributes a decisive role to human performance) (see Oberman: 1963, 176). Therefore, this model is open to an economic interpretation, as we have seen. It allows for understanding the human person's relation with God as a trade in which relatively little investment may create very great profits.

2. Interpretation of the Basic Structure of Martin Luther's 95 Theses

Theses 5 and 6, based on theses 1 to 4, seem to be the center of Luther's 95 theses. As thesis 6 shows, Luther holds the understanding that forgiveness of sins is based on repentance: "The pope cannot remit any guilt except by declaring and confirming its remission by God." (Wengert: 2015, 35/WA 1: 233,20). This is not meant as a criticism of the pope; rather, it is the opinion – widespread in medieval times – that a priest can only declare that God has already forgiven the sins of a truly repentant person. According to the divine pact, God will not deny his grace to someone who has done what is in his or her power (*facienti quod in se est Deus non denegat gratiam*). What is in a person's power is to repent truly out of love for God. If a person does this, her sins will be forgiven, and in the sacrament of penance, the priest can only *declare* that God *has already* forgiven the sins of the penitent. This is what Luther wished to say in thesis 6. Nevertheless, Luther also emphasizes that a penitent is required to go to a priest: "God remits the guilt of absolutely no one unless at the same time God subjects in all things the one humbled to God's vicar, the priest" (thesis 7) (Wengert: 2015, 36/WA 1: 233,23f).

However, Luther deeply transformed this concept of *facere quod in se est* by two important changes: (a) Repentance or turning to God is not an act of the human person out of her natural power but the work of the Holy Spirit.[12] (b) Even if grace is given to a person, it does not change her completely so that she would be able to love God "with all your heart, and with all your soul, and with all your mind, and with all your strength" (Mark 12:29). And not offering one's whole person to God means to violate his will and thus to sin. In this situation, Luther refers to 1 Cor 11:31: "[I]f we judged ourselves, we would not be judged." Thus, being penitent is the way to receive forgiveness for one's sins: loving God through the grace given by God and at the same time acknowledging that one is not able to love God with one's whole heart and denying the self-seeking dynamics of

12 *Disputation against Scholastic Theology*, theses 26–28 (LW 31: 11/WA 1: 225,17–26).

oneself. In line with this understanding, Luther begins his 95 theses as follows: "Our Lord and Master Jesus Christ, in saying, 'Do penance …,' wanted the entire life of the faithful to be one of penitence." (Wengert: 2015, 34/WA 1: 233,10f). Already this starting point indicates that when it comes to the punishment for sins, Luther will only focus on its medicinal function (i.e. being penitent in the way described)[13] while completely leaving out their satisfactory aspect (i.e. coping with the requirements of God's justice). This presupposes a different concept of God's righteousness. It is astonishing that Luther did not identify this point as the basic point of controversy in his theses.

In the famous preface to his Latin works, Luther is looking back at his beginnings. He mentions that he seriously struggled with Rom 1:17 ("For in it [the gospel], the righteousness of God is revealed"). He understood this word "righteousness of God" philosophically, that God acts as a just judge who punishes the evildoer and rewards the one who acts well, but Luther found himself to be a sinner and thus expecting the punishment of God. Why should this be understood as gospel? He overcame this difficulty when he realized that the "righteousness of God" does not simply describe God in himself but God as communicating his righteousness to human beings. God is righteous in making sinners righteous (see LW 34: 336ff/WA 54: 185,12–186,20). In his early lectures, Luther understood this in the following way. For example, the psalmist says in Ps 72:2, "Give the king your justice [*iudicium*], O God, and your righteousness [*iustitia*] to a king's son." According to Luther, God's righteousness condemns and makes sinners condemn their own unrighteousness, but by confessing their unrighteousness by heart, word, and deed, they are being justified (see LW 10: 403–410/Vogelsang: 1963, 151,10–157,10). At the time of the 95 theses, Luther saw this as the way in which the grace of God is present in human beings and by which they are justified. In this concept of the righteousness of God, there is no place for the penalties that God requires, except the way just described. Apart from accusing and confessing one's own unrighteousness and bearing the sufferings of life, which may happen as diseases, famines, droughts, wars, etc., there were no other divine penalties that the sinners had to bear and which someone else could bear on their behalf.

Presupposing this understanding of the righteousness of God, Luther states in thesis 5: "The pope neither desires nor is able to remit any penalties except those imposed by his own discretion or that of the canons." (Wengert: 2015, 35/WA 1: 233,18f). However, people in Luther's time bought indulgence letters with the understanding that there were penalties imposed by God – as a consequence of his righteousness – and that they would be remitted when the penitents showed

13 To be more precise: Luther's understanding of penitence is a tremendous development of what the scholastics called the medicinal aspect of punishment.

the indulgence letter to the priest after contrition, confession, and absolution. The penalties imposed by a priest had precisely the purpose to allow penitents to do works of satisfaction in order to cope with the requirements of divine righteousness. A priest imposing too weak penalties on the penitents would be of no help to them because in purgatory they would have to suffer all the penalties that they had not resolved during the time of their lives. Therefore, if penitents were only relieved from penalties imposed by a priest through indulgences, there would not be a great interest in them since the main concern of the penitents was to be freed from the divinely imposed penalties that they eventually would have to suffer in purgatory. Luther's thesis 5 implicitly denies the underlying concept of the divine righteousness. Luther's opponents immediately reacted against thesis 5 by claiming and insisting that divine righteousness actually requires that no sin be remitted without a certain punishment.

Tetzel, for example, objected: "This satisfaction (since God does not suffer any offense without penalty) happens by punishment or by an equivalent that is accepted by God."[14] Also Eck and Cajetan insisted on the existence of a divine righteousness that requires penalties for each sin. Luther, challenged by his opponents, now explicitly stated:

> No one can defend the position with any passage from Scripture that God's righteousness desires and demands any punishment or satisfaction from sinners except for their heartfelt and true contrition or conversion alone – with the condition that from that moment on they bear the cross of Christ and practice the aforementioned works [prayer, fasting, alms] (but not as imposed by anyone). (Wengert: 2015, 61/WA 1: 244,15–20, *A Sermon on Indulgence and Grace*, 1518).

In the *Asterisci*, Luther explicitly stated against Eck:

> God who forgives sin at the same time forgives guilt and punishment, with the understanding that it is enough of penalties for the sinner if he will live rightly and struggle with his vices and corrupt habits, especially the ones whom he has grown accustomed to.[15]

Luther, of course, knows that the Bible speaks of God's punishment several times, for example in the case of David's adultery with Bathsheba. According to 2 Sam 12:13–14, David repented, and his sin was forgiven; nevertheless, the newborn baby died as a punishment of God. But Luther argued that if God in certain cases actually punishes people, then this is his will, and the church cannot arrogate to herself the power to take away this punishment. In a case similar to that of David,

---

14 "3. Hec satisfactio (cum Deus delictum absque ultione non patiatur) per penam fit vel aequivalens in acceptatione divina" (Fabisch/Iserloh: 1988, 322).

15 WA 1: 284,15–17: "[…] Deus remittens peccatum simul culpam et poenam remittit, sciens sat poenarum esse peccatori, si bene vivat ac cum viciis pravisque moribus, praesertim inolitis, pugnet."

the pope's indulgence thus would not keep the baby alive. The pope cannot remit such a penalty. Even though there are such penalties, Luther's main understanding of punishment for sin emphasized its justifying and healing dimension.

The decisive step in overcoming the economic thought structure with respect to indulgences lies in Luther's focusing exclusively on the medicinal aspect of punishment – i. e. on penance. Concerning one's healing process, nobody can be replaced by someone else. Thus, there is no space for any trade. The understanding of the irreplaceability of a person is connected with a certain understanding of the righteousness of God.

Since Luther focuses on penance and thus on the healing aspect of struggling with sin, indulgences can only relate to the penalties imposed by priests. Since medicine is only for persons living on earth, penalties that have not been served in a person's lifetime cannot be transferred into a situation after death, into purgatory: "Those 'tares' about changing the canonical penalty into the penalty of purgatory certainly seem to have been 'sown' while the bishops 'were sleeping.'" (thesis 11; Wengert: 2015, 36/WA1: 233, 31f, see Matt 13:25). But what to do if a person, according to the traditional understanding, were concerned that she was not able to serve all penalties as long as she lived? In his *Sermon on Indulgence and Grace*, Luther declares:

> [N]othing is being said [by arguing] that the punishment and works may be too much, that the individual may not complete them because of the shortness of life, and therefore there is need for indulgences for such a person. I respond that this has no basis in fact and is pure fiction. For God and the holy church impose on no one more than they are able to carry, as St Paul also says [1 Cor. 10:13, paraphrase]: "God will not let [anyone] be tested beyond [what that person can endure]." (Wengert: 2015, 63/WA 1: 245, 5–10).

This argument presupposes a different understanding of the righteousness of God.

Thus, if the problem of a too heavy weight of countless penalties no longer existed, the question came up: What then about the purgatory? There no longer seemed to be a reason for assuming the existence of something like the purgatory. Luther offers a highly interesting interpretation of purgatory. We can call it an existential interpretation of it. Luther's starting point is 1 John 4:18: "There is no fear in love, but perfect love casts out fear; for fear has to do with punishment, and whoever fears has not reached perfection in love." If a person dies with an imperfect love for God, she will suffer because of her fear of God. This suffering constitutes purgatory. Theses 14 to 16 read as follows:

> Imperfect purity or love on the part of the dying person necessarily brings with it great fear. The smaller the love, the greater the fear. This fear or horror is enough by itself alone (to say nothing of other things) to constitute the penalty of purgatory, since it is very near

the horror of despair. It seems that hell, purgatory, and heaven differ from each other as much as despair, near despair, and assurance. (Wengert: 2015, 36/WA 1: 234,3–8).

If this is so, getting out of purgatory can only happen if love for God is growing: "It seems necessary that, for souls in purgatory, as the horror decreases so love increases." (thesis 17; Wengert: 2015, 37/WA 1: 234,9f). The cause for the decrease of horror is the increase of love for God. But how can love increase in purgatory? In the earlier *Treatise of Indulgences*, Luther stated that indulgences may play a role in this respect, namely as prayers of the church to God that he may grant the person in purgatory an increase of love for him (See *Tractatus de indulgentiis*, WA BR 12: 5–10, no. 4212a). Thesis 26 declares: "The pope does best in that he grants remission to souls [in purgatory] not by 'the power of the keys,' which he does not possess [here], but 'by way of intercession.'" (Wengert: 2015, 37/WA 1: 234,27f).[16] With respect to souls in purgatory, the popular saying was: "as soon as a coin thrown into the money chest clinks, a soul flies [out of purgatory]."[17] This is a trade in the strictest sense: A living person pays a certain amount of money so that a deceased person staying in purgatory receives liberation from her punishment. In this case, the economic model is overthrown by Luther for two reasons: He denies that the pope has jurisdictional power over the souls of the deceased. The pope together with the whole church can pray for them, but the fulfillment of the prayer lies in the hands of God. Thus, Luther rejects narrowing the power of the pope's prayer to the power of the keys. In addition, according to the traditional understanding, satisfactory penalties could be detached from the person and be taken over by a substitute; but this is not possible when purgatory is understood as suffering due to a lack of love for God and not as the place where unresolved penalties have to be served by the deceased. Thus, there are two reasons why the economic model is not accepted by Luther.

In thesis 28, Luther brings together the theological understanding of this trade and the financial interest of the church: "It is certain that when a coin clinks in the money chest, profits and avarice may well be increased, but the intercession of the church rests on God's choice alone." (Wengert: 2015, 38/WA 1: 234,31f). In order to improve the financial interests of the church, the promised return of the financial investment in indulgences was emphasized and extended; however, Luther insists that the church is not able to guarantee the promised value since this is in God's hands alone.[18]

16 Luther refers to Sixtus IV's Encyclical letter "Romani Pontificis provida" of 1477 (Denzinger/Hünermann: 1999, nos. 1405–1407).

17 Quoted by Luther in thesis 27 (Wengert: 2015, 38/WA 1: 234,29f).

18 Even though it is appropriate to mention the financial interests of the church in dealing with indulgences, one should also note that poor people had to pay only a very small amount in order to receive an indulgence letter. There were many responsible persons in the medieval

In the time of the 95 theses, Luther binds the remission of guilt and penalty to true repentance. Thus, there is no need for investing money in indulgence letters because what they promise to offer, the true – truly repentant – Christians receive through their repentance. Thesis 36 states: "Any truly remorseful Christian has a right to full remission of guilt and penalty, even without indulgence letters." (Wengert: 2015, 39/WA 1: 235,7f). Luther describes in theses 1 to 4 what true repentance is: "hatred of self" (*odium sui*) that produces outwardly "various mortifications of the flesh."(Wengert: 2015, 35/WA 1: 233,14–16). Hatred of self is not directed against the human being as created by God but against the self-seeking structure of human persons that cannot be separated from them. "Seeking one's own benefit in everything" (*in omnibus quaerere quae sua sunt*) is one of Luther's definitions of sin (See Dieter: 2001, 80–107). The "various mortifications of the flesh" include the traditional works that were imposed on a penitent: alms, fasting, and praying (See *A Sermon on Indulgences and Grace*, nos. 6 and 3, Wengert: 2015, 60/WA 1: 244,1–6.15–24). Thus, there is a contradiction between emphasizing true repentance and the advice to buy indulgence letters since true repentance is committed to fulfilling the works of giving alms, fasting, and praying, and it does not wish to get rid of them. On the contrary, it is a sign of true repentance to accept those works willingly. If one wishes to be free from those penalties for sin, he only demonstrates the self-seeking tendency of his whole person and that he is not willing to struggle against it. Thus, Luther says in theses 39–40:

> It is extremely difficult, even for the most learned theologians, to lift up before the people the liberality of indulgences and the truth about contrition at one and the same time. The "truth about contrition" seeks and loves penalties [for sins]; the "liberality of indulgences" relaxes penalties and at the very least gives occasion for hating them. (Wengert: 2015, 39/WA 1: 235,14–17).

A consequence of this is what Luther expresses as a paradox in thesis 23: "If any remission of all penalties whatsoever could be granted to anyone, it would certainly be granted only to the most perfect, that is, to the very fewest."(Wengert: 2015, 37/WA 1: 234,21f). This means: There are only very few who deserve to receive indulgences, but they do not need to buy indulgence letters; they receive remission of penalties without them. Consequently, buying indulgence letters is done in vain. In his *Sermon on Indulgences and Grace*, Luther makes a different point in order to make some sense of indulgences:

> Indulgences are tolerated for the sake of the imperfect and lazy Christians, who either do not want to practice good works in a lively way or want to avoid suffering. For

church who wanted to offer indulgences as means of pastoral care and spiritual aid. See Hamm (2016).

> indulgences do not demand improvement but tolerate and accept such people as imperfect. For this reason, one should not speak against indulgences, but one must also not speak in favor of using them. (Wengert: 2015, 63/WA 1: 245,26–30).

The *Summary Instruction* of Archbishop Albrecht of Mainz offers four principal graces with respect to indulgences. The third grace is this:

> Participation in all goods of the universal church, which consists in this that those who contribute to the building of St Peter ['s Basilica] and their deceased parents who died in love for God will participate now and forever in all intercessions, petitions, alms, fasting, prayers, and any kind of pilgrimages, also to the Holy Land, stations in towns, masses, canonical hours, disciplines, and all other spiritual goods that happen and can happen in the universal, most holy Church Militant and in all her members. The faithful acquire this participation when they buy the indulgence letters. Preachers and confessors must strongly insist on this power convincing the faithful that they do not neglect this and miss to buy indulgence letters. (Köhler: 1934, 115).

According to this *Instruction*, the faithful have to pay for entering into the realm of the spiritual wealth of the church and being able to benefit from it. Buying an indulgence letter is the ticket that allows for participating in all goods of the universal church. This is an appealing trade since it promises eternal return for investing temporal goods. Luther holds a very different position: "Any true Christian, living or dead, possesses a God-given share in all the benefits of Christ and the church, even without indulgence letters." (Wengert: 2015, 39/WA 1: 235,9f, thesis 37).

Another economic thought structure is addressed by Luther in theses 56 to 68 – the concept of the "treasure of the church." In the institution of indulgences, there is a joyful exchange between a human contribution (pilgrimage, visiting a church, offering money, etc.) and a divine response communicated by the church. The church had to find a middle way between (a) continuing to insist that each sin deserves a temporal penalty and (b) alleviating the loads that came out of the inevitably accumulating temporal penalties on the sinners. The idea of the treasure of the church allowed for emphasis of both aspects. Penitents could receive indulgences out of this treasure, and this treasure was needed because so many penalties had to be carried and compensated. Buying indulgence letters meant that the penitents could contribute a little to the remission of their penalties while the main contribution came from the treasure of the church. Thus, a certain price had to be paid, differentiated according to the financial possibilities of the penitents. Compared with the relief that penitents could gain by this trade, their investment was not very high.

Luther carefully discusses the concept of the treasure of the church claiming that this treasure has not yet been appropriately identified. "The treasures of the church, from which the pope distributes indulgences, are not sufficiently discussed or known among Christ's people." (Wengert: 2015, 41/WA 1: 236,10f, thesis 56). The connection between the theological understanding of the treasures of the church and the financial interests of the church is ironically addressed in thesis 57: "That [these treasures] are not transient worldly riches is certainly clear because many of the [indulgence] declaimers do not so much freely distribute such riches as only collect them." (Wengert: 2015, 41/WA 1: 236,12f). The concept of treasures is an ambivalent concept with different meanings. A treasure can be in a closed box for which only one person has the key, but a treasure can also be a precious good that is freely available. The beauty of a landscape can be understood as the treasure of a certain area. Everybody who stays there may enjoy it and benefit from it. It is, as economists say, a public good, but it can be made a private good if a fence surrounds the area and one has to pay a fee when entering that area. One has to keep in mind these different meanings of "treasures" when reading Luther's theses. Thesis 58 reads: "Nor are they [the treasures of the church] the merits of Christ and the saints because even without the pope, these merits always work grace for the inner person and cross, death, and hell for the outer person," (Wengert: 2015, 42/WA 1: 236,14f) while the famous thesis 62 says, "The true treasure of the church is the most holy gospel of the glory and grace of God." (Wengert: 2015, 42/WA 1: 236,22f). But "the most holy gospel" also always works "grace for the inner person" – this is the argument in thesis 58 declaring why the merits of Christ cannot be the treasure of the church. One can only solve this contradiction if one realizes that the "treasures of the church" in thesis 58 is understood as a private good, which the pope has at his disposal and alone is in charge of, while the "treasures of the church" in thesis 62 are a public good from which every true Christian is benefitting even without any special permission of the pope. The difference between thesis 58 and 62 is not in terms of the content but in the understanding of the treasures of the church as "private goods" or as "public goods," of course with the difference of the role of the saints. One can see how a certain understanding of the economic metaphor of the "treasure" overcomes the economic thought structure in soteriology. In addition, Luther connects the theological interpretation of "treasure" with the financial interests of the church:

> Therefore, the treasures of the gospel are nets with which they formerly fished for men of wealth. The treasures of indulgences are nets with which they now fish for the wealth of men. Indulgences, which the declaimers shout about as the greatest "graces," are indeed understood as such – insofar as they promote profits. Yet, they are in truth the least of all when compared to the grace of God and the goodness of the cross. (Wengert: 2015, 42/WA 1: 236,27–34, theses 65–68).

Luther also struggles with the economic thought structure when addressing the question of good works. Theses 42 to 44 read as follows:

> Christians are to be taught that the pope does not intend the acquiring of indulgences to be compared in any way with works of mercy. Christians are to be taught that the one who gives to a poor person or lends to the needy does a better deed than if a person acquires indulgences because love grows through works of love and a person is made better; but through indulgences, one is not made better but only freer from penalty [for sin]. (Wengert: 2015, 40/WA 1: 235,20–25).

This translation using the phrase "acquiring indulgences" is correct, as opposed to older translations that used "buying indulgences." To emphasize it again: Indulgences – as the remission of punishment – were not bought; rather, indulgence *letters* were bought that gave the right to receive the remission of penalties after the remission of guilt had taken place in the sacrament of penance. In order to gain indulgences, giving money was not the only possibility. Instead, one could undertake pilgrimages, visit churches, etc. Giving money for a special, designated purpose, e.g. to build a church, is a good work, but in the case of indulgences, this good work is – through a decision of the pope – connected with the (total or partial) remission of penalties for sins. Every good work has a certain merit, but in the case of indulgences, the good work has huge effects. A small cause (the good work) has enormous effects because in this case, the pope is willing to open the treasure of the church. Many churches in Europe that are now Lutheran churches were originally built with the money given for indulgence letters.

But why is giving alms a better work than acquiring indulgences? If people spend money on indulgence letters, they indeed do a good work, but they do it with the expectation that they will receive a great benefit from this investment. They act according to the economic model of purchase, acquisition, and profit, but this actually strengthens human beings' self-centeredness in that they seek their own good in everything, also in good works. In contrast, giving alms means helping a person in need without necessarily expecting a reward. In addition, Luther argues that the pope can only act out of love for the faithful. Thus, he cannot wish that the needs of poor persons would be neglected in order to buy an indulgence letter that supported the building of St Peter's Basilica. "Christians are to be taught that anyone who sees a destitute person and, while passing such a one by, gives money for indulgences does not buy [...] indulgence of the pope but God's wrath." (Wengert: 2015, 40/WA 1: 235,26f, thesis 45).

In theses 80–91, Luther offers a series of sharp questions and arguments expressed as critical questions of lay people and requires that these be addressed because the church would otherwise be ridiculed. These questions also comprise economic practices and models. "Namely, why does the pope not empty purgatory for the sake of the holiest love and the direct need of souls as a matter of the highest justice, given that he redeems countless souls for filthy lucre to build the Basilica [of St Peter] as a completely trivial matter?" (Wengert: 2015, 44/WA 1:

237,22–25, thesis 82). The Roman response would be something like this: There must be a certain, even small contribution from the side of the penitent (or his friends and relatives) in order to open the treasure of the church; otherwise, the principle that God does not forgive a sin without punishment would be violated. Nevertheless, this answer is not convincing: The pope is aware that millions of faithful suffer in purgatory, but even though he is able to relieve them from their suffering and should do so out of love, he does not – he does this only when a friend or relative of the suffering person has paid for acquiring the indulgence and communicated it to the deceased. One may wonder whether this fulfills the requirement of divine righteousness. The paradox of this situation for Luther is that the pope in his self-centered love offers remission of penalties only for money while those penalties themselves are the consequences of people's self-centered love.

Another sharp argument is presented in thesis 83: "Again: Why continue funeral and anniversary masses for the dead instead of returning or permitting the withdrawal of the endowments founded for them since it is against the law to pray for those already redeemed?" (Wengert: 2015, 44/WA 1: 237,26–28). This is a very serious objection. People gave a lot of money to abbeys or brotherhoods that promised to celebrate masses at the anniversaries of the death of a certain person. This would help the deceased to get out of purgatory earlier than without this help. But when a relative of the donors received a plenary indulgence for the deceased, this person could leave purgatory immediately and go to heaven. Since it is not allowed to pray for people who are already in heaven, the anniversary masses should be stopped, and a certain part of the donated money should be given back. Actually, such endowment contributed considerably to the economic basis of monasteries and friaries. Again, one can see how closely economic and financial aspects of the church's life and economic models in theology were linked together.

In thesis 89, Luther addresses the practice of the indulgence campaigns that canceled earlier indulgence letters either for the time of the campaign or a certain area. Luther quotes an objection of lay people: "Since, rather than money, the pope seeks the salvation of souls through indulgences, why does he now suspend the documents and indulgences previously granted although they have equal efficacy?" (Wengert: 2015, 45/WA 1: 238,6–8). Again, one can describe the criticized behavior in economic terms: The organizers of the indulgence campaigns were afraid of a market saturation, and they wanted to uphold the demand for indulgences from the faithful on a high level; thus, they devaluated earlier indulgence documents. But this practice diminished the credibility of the indulgence commissioners since people had paid for a document that ought to be valid for their whole lifetime but now lost its value on the request of the pope who had previously authored it.

3. Consequences for Human Self-understanding

It has often been emphasized that Luther contributed substantially to the modern understanding of subjectivity (see the overview in Bornkamm: 1970, 13–197). In his discussion of the institution of indulgences, which very many people at that time made use of, Luther did not only change the economic activities of the church and the economic thought structure in theology; he also developed certain aspects of the understanding of the human person.

The backdrop against which Luther presented his 95 theses was an understanding of the relation between human beings and God in economic terms – the model of a trade: Temporal goods were given, and eternal goods were received (or hoped for) by the buyers. Meanwhile, the church, which transferred these eternal goods, received temporal goods in exchange and became wealthy. Today, it seems astonishing that it was the debate about the practice and understanding of penance that triggered the development of the understanding of subjectivity. For Luther, true contrition begins with the love for God so that this love cannot be the final point of a process that begins from a different starting point. He experienced this understanding as an important insight that helped him overcome serious problems with penance.[19] But if sin is the self-centeredness of the human being who seeks his or her benefit in everything (*in omnibus quaerere quae sua sunt*), how then is contrition possible at all? If contrition includes true knowledge of oneself, but the sinner is the one who deceives himself or herself, what makes contrition of the sinner possible? The starting point of contrition cannot be in the penitents; rather it has to come from outside of the human being, from an inspiration from God, from the gift of love for God that allows for realizing the lack of love for God in the penitents – through the divinely given love for God! Contrition is the painful acknowledgment of one's self-centeredness and lack of love for God. This corresponds to Luther's new understanding of "the righteousness of God" that does not denote an attribute of God in himself but his relation to the human beings. God practices the *iustitia Dei* in such a way that he leads human beings, who are sinners, to acknowledging their sinfulness, but through this acknowledgment they are justified, according to the saying of the apostle Paul, already quoted: "[I]f we judged ourselves, we would not be judged" (1 Cor 11:31). Contrition as this acknowledgment cannot be limited to some words or motions in the heart; it also includes the readiness to suffer evil in order to struggle against one's self-centeredness. Thus, Luther is so strongly opposed to indulgences because they hinder the working of God's righteousness in the sinners. Luther argues that sufferings of any kind, which are not self-imposed,

19 Luther tells about this experience in his letter of dedication for his *Resolutiones* (the proofs for the 95 theses) to his superior John of Staupitz (LW 48: 65f/WA 1: 525,1–23).

should be welcomed since they are means of fighting against the sinful structure of human beings, whereas self-determined practices, even ascetic practices, often express the self-seeking nature of the sinner rather than being a help to overcome it.

Two decisive aspects of Luther's understanding of subjectivity become clear: (a) The self is constituted from outside the human being, and (b) what comes from outside has to become something deeply internal. Both aspects belong together. In doing penance, the person cannot be replaced by another person – thus indulgences endanger the process of justification and healing of the person. But indulgences are not needed because God's righteousness does not require a specific penalty for each sin that can be paid by anyone. Rather, God in his justice is focused on making human beings righteous, which happens in repentance. This is the "punishment" that God imposes, but it is very different from the penalties that, according to the tradition of indulgences, are required by divine justice. In this perspective, nobody can be substituted by someone else; thus, no trade is possible in order to get rid of the punishments. Since it is repentance that induces grace and forgiveness of sins, each truly repentant Christian participates in all goods of the universal church. Thus, the concept of the treasures of the church, which are at the pope's disposal, is overthrown and replaced with the understanding that the gospel is the treasure of the church and open to all. The treasure of the church is no longer a private good, but it has become a public good of the church. Good works are to be preferred to indulgences since indulgences are acquired for the penitent's sake while good works should be done for God alone and not with the added wish of receiving something else in exchange. A truly repentant person will not perceive penalties (like almsgiving, fasting, praying, etc.) as something negative but as something positive, like medicine – wishing to be free from the penalties would be acting in the self-seeking line of the "flesh" that is the source of sin. Since purgatory is understood as emerging from a lack of love for God, no vicarious paying of debts of a person in purgatory is possible or makes any sense – no offering of money can free a deceased person from purgatory; this can happen only through prayers to God that he may increase the person's love for him. One could summarize Luther's criticism as follows: Indulgences are a misleading solution for a problem that does not actually exist.

Luther's theology developed further after the spreading of the 95 theses. Later, Luther did not so much emphasize the aspect of penance and contrition as the divine promise of forgiveness in the sacrament of penance. Every promise requires that the person to whom the promise is given trusts in this promise. Yet again, we see the same structure as before: What is constitutive comes from outside the human person – the promise of grace – but this promise must become internal, as faith in it, in trusting it. Only then does it reach its goal and become effective. Luther stresses both aspects, promise and faith, as the two sides of the relation that belong together in constituting the person. Because he himself experienced to be bound in God's words of promise, he was free from all other influential forces. At the Diet of the German Empire in Augsburg in 1521, when Luther was called to recant his teaching, he gave the famous answer: "I am bound by the Scriptures I have quoted and my conscience is captive to the Word of God. I cannot and I will not retract anything, since it is neither safe nor right to go against conscience." (LW 32: 112/WA 7: 838,6–8). Claiming the freedom of the conscience does not mean that he can think and act however he wishes; it means that he claims not to be forced to act against his convictions, being bound by the words of God. He calls for freedom because he himself experiences to be a captive of his conscience. This "captivity" is not enforced from outside, even though it comes from outside, but the words of God have become the innermost part of him, his conscience.

This concept of subjectivity and the self, deeply rooted in theology, has influenced the modern development of an understanding of the self. Its double aspect (*external* constitution of the *inner*) is still a challenge today since post-modern subjectivity is often closed in itself and tends to become arbitrary and at the end loses its freedom. Luther, instead, challenges us to be aware of the constitutive role of what has been called "the categorical gift" (see Bayer: 2007, 186–189) of God that is to become our self.[20]

Bibliography

ANGENENDT, ARNOLD (1994), Deus, qui nullum peccatum impunitum dimittit: Ein "Grundsatz" der mittelalterlichen Bußgeschichte, in: Matthias Lutz-Bachmann (ed.), Und dennoch ist von Gott zu reden, Freiburg: Herder, 142–156.

ANGENENDT, ARNOLD (2013), Offertorium: Das mittelalterliche Messopfer, Münster: Aschendorff.

AQUINAS, THOMAS (1252–1256/2011), Scriptum super libros sententiarum, liber IV, http://www.corpusthomisticum.org/snp4020.html (seen 06. 03. 2017).

BARBEL, JOSEPH (ed.) (1960), Augustinus, Enchiridion de fide spe et caritate: Handbüchlein über Glaube, Hoffnung und Liebe, Düsseldorf: Patmos.

BAYER, OSWALD (2007), Zugesagte Gegenwart, Tübingen: Mohr Siebeck.

BORNKAMM, HEINRICH (1970), Luther im Spiegel der deutschen Geistesgeschichte: Mit ausgewählten Texten von Lessing bis zur Gegenwart, 2nd ed., Göttingen: Vandenhoeck & Ruprecht.

20 For an illuminating presentation of Luther's understanding of the relation between gift and faith, see Holm (2006).

BRADY, IGNATIUS C. (ed.) (1981), Petrus Lombardus, Sententiae in IV libris distinctae, tomus II, Spicilegium Bonaventurianum 5, Grottaferrata: Editiones Collegii S. Bonaventurae ad Claras Aquas.

COGHILL, NEVIL (ed.) (2003), Geoffrey Chaucer: The Canterbury Tales, London: Penguin Books.

COURTENAY, WILLIAM J. (1972), The King and the Leaden Coin: The Economic Background of "Sine Qua Non" Causality, Traditio 28, 185–209.

DENZINGER, HEINRICH/PETER HÜNERMANN (ed.) (1991), Enchiridion symbolorum, definitionum et declarationum de rebus fidei et morum, 37th ed., Freiburg: Herder.

DIETER, THEODOR (2001), Der junge Luther und Aristoteles: Eine historisch-systematische Untersuchung zum Verhältnis von Theologie und Philosophie (TBT 105), Berlin/New York, NY: de Gruyter.

DINZELBACHER, PETER (1999), Die letzten Dinge: Himmel, Hölle, Fegefeuer im Mittelalter, Freiburg: Herder.

DÜRING, ADOLF VON (trans.) (2008), Geoffrey Chaucer, Die Canterbury Erzählungen, Cologne: Anaconda.

FABISCH, PETER/ERWIN ISERLOH (ed.) (1988), Dokumente zur Causa Lutheri (1517–1521), part 1, Münster: Aschendorff.

HAMM, BERNDT (2011), Den Himmel kaufen: Heilskommerzielle Perspektiven des 14. bis 16. Jahrhunderts, in: Berndt Hamm, Religiosität im späten Mittelalter: Spannungspole, Neuaufbrüche, Normierungen, Tübingen: Mohr Siebeck, 301–334.

HAMM, BERNDT (2016), Ablass und Reformation: Erstaunliche Kohärenzen, Tübingen: Mohr Siebeck.

HOLM, BO KRISTIAN (2006), Gabe und Geben bei Luther: Das Verhältnis zwischen Reziprozität und reformatorischer Rechtfertigungslehre (TBT 134), Berlin/New York, NY: Walter de Gruyter.

KÖHLER, WALTHER (1934), Dokumente zum Ablassstreit, 2nd ed., Tübingen: J.C.B. Mohr (Paul Siebeck).

LAUDAGE, CHRISTIANE (2016), Das Geschäft mit der Sünde: Ablass und Ablasswesen im Mittelalter, Freiburg: Herder.

LE GOFF, JACQUES (1984), Die Geburt des Fegefeuers: Vom Wandel des Weltbildes im Mittelalter, Stuttgart: Klett-Cotta.

LUTHER, MARTIN (1513–1515), First Lectures on the Psalms (LW 10/Vogelsang: 1963, 38–221).

LUTHER, MARTIN (1517), Disputation against Scholastic Theology (LW 31: 9–16/WA 1: 224–228).

LUTHER, MARTIN (1517), Ninety-Five Theses (Wengert: 2015, 34–46/WA 1: 233–238).

LUTHER, MARTIN (1517), Treatise of Indulgences (WA BR 12: 5–10, no. 4212a).

LUTHER, MARTIN (1517), A Sermon on Indulgence and Grace (Wengert: 2015, 57–65/WA 1: 243–246).

LUTHER, MARTIN (1518), Luther's Asterisks against Eck's Obelisks (WA 1: 281–314).

LUTHER, MARTIN (1518), Explanation of the Ninety-Five Theses (LW 31: 83–252/WA 1: 525–628)

LUTHER, MARTIN (1521), Luther at the Diet of Worms (LW 32: 105–131/WA 7: 825–857).

LUTHER, MARTIN (1545), Preface to the Complete Edition of Luther's Latin Writings (LW 34: 327–338/WA 54: 179–187).

OBERMAN, H.A. (1963), The Harvest of Medieval Theology: Gabriel Biel and Late Medieval Nominalism, Cambridge, MA: Harvard University Press.

STEGER, PHILIPP (ed.) (2006), Peter Abaelard, Scito te ipsum [Ethica]: Erkenne dich selbst, Hamburg: Meiner.

TANNER, NORMAN P. (ed.) (1990), Decrees of the Ecumenical Councils, vol.1, London/ Washington DC: Sheed & Ward/Georgetown University Press.

VOGELSANG, ERICH (ed.) (1963), Luthers Werke in Auswahl, vol. 5: Der junge Luther, Berlin: de Gruyter.

WASSERSCHLEBEN, FRIEDRICH W.H. (1958), Die Bußordnungen der abendländischen Kirche, 2nd ed., Graz: Akademische Druck u. Verlagsanstalt.

WENGERT, TIMOTHY J. (ed.) (2015), The Annotated Luther, vol. 1: The Roots of Reform, Minneapolis, MN: Fortress Press.

WERBECK, WILFRID (1972), Valor et applicatio missae: Wert und Zuwendung der Messe im Anschluss an Johannes Duns Scotus, ZThK 69, 163–184.

Vítor Westhelle

Faith and Love

The Lutheran Shaping of the Social Imaginary

1. Institution and Constitution

The relationship between faith and love in Martin Luther is at once complex and yet as simple as to cut a Gordian knot. Its complexity and its simplicity are shaped by a particular "social imaginary" as the concept has been used by Charles Taylor (2007, 159–211). This imaginary is made of stories, legends, songs, etc. – shared by a large group of people – that implies beliefs and convictions and from its start brings to the fore religious sentiment and imagery (ibid., 172). This insight had been implied by Max Weber in his celebrated *Protestant Ethics and the Spirit of Capitalism* (1939), which was then also applied by Ernst Troeltsch (1931) and Peter Berger (1967) for the study of social ethics in different forms of religious formation. However, the explicit use of "imaginary" and how it shapes individual identities and social relations finds its inception not in Weber but in the psychoanalytical work of Jacques Lacan (1997) and in the social philosophy of Cornelius Castoriadis (1997). This explicit use of the "imaginary" is buttressed by another tradition that had its origin in Hegel's notion of religious representation (*religiöse Vorstellung*) as the "stable image of unstable appearances" (Westhelle: 1984) and came to life again in Karl Marx's (1977) notion of the ideological superstructure that overdetermines social real existence.[1]

Even if Taylor does not overtly claim this latter tradition, he is genealogically beholden to it.[2] The issue at stake displays itself in his understanding of the "immanent frame" of modernity and whether it is closed or open. Taylor argues

1 The notion of "overdetermination" was used by Louis Althusser (1970, 87–128) to account for the role of the immaterial in transforming materiality.

2 In fact, he goes further back to Hugo Grotius' and John Locke's theory of natural law as founded immanently by the divinely endowed rationality, which sustains itself autonomously without the necessity of revelation. This position grows out of the Reformation distinction of regimes, the spiritual and the earthly (cf. Taylor: 2007, 126ff).

that it can be both – this against “the mainstream secularization theory, the view that modernity must bring secularization in its train […], [which] goes back at least to Weber” (Taylor: 2007, 550).

Taylor supports his position offering a distinction of “frames” that shape the imaginary, which need to be distinguished. One is the role that a theoretical *innovation* (Reformation ecclesiology is used as one example [ibid., 196]) plays in shaping the imaginary. The distinction of the other two frames is the crux of the argument. The first is the *economy* in which the imaginary is transmuted and infiltrated by a notion of “poietic agency” obtaining “efficient causation” (ibid., 177f; cf. also his note 20 on p. 795f.). The other main frame is the *public sphere* “as a common space in which the members of society are deemed to meet through a variety of media” (ibid., 185). By recognizing the distinction of these two frames or paradigms, by which the imaginary is framed, reshaped, and transformed, we are in the Hegel-Marx camp. The Hegel-Marx camp works with this distinction and tries to account for the “open immanent” option of Taylor, allowing for the effective creation of novelty in the *economy*, aside from the *public sphere* of politics. These two frames represent distinct forms by which the intervention into and the composition of the imaginary takes place. So we have, on the one hand, the economic paradigm working with the idea of “poietic agency” to describe the mechanism in and through which the imaginary is shaped and is reshaped by it. This mode of intervention has an *instituting* force in society. The political paradigm, on the other hand, working with the idea of “horizontal” inter-subjective consonance in society exerts a *constituting* function in a social formation.

The Weber-Troeltsch tradition sees religion as having a constituting role in society while the Hegel-Marx heritage, by discerning between economy and politics, offers an interpretation of the role of religion in shaping the imaginary as having an instituting, creative (*poietic*) capability, alongside its constituting function.[3] The difference between the constituting and the instituting functions is that the former sees the social imaginary woven into the texture of a social formation for which Weber’s use of the “spirit” metaphor is fitting. The instituting capability focuses on imagery associated with creation inserted into the social imaginary, without its overtly religious cradle necessarily remaining a constitutive part of it. This explains the argument that religious factors may institute a given social formation that can become thoroughly secularized; in this case, the religious factor does not remain, in its original form, constitutive. The instituting force shapes the imaginary of how a society understands its material sustainability and influences its mode of production and reproduction. The constituting function, on the other hand, molds and intervenes in the imaginary

3 So also Taylor (2007, 185) gives primacy to the economy.

shaping social relations of the public sphere through legislation, cultural mores, market relationship, civil society, and state politics. The more the instituting force is at work, the less the constituting is manifest, and vice versa. As we shall see, the social ethos is going to show itself differently in societies in which the primarily intervening factor in the formation of the imaginary is of an instituting or a constituting nature even as both play a role. Two different paradigms are thus presented. One is political; the other, by discriminating between politics and economy, gives primacy to the economic paradigm.

The recognition of the distinction between institution and constitution offers a non-exclusivist approach. In any society, both are at work, as well as the third factor – the impact on the imaginary made by innovative theories. The three, entwined as a Borromean knot, can be discerned, *a posteriori* of course, as to their respective workings and relative importance. Hence, the quest is a twofold one. First, one needs to examine which is the primary factor that shapes the imaginary and establishes the peculiarity of a given socio-cultural formation giving cohesion to the imaginary. But of decisive importance is also to examine the lenses through which a society is investigated and its imaginary deciphered. Being attentive to the instituting capability turns the examiner's gaze primarily into the human relationship with the rest of nature, i. e. to the economy and to labor as the decisive factors for sustainability, without neglecting the inter-subjective constitution of society, namely, politics. The task is then to look simultaneously at both, the signified (the society described) and the signifier (the one offering the description and the thought tradition subscribed to).

The religious factor as a superstructural and overdetermining element in a particular social formation intervenes into the imaginary with an instituting force and a constituting function. These can be recognized, then, by prying into the production of means to sustain life and reproduce it – that is, the "public" household, the economy – and also into the mode of social interaction, cultural mores, legislation, state apparatuses, all that pertains to intersubjective sociability, politics in *lato senso*. It is important not to blend the two in a diluted mix but keep them discrete, even when and because the nature of the imaginary is complex and cannot be defined *a priori*; the instituting and constituting interventions in the imaginary can be recognized only *a posteriori*, so the different configuration of social imaginaries can be discerned, offering more nuanced variances among societies.

2. The Lutheran Ethos, or How Does This Play Out?

By discerning between economy and politics, the tradition that can be traced to Hegel and Marx finds its root in the medieval tripartite division of society – church, household, and politics – that was adopted by Luther, who turned them from static statuses into dynamic publics in his *Dreiständelehre*. In order to understand the instituting power in shaping the imaginary, this distinction must be taken into account, namely the distinction between two publics that Luther called the *politia* and the *oeconomia*. The latter is the household as the public space, in which production for the sustenance of life and reproduction takes place, and not the privatized *oikos* of post-Industrial Revolution modernity.

A quest for the significance of Luther and Lutheranism in lending a mark to economic and political programs that had an impact in piercing through the social imaginary is pertinent here. Even without explicit help from Luther's works, even if no Lutheran spirit can be recognized as a constitutive part of it, the instituting force did its work. Until recently, research on the religious roots of modern societies has focused on the contrast between Roman Catholicism and the Reformation heritage. Such is the theme of the classical studies by Max Weber (1939) and Richard Tawney (1926). Luther appears only to set the stage for Calvin, Calvinists, and the Puritans. The method was to establish the theoretical sources constitutive in shaping social practices but ignoring the instituting force that affects its mode of production and reproduction for the sustenance of life. Attention was given to the constitutive function of the political paradigm, but the economy was neglected. With the post-Industrial Revolution privatizing of the *oikos*, its distinct public character, defined by the means to produce the sustenance for earthly existence and the reproduction of life, was lost. Whatever was left of its public character, as labor and the market, was subsumed under politics or blended into "political economy," a concept that surfaced only at the time of the Industrial Revolution in the eighteenth century.

Sociologist Sigrun Kahl (2005, 91–126) offers an analytical approach in which the instituting force of religious convictions shaping a social ethos is at the core of her research. She offers a comparative study, not to explore the progress of the capitalist "spirit" and the political organization of the market but to explore the religious roots of modern poverty policies in countries whose major religious constituencies belong to three distinct confessional families, Roman Catholic, Lutheran, and Reformed Protestant. This move implies the distinction between *oeconomia* and *politia*, and the focus is on the former. She is cautious of generalizations – particularly of different religious formations in Western societies – due to the progressive intermingling of traditions and rejects the claim that the religious factor is the independent variable of socio-political and economic diversity in Western modernity (although she gets very close to such a claim). She presents a typological distinction of profiles in countries shaped more typically by each of the three traditions and their imaginaries. The typology, however, does not follow the Weberian "ideal type" approach but looks *a posteriori* to the actual shaping of social policies regarding poverty and how it is treated, which is primarily an economic problem, for it pertains to the sustenance of life. "The fundamental tension in poor relief is that between granting economic support *and* ensuring that everybody who can work in fact does. Each tradition has solved this goal conflict differently" (ibid., 121). After several disclaimers regarding some generalizations, Kahl explicitly calls upon "religious roots" to account for the differences in instituting given social formations. "Despite the immense changes the welfare state brought about, much of the national continuities in attitudes towards, and policies against, poverty can be traced back to religious roots" (ibid., 123) After rich documentation pertaining to poverty and manners to address it, the theological grounding argument is named. "Catholic social doctrine continues to view the beggar as closest to Christ. Therefore, poverty does not carry a stigma, and good works, especially almsgiving, guarantee salvation; in Calvinism, it is a mark of lacking grace; and in Lutheranism, poverty itself says nothing about one's state of grace." (ibid., 120f).

The consequence is that the link between grace and salvation and social responsibility is severed in societies shaped by the Lutheran ethos, opening the social dimension of existence to be more readily secularized. "In countries under Catholic or Reformed Protestant dominance, poor relief was not secularized as early and as comprehensively as in the Lutheran countries" (ibid., 120f). The issue is finally brought squarely to the central category that defines the *oeconomia* – the question of labor, the human faculty through which the means for the sustenance and reproduction of life is obtained.

> Each strategy creates particular problems within the work-welfare trade-off: integration strategies historically rooted in Catholicism provide social assistance benefits or other local support but permanently exclude the long-term unemployed from work. Integration strategies rooted in Lutheranism prevent economic hardship and provide work but institutionalize an inferior kind of work outside the labor market. Integration strategies historically rooted in Reformed Protestantism promote (low wage) labor market integration at the expense of guaranteeing an economic and social minimum. (ibid., 122f).

In order to pursue the theological ground from which the peculiarity of Lutheran social ethics ensues, the way in which Luther set the issue over against Catholic theology must be looked into. Further, we need to attend to the positive task of defining the contours for a social ethics implicit or even explicit in Luther's theology. Far from an underdeveloped social ethics that Calvinism brings to completion, it offers a different ethical matrix for social life on earth, a road not taken by others.

3. Bondage of the Will

The *locus classicus* for looking into the departure from Catholic theology and its ground for social ethics is Luther's 1525 text *The Bondage of the Will* in which the Reformer takes issue with Erasmus on the question of the freedom of choice (*arbitrio*). Luther starts by dismissing all arguments for freedom of choice that are not grounded in the scriptures. Erasmus, in his criticism of Luther in the *Diatribe* (written in response to Luther's *Assertio* of 1520, which was the text of Luther's response to the excommunication bull of Leo X) had agreed to argue on the basis of the scriptures. However, on the issue of choice Erasmus argues that the scriptures are often not clear, for which the magisterium of the church must be called upon to adjudicate (LW 33: 24f/WA 18: 606). Luther argues for the clarity of the scriptures (*claritatis scripturae*); the introduction of categories such as necessity of consequence, necessity of the consequent in God's foreknowing, merits *de congruo* or *de condigno*, and others, are presented as plain sophistry introduced presumably to illuminate what was made obscure. "[T]he scriptures are perfectly clear" (LW 33: 99/WA 18: 659,18f). This was the first point, to settle the hermeneutical ground.

From there, the argument goes on to dismantle Erasmus' attempt to find in the scriptures evidence for the exercise of freedom of choice. Here, Luther makes an important distinction. In the scriptures, whenever there is a call for human responsibility and the implied choice to be exercised, it is geared toward "dealings with lower creatures" (LW 33: 119/WA 18: 672,9f). This is grammatically expressed by the use of the indicative. The imperative does not indicate a choice, only the incapability of exercising; it entails no promise; it is pure law (LW 33: 127/WA 18: 677,7–27). However, in the earthly realm humans cooperate with God; while the agency is still divine, the execution is human (LW 33: 155.241–245/ WA 18: 695,37–696,11.753,12–755,18). Ultimately, the work is still God's.[4] But in the spiritual realm, God alone operates all in all. Luther is clear here, using the distinction of the two regimes (*Zweireichelehre*), the earthly and the spiritual, that he claims to obtain from the scripture itself. *Coram deo* human free choice plays no role.

4 "First, the Bible speaks and teaches about the works of God. About this, there is no doubt. These works are divided into three hierarchies: the household [*Oeconomiam*], the government [*politiam*], the church [*ecclesiam*]" (LW 54: 446/WA TR 5: 218,14ff, no. 5533).

This same point is made a decade later, in the *Disputatio de homine* (1536) in which – while discussing the four Aristotelian causes – Luther grants a certain human sovereignty and rational autonomy regarding the material and the formal cause but none as far as the efficient and the final cause is concerned (LW 34: 137f/WA 39 I: 175,1–177,14).[5] The efficient cause pertains to God's agency alone in creating the world and preserving it while the final cause pertains to divine foreknowledge and predestination. Humans do not have any say in it. But in God's left hand, to use Luther's metaphor for the earthly regime, God "does not work without us because it is for this very thing he has recreated and preserves us, that he might work in us and we might cooperate with him" (WA 18: 754,4ff, my translation).

The point about foreknowledge and predestination is clearly stated already in the *Bondage of the Will.* However, there is a definite proviso that is repeated again and again. And this is the point in which there is a clear divide that suggests an explanation for the difference Kahl pointed to between Lutheranism and Calvinism as to the relationship between poverty and the state of grace and salvation. This pertains to the hiddenness of God that suspends all possible causal connection of the reception of grace to things revealed in the scriptures or any other visible, rational evidence. The argument is so radical that not only miracles or even sanctity are dismissed as serving as evidence to God's mercy (LW 33: 72/ WA 18: 640,10–641,3), but also the commandment to love God is not ours to fulfill. We cannot love God by our choice. Therefore, the love of God cannot be demonstrable outwardly (LW 33: 133/WA 18: 681,12–24). This means that God's election belongs to inscrutable mystery. A "distinction between God preached and God hidden, that is, between the Word of God and God himself" must be drawn (LW 33: 140/WA 18: 685,25ff). Hence, the qualitative difference between external evidence and faith is so stated that outward sanctity in works of love bears no evidence of election. Those whom the church call saints maybe so, but so is also everyone who is baptized. Sanctity is defined "by the rule of love, not by the rule of faith" (LW 33: 88/WA 18: 652,1). This means that the true church remains a hidden church even "not so as to have it called the Church" (LW 33: 87/WA 18: 651,3f). "The Church is hidden, the saints are unknown" (LW 33: 89/WA 18: 652,23). Such is the radical severance of any logical cause-and-effect connection between election and earthly responsibilities, which takes any spiritual value out of the rational equation of earthly responsibilities in the three publics one is called to serve.

5 The same distinction is made is the *Lectures on Genesis* (cf. LW 1: 127/WA 42: 95,25–96,4[on Gen 2:21).

4. Love and Grace

Is there, then, a spiritual way of connecting faith and love, two of the three traditional cardinal virtues of 1 Cor 13 (which Luther also affirmed), namely, faith, hope, and love? How do we connect the external to the gift, to grace? In his commentary on the Sermon on the Mount, Luther's tries to explain the relationship between the undetermined faith that belongs to the *vita passiva* and the love that is determined and active and shows itself. This is the reason that it should be kept in secret (*en tō kryptō*, Matt 6:2, 5, 16). It is not invisible! Secrecy is rather a question of hiding. This is the point: Love is to be kept from sight so that the act seen by the receiver only as an outcome comes as an authentic gift and not commerce. And the One who sees in secret will reward the giver.

This is not the economy of circular exchange, which happens when the subject of the act of mercy is rewarded by displaying the act in the open as propaganda, but still, it is an economy, a *commercium*. This reward from the One who sees in secret is absolute surplus value because the reward of publicity is sacrificed when love is kept out of sight, yet all the same visible! This is how love of the enemy needs to proceed. It is a secret love of the pure heart that dispenses mercies without necessarily ceasing the outward hostility. Love appears here as a disruption in the circular economy of exchange. The exchange becomes asymmetric. The gift bestowed by the secret love disrupts the economy and yields no compensation, except by the One who sees in secret, to whom alone glory is due.

For Luther, the Sermon on the Mount is not to be taken as counsel or advice for the few who want to achieve perfection while remaining at most a desideratum for the average Christian. This is one motif that the Reformer repeats over and over again to counter the qualitative difference between heaven and earth, according to which the difference is not a matter of gradation, an axiological ordering between lower and higher, higher and lower, as he accuses the systems of knowledge and power of his day of seeing it. Luther opens the preface, which he himself wrote for the publication of his transcribed sermons on the Sermon on the Mount, by attacking the difference between *praecepta legis* and *consilia evangelica* and the ordering of them so that the counsels are seen "merely as advice to those who want to become perfect" (LW 21: 3f/WA 32: 299ff). No, he says. The distinction is not one between different classes or castes of people; it is a distinction within the person herself, between the heart and the deed. To use Luther's expressions, between one's own being in itself, inwardly, *coram deo*, and its being outwardly for others, *coram hominibus/mundo* (LW 27: 30/WA 40 II: 37f). What bridges the two is kept out of sight, is kept in secret, for the eyes of only the one who sees in secret. In the commentary on Paul's Letter to the Galatians where he expounds on the Apostle's affirmation that faith is made effective through love (Gal 5:6), Luther points out that the subject is faith. Faith acts; love is a "tool" through which faith operates (LW 27: 30/WA 40 II: 37f).

In his *Confession Concerning the Lord's Supper* from 1528, Luther elaborates on this question of faith and love making explicit the distinction between the blessed or saved and the holy or saint already announced in *The Bondage of the Will.* This pertains precisely to the problem that is being addressed regarding the unique character of Lutheran social ethos and its intervention in the social imaginary where the Lutheran Reformation was largely accepted: "For to be holy [*heilig*/saint] and to be saved [*selig*/blessed] are two entirely different things. We are saved [*selig*] through Christ alone; but we become holy [*heilig*] both through this faith and through these divine foundations and orders" (LW 37: 365/WA 26: 505,18ff). As a Christian, one is not excused from participating in any or all of the divinely instituted orders, as Luther states in the *Confession* of 1528, listing them: "But the holy orders and true religious institutions established by God are these three: the office of priest, the estate of marriage, the civil government. All who are engaged in [...] these are engaged in works, which are all together holy in God's sight" (LW 37: 365/WA 26: 504,30ff).

This brings us back to the question about the connection between the two – the holy and the saved, sanctification and justification. Simply put, can one be blessed and saved without being holy or saintly? Alternatively, the reverse, can one be holy without being blessed? Luther admitted that the "godless may have much about them that is holy without being saved thereby" (LW 37: 365/WA 26: 504,20ff). Is there some form of causal relationship implied here? How can he know, by his own argument, who is faithful? Before this question is answered, a digression is called for.

5. Unio Hypostatica

Luther's strong and qualitative differentiation between the hidden realm of grace and the visible manifestation of love is predicated on a peculiar Lutheran teaching and interpretation of the Chalcedonian *communicatio idiomatum*, the union and not mixing of the two natures in Christ. Luther's interpretation of one of its categories or genre, which was later dubbed the *genus maiestaticum*, started to mark the difference between the Lutheran and the Reformed traditions as early as the dispute with Zwingli at the Marburg Colloquy of 1529. A year before, Luther, who thought that he did not have much time left in life, decided to write his theological *Confession Concerning the Lord's Supper* (LW 37: 151–372/WA 26: 261–509), referred to above. However, this text is better known for setting up the argument that at Marburg would underscore the Lutheran stance on real presence.[6] But in this text, he goes even further than affirming the real presence. He presents three modes of Christ's presence. The first is the historical Jesus; the second is the sacramental presence in the visible elements entailing a promise. But then he presents the third mode of presence where Christ is indivisible with God and present everywhere, as these words that have already been quoted many times convey:

> You must place this existence of Christ which constitutes him as one person with God far, far beyond things created, as far as God transcends them; and, on the other hand, place it as deeply in and as near to all things as God is in them. For he is one indivisible person with God, and wherever God is, he must be also, otherwise our faith is false (LW 37: 223/WA 26: 336,15–19).

This is the crucial aspect of Luther's theology. Christ is present where the right hand of God is (to use the creedal metaphor discussed at Marburg), and that means: everywhere! And yet, he is present in a clothed or masked way, which is the outward matter we see and our senses detect. Luther expressed this "wrapping of God" with a series of metaphors: mask (*larva*), clothing (*vestitus*), wrapping (*involocrum*), which are the external manifestations of God's presence in Christ according to the flesh, i. e. in nature, in "majestic matter," as he qualified it. This third mode of presence should not surprise those familiar with his *Sermon on the Sacrament* of 1526 where, presupposing the real presence in the sacrament, he states, "If it were possible, and I should measure all creatures and describe them in words, you would see wonders just as great, nay, even greater, than in this sacrament" (LW 36: 338/WA 19: 487,14ff).

But how is this to be conceived? Here, Luther appeals to ordinary experience,[7] as he often does. He suggests the analogy of a crystal with many facets that display a spark or a bubble inside the crystal even as it appears in every one of the many facets when in fact, it is in the middle of it. So he applies the analogy:

> If Christ also sat at one place in the center of the universe, like the bubble or spark in a crystal, and if a certain point in the universe were indicated to me […] by the Word, should I not be able to say, "See, there is the body of Christ […]," just as I say, when a certain side of the crystal is placed before my eyes, "See, there is the spark in the very front of the crystal"? (LW 37: 224/WA 26: 337,15–20).

Indeed, it looks to be on the surface of the facet while in fact, it is at its core. Here, Luther plays with words in his spelling of crystal as *Christall* (modern German *Kristall*), which a strict transmutation into English would render as "Christ-All."[8]

---

6 This, incidentally, was the only point of discord between Zwingli and Luther after expressing agreement on the other fourteen theses bearing the position of the Reformation.
7 "I am not speaking now from Scripture," he says (LW 37: 224/WA 26: 337,14).
8 See the insightful reflection on this passage in Gregersen (1995).

Now, if the incarnation is what establishes the connection (*communicatio*) between the realm of the divine and the material world according to the mutual interchange of properties (*idiomata*), and if the workings of one nature is the workings (*apotelesmata*) of the other, then the gracious work of God operates through love in which faith is effective. So there is no true faith if love does not follow. If there is holiness without confessing faith in Christ, this will break down the union of natures (*unio hypostatica*). The same would be the case if there were the possibility of being blessed without producing holy works. In fact, Bonhoeffer took the notion of "cheap grace" from Luther himself, who used the concept in *The Bondage of the Will* where it is used to reject the *facere quod in se est*, to do the minimum to earn it, turning it "cheap and contemptible" (LW 33: 268/WA 18: 770,36). Luther refers to this cheap faith again in the Galatians commentary where he calls it "lazy" (LW 27: 30/WA 40 II: 37,21).

6. The Regimes

There is enough in Luther's writings to corroborate the Wesleyan accusation that Luther is weak on sanctification, with his emphasis on *sola fide* and the invectives against works and law. These seem indeed to corroborate this breaking down of the hypostatic union, which is only mildly assuaged by the metaphor of the tree and its fruits. However, even this analogy breaks down because one might conceive of a tree without fruit but never the fruit without a tree. To state, as Luther does, that there may be holiness among those not being saved is an untenable statement (LW 37: 365/WA 26: 504,20ff). If the elect are unknown and the true church hidden, logically one cannot know if the work of love is a manifestation of the love worked by faith or not, i.e. whether it is true love. Love does not serve as evidence, for "it is in the nature of love to be deceived" (LW 33: 88/WA 18: 652,4). Hence, love, as it makes its appearance is no evidence of election, for one does not know true love except in faith, which cannot be demonstrated outwardly. This is why Sigrun Kahl can say that poverty (or, for that matter, prosperity) "says nothing about one's state of grace" (Kahl: 2005, 120f). We may add that neither can the attitude toward it be judged in the tribunal of faith but only of reason, which is deceitful.

Luther's teachings on the two regimes, the worldly and the spiritual, is something that he eventually shared with other reformers such as Zwingli, Melanchthon, Bucer, and Calvin.[9] It has been interpreted throughout history in several ways. For example, in German theology, in response to its abuse during

9 This is also the theological ground for Taylor's and Grotius-Locke's theory of immanently and rationally framed natural laws.

the Nazi period, there was a tendency to read it as an extension or even foundation of the law/gospel distinction. In the USA, with its indebtedness to the Hobbesian/Lockean type of liberalism, it has been almost equated with the separation of church and state. With the publication in 1970 of Ulrich Duchrow's seminal work, *Christenheit und Weltverantwortung* (1970), an amazing amount of research on the topic since the 1930s was put to rest. Some of its lessons have been ignored, others have been learned. Among those learned was that the spiritual regime (or kingdom, regiment) is not a symmetrical figure of the earthly, in which the earthly would be the shadowy Platonic projection of the spiritual. It is also not Augustine's two divergent roads offering the pilgrim a choice of which to follow, to bliss or to gloom. Neither is it a distinction between content and form as the Barthian-Lutherans would frame it. It is even less in any sense a direct expression of the relationship between church and state (a penchant of US interpreters). Finally, it is also not what post-Vatican II progressive Roman Catholic theologians consider it to be: a post *corpus christianum* revision of the two planes theory, the natural and the supernatural. In sum, it is not as if two vectors ran parallel to each other – to meet only in the future eschatological horizon – and were occasionally related through the ministry (*Amt*): proclamation, sacraments, and charity. Positively stated, the two regimes describe asymmetric dimensions that do not concur, but where the spiritual produces incidents in the earthly order and is subjectively apprehended[10] as something that happens and breaks through the order of things and, in that, reveals the masks under which the divine is hidden. Through these masks shines the light that convicts the world and promises a good life in the midst of the ordeal of a perennially decaying world.

7. Apocalyptic

Henceforth, one may surmise that the Lutheran incisive transformative incision into the social imaginary was this affirmation of the union of faith and love but with the simultaneous denial of how they stand to each other, i.e. the logical (Luther: dialectical) relation between the two. This relation can be known not by reason but only by faith that is non-demonstrable. And then the incision cuts deeper as Luther's apocalyptic move comes into play.

As in early Jewish apocalyptic, the presence (*parousia*) of the Messiah is accompanied by the manifestation of the Anti-Christ, an entity that does not come from above but is at work in the midst of the "orders of creation," or the public spheres of economy, politics, and the church. As sin is a universal

10 This is what Luther meant by the affirmation that "experience makes a theologian."

original condition (*peccatum originale originatum*, Gen 3); it is also always at work (*peccatum originale originans* – "because all have sinned," Rom 5:12). And what does sin accomplish? To carry on Luther's metaphor, the work of the Devil is what cracks the mask, tears the clothing, rips the wrappings of the divine, effaces the facets of the crystal. In other words, it destroys nature, human and otherwise, and corrupts the institutions ordered for its protection. And this protection – the mask, the clothing, the wrapping – shields us from the exposure to the *deus nudus*, the ominous *tremendum* of Rudolf Otto. At this point, Luther's disconcerting paradoxes again throw us off balance because this is precisely also the point in which messianic presence is at hand. The *parousia* of Christ becomes manifest, showering us with faith, love, and hope. And for what? To rapture us to heaven? Or to throw us into the abysmal black hole of a naked god? No! Rather, it is to darn the ripped clothing, to mend the mask, to restore the wrapping. This he expresses in theological concepts but in paradoxical terms: *ad deum contra deum confugere*, "to flee from and find refuge in God against God" (WA 5: 204,26f).

Luther's apocalyptic gesture is paradoxical in that it does not suspend ethics. The legendary saying, at times attributed to Luther, that if he knew that the end of the world would come tomorrow, he would still plant an apple tree, indeed is fitting to represent his paradoxical apocalyptic. Behind the mask, the metaphor for our public responsibility is always the emptiness to the *deus nudus*; and both are simultaneously present.

If a sociological study, like the one Kahl has done on poverty, would be done on the question of the care of creation and ecological responsibility or on the question of refugees and immigrants assailing Europe today, a differentiated profile of the social imaginary should emerge in countries where Lutheranism prevailed. The suspicion is that not only would there be a sense of public responsibility, but also that the failure to attend to the issue would bring catastrophic consequences of apocalyptic proportions even if and because this apocalyptic incision is kept in a secular form, without the religious figurative adornments.

8. Usury

Finally, I will present an illustration of how this incision into the texture of the imaginary can genealogically find its place, for example in Luther himself, using the last of Luther's three writings against usury (in 1519/1520, 1524, and 1540). The language exemplifies Luther's use of apocalyptic verbiage and imagery, channeling at times motifs not unlike the description of the Beast of the Sea (i.e.

the market)[11] of Revelations 13. And yet, simultaneously it is a call for human public responsibility in the *oeconomia*. Here, we find the framing of the relation of faith and love, viz. its failure together with an apocalyptic intimation.

In this text, Luther does not abandon the concrete ground in addressing a socioeconomic problem; he is adamant in not allowing a "spiritualization" of the issue. And last, but decisively, he is tackling what he regards as a superlative manifestation of evil at the time – the practice of usury which was the main tool in the implementation of the emerging financial capitalism. The usurer is the primate of the contemporary *homo pecuniosus*. The choice of this text from 1540 was not made on the basis of its moral implications (as if it could provide us with anachronistic criteria to pass judgment on late-modern capitalism) but to exemplify how this incision into the imaginary reshaped it. The treatise is entitled *An Admonition to Pastors to Preach against Usury*.

Luther starts by exposing misconceptions regarding the practice of usury, namely, the presumption that by lending money the usurer is actually providing a service to the people. Foreshadowing the modern criticism of ideology, he writes:

> Whoever takes more or better than he gives is doing usury, and this is no service at all but wrong done to his neighbor as when one steals and robs. All is not service and benefit to a neighbor that is called service and benefit. For an adulteress and adulterer do one another a great service and pleasure. […] The devil himself does his servant inestimable service (WA 51: 338,32–339,25).[12]

To make his case, the Reformer does not appeal to dogmatic or ecclesial authority. He draws on classical philosophy (Seneca, Aristotle, among others) to demonstrate his point: "We must spare our theology hereupon" (WA 51: 344,30f). At the court of reason and for the sake of equity (WA 52: 344,25f), he pleads his case that usury is an unnatural (*wider die Natur*, i.e. not part of the relationship of humans with the rest of nature) mode of producing value.[13] This would not be a problem in itself if it were not for the fact that usury cannot create value without (mis)appropriating "alien labor" (WA 51: 351.21–27).[14] And the verdict is peremptory and consistent with his view of the purview of reason: "Even if we were not, Christian reason alone would tell us all the same that a usurer is a murderer" (WA 51, 361.34–362.17).

After having argued so far without appealing to theology, he starts to address Christians: "The heathens were able by the light of reason to conclude that the usurer is a double-dyed thief and murderer. We Christians, however, hold them in

11 For the use of the imagery as an allegory for the market see Westhelle (2005).
12 Translation by me (parts of Luther's *Admonitions* are translated in Eric Kerridge, Usury, Interest and the Reformation, Aldershot: Ashgate, 2002).
13 For Aristotle's argument, see *Treatise of Government*, Book 1, ch. 10.
14 Elsewhere, he calls it *sudore alieno* (WA 44: 50,25).

such honor that we fairly worship them for the sake of their money" (WA 51: 261,30ff). And the attack goes on with apocalyptic zest:

> Therefore is there on this earth no greater enemy of man (after the Devil) than a gripe-money and usurer, for he wants to be God over all men, [...] a usurer and money-glutton [...] he may have the whole world to himself, and every one may receive from him as from God and be his serf forever. [...] The usurer wants to condemn the whole world to hunger, suffering, and misery (WA 51: 396,28–397,19).

What are we to do? The language becomes shocking and appalling: "And since we break on the wheel and behead highwaymen, murderers, and housebreakers, how much more should we break on the wheel and kill, [...] hunt down, curse, and behead all usurers?" (WA 51: 421,24ff). Luther refuses to make the spiritual leap from the concrete political order to the universal condition of human sinfulness as a palliative by which sin is denounced while the sinner is justified. Is this not a problem to be solved by sincere repentance alone, knowing that, after all, justification is for the sinner qua sinner? The response resounds clearly and coherently:

> They say that the world could not be without usury. This is certainly true. For so strong and stiff can no government in the world ever be and has never been [...], and even if a government could prevent all sin, there would still be original sin. [...] But if with this [argument] they think they are excused, let them see (WA 51: 353,32–354,28).

Preachers who fail to raise their voice from the pulpit against usury and usurers and even associate with them "make a comedy of their preaching office [...] and turn themselves against the truth. [...] Such people cannot promote the gospel" (WA 51: 409,19–22).

Sin is not to be fought in a disembodied piety, but it is always to be fought where it appears: in the flesh, in matter, because that is where the gates to condemnation as well as redemption open themselves. Quoting Luther again shows the instituting motif in using creation and incarnational language: "If our gospel is the true light, then it must truly shine in the darkness. [...] If we do not want suffering, if we want to transform the world [*die Welt anders haben*], then we must go out into the world or create [*schaffen*] another world, which will do whatever we or God wants" (WA 51: 409,27–32). And Luther adds: "God's marvelous power and wisdom must have its signs [*Spuren*] and must be grasped herein [*hierin*]." What are these traces, these signs that may be grasped in here? The answer is straightforward in the same text: "earthly peace to increase and sustain [*mehren und nehren*] the human race" (WA 51: 354,29ff). And this peace that promotes development and sustainability is concretely undermined by the practice of usury, which for the Reformer at the time rated with singular highest prominence among the manifestations of sin (cf. Rieth: 1996).

9. Love's Public Rational Responsibility

The text on usury is exemplary, for it shows the supposed logical inconsistency in the Reformer, the same one that Otto denounced in Schweitzer. The latter maintained that the evangelical story combines a "marvelous ethics" alongside a thoroughgoing (*konsequente*) eschatology, which is indeed echoed by Jesus' saying, "Occasions for stumbling are bound to come, but woe to anyone by whom they come!" (Luke 17:1; Matt 18:7). How can this combination of an apocalyptic stance (the world is going to hell in a handcart) and a vigorous defense of justice, reason, and fairness for the promotion of the common good be explained (Otto: 1943, 59)?[15]

The grounds for the so-called inconsistency can be elucidated either by some circumstantial peculiarities or deeply felt theological convictions. Although Luther had said that there was no saint that was not well versed in politics and economy, his temperament did not thrive in those fields, even if his impact on them has been significant. His base remained in theology, with frequent incursions into those other fields but never on their own autonomous grounds. To say it differently, if the young Luther would be placed in the second half of the twentieth century, alas, he would be a dismal failure in *Realpolitik* and would not be admitted to study monetarism at the School of Economics of the University of Chicago. Despite having been exposed and influenced by the nominalism of the *via moderna*, his understanding of the exchange value of merchandise was that of a realist. He followed the prevailing medieval Aristotelian theory of the sterility of money and saw value determined and imbued in merchandise by labor. In that, he was even less refined than the late medieval Roman moralists who, under the spell of money's sterility, could come up with a justification for a quasi-interest principle of charging a fee for a loan on account of depreciation by deterioration due to the handling of currency.

Luther was light years away from his younger reformation colleague, John Calvin, who recognized the economic validity of earning interest for lending money. The interest rates charged would have to be subject to strict and reasonable regulation. As Richard Tawney remarked when comparing Calvin to Luther, "The significant feature in his [Calvin's] discussion of the subject [of usury and interest] is that he assumes credit to be a normal and inevitable incident in the life of a society" (Tawney: 1926, 95).[16] Max Weber, who begins his *Protestant Ethic and the Spirit of Capitalism* with the importance of Luther's

15 Otto intends to call attention to this inconsistency as a genuine trade of religious experiences of people also like Francis and Luther (see p. 62).

16 It should be noted that later in his career, Luther admitted some flexibility on the question of regulated interests as insurance for a debtor's insolvency (cf. zur Mühlen: 1978).

understanding of vocation (*Beruf*) for the ensuing development of a worldly asceticism, has hardly anything to say in favor of Luther as far as his contribution to the development of capitalism is concerned: "[I]t is hardly necessary to point out that Luther cannot be claimed for the spirit of capitalism in the sense in which we have used that term above, or for that matter in any sense whatever" (Weber: 1939, 82). Indeed, Luther's home base was theology. If, however, he did not contribute much to capitalism as such, it is because his sway in economy, politics, and society was grounded in theology, not subjected to political negotiations or economic calculations.

Luther's scathing attack on usury is due to the misery it engenders, thus disturbing the earthly peace necessary for the pursuance and advancement of the common good. And this good is predicated on the result of labor which, for Luther, was the source of earthly, material value for the promotion and sustenance of life sustained by God's promise to Adam before the Fall (cf. Rieth: 1996, 217f; Bayer: 1998). If we consider what Luther has written about the "third mode of presence" of Christ, labor, as the human engagement with nature, plays a critical role. The disregard for and exploitation of labor undermines a "metabolism"[17] that takes place when the *adam* cultivates *adamah* producing and reproducing herself, participating and transforming human beings and the rest of nature in which the majestic presence of God in Jesus/matter dwells. Therefore, Luther describes the work performed in the three institutional spheres (*ecclesia, oeconomia, politia*) as bringing forth "God's gifts," adding: "These [gifts] are masks of God, behind which He wants to remain concealed and do all things" (LW 14: 114f/WA 31 I: 434,7–11). The use of the mask motif is significant in the imagery that the metaphor evokes and how it intervenes. Usury (or sin in general) destroys the dignity of labor and damages the masks of God, exposing thus the reality of the abyss of the *deus nudus.* This is why the masks themselves and the work in them accomplished – the peace, protection, sustenance, and procreation they provide – are of no soteriological import. It goes without saying: *sola fide!* But active responsibility toward the public is the means through which the promises embedded in this earthly divinely instituted orders come to fruition: protection, sustenance, and growth (Luther: *wehren, nehren, mehren*). This is why if we say *pax mundi non speranda,* we also must add *pax mundi exspectare est.* The peace of the world is not a function of hope, but it is a longing for, a looking forward to what can be attained herein as something finite and not unambiguous.

With this move, love, which faith enacts, can only move outwardly, toward the world and be made visible there. There is no causal connection that can be established between love and faith. Love is beholden to reason, which in fact rules

17 *Stoffwechsel,* metabolism, is how Karl Marx explains labor in *Das Kapital* (1962, 192).

over the earthly sphere in the three publics that Luther distinguished. There, love is rational for the achievement of equity (*Billigkeit*).

In the *Confession* of 1528 after presenting the three publics, Luther adds: "Above these three institutions and orders is the common order of Christian love in which one serves not only the three orders but also serves every needy person in general with all kind acts of benevolent deeds" (LW 37: 365/WA 26: 505,11 ff). Love is the canopy that shelters rational human responsibility in the three public spheres instituted by God for the achievement of an equitable kingdom of this world that is perennially passing. Reason is love's public procedure that unfolds itself, according to the different operations of the human faculties, in the three distinct publics (*ecclesia, oeconomia, politia*). However, this cooperation cannot be argued backward to justification, for in faith justifying grace remains in-dwelling presence (*parousia*) in its apocalyptic immediacy.

Bibliography

Althusser, Louis (1970), For Marx, trans. Ben Brewster, New York, NY: Vintage.

Bayer, Oswald (1998), Nature and Institution, LuthQ 12/2, 125–159.

Berger, Peter (1967), The Sacred Canopy: Elements of a Sociological Theory of Religion, Garden City, NY: Doubleday.

Castoriadis, Cornelius (1997), The Imaginary Institution of Society, trans. Kathleen Blamey, Cambridge, MA: MIT Press.

Duchrow, Ulrich (1970), Christenheit und Weltverantwortung: Traditionsgeschichte und systematische Struktur der Zweireichelehre, Stuttgart: Ernst Klett.

Gregersen, Niels Henrik (1995), Natural Events as Crystals of God, in: Viggo Mortensen (ed.), Concern for Creation: Voices on the Theology of Creation, Uppsala: Tro & Tanke, 143–155.

Kahl, Sigrun (2005), The Religious Roots of Modern Poverty Policy, AES 46/1, 91–126.

Lacan, Jacques (1997), Écrits: A Selection, trans. Bruce Fink, New York, NY: W.W. Norton & Co.

Luther, Martin (1519–1521), Lectures on Psalms I (LW 10/WA 5).

Luther, Martin (1525), The Bondage of the Will (LW 33/WA 18: 600–787).

Luther, Martin (1526), The Sacrament of the Body and Blood of Christ – Against the Fanatics (LW 36: 335–361/WA 19: 482–523).

Luther, Martin (1528), Confession Concerning Christ's Supper (LW 37: 161–372/WA 26: 261–509).

Luther, Martin (1531/1535), Lectures on Galatians (LW 26–27/WA 40 I–40 II).

Luther, Martin (1532), Exegesis of Ps 147 (LW 14: 109–135/WA 31 I: 430–456).

Luther, Martin (1532), Commentary on the Sermon on the Mount (LW 21: 3–294/WA 32: 299–544).

Luther, Martin (1535–1545), Lectures on Genesis (LW 1–8/WA 42–44).

LUTHER, MARTIN (1536), The Disputation Concerning Man (LW 34: 137–144/WA 39 I: 175–180).

LUTHER, MARTIN (1540), An Admonition to Pastors to Preach against Usury (WA 51: 331–424).

LUTHER, MARTIN (1542–1543), Three Rules Used for Translating the Bible (LW 54: 445f/ WA TR 5: 218, no. 5533).

MARX, KARL (1962), Das Kapital: Kritik der politischen Ökonomie, Berlin (GDR): Dietz Verlag.

MARX, KARL (1977), The Eighteenth of Brumaire of Louis Bonaparte, New York, NY: International Publishers.

OTTO, RUDOLF (1943), The Kingdom of God and the Son of Man: A Study in the History of Religion, trans. Floyd F. Filson/Bertram Lee-Woolf, London: Lutterworth.

RIETH, RICARDO (1996), "Habsucht" bei Martin Luther: Ökonomisches und theologisches Denken, Tradition und soziale Wirklichkeit im Zeitalter der Reformation, Wien: Böhlau.

TAWNEY, RICHARD (1926), Religion and the Rise of Capitalism: A Historical Study, London: John Murray.

TAYLOR, CHARLES (2007), A Secular Age, Cambridge, MA: The Belknap Press of Harvard University Press.

TROELTSCH, ERNST (1931), The Social Teachings of the Church, 2 vol., trans. Olive Wyon, Chicago, IL: University of Chicago Press.

WEBER, MAX (1939), Protestant Ethics and the Spirit of Capitalism, trans. Talcott Parson, London: G. Allen & Unwin.

WESTHELLE, VÍTOR (1984), Religion and Representation: A Study of Hegel's Critical Theories of Vorstellung and their Relevance for Hegelianism and Theology, unpublished PhD Thesis, Lutheran School of Theology at Chicago.

WESTHELLE, VÍTOR (2005), Revelation 13: Between the Colonial and the Postcolonial, a Reading from Brazil, in: D.M. Rhoads (ed.), From Every People and Nation, Minneapolis, MN: Fortress Press, 183–199.

ZUR MÜHLEN, KARL-HEINZ (1978), Article "Arbeit VI: Reformation und Orthodoxie", TRE 3 (1978), 635–639.

Hans-Martin Gutmann

Intimacy, Shame, Justification

Martin Luther's Theology as an Answer to the Early Modern Crises of Communalization and Individualization

1. Intimacy, Not Order

The imagination of communalization is necessary for the success of actual communal life with others and the capacity for selfhood.[1] Mental images of community are important for sociality and individuality. This dependence and its meaning for Modernity have been examined in many ways. Empirical inquiries indicate, for example, that today users of social media need to imagine successful communities and that these imaginings are productive for the existence and stability of communalization. This dependence was also true in the period of the Reformation.

Communication succeeds when and because the parties involved are able to mobilize autobiographical and environmental resources as mental images. In these mental images, participants can imagine the success of the good life. Without these imaginative resources, which might be called "fundamental trust" in the tradition of psychoanalysis (Erikson: 1973), or "a good enough mother" (Schulte-Markwort: 2015), or even of a functional transitional object in intermediary spaces, neither the communal life with others nor a healthy relationship to the self is possible (e.g. Winnicott: 1990).[2]

Charles Taylor opened this phenomenon up from the concentrated themes of the mediated worlds to possibilities for understanding Modernity in general when he spoke of "social imaginary." He said:

> What I'm calling the social imaginary extends beyond the immediate background understanding which makes sense of our particular practices […] this understanding supposes, if it is to make sense, a wider grasp of our whole predicament, how we stand to

1 This necessity is as valid in the media culture of contemporary Modernity as in the Reformation period (cf. Hepp/Berg/Roitsch: 2015).

2 See Kohut (1983) for theoretical perspectives on narcissism.

> each other, how we got to where we are, how we relate to other groups, etc. (Taylor: 2007, 172f.).

From this perspective, Martin Luther's theology comes into view in a surprising new way. When it comes to topics related to communal life like marriage and family, political policies, and business, Luther's theology is often understood as a theology of order. However, this approach shortchanges Luther's theology. In his texts on faith, the family, and communal life in a polity, Luther is concerned with the *formation of intimacy*, an experiential possibility that in many respects was new in the Reformation period. Luther's subject matter was not primarily order, but rather lived relationships. The possibility of forming intimacy in social space is dependent on mental images of success. And precisely here, the relevance of Luther's theological reflections on "faith" must be fully appreciated (cf. Gutmann: 1991).

The communal life with others is like the self-relation of the I to the self. Both orientations of conduct require imagined images of successful lives. Here lies an important task for all religious narrative traditions and symbolic worlds, including Protestant Christianity. In its origins, Reformation theology made use of inner images that supplied resources for the "social imaginary." In no way is the need for these resources new. And in no way does it indicate a problem that first arose in contemporary Modernity. Rather, it has plagued people since the beginning of the era.

The social movements of the Reformation period brought with them social, political, and religious changes for large groups of people. People became socially homeless en masse and had to orient themselves to changing social realities. Countless new cities were established as a result of expanding silver mining. This led to the dissolution of traditional relationships and the development of new and often random population groups. In addition to the religious reform movements, uprisings against feudal lords amongst peasants in the countryside and the urban citizenry upset the state of affairs that had been rehearsed for centuries. However, Luther's theology also found its plausibility in this upheaval. It offered "social imaginaries," in Taylor's terminology, that made manifest for many people of this time that such upheavals were manageable.

2. The Shift from Outer to Inner Governance

The Reformation brought about a mass movement and affected the lifestyles of many people through pamphlets, worship services, and public demonstrations because certainty that one could be made right before God through the empty performance of religious ritual had been largely lost (cf. Oberman: 1987).

Reformation theology answered this problem through the shift from outer to inner governance, from external conduct to interiority, from ritual observance to faith.

This radical change can be traced autobiographically in Luther's theology itself. In the period leading up to Luther's lectures on the book of Hebrews (1517–1518), he understood faith in the righteousness of God in terms of humility, as humbleness.[3] But in the Hebrews Lectures, Luther came to understand the righteousness of God, not as a type of punitive justice, but as a righteousness that God gives. Faith was no longer bound up with external agency and behavioral patterns – the righteousness of God could no longer be infused purely through participation in the sacrament of faith. Here, Luther came to a fundamentally new insight: the *faith* of the recipient is the foundational element in what occurs between God and the human person; through it, the human person is made just.

In these tumultuous months during 1517–1518, the basic decisions for the construction of Luther's Reformation theology were made. Despite emerging possibilities for communalization in Protestantism, the move from "behavior" to "interiority," from "ritual" to "faith" was, however, decidedly risky. Ethnographic and cultural anthropology research in many societies has shown that, in many historical upheavals, decline in the self-evidence of rituals and decreasing plausibility for participating in them coincides with a rapid erosion of social cohesion, indeed, with a death of sociality altogether (cf. Douglas: 1970).

The risk of the new orientation of Reformation theology reinforced itself in that the "Law" (*Gesetz*) of God was no longer understood as a guide to everyday life. In the traditional sense, laws (*Gebote*) pertained to and ordered life before God, other people, and one's self. Now, in Luther's understanding, the law of God was understood to convict the human person of sin because the essence of the law did not pertain to the laws of the second table that oriented behavior. Instead, the first commandment stood as the core of the law. God's law confronted the human person with the fact that he cannot let God be God because he himself wants to be like God.

> Although the commandments teach things that are good [...] the commandments show us what we ought to do but do not give us the power to do it. They are intended to teach man to know himself, that through them he may recognize his inability to do good and may despair of his own ability (LW 31: 348/WA 7: 52,25–29).

3 On this point, I follow Bizer (1958, esp. 22ff, 100ff).

The law of God leads the human person to this realization in order that he despairs of himself. This is risky for the psychological stability of individuals. The devaluation of "law" (*Gesetz*) as a mandatory norm for behavioral control, the establishment of law as the destruction and depression of the human person in his delusion of grandiosity also corresponds to a de-emphasis on the psychological apparatus of the person – in psycho-analytic terms, the "super-ego" is no longer the decisive instantiation for the inner regulation of the affect, rather it is the "ideal self." The person crashes into his grandiose desire to be like God. Narcissism is the key psycho-dynamic constellation for these persons. The foundational psycho-dynamic conflict in the Reformation and leading into Modernity was not *guilt*, but rather *shame.*

Shame is the greatest threat to the narcissistic personality that is governed by aspirations to grandiosity. Shame confronts the individual with the realization that he has not attained his ideal self and that he never will.

According to Heinz Kohut, the narcissistic individual is incapable of abandoning the early childhood condition of an "undisturbed, primarily narcissistic orientation, a psychological state whose own perfection precedes the simplest differentiation in later stages of perfection (i. e. perfection in areas of power, knowledge, beauty, and morality)" (Kohut: 1983, 85). This occurs in such a way that the child holds onto warm feelings as part of its own psychological structure in adulthood. Additionally, in all relationships, the grown adult tends to seek out that strong sense of being united, cared for, and balanced, just as it is experienced in the early childhood relationship with one's mother.

Shame is destructive for human subjectivity. Shame destroys the subject. Guilt shatters relationships, but these can be repaired in some successful situations. Shame, on the other hand, hands the individual over to the "Tribunal of Stares" (*Tribunal der Blicke*), as the German literature scholar, Claudia Bentien, titled her insightful study (Bentien: 2001). Shame is bound up with being exposed. The identity, self-worth, and social status of anyone who is delivered to the Tribunal of Stares on the basis of a disastrous offense, even if it is unintentional, is irreparably harmed by the mercilessness of the desirous-destruction of the glares of many people.

A central story in the Old Testament prehistory, the tale of Cain and Abel (Gen 4:1–16), could be interpreted through the creative lens of literary criticism (Bastian/Hilgers: 1990). According to this interpretation, shame is abrogated through guilt. God receives Abel's sacrifice with delight even as he disregards Cain's sacrifice. Thus, Cain's gift in return for God's blessing is rejected without ground or obvious motivation. This must have caused Cain's shame, devastating him in his social and individual existence. The outlet that Cain sought is, itself, the culpable act: the murder of his brother. Specific guilt suspends endless shame. Moreover, Cain is not put to death for his act. Rather, he receives a sign from God that protects him.[4] The biblical narrative even introduces him as a cultural founder.

Shame destroys the human subject. We have convincing theories for the development of cultural history that help to explain this dependence. Paul Ricœur saw shame to be bound up with the ancient experience of defilement, of impurity resulting from overflowing, polluting evil coming from outside the self (Ricœur: 2002). Norbert Elias, on the other hand, understands feelings of shame and embarrassment as instances of mental control over the affects: it is not fear of punishment, but rather shame that prevents people from automatically following their tribal instinct (Elias: 1978). This kind of tribalism remains ever precarious. It remains unconscious and barely restrained, hiding itself growing capacities for introspection and self-reflection for individuals.

3. The Theological Construction of the Notion of an Intimate Interior Space

From a theological perspective, the problem of shame in the contrast of "Law" and "Gospel" is virulence, hostility.[5] In Law and Gospel, God is encountered as a power that can drive people to the point of self-destruction in despair (Law) and at the same time to embrace them in a transaction, a "happy exchange" that re-establishes the human core of the person (Gospel).

In a Reformation understanding of "Law," Law delivers the person to a disastrous, destructive experience of shame, which must annihilate her as the subject of her own life. What positive solution does Luther's theology provide to escape this destructive experience? This question probes at the imagination, which is built on the conceptual dependence between "promise" and "gospel." This has to do with the *conceptualization of an intimate interior space* in which the relation between God and the soul of the believing person finds a home. More precisely, this space is first formed through the relation between God and the person in faith: an imagined relational space like that between a *bride and a groom.*[6] In the foundational Reformation treatise of 1520, *The Freedom of a*

4 This mirrors the narrative pattern in many classical myths and persecution texts: the one who is "guilty" of violence becomes the victim of violence (cf. Girard:1982).

5 It is important to note that the distinction between Law and Gospel has to do with a foundational religious logic. Law does not refer here to the Torah, the so-called legal Judaism or even the Old Testament. Were these identified with Law, then the door to an anti-Jewish argument would be opened up. On a fundamental discussion of the problem of anti-Judaism with regard to the topic, see Volkmann (2002).

6 In the sociology of space, "spaces" are understood as fundamentally relational and, therefore, in terms of human perception and conceptions of action. The reverse – as though a space

Christian (LW 31: 343–377/WA 7: 49–73), Luther described the essence of Christian freedom as the freedom of the inner person using the intimate image of a wedding: the grace of faith lies in the idea that the soul is bound up with Christ like the bride with the bridegroom. Christ and the soul become "one flesh."

Historically, this intimacy is a prerequisite. Inner images of successful intimacy between loved ones is a resource that believers can recall in their relationship to God. This resource feeds on the emergence of such intimate spaces in the social life of people. But Luther reverses this order. In his understanding of an intimate inner space does not simply refer to real social living conditions. It is an idealized conception that can have consequences for the way people perceive and shape their everyday life insofar as it is fed by the power of the imagination and linked with such a picture of success.

In Luther's time, various types of marriages and families existed side by side. In the landed gentry, we find multiple generations, relatives, and unrelated household staff living together in the "house," in the "large household family" under the lordship of the housefather and sharing considerably in the productive work in the life of the housewife.[7] In the late middle ages, marriages between the houses of landed upper-class families were primarily made through family contracts between the father of the bride and the bridegroom. The male leaders of the household forged the marriage between the engaged couple through a "gift and vow." Intimacy was necessary neither in the initiation of the couple's relationship nor in the couple's social life because of the largely absent separation between work and living quarters in the houses of rural populations and the urban craftsmen (Schröter: 1985).

In the rural and urban lower classes around the time of the Reformation, among craftsmen and day laborers, the poor and the "have-nots," the small family was predominant. Working conditions, housing situations, and the lack of separation between public and private life in this context did not allow for intimate spaces. The social control of the surrounding society not only pressed in on the intimacy of the married couple, but even constituted it. In the lower classes, a marriage was established through "rumors," through public awareness in the neighborhood that a man and a woman shared a table and bed together.

Some clues from the Reformation period also indicate that different strata of urban bourgeoisie separated themselves from one another in areas of work and family life, in public and private life. Intimate relationships could be established between the married couple and between parents and children. In this setting, it

preexisted and the perception of the space and action, then, take place *in* a *given* space (cf. Löw: 2001). On the reception in practical theology, see Woydack (2005).

7 Katharina von Bora, Luther's wife, owned a farm with vineyards and a beer brewery. She also supervised garden and farm work and the workers.

was thought that the woman was uniquely equipped by "nature" and the "character of her sex" for work in the intimate area of life, for relationship building, for work out of love for her husband and children while the husband proved himself in the publicity of the "world," in politics and business.[8] The Reformation made possible the expansion of the intimate family type in various ways, through church order, through marriage ceremonies in the Protestant church, through public statements.[9]

It is the *imagination* of such *intimate relational spaces* that, historically, arise in the social realms of life that Luther offers in his theological reflections as a mental image of the relationship between Christ and the believer. This imagination can remove the destructive experience of shame. Experiences of shame can always emerge in everyday life; intimate relationships are never exclusively harmonious. The model of intimacy that Luther propagates excludes women from public communication and work; to the extent that the form of intimacy in everyday life is not successful, imagined success stories become all the more urgent. But public communication, which Luther saw in the estates of *politia* and *ecclesia*, in politics and the church, is by no means always the domain of conflict-free, harmonious relations.

4. Between Conceptualization and Reality

In contrast to real life social possibilities, the conception of intimacy that Luther develops in his writings on faith is strongly idealistic. Faith binds the soul to Christ as a bride with a bridegroom. Christ and the soul become one flesh, and a "real" marriage exists between them of which human marriages are but imperfect images. Everything that belongs to Christ and to the soul becomes common to both, good and bad. Everything that belongs to Christ is attributed to the soul, and everything belonging to the soul is attributed to Christ as his own. "Now let faith come between them and sins, death, and damnation will be Christ's, while grace, life, and salvation will be the soul's; for if Christ is a bridegroom, he must take upon himself the things which are the bride's and bestow upon her the things that are his" (LW 31: 351/WA 7: 55,1–4).

How does the intimate relational space that is imagined through faith in the Gospel contrast with the experience of conflict in everyday life? How does Lu-

8 Thus, this development does not arise until the Romantic period, as is widely accepted in family history research (cf. Hausen: 1978, 177ff). See also Gutmann (1991). The developments mentioned here are subsequently traced in the interpretation of exemplary texts by Luther.

9 The Reformation also contributed to the exclusion of women from professional work beyond the family, limiting her to work in the home.

ther's theological concept differ from the social realities of real people? On this point, there is a clear ambivalence.

On the one hand, there are massive clues that Luther understood everyday reality – in the "estates" of *oeconomia*, *politia*, and *ecclesia* – in the sense of a "harmonious community." In 1530 and 1531, in the years of the Diet of Augsburg and the founding of the Schmalkaldic League, Luther gave a lecture on the Song of Solomon, a central biblical text for medieval mystical piety.[10] Here, Luther broke with the interpretative tradition of the Middle Ages in a peculiar way (see Ohly: 1958). In the twelfth century, the main focus of interpretation shifted towards an internalization of God's salvific history of the world to the history of mystical experience in the soul. Exemplary for this move is the interpretation of the bride figure, whose union with the bridegroom is poetically rehearsed. While the bridegroom is understood as Jesus Christ, three possible interpretations are identified for the role of the bride: namely, the *church*, *Mary*, or the *soul* of the believer.

Keeping this tradition in mind, Luther's interpretative decision in his analysis of the Song of Solomon in 1530/31 is surprising. In his view, the bride in the poem is not the church, Mary, nor the soul of the believer. Instead, Luther understands the bride as the *state (der Staat)*, or more precisely, the community permeated by the Reformation. The Song of Solomon deals with the state: "that we may know that the greatest gift is *politia*." (WA 31 II: 590,17f).[11] While life in the sphere of the household is achieved somewhat naturally – in conflict-free subordination – specific instruction is required for the multifaceted conflicts encountered in the political realm (WA 31 II: 590,6ff). Luther read the Song of Solomon in this light: as a guide to help men get along better in their duty. "To govern a principality [is] different from [governing] a home." (WA 31 II: 591,3).[12]

The result of this interpretive decision in the Lectures is a near complete removal of the erotic symbolism in the biblical text. For example, when the term "kiss" is utilized, Luther determines this term to actually refer to the experience: "and with certainty to confirm and not to doubt that God loves us and the duchy of Saxony." (WA 31 II: 595,8f).[13] The breasts, perfume, virgins, bedchamber, lover, and the bosom of the woman are understood in similar ways. For Luther, all

10 See Gutmann (1991, 179ff, 212ff) for more details on the following. I see a methodological advantage to investigating texts in Luther's writing that are deemed outside the central texts. From these peripheral texts, it is possible to garner information about attitudes towards life and even about the power of inner images because the text is not concentrated on a thoroughly shaped theological proposition.

11 "[...] ut sciamus, quam maximum donum sit polita" (Rörer's notes).

12 "Ein furstenthumb zu regirn aliud quam domum" (Rörer's notes).

13 "[...] et certo statuere et non dubitare, quod deus nos amet et ducatum Saxoniae [...]" (Rörer's notes).

of these erotic images refer to God's union with his people in the Reformation community (WA 31 II: 628,18ff). The public area of state-political life that is ordered by rules meets the domain of intimacy, bestowing as much maternal protection as sexual attraction radiates: "you are the most beautiful woman, no one goes after your like in the world." (WA 31 II: 620,9f).[14]

The Reformation "state" is, in Luther's opinion, the harmonious community. However, this community must be secured through the occasionally conflict-ridden and arduous work of men. In order to manage this, they must approach their work as an intimate, even erotically-charged attraction. The intimate sphere of life is de-eroticized while the public eroticized. The explosive nature of Luther's Lectures comes not least through the designation of public life to men and private life to women. Wives sit at home, as Luther puts it in his *Genesis Lecture*, "like a nail driven into the wall" (LW 1: 202/WA 42: 151,25f). The public life, now defined as the realm of intimacy – authority, administration, church, and economic activity – is, for Luther, the realm of men. Men must prove themselves even when peace in the harmonious community proves itself to be persistently brittle and when conflict in the state and family must be endured.

In this sense, the word of God takes on a central importance for the "harmonious community"–in the sense of a conceptualization of living without conflict, denying all differences. The real problem for the preservation of public peace lies, in Luther's opinion, in the individual disposition: obedience, reverence, and peace must be retained to gain the upper hand over the potentially chaotic power of desire. If behavioral conditions are managed at an individual level, a harmonious, conflict-free life can also be achieved in the state: people with "good affects" who labor for good works also stand for a peaceful political life in the public realm. Interiorly, this community is characterized by tranquility, harmony, and peace; outwardly, by the militaristic and ideological resistance of the enemy.

With his model of a "harmonious community," Luther grabs onto and escalates a theological-political discourse that had been alive since the High Middle Ages, namely the traditional idiom of the "three orders" (cf. Duby: 1978). Pray, fight, and work. *Orare, bellare, et laborare.* However, Luther abolishes the traditional hierarchy of the three orders that sees the orators atop the hierarchical structure followed by the warriors and the laborers: priests/pastors are denied

14 "[…] es formosissima mulier, nulla plus petit similis in orbe terrarum" (Rörer's notes). Luther justifies this position by stating that: "you have the law, the prophets, the teachers, and the preachers. She does not know herself as the most beautiful, it is, therefore, necessary to reveal [it], so that she may know herself as the most beautiful." (WA 31 II: 620, 10ff) "[…] quia habes leges, prophetas, doctores, praedicatores. Ipsa ignorat se formosam, ideo oportet indicare, ut sciat se formosam" (Rörer's notes).

every authoritative competence. Rather, they fulfill a much more specific function for the community.

Luther redefines the relationship between the *bellatores* and the *laboratores* – in Luther's terminology, the estates of *politia* and *oeconomia* – such that *oeconomia* is genetically and quintessentially defined as the origins of *politia*. At the same time, he no longer understands the *laboratores* as objects of exploitation, but as subjects of obedience and objects of protection within dependent feudal relationships with the *bellatores*.

In his lectures in the Song of Solomon, Luther takes his earlier position in texts such as "On Good Works" (1520) one step further. But now, the estates of *oeconomia* and *politia* are no longer clearly distinguished. *Politia* is seen more as a characteristic of *oeconomia:* namely, as a power relation that is to be determined by mutual care and service to all. *Politia* also becomes a way of interacting that is characterized by intimacy (the state as a "bride," which is also described using the entire intimate erotic metaphor of the Song of Solomon – kiss, breasts, and bedchamber). In the Lectures, *politia* is *oeconomia*. Thus, one could say that, in Luther's understanding, the harmonious community encompasses state and church within one household.[15]

With this, Protestantism in Germany since the Reformation period concocts the idea that the community as a whole can be permeated by the Christian spirit and can take shape as a society of interconnected Christian persons.[16] This attitude and understanding of life has remained an effective undercurrent in the history of Protestantism, surfacing again and again in efforts to shape and form society.[17]

The impact of this social model is also problematic for self- and world-relations insofar as the boundary between "inner" and "outer" is rigidly determined. The assumption that a harmonious community can be insulated from all human, social, and ecclesiastical conflicts can lead to the deterioration and repudiation of the very ambiguities that give vitality to life. The idealized social conception of a

15 "I am in that way of life, that it most certainly pleases God. He gave me the office of governing the security of the commonwealth, having a wife, to fight against Satan." (WA 31 II: 635,5ff.); "In eo genere vitae sum, quod deo certissime placet, dedit mihi officium, regendi promissionem Civitatis, habendi uxorem, adversatur Satan […]" (Rörer's notes).

16 With this claim, I also object to a predominant interpretation within Lutheran theology exemplified (e.g., example by Elert (1952) 9).

17 For example, in Protestant orthodoxy and Pietism during the 17th century; in the revival movement and the missionary movements of the 19th century; in Johann Hinrich Wichern's attempt to reawaken the poor population of industrialized Germany in "inner mission" as a social and ecclesiastical process since the founding of the "Rauhes Haus" ("Rough House") in 1833; in the various breakouts of Christian Socialism, including the socially responsible Christianity of the early CDU in the beginning of the Federal Republic of Germany.

harmonious community exists within this ambivalence of the image of an ideal society.[18]

5. Harmony and Conflict

However, there is also a countermovement to the idealistic imagination of a "harmonious community" in Luther's theological reflection. Luther in no way envisaged the intimate relational space of faith as static. This space is full of movement, full of conflict, full of antagonistic exchanges. It is all or nothing, life or death, justice or sin.

The intimate relational space of faith, in the imagined picture that Luther portrays here, permits an exchange of gifts, a "happy exchange and conflict." Christ and the soul become "one flesh… such that everything that belongs to them (i.e., Christ and the soul) becomes communal, both good and bad, so that the believing soul can boast and rejoice over everything that is Christ's as her own. And all that the soul has, Christ lays down as his own." If we compare this, something inconceivable emerges: Christ is full of grace, life, and salvation; the soul is full of sin, death and, condemnation. But faith comes as a mediator between Christ and the soul. The result is that sin, death, and hell belong to Christ, but grace, life, and salvation belong to the soul. According to the bridal metaphor, the bridegroom must simultaneously accept everything that the bride has and give to the bride everything that is his. For when he gives her his body and his very self, how can he not give her all that is his? "Moreover, how could it be that whoever accepts the body of the bride, should not also accept all that the bride has? Here is the loveliest display – not only of unity, but of a salutary conflict, of victory, of salvation, and redemption." (LW 31: 351 f/WA 7: 54,35–55,8)

In this text, Luther depicts the interaction between God and the person in the intimate relational space of faith as a gift exchange. Just like gift exchange in the everyday realities of social life,[19] gifts must be given, received, and reciprocated. The incomparable uniqueness of this particular gift exchange lies above all in the fact that *everything* is exchanged for *nothing*: righteousness for sin, the most

18 The negative-destructive side of idealized notions of a "harmonious community" is Luther's anti-Judaism (see Kaufmann: 2011; Ebach: 1998). The evil failures of the Reformer and the destructive historical effects of his anti-Jewish diatribes cannot easily be kept in silence as Luther's lack of understanding reflected in his crass rejection and condemnation of the social uprisings of his time. Ultimately, the latter extends from a lack of understanding of the life circumstances and behavioral concepts of the poor.

19 The feudal social order, which was in crisis in Luther's time, must be understood as a gift exchange. (cf. Duby: 1978; Mauss: 1978).

valuable for nothingness. Moreover, the very one who initiates this exchange, namely God, regards this interaction as *just.*

This notion fundamentally upends the traditional obligations of exchange in feudal culture, but also the rules requiring an equivalent exchange grounded in the capitalist economy during this period. In the faith relationship, the rules of reciprocal obligation are transgressed without violating the relationship. In fact, the relationship between God and the person in the intimate space of faith is grounded precisely in this unequal exchange. Obviously, this liberating experience provokes serenity, laughter, and joy, especially in the disempowered partner of this interaction: "happy exchange and conflict."

In his Freedom Treatise from 1520, Luther formulated in concentrated form what he had already conceived during the explosive months of the beginning of the Reformation in 1517–1518. In the *Lectures on Hebrews*, Luther used metaphorical language to give shape to the connection between intimacy, gift exchange, and the exchange of subjects that occurs in the relational space of the faith relationship between God and the human person. In these reflections, the person's faith, his "*fides*," is a glue, a binding agent, a "copula" between the "*Verbum*" of God, Christ, and the human heart or the soul as the core of the person. "For through faith a man becomes like the Word of God, but the Word is the Son of God" (LW 29: 155/WA 57 III: 151,14f). Interpreting Heb 4:2, Luther described the event between the Word of God and the human heart as bilateral preparation, gluing, and commingling: three elements – faith, Word, and heart – become one.

> "Yet this of little importance, for that uniting or combination of the Word and the hearts is reciprocal. For these three – faith, the Word, and the heart – become one. Faith is the glue or the bond. The Word is on one side; the heart is on the other side. But through faith they become one spirit, just as man and wife become "one flesh" (Gen. 2:24). Therefore it is true that the heart is combined with the Word through faith and that the Word is combined with the heart through the same faith" (LW 29: 160/WA 57 III: 156,19–157,4)

The expressions "*mixtura*," "*copula*," union between beloveds, glue, and binding agent let loose the imagination, giving expression to the fusion and commingling as radical nearness and intimacy. Nevertheless, these expressions invoke an interaction loaded with conflict. Namely, they connote an exchange in which the human person is completely altered through his death and renewal. The person is removed from the world, from creatureliness, sensuality, the quest for wealth and social position while, at the same time, his Creator supplies the suffering and consent to death.

In his death on the cross, Jesus consumes sin and death. Through death, comes life.

> We Christians should learn, in order that we may die joyfully. For just as it is impossible for Christ, the Victor over death, to die again (cf. Rom. 6:9), so it is impossible for one who believes in Him to die [...] For just as Christ, by reason of His union with immortal divinity, overcame death by dying, so the Christian, by reason of his union with the immortal Christ [...] also overcomes death by dying (LW 29: 136/WA 57 III: 129,15–24).

Luther describes the change that occurs here in the human person as a complete transformation, through conformity, commingling, and identification of the "heart" with Christ; in faith, the human heart is made like Christ. Christ takes the place of the "old man." The commingling, conceived as a marital intimacy, leads to an exchange of *sin and righteousness*. In the Hebrew Lectures, Luther captures this entire conceptual framework of intimacy, commingling, and exchange of sin and righteousness in the notion of "*Sacramentum*."

This imagined intimate relational space of faith is a place of refuge, an alternative place to which the person can flee from the constraints and conflicts of daily life. Faith is a place of power, a "furnace full of love," that can provide vital energy for life. "God has poured out upon us all his treasures," as Luther put it, so that we now live in "a glowing furnace full of love, reaching from the earth to the heavens." (LW 51: 95/WA 10 III: 56,1 ff). At the same time, the real, actual form of human existence is found here, even if it is never fully realized under the conditions of everyday life. In the reception history of Luther's theology, the formula "*simul iustus et peccator*" has often taken on the flavor of a denial. It is as though God's enormous gift, the abundant gift of righteousness that first makes man what he really is before God, is more like a kind of dangerous utopia. And as such, it is now necessary to protect believers from it, to suppress complete ecstasy in their everyday life now and literally to chuck it from the basket. However, whoever attends to the normal forms of communal relationship in the promise of justification will soon see that this is not the greatest danger threatening Protestant Christianity today.

6. The Coming Grandiose Experience

Images of successful Being-Able-to-Live in both intimate and public space open up opportunities to internalize powerful inner images, "imaginings" in a psychoanalytic sense that can provide support and an antithesis to experiences of shame in everyday life. The complete transformation that Luther imagined through conformity, commingling, and identification of the "heart" with Christ is without a doubt a *grandiose experience* for the believer. However, this grandiose experience comes to the person from the outside, from God, not through his own achievements, self-improvement, or illusions of omnipotence.

This is a perspective that is as valuable today as it was in the historical period of the Reformation. It takes the imagined experience of the relational space in which God becomes a significant other for me and removes all lived negative experiences of denigration and social humiliation. This emerges in daily social life through the living shape of the gospel in the communal forms of the Church. It is a gift of God given according to faith in the Gospel, not the work of one's own strength, that comes in the work of the Holy Spirit. This insight can leave Christians calm and relaxed for their shared work in necessary organizational tasks for the social form of faith.

The inner image of a completely successful space of intimate relationship in the *Gospel* is, in Luther's theological interpretation, the positive counter-image that disempowers the destructive, shame-provoking image of *the Law* that depresses the person's desires for grandiosity. The person who has entrusted himself to faith in the Gospel can imagine this protective, tender, and loving relational space as a life-giving resource, as a healing inner image against, not only, the destructive effects of the Law, but also against all social, economic, and political experiences of daily life in which he is devalued and rejected as unlovable. In the Freedom Treatise (1520), Luther spoke of the Christian freedom of the "inner man," which cannot be maligned or damaged by any lack of freedom experienced in everyday life. God in Jesus Christ can always be imagined as the "significant other" (cf. Mead: 1934) who can destroy and correct destructive experiences with others in everyday life, and thus can motivate a new, life-promoting solidarity in everyday life (Cf. WA 7: 38).[20]

Bibliography

Bastian, Till/Mischa Hilgers (1990), Kain: Die Trennung von Scham und Schuld am Beispiel der Genesis, Psyche 44/12, 1100–1112.

Bentien, Claudia (2001), Tribunal der Blicke: Kulturtheorien von Scham und Schuld und die Tragödie um 1800 (Literatur – Kultur – Geschlecht, Kleine Reihe 30), Cologne/Weimar/Vienna: Böhlau Verlag.

Bizer, Ernst (1958), Fides ex auditu: Eine Untersuchung über die Entdeckung der Gerechtigkeit Gottes durch Martin Luther, Neukirchen: Neukirchener Verlag.

Douglas, Mary (1970), Natural Symbols: Explorations in Cosmology, London: Penguin Books.

Duby, Georges (1978), Les trois ordres ou L'imaginaire du féodalisme, Paris: Gallimard.

20 "Sieh, so müssen Gottes Güter von einem zum anderen fließen und gemeinsames Eigentum werden, dass jeder sich so um seinen Nächsten annimmt, als handele es sich um ihn selber. Von Christus her fließen sie zu uns; denn er hat sich in seinem Leben unser angenommen, als wäre er das gewesen, was wir sind. Von uns aus sollen sie denen zufließen, die sie brauchen, und zwar ebenso völlig."

EBACH, JÜRGEN (1998), Luthers Auslegung der Psalmen, in: Jürgen Ebach, Weil das, was ist, nicht alles ist (Theologische Reden 4), Frankfurt am Main/Bochum: Gemeinschaftswerk der Evangelischen Publizistik, 246–264.

ELERT, WERNER (1952), Morphologie des Luthertums, vol. I, 2nd ed., Munich: C.H. Beck.

ELIAS, NORBERT (1978), Über den Prozeß der Zivilisation. Soziogenetische und psychogenetische Untersuchungen, vol. I–II, 6th ed., Frankfurt am Main: Suhrkamp.

ERIKSON, ERIK H. (1973), Identität und Lebenszyklus: Drei Aufsätze, Frankfurt am Main: Suhrkamp.

GIRARD, RENÉ (1982), Le Bouc émissaire, Paris: Grasset.

GUTMANN, HANS-MARTIN (1991), Über Liebe und Herrschaft: Martin Luthers Verständnis von "Intimität" und "Autorität" im Kontext des Zivilisationsprozesses (GTA 47), Göttingen: Vandenhoeck & Ruprecht.

HAUSEN, KARIN (1978), Die Polarisierung der Geschlechtscharaktere – eine Spiegelung von Erwerbs- und Familienleben, in: Heide Rosenbaum (ed.), Seminar: Familie und Gesellschaftsstruktur: Materialien zu den sozioökonomischen Bedingungen von Familienformen, Frankfurt am Main: Suhrkamp, 161–194.

HEPP, ANDREAS/MATTHIAS BERG/CINDY ROITSCH (ed.) (2014), Mediatisierte Welten der Vergemeinschaftung: Kommunikative Vernetzung und das Gemeinschaftsleben junger Menschen, Wiesbaden: Springer VS.

KAUFMANN, THOMAS (2011), Luthers "Judenschriften": Ein Beitrag zu ihrer historischen Kontextualisierung, Tübingen: Mohr Siebeck.

KOHUT, HEINZ (1983), Narzißmus. Eine Theorie der psychoanalytischen Behandlung narzißtischer Persönlichkeitsstörungen. 4th ed., Frankfurt am Main: Suhrkamp.

LÖW, MARTINA (2001), Raumsoziologie, Frankfurt am Main: Suhrkamp.

OBERMAN, HEIKO A. (1987), Luther: Mensch zwischen Gott und Teufel, Berlin: Siedler.

LUTHER, MARTIN (1517), Lectures on Hebrews (LW 29: 109–241/WA 57 III: 1–238).

LUTHER, MARTIN (1520), The Freedom of a Christian [German version] (WA 7: 20–38).

LUTHER, MARTIN (1520), The Freedom of a Christian [Latin version] (LW 31: 343–377/ WA 7: 49–73).

LUTHER, MARTIN (1522), Eight Sermons at Wittenberg (LW 51: 70–100/WA 10 III: 1–64).

LUTHER, MARTIN (1530–1531), Lectures on the Song of Solomon (WA 31 II: 586–769).

LUTHER, MARTIN (1535–1545), Lectures on Genesis (LW 1–8/WA 42–44).

MAUSS, MARCEL (1978), Die Gabe: Form und Funktion des Austauschs in archaischen Gesellschaften, in: Marcel Mauss (ed. Wolf Lepenies/Hanns Henning Ritter), Soziologie und Anthropologie, vol. II, Frankfurt am Main/Berlin/Wien: Ullstein, 11–144.

MEAD, GEORGE HERBERT (1934), Mind, Self, and Society, Chicago: University of Chicago Press.

OHLY, FRIEDRICH (1958), Hohelied-Studien: Grundzüge einer Geschichte der Hoheliedauslegung des Abendlandes bis 1200, Wiesbaden: F. Steiner.

SCHULTE-MARKWORT, MICHAEL (2015), Burn out Kids. Wie das Prinzip Leistung unsere Kinder überfordert, Munich: Pattloch.

RICŒUR, PAUL (2002), Symbolik des Bösen. Phänomenologie der Schuld, vol. II, 2nd ed., Freiburg im Breisgau: Verlag Karl Alber.

SCHRÖTER, MICHAEL (1985), "Wo zwei zusammenkommen in rechter Ehe…": Sozio- und psychogenetische Studien über Eheschließungsvorgänge vom 12. bis 15. Jahrhundert, Frankfurt am Main: Suhrkamp.

TAYLOR, CHARLES (2007), A Secular Age, Cambridge, MA/London: The Belknap Press of Harvard University Press.

VOLKMANN, EVELINA (2002), “Gesetz” und “Evangelium” in der Predigt, in: Hans Martin Dober/Dagmar Mensink (ed.), Die Lehre von der Rechtfertigung des Gottlosen im kulturellen Kontext der Gegenwart. Beiträge im Horizont des christlich-jüdischen Gesprächs (Hohenheimer Protokolle 57), Stuttgart: Akademie der Diözese Rottenburg-Stuttgart, 106–123.

WINNICOTT, DONALD W. (1990), The Maturational Processes and the Facilitating Environment: Studies in the Theory of Emotional Development, London/New York, NY: Karmac Books.

WOYDACK, TOBIAS (2005), Der räumliche Gott: Was sind Kirchengebäude theologisch?, Berlin: EB-Verlag.

Bo Kristian Holm

Dynamic Tensions in the Social Imaginaries of the Lutheran Reformation

1. Identifying a Lutheran Social Doctrine

Research on the relation between Lutheranism and the formation of society is challenged by basic methodological ambiguities. When it comes to explicit social doctrines, Lutheranism appears to be relatively sparse compared to other confessions like Roman Catholicism or the Reformed traditions. Although it is possible to construct some kind of social doctrine out of Luther's writings that deal with social issues, an elaborate commentary on social doctrines does not exist. One could argue with Harold Berman (2003, 71) that scholars have largely overlooked the abundant material on legal philosophy in the work of Melanchthon. However, the interest of this chapter is the potential impact of Lutheran theology upon daily life and the formation of worldly institutions, not philosophical discourses per se. In the quest to identify effective methodological approaches for studying the potential impact of theology on social life, as it is the aim of this volume, there are more fruitful possibilities than simply to look for explicit social doctrines. One such possibility is to approach the core elements of Lutheran theology in itself as a social doctrine.

1.1. The Social Dimension of the Doctrine of Justification by Faith Alone

Some approaches in the history of Reformation research move in the direction of approaching Lutheran theology as a whole as a social doctrine. The current effort could be likened to the situation around 100 years ago when leading historical and sociological scholars primarily in Berlin discussed the relation between Protestantism, sociality, and modernity. In the years around World War I, the leading German theologian, Karl Holl, who initiated the German *Luther-renaissance*, was deeply involved in the inquiry into the cultural significance of the Reformation in discussion with Ernst Troeltsch and Max Weber. Weber and Troeltsch did not see any major connection between Luther and modernity. Holl disagreed and sought to show that this was exactly the case. Rejecting any kind of historical analysis inspired by Marxism, Holl opined that theology and religion were the driving forces of Western history. Holl's (1959) work on the cultural significance of the Reformation countered the claim that modernity's progress was indebted to society's liberation from religion. Instead, Holl argued that the fundamental force of the Reformation was its impact on the individual. Holl located this impact in a pre-linguistic experience of conscience, in the idea of a total renunciation of the self towards both God and the communal life.

Holl identified the impact on the individual state of mind as the driving force of the Reformation, but it is methodologically problematic to focus solely on individual experience. An alternative is needed and this alternative must be able to both analyze confessional cultures as social forces and Lutheran theology as a social doctrine.

Both aspects are vital: both the intellectual self-reflection of a culture and the everyday practices. The concept of confessional culture can encompass both (cf. the introductory chapter), but we need a methodological approach that can do the same. The problem with individual experience is that they are in themselves inaccessible. However, worldviews are more ascertainable because worldview is expressed in different kinds of material culture, from paintings and hymns to legal documents. Therefore, the concept of "social imaginaries" as it is used, for example, by Charles Taylor offers an attractive alternative to Holl's concept of prelinguistic experience.

This chapter investigates how Lutheran theology's most important impact on the shaping of society emerges from "social imaginaries" attached directly to its key theological assumption, namely, justification by faith alone, rather than in its explicit social teachings. The most important source for Lutheranism's influence on the formation of society is, therefore, to be found in its central theological ideas. These ideas function as both a background for and as a possible corrective to explicit social doctrines. What constitutes the individual's being "selig" (blessed), to use the term that refers to the individual's salvation in Luther's *Confession Concerning Christ's Supper* (see Westhelle's chapter) forms the framework for the same individual's being "heilig" (holy), that is for living a Christian life in the world. Taylor's concept of "social imaginaries" (cf. the introduction) offers a useful tool for identifying connections between theology and social formation. If the primary theology of a confessional culture contains "social imaginaries" used for explaining the individual's new relationship with God and, subsequently, the Christian's relation to the world, then these social imaginaries have a strong likelihood of impacting the "imaginaries" that form the perceptions of social realities in the world. Therefore, these social imaginaries offer a firm basis for investigating the proximity of connections between perceptions of social practices and key theological ideas.

This approach is not totally new. Weber, Holl, and Troeltsch among many others were aware of the connection between central theological ideas and the formation of society. This chapter aims to dig a little deeper by looking for dynamic tensions in the "social imaginaries" of the Reformation. Focus will be on the first generation Lutheran theology *in casu* Luther and Melanchthon.

In his work on the legal history of the Reformation, John Witte Jr. has identified a twofold legacy of the Lutheran Reformation – one points towards hierarchy and absolutism, the other points towards egalitarianism and republicanism and highlighted the importance of the use of metaphors in relation to worldly power (Witte: 2002, 108–113; 298–303). The study of the social metaphors in the Reformation indicates that, in a variety of ways, this duality is already implicit in key imagery of Reformation theology. Both Luther and Melanchthon used metaphors from the intimate spaces of the family: marriage and the parent-child relations. These metaphors were helpful for articulating the central doctrine of the Reformation, the doctrine of justification and of justifying grace. As Gutmann has pointed out, this use of family metaphors may have had a major significance – while family imagery was universally accessible, family metaphors represented them in an idealized way.

These family metaphors are significant supplements to the dominating court room imagery in the Lutheran tradition. Gerhard Ebeling linked this imagery to the *coram*-structure as the basis for the individual's understanding of him- or herself, of God, and of the world. In Ebeling's interpretation of Luther, every individual is in all aspects of life placed on trial in a courtroom, either in front of God, the world, or one's self, *coram deo, coram mundo,* or *coram seipso* (See Ebeling: 1970, 173). No matter how important the court room imagery may be, it is limited in its expression, especially when it comes to social aspects. The inner tension between diverse core metaphors opens up a dynamic field of shifting focus and emphasis. Despite inner tensions and variations, there is nevertheless a common direction in the use of metaphors that drives a specific understanding both of the individual's relation to God and also to the world. The investigation of basic "social imaginaries" makes possible new ways of understanding the relation between theology and societal change.

It is possible to identify two primary types of social metaphors in use, the nuptial and the father-child imagery. Each image contains two alternative per spectives on social roles and norms. This also reflects a certain inherent ambiguity in Luther's doctrine of the three estates – a doctrine that could itself be seen to expand one of these fundamental social metaphor, namely, the father-child imagery.

This study concentrates on these two central metaphors and the relation between sacrament and worldview. Not only is the link between sacrament and worldview critical for our investigation, it is also closely related to the use of family metaphors. We will begin by attending to Luther's use of the nuptial metaphor. This metaphor both appears at a crucial stage in Luther's development and demarcates him from his fellow reformer, Philipp Melanchthon, who very seldom used marital imagery.[1] Instead, Melanchthon clearly favored the father-child metaphor, which will be the subject of the second section. The father-child imagery is the most widely used social metaphor in the reformers' theology, covering both theological and political themes. The political sense is apparent in Luther's exposition of the fourth commandment in the *Catechisms.* For this reason, the third section examines Luther's political interpretation of the Song of Solomon, which Gutmann also discusses in his chapter. Finally, Luther's mature writings on the Lord's Supper offer yet another view of the relationship between human beings and the divine, revealing a specific view of life in the earthly realm that could be described as "sacramental realism." This perspective builds the framework for Luther's doctrine of the three estates, which then becomes important for societal development in Lutheran countries, such as Denmark.

1.2. Lutheran Relationality

A presupposition of this chapter is that Luther's view of human beings is deeply embedded in a social relationship of giving and receiving. This goes both for his doctrine of justification and for his sacramental theology. To investigate sociality within these core theological ideas opens up new ways of understanding the connection between theological ideas and earthly behavior. The premise for this investigation is, therefore, taken from social-anthropological research: the glue that holds societies together is reciprocity, or exchange.[2] At the same time, the approach is profoundly theological. A Lutheran notion of divine presence cannot be understood apart from its incarnation in the realities of this world.

Gift theories offer a promising approach to central issues in Lutheran theology. The concept of the gift itself combines two vital aspects both of Lutheran theology, in particular, and of social life, in general. Gift theories connect the physical or natural world of gifted objects with the spiritual or mental world of giving; the *donum* and the *favor dei*; the gift and the giver's intention in the act of giving. The connection to Lutheran theology is clear: to receive a gift as a good gift, one must have faith in the benevolence of the giver, in his *favor.* Seneca and the Wittenberg reformers converge to a remarkable extent in their common

1 See however his *Loci communes,* Melanchthon (1521/1997, 196): "Lex ira vox est et mortis, evangelium pacis et vitae et in summa vox sponsi et sponsa, sicut propheta dicit."

2 A development of the consequences of this premise for the overall understanding of Luther's theology can be found in Holm (2006).

emphasis on the inner aspect of giving, the benevolence of the giver, the confidence of the receiver.[3]

The doctrine of grace is a theory of exchange. Troeltsch saw the foundation of a Lutheran social doctrine to be Luther's new understanding of grace (Troeltsch: 1965, 436f). In his extension of the Weberian perspective on religion's impact on social development, the French philosopher and ethnologist Marcel Hénaff (2003, 296) has argued that the Church's doctrine of grace is the theological counterpart to anthropological gift theories. This understanding can be adapted to fit a Lutheran context. The doctrine of justification is the Lutheran analogue to anthropological theories of gift giving (cf. e.g. Saarinen: 2005; Holm: 2006). At this point, the thesis is relatively uncontroversial; the discussion begins with attempts to clarify how the exchange in justification relates to inter-human exchange. This discussion has been particularly lively in theology (cf. Dalferth 2009; Hamm: 2015). Does a theological notion of a pure gift of grace stand in contrast to any kind of exchange, or does the idea of grace in a Lutheran perspective involve a particular kind of exchange or mutuality? The strength of family metaphors in Lutheran theology seem to be intimately connected with the metaphors' capacity for articulating a mutual relation of giving and receiving that differs from an exchange economy.

2. The Lutheran Theological Use of the Nuptial Metaphor

2.1. The Ambiguity of the Nuptial Metaphor

The nuptial metaphor is well known in monastic theology. Luther was familiar with it through his own career as an Augustinian friar. Nevertheless, Luther does not begin to use the nuptial metaphor in any kind of theologically profound manner until relatively late in his formative years. He uses it for the first time at the end of his Sermon on St Andrew's Day in 1516 and with real significance in the *Explanations of the 95-theses* from 1518 and the contemporaneous "Sermon on Two Kinds for Righteousness" (LW 31:293–306/WA 2: 145–152). Luther's use of the nuptial metaphor is always closely linked with the structure of the "happy exchange." Although this phrase was first used *expressis verbis* around 1519, it has been a key element in Luther's theology since his *Lectures on Romans* from 1515–16.

3 Risto Saarinen (2007) has shown how the relation between the gift on the one hand and the real beneficium on the other hand (i.e. the benevolence in which a gift is given) moves from stoic literature as Seneca's *De beneficium* into the theology of both Luther (*Against Latomus*) and Melanchthon (*Loci communes*).

Luther's use of the nuptial metaphor can be found in two arenas: the doctrine of justification and the understanding of the earthly regime i. e. both in theology and politics. We will begin at the center with the theology and take up the political part later on.

In German, the word *Verkehr* can refer to erotic activity (*Geschlechtsverkehr*), correspondence (*Schriftverkehr*), or even commerce (*Geschäftsverkehr*). But it is most widely used as a term for "traffic." In earlier forms of German, *Verkehr* could also have the meaning of social connection, as in Wilhelm Herrmann's book *Der Verkehr des Christen mit Gott im Anschluss an Luther dargestellt* (Herrmann: 1906). The variety of meanings is crucial in relation to nuptial images and the related erotic metaphors in theology. On this point, Wilhelm Herrmann's use of both the word *Verkehr* and his reservation about the erotic elements in Luther's use of the bridal metaphor is illuminating. According to Herrmann, Luther borrowed the imagery of bridal love to illustrate the Christian's relations to God as it is mediated through Christ from Bernhard of Clairvaux, but Luther used it in a way that moves Luther's theology far beyond Bernhard's (Herrmann: 1906, 223–238. Cf. Holm: 2006, 27 ff; Holm: 2009a, 33; Pedersen: 2015). In Herrmann's reading, Luther's use of the bridal image is liberated from the sensuality that burdened pietism: Luther was, in Herrmann's words, far away from the pietistic idea of the "sweet Jesus." For Herrmann, the crucial point was the *Verkehr* between God and the Christian, of which the bridal love can be metaphor, but only when it is purged of its erotic connotations, primarily of sensuality.

2.2. The Necessary De-Erotizing of the Nuptial Imagery

Herrmann's concerns are by no means unique. There is also a possible structural problem inherent in erotic metaphors that Herrmann overlooked:[4] erotic love is a matter of longing for what it does not have. This problem goes beyond the question of mere distaste for sensuality; it makes the nuptial metaphor too ambiguous for theological use. This nuptial metaphor's structural problem within Lutheran theology can only be solved by de-eroticizing the erotic image. By focusing on how Luther separates the nuptial imagery from its erotic overtones, the social potency of the image becomes clear. The nuptial metaphor enters into a strange complex of juxtaposed hierarchical and egalitarian tendencies when used as Luther does in theology and politics.

Luther's early theology is marked by a vehement rejection of all formulations or notions that suggest any degree of divine-human reciprocity (cf. e. g. WA 57 II:

4 As Troeltsch (1965, 441) criticized, Herrmann's understanding of the "Verkehr" between God and human being bypasses both Luther's sacramental theology and Incarnation Christology.

69,15f.26). As argued elsewhere (Holm 2006, 48–69), the shift from Luther's early theology to his mature theology occurs simultaneously with his integration of metaphors and terms implying a sense of mutuality or economy. This appears in the simultaneous self-giving in the nuptial metaphor[5] or the use of the term "*bezahlen*" (to pay) both in relation to God and to the fellow human beings.[6] The latter social nuance resulted from Luther's integration of the classical definition of "righteousness" as "paying each one his due" (*unicuique quod suum est tribuere*). Luther's use of the marriage metaphor plays an important role in this development.

The change can be clearly seen in the difference between Luther's original 95 theses on indulgences from 1517 and the subsequent *Explanations of the Ninety-Five Theses* from 1518, in which Luther offers an explanation of the theses that far transcends their original meaning. In 1517, thesis thirty-seven states: "Any true Christian, living or dead, possesses a God-given share in all the benefits of Christ and the church, even without indulgence letters" (Wengert: 2015, 39/WA 1: 235,9ff).[7] In his later Explanation, he brings in Song of Sol. 2:16, which says, "My beloved is mine and I am his." This inclusion grants his *Explanations* a meaning that heavily expands the original focus on the benefits of Christi available to the believer without indulgence letters. The explanation focuses on Christ as the possession of the Christian:

> It is impossible for one to be Christian unless he possesses Christ. If he possesses Christ, he possesses at the same time all the benefits of Christ. For the holy Apostle says in Rom. 13 [:14]. Put on the Lord Jesus Christ. And in Rom. 8 [:32] he says, Will he not also give us all things with him? And in 1 Cor. 3: [:21–22] he says, "All things are yours, whether Cephas or Paul, or life or death." And in 1. Cor 12 [:27] he says, "You are not your own, but individually members of the body." And in other places, where he describes the church as one body, one bread, we are altogether in Christ, members of one of another [1 Cor. 10:17]. And in the Song of Salomon we read, "My beloved is mine and I am his" [Song of Sol. 2:16]. By faith in Christ, a Christian is made one spirit and one body with Christ. For the two shall be one flesh [Gen. 2,14]. This is a great mystery, and I take it to mean Christ and the Church [Eph. 5:31–32].

Luther here accentuates the oneness of Christ and the Christian as a result of mutual self-giving in the happy exchange as the central dynamic:

> Therefore, since the spirit of Christ dwells within Christians by means of which brothers become co-heirs, one body, and citizens of Christ, how is it possible for us not to be participants in all the benefits of Christ? Christ himself has all that belongs to him from the same Spirit. So it happens through the inestimable riches of the mercies of God the

5 As in Luther's *Treatise on the Freedom of a Christian* (LW 31: 351/WA 7: 54,31–55,6).
6 As in Luther's *Preface to Romans* from 1522 (LW 35: 365–380/WA DB 7: 2–27).
7 To this and the following, see Holm: 2009b, 87; 100f.

> Father that a Christian can be glorified with Christ and can with confidence claim all things in Christ. Righteousness, strength, patience, humility, even all the merits of Christ are his through the unity of the Spirit by faith in him. All his sins are no longer his; but through that same unity with Christ everything is swallowed up in him. (LW 31: 189 f/WA 1: 593,7–24).

Luther further draws on the nuptial metaphor to explain the most central aspects of the doctrine of justification in his *Treatise on the Freedom of a Christian* from 1520 and, prior to that, in his *Sermon on Two Kinds of Righteousness* from 1519 (Stjerna: 2016, 9–25/WA 2: 145–152), but the point is exactly the same – just as it is in one of Luther's most important hymns: "Nun freut euch, liebe Christen g'mein" (Dear Christians, One an all rejoice). The divine justification of the human being integrates the human being into a relationship of mutual self-giving like the one between a groom and bride. In *Sermon on Two Kinds of Righteousness* Luther makes this even stronger. He uses the explicit dialogical formula of the mutual "I am yours." Centuries later, the Lutheran composer Johann Sebastian Bach exemplified the impact of Luther's imagery when he put this theme into music in the cantata "Ich hatte viel Bekümmernis" (BW 21). The *Explanations* make it quite clear, however, that other social images are also relevant, such as the union of members in one body through which all are brothers (and sisters) and, therefore, co-heirs. Nevertheless, the crucial emphasis remains the union of bride and groom by which the couple gain joint property.[8] The dynamics here are crucial: the exchange of property, justification for sin, depends on a prior union established through mutual self-giving.

Traditionally, interpreters of Luther's doctrine of justification have highlighted the forensic metaphors, but in the search for social metaphors the court room metaphor proves lacking. The court room imagery ends with a guilty conviction or an acquittal through the imputation of an alien righteousness. The social element of reintegrating the guilty into the social life is cast to the side. This could be the reason why Luther gave up on trying to use the judicial metaphor of *cessio bonorum*, the voluntary renunciation of all property to explain the cancellation of punishment (See e.g. *Sermon on Sct. Andrew's Day*, WA 1: 102, 15–18), as an adequate explanation of justification.

The problem with the *cessio bonorum*-metaphor was precisely the challenge of integration. How is the justified sinner to be understood as being integrated into

8 The use of the nuptial metaphor in *Sermon on Two Kinds of Righteousness* and in the *Treatise on the Freedom of a Christian* plays deliberately on the regulation of marriage in canon law, where the marriage becomes effectual in a legal sense by consummation: "Quod animan copulat cum Christo, sicut sponsam cum sponso. Quo sacramento (vt Apostolus docet) Christus et anima efficiuntur vna caro, Quod si vna caro sunt, verumque inter eos matrimonium, immo omnium longe perfectissimum consummator." (LW 31: 351/WA 7: 54,31–34. Cf. Stjerna: 2016,17/WA 2: 147,26–32). To this see further Holm (2006, 64, 114f).

communion with God when the metaphor is that of total renunciation? Cultural anthropology can help to isolate the problem. If the renewed relationship between God and the human person is to be understood as a real relationship, metaphors involving a clear dimension of sociality are highly necessary. Because social metaphors inevitably incorporate a certain element of mutuality, however, they are simultaneously perplexing given Luther's quest against works righteousness and doctrine of justification by faith alone. Therefore, social metaphors must be utilized in a way that safeguards justification by faith alone and divine action as the sole determination of justification.

By using love, *in casu* the nuptial metaphor, as the cornerstone for explaining the relation between Christi and human being, Luther creates a new way of understanding justification. While social exchange generally disguises the reciprocal aspect of gift-giving by giving something different and with a delay, love is an exception to this rule. In the exchange of love, the gift given is replaced by the self and the mutual self-giving happens in a moment of fulfillment (cf. Holm: 2009b, 102–110). It is crucial that Luther uses the aspects of symmetrical self-giving in the nuptial metaphor and not the hierarchical relation between groom and bride. The latter was used in Paul and in patristic and medieval theology to represent either the church or the soul. Luther protects the theologically necessary asymmetry of the God-human relation by combining the nuptial imagery with the marital narrative in Hosea (Hos 12). The unworthy woman is lifted up to new dignity through her union with the groom. Luther's use of the nuptial metaphor thereby becomes a model for elevating the unworthy up to new dignity, and for integrating the human being outside of social relations into a relation of mutual self-giving. This closely follows the underlying contours to Luther's admonition to be like Christ to one's neighbor in *The Freedom of a Christian* (LW 31: 371/WA 7: 69, 1–11).

3. The Lutheran Use of the Father-Child Metaphor

Both Luther and Melanchthon utilize the father-child metaphor. Melanchthon clearly seems to prefer it over the nuptial metaphor, which is largely absent from his corpus of work with only a few exemptions. Melanchthon functions here as the prototypical example of the use of the father-child imagery in Reformation theology.

In his *Loci communes*, Melanchthon is more hesitant than Luther to use family metaphors. In the *Locus* on the Gospel, Melanchthon occasionally quotes Jeremiah 7:34, comparing the voice of the Gospel with the voice of groom and bride (Melanchthon 1521/1997, 197). The first crucial place where Melanchthon uses family metaphors is, however, the sixth *Loci* on justification and faith.

In my translation the text here reads

> And do not doubt your confidence that now you no longer have a Judge in heaven, but a Father, who cares for you, without any difference from the way human beings act when parents take care of their children. (Melanchthon: 1521/1997, 218).[9]

Up to this point, grace and justification have primarily been understood to reveal God's mercy. Here, the emphasis on the *misericordia dei* lays the groundwork for understanding God as a Father instead of as a Judge, replacing the court room with family care. In the following paragraph, Melanchthon emphasizes that God's wish to be called Father is a sufficient reason for trusting his good will. The trust in God's mercy is, for Melanchthon, another reason for trusting God as the giver of everything necessary for life (cf. Melanchthon: 1521/1997, 232). In this way, Melanchthon connects the doctrine of justification to the doctrine of creation (on the importance of this connection, see Holm: 2017).

Luther joins Melanchthon in this move with great impact on Lutheran theology, most clearly seen in Luther's *Small Catechism.* Here, the recognition of the world as a divine gift, given out of pure fatherly and divine goodness and mercy depends on the work of the Son through whom human beings see into the heart of the Father (Beintker: 1989, 2; Link: 1991, 27). Although we do also find creation theology in the works of the young Luther, for an elaborate discussion one must look to the later Luther, and the later Luther clearly follows the path of Melanchthon's *Loci 1521.* In this early work, Melanchthon sees divine gifts in the most ordinary things of daily life, anticipating Luther's explanation of the first article of the Creed in the *Small Catechism.* This way of looking at the world becomes important for Luther's appreciation of earthly life within in the three estates.

In Melanchthon's presentation, however, the father-child relation between God and human being also results in a kind of mutuality as the consequence of the reestablished relation between God and human being. Under the headline *De fidei efficacia* Melanchthon explains how, as a result of the faith in God's mercy, the heart cannot but love God in return as a gesture of gratitude for his overwhelming mercy. This encompasses the content of Rom 8:15b: "When we cry, 'Abba! – Father!" which in Paul is intimately related to the spirit of adoption (Rom 8: 15a).

In this way we also find a mutuality of love between God and human being in Melanchthon. However, Melanthchon clearly separates the human response from the divine initiative. Human reciproation follows faith as love towards God and neighbor. In a structural continuation of Luther's understanding of Chris-

9 "[...] eius fiducia nihil dubita, quin iam non iudicem in coelis, sed patrem habeas, cui tu sis curae non aliter atque sunt parentibus filii inter homines." Trans. by author.

tians being Christ for each other in the *Freedom Treatise*, Melanchthon can speak here of the believer making himself a servant of both God and human beings (Melanchthon: 1521/1997, 260). Among fellow Christians brotherly love should increase (ibid., 262). In a previous *locus*, Melanchthon praises common property and relates the earthly life of the Christian to the common good. With this, a crucial term for post-Reformation sociality is formed.[10]

4. Equality and Hierarchy in the Reformers' Use of Metaphors

Both Luther and Melanchthon searched for metaphors capable of describing the renewed fellowship between God and the justified human being. Family metaphors offer an effective way for describing the renewed relation between God and human being without falling back into economic models for understanding the relationship. Instead, family metaphors establish a domain of confidence. Luther uses the father-child metaphor, but the nuptial metaphor is scarce in Melanchthon. In both kind of images, equality between God and human being is also related to in-equality. God shares his divinity with human beings, who remain recipients of divine salvation. In search for "social imaginaries" with the capacity for shaping society, it is noteworthy that from the very beginning Lutheranism contains two core metaphors for understanding the relation between God and human being, especially because they deal with the relation between equality and un-equality in distinct ways.

The father-child metaphor is unmistakably asymmetrical with regard to the leading social relation emphasizing inheritance. However, it also involves a high degree of equality when it comes to family lineage. Conversely, the nuptial metaphor, as Luther uses it, emphasizes the symmetrical relation of mutual self-giving in love, even as the status of groom and bride are absolute opposites. The righteous groom marries the sinful whore (cf. Hos). The differences between the images could be listed in the following simple way:

Metaphor	**Family "hierarchy"**	**Internal status**	**Emphasis**
Father – Child	Asymmetrical	Equality	Future inheritance
Subcategory – adoption	Asymmetrical	Equality	*Present status*
Groom – Bride	Symmetrical	Inequality	Present union

Table 1

10 According to e.g. Schneider-Ludorf (2012) considerations for the common good became the only legitimate reason for donating wealth to foundations after the Reformation,

If the father-child metaphor is used to describe the relation between God and human being, it structurally emphasizes the future aspect of the relation: the human being now has the status of an heir, but the inheritance does not come until the future life. A father-child-like relation necessarily emphasizes the hierarchical dimension of subordinance and obedience – particularly within patriarchal societies. For Melanchthon who generally follows Paul much more closely than Luther, the subcategory "adoption" is crucial. Adoption differs from the main variant by emphasizing the present status of the adopted child who now has a merciful father instead of a severe judge. Melanchthon uses the metaphor of adoption primarily in a quotation of Rom 8:15 either in relation to the central locus *De gratia* in the first and third version of the Latin *Loci* (CR 21:158; CR 21: 807: 892) or in relation to the distinction between Old and New Testament (CR 21: 459), that is, in two crucial contexts related to the doctrine of justification.

The tendency toward hierarchy is balanced by underlining familiarity; father and child are members of the same family. Obedience then is kept within the family, so to speak, even when the metaphor is used for understanding worldly relations as Luther does in his theory of command and obedience within the worldly regime using the fourth commandment (to this see Stopa's chapter).

By way of contrast, the marriage metaphor emphasizes the present union consisting in the symmetrical self-giving of Christ the bridegroom and the soul his bride. In continuity with Hosea's marriage and the happy exchange, the inequality between the partners is maintained. The unworthy woman is raised to new dignity by the marriage itself through the transfer of goods and properties.

It is this focus on the union as present that eradicates the erotic connotations of the metaphor. Erotic metaphors and language are fundamentally based on the idea of distance and longing. This has been the case since the very first poets used written language for love poetry, brilliantly described in Anne Carson's book on ancient Greek lyrics. Although she starts by pointing at the simultaneity of pleasure and pain in erotic poetry (Carson: 1986, 3), she rapidly introduces etymology to point at Eros' concern for what it does not have and, thus, at Eros' inherent dilemma: it cannot have what it wants.[11] This perspective from the ground of erotic imagery indirectly clarifies Luther's use of the nuptial metaphor. The union of Christ and the soul is a union of fulfillment that cannot be exceeded.

The ambivalence of Eros has both possibilities and limitations for Luther's doctrine of justification. One of the main points of Luther's theological anthropology is that the justified sinner has an ambivalent existence with a positive

11 Carson (1986, 10): "The Greek word *eros* denotes 'want,' 'lack,' 'desire for that which is missing.' The lover wants what he does not have. It is by definition impossible for him to have what he wants, as soon as it is had, it is no longer wanting. This is more than wordplay. There is a dilemma within eros that has been thought crucial by thinkers from Sappho to the present day."

outcome. On the other hand, Luther sees the issue of longing to be settled. The thing the sinner does not want and the justified wants is already reality. Therefore, longing is no longer necessary. This dimension of the Christ-soul relationship cannot be grasped by the erotic metaphors unless the erotic element of ambivalent longing is cancelled out.

While monastic theology could still use the aspect of longing to imagine the pursuit of unity with the divine, Luther could not. The consummated marriage in Luther is consummated in exactly the sense that no further addition is needed. The nuptial imagery is de-erotized, because faith is confidence and reception of all that God has and is.[12]

This means that Luther's theological use of the nuptial metaphor to emphasize present gain actually stresses the present in a radical sense. The role of longing must be replaced by the gift of presence and, therefore, also of union. The doctrine of justification is a way of articulating that what the human being has been longing for is already reality, but in a way that is totally unexpected. This is the reason Luther combines the bridal image with the image of the whore's marriage in Hosea.

In this case the basic erotic metaphor is neutralized. Luther's theology is for theological as well as structural reasons fundamentally un-erotic.[13] On the other hand, this could be one of the most important preconditions for the fact that the erotic life so long as it is realized within an order, such as marriage, is no longer understood to necessarily be at odds with the ideal Christian life after the Reformation. The spiritual relation to God and the worldly relation to a spouse are no longer in competition.

Both Luther and Melanchthon look for metaphors that can convey the reality of the salvific community with God. The metaphors of father-child and groom-bride have almost the same function here, as does the sacrament of the altar, to which we will return in a moment. In comparison with the father-child metaphor, the marriage metaphor integrates elements of mutuality, self-giving, life (of the new human being), and death (of the old human being) in a way that the father-child metaphor cannot do. However, as table 1 shows, both metaphors contain asymmetrical-hierarchical and symmetrical-egalitarian connotations, which gives the metaphors an inherent and inevitable dynamic. The hierarchical ele-

12 According to Gutmann (1991, 237), Luther replaces the medieval view with his own early use of the nuptial imagery, focusing on the merging of bride and groom into a union through a gift exchange (happy exchange) in which Christ gives justice and takes away sin. However, this characteristic lacks precision, since the exchange of gifts (justice and sin) happens as a consequence of the mutual self-giving of Christ and the human being.

13 Gutmann (1991, 184–211) also discusses Luther's de-eroticizing of nuptial imagery, but focuses on Luther's political interpretation of erotic metaphors. See also Gutmann's chapter in this volume. I am arguing that a de-eroticizing also happens at a more basic structural level.

ments are to some extent destabilized by the emphasis on the family relations: the son is from the same family as the father, the bride is raised to equal status with the groom.

4.1. Luther's Political Use of the Nuptial Metaphor

Luther's political use of the nuptial metaphor in the early 1530s is quite illuminating for fully grasping the inner dynamic of the social metaphors in the Reformation. Gutmann has given a fine interpretation of the somewhat neglected lecture on the Song of Solomon from 1530. What is needed here is almost exclusively to relate his points to the main argument of this chapter. Luther does not see the Song of Solomon as a love poem, as some might read it, or about the relation between Christ and the Church or the soul, as was the tradition from the early Church onwards. Rather, the Song of Solomon was about politics. Luther conducts a type of genre study and concludes that kings cannot write directly about political matters, but must disguise it. That is what Solomon does in the Song of Solomon, which then becomes a description of the political order and of the state as a gift of God (WA 31 II: 587,26ff. Cf. Gutmann: 1991, 179f). The God given role of the state is to secure peace, justice, and discipline

In Gutmann's reading, Luther transfers the mystical nuptial imagery of the union of God and the human being to the political sphere in order to propose a new understanding of the relation between God and state. As a gift of God, Luther describes the life of the state through erotic imagery in order to separate it from the alternatives, the traditional culture and the early modern bourgeois capitalist economy (Gutmann: 1991, 237). Luther's new interpretation is meant to be an explicit alternative to the search of mystical experience in monastic piety that is located outside of the household.

Luther's new interpretation clearly distinguishes between private and public life. At the same time, public life is modeled by the structures of private family life. This supports a certain internal cohesion of the state and deepens the understanding of the earthly life as ordered into three estates, all of which are structured according to the household model. Instead of the cloister, the life with God is specifically to be found in the political life of the state and in the economic life of the household. Furthermore, Luther abandons clear distinction between *oeconomia* and *politia.* The state's responsibilities resemble that of the household. According to Gutmann, Luther's understanding of the state can be characterized as the notion of a harmonious community. In this way, politics is not primarily a matter of power, but a matter of care. Political life is not a life apart from God, but a life with God. Accordingly, communal life should not be governed by mistrust, but by confidence, as Luther states in his explanation of the eighth commandment: "We are ... not [to] tell lies about our neighbors ... Instead we are to come to their defense, speak well of them, and interpret everything they do in the best possible light" (BC 353/WA 30 I: 288,13–17).

The ideal of a harmonious community exists within the ambivalences of the real society and not in the monastery. This parallels the dynamic instability of hierarchy and equality in the family metaphors. At the same time, Luther's critique of mystical interpretations of the Song of Solomon should prevent the "Schwärmer" use of mystical imaginaries to free themselves from bonds like the external word, the sacraments, and the political order. The imagined harmonious political domain, marked by tranquility and peace, should be protected from all that could ruin this peace. The positive embrace of worldly life gets joined to the exclusion of possible threats.

4.2. The Advantage of Family metaphors

In order to analyze the possible impact of theologically-formed imaginaries on real life forms, the dynamic sketched within these metaphors themselves needs further attention. One advantage to family metaphors is that they use ideas from a pre-existing reality, although, as Gutmann points out, always in an idealized way (see also Troeltsch: 1965, 566). The father-child relation is always already a given; even in the adoptianistic subcategory we find in Melanchthon, thanks to Paul (the main agent in the father's adoption of his new child is always the father, never the child). Luther's use of bridal imagery always refers to something that is already the case in actual use – as is most clearly seen in Luther's use of the image in *Sermon on Two Kinds of Righteousness* and *On the Freedom of a Christian.* This is also true of Luther's use of the father-child relation as a general way of understanding society, as is the case in the doctrine of the three estates, to which we also will soon return. The metaphor describes a reality already in existence and in which the individual already participates, and in which certain deeds are required – as a consequence, not as a precondition.

The use of family metaphors outside as well as inside the doctrine of justification accentuates the social dimension of Luther's theology. The imagery he and Melanchthon use gives an immediate possibility for rearranging the individual's "social imaginaries." He or she can now see him- or herself as God's partner or child. As a result, the admonition to act as God has acted towards the individual is able to find some kind of resonance in the individual and, therefore, also in society.

The family metaphors helped Luther to integrate the necessary aspect of social mutuality into Reformation theology. This is most clearly seen when Luther highlights the mutual self-giving of Christ and the believer, but it is less clear in the focus on hierarchical relations in his use of the father-child metaphor.[14] In the moment the father-child metaphor is transferred onto any other social relation, the mutual responsibilities become clear. The "father" is obligated to his "children" just as the "children" towards their "father." This is true in the family as well as in church and state (see Koefoed's chapter). The obligations truly exist within a hierarchical relationship, but within the relationship both master and servant have the possibility of imagining one another as principally equal in relation to God and therefore also in relation to their respective duties. No duty is more worthy of God's praise than another. Luther's interpretation of the Song of Solomon supports this. By using family metaphors to also describe interpersonal exchange, the economic exchange is covered by the veil of intimate familiarity where goods are exchanged by another system of measure than in bargain or similar kinds of economy.

5. Social Aspects of Luther's Understanding of the Lord's Supper

In order to grasp the inherent "social imaginaries" in Lutheran theology it is necessary to broaden our perspective to include the Lord's Supper. Although the nuptial metaphor plays a central role in Luther's writings around 1520, it slowly decreases. Instead, the Lord's Supper in some ways replaces the nuptial metaphor as the primary form of social imagery. In two of Luther's interrelated writings, *On the Freedom of a Christian* and *On Good Works*, the nuptial imagery in the former and the Lord's Supper in the later seem to have similar functions.

Luther's writings on the Lord's Supper offer at least three important perspectives for the relation between sacrament and sociality. I briefly introduce them here according to the three phases of his writings, read through some of Luther's recent interpreters.

Luther's 1519 *Sermon on the Lord's Supper* is normally emphasized for its critique of a use of the sacrament that undermines the social cohesion of the congregation. This emphasis on the social dimension of participation in the Lord's Supper is characteristic for the first phase of Luther's sacramental writings.

According to Wolfgang Simon (2003; 2008), the second phase, normally characterized by Luther's critique of the sacrifice of the mass, actually entails a new understanding of the sacrifice of the mass that underscores Christ's giving of himself to the believer, but also of the believer to God in faith. This relation then converges with Luther's use of the nuptial metaphor and stresses the social

14 In Melanchthon's atypical use of the marriage metaphor in the book of Hosea, he focuses solely on the groom as the active agent, cf. Hos 2:21 (Melanchthon: 1521/1997: 252).

dimension of the sacrament of the altar by focusing on the divine-human relation.

Luther's vehement defense of the real presence of Christ in his controversy with Zwingli and Oecolampadius was widely neglected in mainline Lutheran theology in th twentieth century for its lack of consistency and its return to metaphysical thinking. The last 15 years have changed this picture.[15] Using the phrase "Luther's sacramental realism," Ronald Thiemann (2013, 29) has argued that Luther's insistence on the presence of Christ in ordinary bread and wine was a radicalization of the idea of the humble sublime. Thiemann argued that this laid the foundation for the sacralization of everyday life – an explicit critique of Charles Taylor's secularization thesis. Only the God who humbles himself and gives himself can offer comfort and confidence to the conscience of the human being. If God shows himself by being present in the ordinary earthly elements of bread and wine as an act of self-giving, then this reflects a divine benevolence towards human beings that can be rediscovered in worldly matters and orders. This interpretation of Luther's doctrine of the Lord's Supper has clear similarities to Melanchthon's combination of creation with the doctrine of justification, although Melanchthon himself never took over Luther's elaborate theology of divine presence in the sacramental elements.

Against this backdrop, Cranach's well-known Wittenberg Altarpiece can be understood as a clear depiction of some of the fundamental social imaginaries of the Reformation. Here, sacrament and everyday life is related through the open windows of the dining hall of the Lord's Supper. The general Renaissance interest in landscape painting, which corresponded to a certain and rather widespread interest in stoicism's nature-God (cf. Starobinski: 1997, 64), is here construed onto a genuinely Lutheran setting. However, this Lutheran setting corresponds with remarkable similarity to both Seneca's understanding of God giving through the riches of nature in *De beneficiis* on the one hand and, on the other, Melanchthon's description of the giving Creator in the article on justification in the 1521 *Loci* (cf. Holm: 2017). This form was later repeated in Luther's explanation of the first article of faith in the *Small Catechism.*

Luther's explanation of the three estates in the concluding confession of *Confession on the Lord's Supper* should be understood to be intimately related to Luther's defense of the doctrine of sacramental real presence. This means again that the sacramental theology of the older Luther has the same social orientation as his earlier writings. Therefore, the Lord's Supper can potentially function as a "social imaginary" in which the individual sees him- or herself as individual recipients of divine self-giving in a way that can be transposed from the altar to

15 Particularly through new research in Luther's use of the doctrine of *communicatio idiomatum.* See Steiger (2000).

the world. In this interpretation, Luther establishes an intimate connection between participation in the Lord's Supper and life in a world structured by the three estates as markers of divine presence. In this way, the three estates becomes a vital part of what Thiemann has called Luther's sacramental realism.

6. Luther's Doctrine of the Three Estates as Social Imaginary Formed by Luther's "Sacramental Realism"

The doctrine of the three estates occupies a central position in Luther's *Confession* from 1528. The way Luther explains the three estates – *ecclesia, oeconomia*, and *politia* – depends on the specific context of his individual writings. However, some general characteristics of Luther's understanding of the three estates indicate the potential of his reinterpretation of this doctrine for forming "social imaginaries" (For a more detailed discussion see the chapters by Andersen, Sommer, and Westhelle). According to Luther all three estates or orders can be developed on the basis of the fourth commandment. In this way the relation to the father and, to a lesser degree, to parents becomes the general matrix for understanding social relations.

In the search for ambivalent features with dynamic potential within Lutheranism, the use of the father figure as general matrix opens up an egalitarian impulse in an otherwise hierarchical societal form. In the end, all authorities are variations of the same function, the function of a father caring for his household. At the same time, precisely this element facilitates the individual's acceptance of being subjected to another person's authority. Although Luther clearly distinguished between private matters and public life,[16] he also had a tendency to break down the boundary between the responsibility of the prince as head of the state and as head of the national household.

Luther saw all three orders to be necessary for the wellbeing of society. If we follow Luther's elaboration of the three orders in his *Lectures on Genesis*, he assigns each of the three orders clear, but distinct functions. In Luther's exegesis of Genesis 1, God creates the church as the first order, prior to the creation of Adam and Eve. The function of the church is to be the place of thanksgiving for the plenitude of gifts given to sustain life in creation (LW 1: 106/WA 42: 80,41–81,4). The household is created simultaneously with the creation of Eve and becomes the frame for mutual love (Eve is created before Adam had a chance of feeling lonely), procreation, production, exchange, and sociality (LW 1: 115/WA 42: 87,12–14).

16 Koefoed's study in this volume shows how the distinction between public and private is repeated in the distinction between affairs within or outside a household.

Luther's view of the prelapsarian orders corresponds with Luther's understanding of creation as basically the establishment and preservation of community, as Oswald Bayer (2008, 116–119.123) has summarized it. For the very sake of community a third order had to be added after the fall: the state. Its function is clearly to protect the first two orders for the reception and the circulation of divine goods.

Furthermore, this understanding of the three estates corresponds with Luther's *Confession Concerning Christ's Supper* where the three estates are grouped together under the common order of Christian love. In this fundamental functional understanding of the estates, hierarchy and equality meet again. Luther understands the orders to have a clearly hierarchical organization, but with certain variations. Among these variations, the most important is the doctrine of the priesthood of all believers, which in principle grants each individual the same status and duties and makes them equally important. This forms the background for the Lutheran notion of vocation.

7. Conclusion

Family metaphors were used at the center of Reformation theology in order to express a mutual but non-economic, relation between God and the human being. Both of these metaphors as well as the liturgical act of the Lord's Supper had the potential to form the social imaginaries of the individual and, therefore also, of communities. By relating to a familiar world – in both meanings of the word – the individual can easily adopt family metaphors. Thus, these metaphors can function to stabilize the established order or the use of idealized versions can function as destabilizing tendencies. The tensions are also detectable in the simultaneity of hierarchy and equality, symmetry and asymmetry. Metaphors, originally located in theological treatises, have the possibility of wandering out into ordinary language, poetry, and hymns precisely because they were formed to do so. In Denmark, Luther's *Small Catechism*, other kinds of devotional literature, together with the rather intense production of hymns and hymnbooks helped this transition. Thus, the family metaphors of Reformation have to be included in the formative sources for social imaginaries of ordinary people. To get at the full picture, an understanding of both their theological background as well as their social and political implications is crucial for clarifying both the force of theological ideas as well as of actual political development.

The survey of social imaginaries of the Reformation in the form of theologically important social metaphors forms a variety of possibilities for the individual's self-perception. All images and metaphors that the reformers used have an inherent ambiguity within them. They can support both authoritarian and egalitarian impulses in society. Witte's claim of a twofold legacy of the Reformation converges with the characteristics of the key theological metaphors in the work of the reformers.

Bibliography

ALLGAIER, WALTER (1966), Der "Fröhliche Wechsel" Bei Martin Luther: Eine Untersuchung zu Christologie und Soteriologie bei Luther unter besonderer Berücksichtigung der Schriften bis 1521, unpublished Doctoral Dissertation, Friedrich-Alexander-Universität Erlangen-Nuremberg.

BAYER, OSWALD (2008), Martin Luther's Theology: A Contemporary Interpretation, Grand Rapids, MI: William B. Eerdmans.

BEINTKER, MICHAEL (1989), Das Schöpfercredo im Luthers kleinen Katechismus: Theologische Erwägungen zum Ansatz seiner Auslegung, NZSTh 31, 1–17.

BERMAN, HAROLD J. (2003), Law and Revolution, II: The Impact of the Protestant Reformations on the Western Legal Tradition, Cambridge, MA: The Belknap Press of Harvard University Press.

CARSON, ANNE (1986), Eros the Bittersweet, Princeton: Princeton University Press.

DALFERTH, INGOLF U. (2009), Mere Passive: Die Passivität der Gabe bei Luther, in: Bo Kristian Holm/Peter Widmann (ed.), Word – Gift – Being: Justification – Economy – Ontology, Tübingen: Mohr Siebeck, 43–72.

EBELING, GERHARD (1970), Luther: An Introduction to His Thought, trans. R.A. Wilson, Minneapolis, MN: Fortress Press.

GUTMANN, HANS-MARTIN (1991), Über Liebe und Herrschaft: Luthers Verständnis von Intimität und Autorität im Kontext des Zivilisationsprozesses (GTA 47), Göttingen: Vandenhoeck & Ruprecht.

HAMM, BERNDT (2015), Martin Luther's Revolutionary Theology of Pure Gift without Reciprocation, LuthQ 29/2, 125–161.

HÉNAFF, MARCEL (2003), Religious Ethics, Gift Exchange and Capitalism, AES 44, 293–324.

HERRMANN, WILHELM (1906), Der Verkehr des Christen mit Gott im Anschluss an Luther dargestellt, 6. ed., Stuttgart: J.G. Cottasche Buchhandlung.

HOLM, BO KRISTIAN (2006). Gabe und Geben bei Luther: Das Verhältnis zwischen Reziprozität und reformatorischer Rechtfertigungslehre (TBT 134), Berlin/New York, NY: de Gruyter.

HOLM, BO KRISTIAN (2009a), Der Fröhliche Verkehr. Rechtfertigungslehre Als „Gabe-Theologie, in Veronika Hoffmann (ed.), Die Gabe: Ein "Urwort" Der Theologie?, Frankfurt am Main: Verlag Otto Lembeck, 33–52.

HOLM, BO KRISTIAN (2009b), Justification and Reciprocity: "Purified Gift-Exchange" in Luther and Milbank, in: Bo Kristian Holm/Peter Widmann (ed.), Word – Gift – Being: Justification – Economy – Ontology, Tübingen: Mohr Siebeck, 87–116.

HOLM, BO KRISTIAN (2017), Theologische Anthropologie, in: Günter Frank/Axel Lange (ed.), Handbuch Philipp Melanchthon, Berlin/New York, NY: Walter de Gruyter, 395–408.

Joest, Wilfried (1967), Ontologie der Person bei Luther. Göttingen: Vandenhoeck & Ruprecht.

Link, Christian (1991), Schöpfung (HST 7/1), Gütersloh: Güterloher Verlagshaus.

Luther, Martin (1516), Sermon on St Andrew's Day (WA 1: 101–104).

Luther, Martin (1517), Ninety-Five Theses (Wengert: 2015, 34–46/WA 1: 233–238).

Luther, Martin (1518), Sermon on Two Kinds of Righteousness (Stjerna: 2016, 13–25/ WA 2: 145–152).

Luther, Martin (1516–1517), Lectures on Galatians (WA 57 II: 5–108).

Luther, Martin (1518), Explanations of the Ninety-Five Theses (LW 31: 83–252/WA 1: 525–628).

Luther, Martin (1520), Treatise on the Freedom of a Christian, (LW 31: 327–378/WA 7: 39–74).

Luther, Martin (1529), The Small Catechism (BC 347–375/WA 30 I: 243–425).

Luther, Martin (1530–1531), Lectures on the Song of Solomon (WA 31 II: 586–769).

Luther, Martin (1535–1545), Lectures on Genesis (LW 1–8/WA 42–44).

Melanchthon, Philipp (1521/1997), Loci Communes 1521: Lateinisch – Deutsch, trans. Horst G. Pöhlmann, Gütersloh: Gütersloher Verlagshaus.

Melanchthon, Philipp (1543), Loci praecipui teologici, tertia aetas (CR 21: 601–1106).

Pedersen, Else Marie Wiberg (2015), Mysticism in the Lutherrenaissance, in: Christine Helmer/Bo Kristian Holm (ed.), Lutherrenaissance Past and Present (FKDG 106), Göttingen: Vandenhoeck & Ruprecht, 87–105.

Saarinen, Risto (2005), God and the Gift: An Ecumenical Theology of Giving, Collegeville, MN: Liturgical Press.

Saarinen, Risto (2007), Gunst und Gabe, Melanchthon, Luther und die existentielle Anwendung von Senecas "Über die Wohltaten," in: Johannes Brosseder/Markus Wriedt (ed.), "Kein Anlass zur Verwerfung!": Studien zur Hermeneutik des ökumenischen Gesprächs: Festschrift für Otto Hermann Pesch, Frankfurt am Main: Otto Lembeck, 184–197.

Schneider-Ludorff, Gury (2012), Der neue Sinn der Gabe. Stiftungen im Luthertum des 16. und 17. Jahrhunderts, JBTh 27, 277–291.

Simon, Wolfgang (2003) Die Messopfertheologie Martin Luthers: Voraussetzungen, Genese, Gestalt und Rezeption (SuR NR 22), Tübingen: Mohr Siebeck.

Simon, Wolfgang (2008) Worship and Eucharist in Luther Studies, Dialog 47, 143–156.

Steiger, Johann Anselm (2000), The communicatio idiomatum as the Axle and Motor of Luther's Theology, LuthQ 14, 28–33.

Stjerna, Kirsi I. (ed.) (2016), The Annotated Luther, vol. 2: Word and Faith, Minneapolis, MN: Fortress Press.

Thiemann, Ronald F. (2013), The Humble Sublime. Secularity and the Politics of Belief, New York, NY: I.B. Tauris.

Troeltsch, Ernst (1965), Die Soziallehren der christlichen Kirchen und Gruppen, 2nd ed., Aalen: Scientia Verlag.

Wengert, Timothy J. (ed.) (2015), The Annotated Luther, vol. 1: The Roots of Reform, Minneapolis, MN: Fortress Press.

Witte, Jr., John. 2002. Law and Protestantism: The Legal Teachings of the Lutheran Reformation. Cambridge: Cambridge University Press.

Sasja Emilie Mathiasen Stopa

"Honor Your Father And Mother"[1]

The Influence of Honor on Martin Luther's Conception of Society

1. Introduction: Restructuring Society on the Basis of Honor

Martin Luther's Reformation theology entailed a break with ecclesial authorities as he formulated it in the years leading up to his excommunication from the Roman Church in 1521. As such, Luther's theology denounced the previous social structures especially as these structures were secured by the church and maintained through Canon Law (cf. Witte: 2002, 35). The urgent need for Luther to securely reestablish social order increased with the growth of the Reformation into the 1520s and in light of the Peasants War (1525). In accord with the Reformers' *sola scriptura* principle, Luther reorganized society in light of Scripture, more specifically, via the fourth commandment, which states: "Honor your father and mother" (Exod 20:12; Deut 5:16). Luther argued that the commandment concerns not only the relation between parents and children but also all other hierarchical relations in the earthly realm. Thus, the relations between the prince and his subjects and between ecclesial authorities and laity were defined by the fourth commandment.

In this chapter, I examine Luther's exposition of the fourth commandment in order to show how Luther restructures society on the basis of earthly hierarchies defined by honor. I begin by overviewing the pivotal role of honor for Luther's dichotomous understanding of the human being in his relationship to God and to his neighbor. I then analyze Luther's exposition of the fourth commandment in two central texts: *A Treatise on Good Works* from 1520 and *The Large Catechism* from 1529. Both texts view the Decalogue as an expression of God's will, which can only be acknowledged and obeyed through faith. However, Luther composed these texts under very different situations, which influenced their understanding of the human role in obeying this will. After clarifying these

1 "Du solt dein vater und mutter ehren." (BC: 400/WA 30 I: 147,20–21).

differences, I will analyze Luther's conception of society as it is structured by God-given estates or hierarchies. These estates are characterized by the obligation to honor superiors and thus mirror the relation between the human being and God in justification.

Luther sees honor to entail the power and right to rule, and in this way, honor upholds the social hierarchies instituted by God. By contrast, Luther's new understanding of justification underlines that all human beings are equal *coram Deo.* The question that follows is how the hierarchical social structure in honor is to be understood in light of the egalitarian impulse inherent in Luther's reformulation of the doctrine of justification. In his exposition of the fourth commandment, Luther maintains that superiors serve as divine co-operators. Superiors sustain the created order as God's representatives and, therefore, they are due honor and obedience. At the same time, however, Luther stresses that even superiors are subordinate in their relation to God, and he authorizes the Christian to break with earthly authority in consideration of this relation. Furthermore, Luther unfolds the relation of honor as a mutually binding commitment to act out of love and rejects any notion of blind obedience. In that sense, the texts in view in this chapter exemplify the way in which Luther's renewed perception of the human relationship to God in justification molds his comprehension of interpersonal relations and informs the "social imaginary" (Taylor: 2007, 171) of emerging Lutheran confessional culture (cf. Kaufmann: 2006, 9).

2. Honor at the Intersection between the Heavenly and the Earthly Realm

Martin Luther understands the human being as defined by his relationship to God and to his neighbor.[2] Whereas the relationship to God constitutes the human being, interpersonal relationships emanate from this fundamental relation of faith.[3] The notions of honor and glory, which Luther employs synonymously, play a crucial role within this relational anthropology. Rather than denoting a substantial quality, honor and glory are relational concepts that qualify the relation to God as well as interpersonal relations as either appropriate when due honor is given or inappropriate when honor is unjustly claimed or fails to be

2 The relational constitution of the human being has been stressed throughout most of the 20th-century Luther research by for instance Ebeling (1993); Joest (1967); and Bayer (2007). In opposition hereto, Finnish Luther research has asserted the ontological aspects of faith (Juntunen: 1998); cf. Bo Kristian Holm's chapter in this volume.

3 *Fides autem facit personam* ("Faith creates the person," WA 39 I: 282a,16). In this way, Luther supports an eccentric rather than a substantial notion of person (cf. Bayer: 1993, 108; Joest: 1967, 232ff.).

given (cf. Honecker: 1999, 1103). The following analysis will show that Luther continuously describes the proper relationship to God and to the neighbor as characterized by exchanges of honor.

Luther consistently applies the Latin terms *honor* and *gloria* as well as the German term, *Ehre,* to denote worldly and divine honor and glory. In this way, Luther does not distinguish between divine and secular notions of honor and glory. He maintains an intimate connection between the heavenly and the earthly realm as they are created and ordered by God.[4] On the one hand, Luther employs both biblical and theological accounts of the human relationship to God as an interpretive pattern for clarifying interpersonal relationships and understands the relationship between God and the human being to be mirrored in the earthly hierarchies. On the other hand, Luther's conception of honor and glory is determined by the general apprehension of social relations in the Late Middle Ages, in which honor played a crucial role. As part of the increasingly judicial character of medieval society, honor and shame were predominate in the legal system. Honor was protected, satisfaction for lost honor was provided, and shame was assigned (Nowosadtko: 1994).

In this way, the notion of honor marks an intersection between the human being's vertical relation to God and the horizontal relation to fellow human beings and society. This can be seen in Luther's description of parents and secular authority as masks of God, *larvae Dei,* who are to be honored in the civic life (LW 26: 95/WA 40 I: 175,3–5). It is also evident from the way in which Luther aligns the definition of the God-human relationship in the first commandment and the framework for interpreting interpersonal relations in the fourth commandment. Luther asserts that the first commandment is the source of all other commandments (LW 44: 30/WA 6: 209,35f.) and states that the ethics of the earthly realm as expounded in the second table are closely connected to the worship of God as devised in the first table.[5] This interconnection is further established in *On the Freedom of a Christian* from 1520, which rephrases the first commandment in concordance with the fourth: "You shall honor one God" (LW 31: 350).[6] As the first commandment of the second table, the duty to honor parents is conceived as the most important commandment of the second table (BC: 400/WA 30 I: 147,17ff). Luther juxtaposes the call for obedience towards parents with the commandment to obey God: "Let us see whether they can

4 The way in which concepts such as honor and glory interchange between the heavenly and the earthly realm, both of which are ordered by God, testifies to Luther's late medieval mindset, as a sharp distinction between the secular and the divine, or the holy and the profane, belongs to a modern worldview.

5 Accordingly, Luther begins his exposition of the fourth commandment in *The Large Catechism* by summarizing the content of the first three commandments (BC: 400/WA 30 I: 147,5–16).

6 "Du solt eynen gott ehren." (WA 7: 26,13ff; cf. BC: 388/WA 30 I: 134,30ff).

produce a single work that is greater and nobler than obeying father and mother, which God has ordained and commanded next to obedience to his own majesty." (BC: 402).[7] In this way, Luther stresses the parallel nature of the first and the fourth commandments. Both commands require the human being to honor his superiors, then God and then God's earthly masks, namely paternal, ecclesiastical, and secular authorities.

Before turning to these relations of honor, I will examine the way in which Luther's understanding of the Decalogue at the high point of the Reformation in 1520 leads him to determine faith as the precondition for works. In doing so, I aim to outline how earthly relations of honor mirror the human relationship to God in justification. Subsequently, I will spell out Luther's reinstatement of earthly hierarchies on the basis of the fourth commandment as the Reformation is consolidated on more pragmatic grounds in 1529.

3. Faith, Works, and the Honor of God

3.1. Acknowledging God's Will through Faith

Exod 20:12 and Deut 5:16 present the Decalogue to the Israelites as a direct word of Yahweh. Thus, the Ten Commandments stand apart from other Old Testament legislature (Landmesser: 2008, 52). In the New Testament, the Decalogue is encapsulated in the double commandment of love's request to love God and neighbor (Mark 12:29; Matt 22:37–39; Luke 10:25–28). Interpreters in the ancient church and medieval theologians such as Thomas Aquinas follow the traditional condensation of the Ten Commandments into the double love command. Luther's interpretation of the commandments is clearly influenced by this tradition. In the Late Middle Ages, however, the Decalogue regained its importance as a source of Christian ethics in its own right. The fact that Luther expounded the Decalogue repeatedly throughout his career beginning in 1518 with *Eine kurze Erklärung der Zehn Gebote* and reaching its zenith in the Catechisms from 1529 testifies to this increasing influence.

In *The Large Catechism*, Luther defines the Decalogue as a law of the Jews, which Christians are under no obligation to observe. Accordingly, in *Against the Heavenly Prophets on the Matter of Images and Sacraments* from 1525, Luther defines the Law of Moses as a Jewish version of the German law Sachsenspiegel

7 "Las sehen, ob sie yrgent eines erfurbringen kuenden, das groesser und edler sey denn vater und mutter gehorsam, so Gott nehisten seiner Maiestet gehorsam gesetzt und befolhen hat." (WA 30 I: 149,11 ff). However, as will be clarified below, Luther stresses that obedience towards parents is subordinate to the obedience towards God.

(LW 40: 97/WA 18: 81,16; cf. Peters: 1990, 74). Luther goes on to explain why Christians should nevertheless teach and follow the Ten Commandments: "Because the natural laws were never so orderly and well written as in Moses" (LW 40: 97).[8] Thus according to Luther, the Decalogue, which he occasionally explains to be summarized in the Golden Rule (Matt 7:12; Luke 6:31), contains a paradigmatic interpretation of natural law written in the hearts of all people. As such, the Decalogue is binding for Christians. In order to segregate the commandments belonging to the specific Jewish context from the commandments belonging to natural law, Luther introduces the double commandment of love as an interpretive grid. In some texts, Luther simply determines the content of natural law as the double commandment of love and recapitulates the first table in the commandment of selfless love of God and the second table in the commandment of altruistic love of the neighbor.

According to Luther, natural law is unable to grasp the Christian *kerygma*. In his exposition of the book of Jonah, Luther claims, that natural law acknowledges *that* there is a God but is unaware of *who* this God is (LW 19: 54f/WA 19: 206,32ff). Natural law is unable to convey God as God *pro nobis* who reveals himself in Christ in order to justify the human being. This can only be acknowledged through faith. In this way, Luther asserts the cognitive importance of the relationship to God in faith. Luther follows theologians such as Augustine and Thomas Aquinas in claiming that postlapsarian humanity is in need of God's assistance in order to acknowledge God's will expressed in the Decalogue. In *The Large Catechism*, Luther states that the Decalogue is able to help humans recognize natural law only through the Holy Spirit (BC: 404/WA 30 I: 151,2f.).[9] God invokes the conscience through the Decalogue, and in this way, Luther underlines the ethical importance of the conscience despite the fallen nature of the human

---

8 "Darumb, das die naturlichen gesetze nyrgent so feyn, und ordenlich sind verfasset als ynn Mose." (WA 18: 81,18ff).

9 Luther's understanding of the relationship between natural law as formulated in the Golden Rule and the law of Christ understood as the double commandment of love has been discussed by various scholars. In his commentary on *The Large Catechism*, Albrecht Peters (1990, 84) claims that Luther fails to completely bridge the gap between *lex naturalis* and *lex charitatis* as the latter is characterized by a complete renunciation of reciprocity, which distinguishes it from the "as yourself" of the Golden Rule. Antti Raunio opposes this dualistic understanding of the law and describes the Golden Rule as a genuinely Christian law of divine love. According to Raunio (2001, 369ff), the Golden Rule admonishes the Christian to realize this divine love on the basis of his participation in the divine being as love without expecting anything in return. In his book on Lutheran political ethics, Svend Andersen claims that Luther perceives of the ethics of neighborly love as partially in concordance with the Golden Rule in that both promote reciprocity, that is, the ability to put oneself in the place of others. Against the assertion of, for instance, Immanuel Kant and K.E. Løgstrup, Andersen (2010, 303), however, underlines that the ethics of neighborly love is not fully identical with universal ethics and asserts "das 'Mehr' einer christlichen Ethik."

being. The ability to know of good and evil is, however, not a possession of reason or dependent on a certain *habitus* of the conscience but is solely reliant on the Holy Spirit (cf. Peters: 1990, 76). Faith as God's gift in justification is a pre-condition for acknowledging God's law in the commandments. Faith is also a prerequisite for fulfilling this law through works, which is the topic of the following paragraph.

3.2. Obeying God's Will through Faith

Written in 1520, *A Treatise on Good Works* joins two other major works from that year – *On the Freedom of a Christian* and *On the Babylonian Captivity of the Church* – to constitute the culmination of Luther's Reformation theology. In the treatise, Luther deals with a key issue of justification, namely, how to understand the role of works in the relationship between God and human beings. He interprets the Decalogue with the aim of defining Christian works.

The text is defined by a double agenda. On the one hand, Luther highlights that God orders the human being to fulfill his commandments through works. In making this point, Luther responds to the claim of his adversaries that the break with the so-called work-righteousness of the Roman Church leads to a denial of works altogether. On the other hand, Luther maintains that works are done through faith and on the basis of God's preceding justification: "If righteousness consists of faith, it is clear that faith fulfills all commandments and makes all its works righteous, since no one is justified unless he does all the commandments of God" (LW 44: 31).[10]

Throughout the treatise, Luther promotes the Reformation insight that justification takes place *sola fide* without works. Christian works are not performed in order to gain salvation but emanate from the renewed relationship to God in faith. This relation between faith and works of love is prodigiously described in *On the Freedom of a Christian* in which Luther outlines a theological anthropology based on an understanding of the human being as "at the same time free and a servant" (LW 31: 344/WA 7: 50,3). The Christian is on the one hand freed from works in relation to God and receives salvation *sola fide* and on the other hand enslaved in relation to his fellow human beings following the example of Christ. Based on God's preceding gift, the Christian is enabled to imitate the self-giving of Christ in the incarnation and on the cross by giving himself in faith to

10 "Steht dan die gerechtickeit im glauben, szo ists klar, das er allein alle gebot erfullet und alle yhre werck rechtfertig macht, seint dem mal niemant rechtfertig ist, er thu dan alle gottis gebot." (WA 6: 211,4ff). Cf. Rom 3:28.

God and to the neighbor through works of love.[11] Correspondingly, *The Large Catechism* maintains that the human being serves God through faith and the neighbor through works (BC: 406/WA 30 I: 153,18ff). The ability to do works is a dignity bestowed upon the human being by God and founded in the word of God and the commandment itself (BC: 402/WA 30 I: 149,17ff).

In this way, works emanate from the faithful relation to God and a Christian work is thus not characterized by its content but rather by faith and trust in God (cf. LW 44: 24/WA 6: 205,21f). Consequently, Luther denies any separation between holy and profane works and claims that all of God's commandments concern everyday life. In *The Large Catechism*, Luther describes the work of a maid as more pleasing to God than the holiness and severity of a monk: "Is it not a tremendous honor to know this and to say, 'If you do your daily household chores, that is better than the holiness and austere life of all the monks'?" (BC: 406).[12] Luther determines faith as *the* fundamental good work: "The first, highest, and most precious of all good works is faith in Christ." (LW 44: 23).[13] When performing good works, faith acts as a so-called "Werckmeyster" (LW 44: 98/WA 6: 263,28).

According to Luther, all works done in faith appear just in the eyes of God and all works done outside of faith is sin. Thus, human beings sin when trying to fulfill the commandments through faithless works. In this way, the proper relationship to God is a prerequisite for the ethical capacity of the conscience and the work-righteous human being sins even while acting ethically responsible.

3.3. Faith Honors God

As previously mentioned, Luther determines faith to be the cognitive prerequisite for understanding the commandments as well as the necessary precondition for fulfilling them because faith signifies the appropriate relation to God. According to Luther, honor is at the heart of this proper relation of faith. In *On the Freedom of a Christian*, faith is described as the one "who glorifies God and brings forth the works" (LW 31: 353).[14] Luther describes honor as a virtue of faith and claims

11 Bo Kristian Holm (2006, 118–123) has analyzed the reciprocity of self giving between Christ and the Christian by employing the notion of gift.

12 "Ists nicht ein trefflicher rhum, das zuwissen und sagen: wenn du dein tegliche hauserbeit thuest, das besser ist denn aller Monche heilickeit und strenges leben?" (WA 30 I: 153,14ff).

13 "Das erste und hochste, aller edlist gut werck ist der glaube in Christum" (WA 6: 204,25f). Hereby, Luther breaks with the Catholic perception of faith as one of three theological virtues together with love and hope. While maintaining the priority of faith, Luther does, however, suggest a close interconnection between faith, love, and hope (LW 44: 30/WA 6: 210,5ff).

14 "Selbsttäter und Werkmeister, der Gott ehret und die Werke tut" (WA 7: 26,26f). In *The Lectures on Galatians* from 1531, Luther defines faith as trusting in God's promise and giving

that the human relation to God is based on a mutual exchange of honor (LW 31: 350f/WA 7: 53,34–54,30). First, God glorifies the human being by giving him the divine word, Christ, and by inviting him to participate in the alien honor of Christ. Second, the human being is obliged to honor God back through faith in response to God's giving of the Word. This exchange is mutual but radically asymmetrical. The human being who honors God renounces all human claims to honor and acknowledges himself as completely passive in relation to salvation. In addition, this honoring of God takes place through faith, which is a gift of God granted in justification. In this way, Luther avoids any synergistic connotations by maintaining God as the initiator of reciprocity. Furthermore, Luther claims that upon receiving honor God honors the human being in return by regarding him as truthful and just and by bestowing upon him a spiritual kingdom and priesthood. Hereby, Luther introduces the notion of a priesthood of all believers asserting the equality of all human beings in their radical subordination to God.

In this way, Luther interprets faith to mean that the human being renounces all claims to honor and honors God by trusting his promise of salvation. Works done in faith are done in acknowledgment of God's preceding gift in justification and in honor of God. I will now turn to the exposition of the fourth commandment in order to analyze how Luther employs this understanding of the duty of the human being to honor God as a pattern for outlining interpersonal relations.

4. Honor in the Earthly Hierarchies

4.1. Reinstating Ecclesial and Societal Order through the Catechisms

Whereas *A Treatise on Good Works* was written at the dawn of the Reformation, *The Large Catechism* was published nine years later in 1529 expressing an urgent need to reestablish societal and ecclesial order.[15] The immediate cause for the publication of *The Small* and *Large Catechisms* was Luther's participation in a number of visitations in Saxony, which had left him with a discouraging impression of the general knowledge of Christianity not only among the laity but also among its ministers. In the preface to ministers, which became a part of *The Large Catechism* in 1530, Luther describes the reasoning behind the publication: "It is not for trivial reasons that we constantly treat the catechism [...], for we see that unfortunately many preachers and pastors are very negligent in doing so and

honor to God (LW 26: 227/WA 40 I: 360b,12ff). In *A Treatise on Good Works*, Luther describes work-righteous human beings as only honoring God on the outside while actually honoring themselves as idols (LW 44: 32/WA 6: 211,28f; cf. LW 25: 160/WA 56: 179,17).

15 Albrecht Peters has written a thorough commentary on *The Large Catechism* (1990).

thus despise both their office and this teaching." (BC: 379).[16] In the Catechisms, Luther explained the Creed, The Lord's Prayer, the teachings on the sacraments and, as of the 1530 edition, the Confession, in addition to the Decalogue. These explanations were meant to guide teachers, such as the father of the house or the minister. In the church, knowledge of the Catechism was a precondition for receiving communion, and from 1523 onwards, participants in the Confession were questioned in the Catechism. In the general preface to *The Large Catechism*, Luther asserts that the Catechism, which he terms *Kinderlehre*, should be employed in the education of children and simple people and that the father of the house should at least once a week question his children and servants on different parts of its teachings (BC: 383–384/WA 30 I: 129,11–130,5).[17]

Furthermore, *The Large Catechism* is also marked by Luther's controversy with Thomas Müntzer and Luther's experience of the Peasanst War in the middle of the 1520s. Luther had learned that his interpretation of Christian freedom in earlier writings such as *On the Freedom of a Christian* could spur a rebellion against social inequality, resulting in the disintegration of social order. Consequently, in his exposition of the fourth commandment Luther seeks to sustain such order by stressing that the person who fulfills the commandments will be rewarded by God: "Those who are obedient, willing, and eager to be of service, and cheerfully do everything that honor demands, know that they please God and receive joy and happiness as their reward." (BC: 408).[18] In accord with the Old Testament wording, Luther underlines that every commandment entails a divine promise. The fourth commandment promises a long and pleasant life. Luther claims that the pious and obedient will be blessed and emphasizes that he who honors his spiritual and earthly fathers is promised a great reward (BC: 409/WA 30 I: 155,22ff). In this way, the Catechism seems to support an understanding of the human relationship to God based on a notion of *do ut des*; the human being gives God his loyal obedience in order to receive a reward: "If you obey him, you will be his dear child; but if you despise this commandment, you will also have shame, misery, and grief as your reward." (BC: 407).[19]

It is remarkable that Luther only stresses the crucial *sola fide* of the major Reformation works of 1520 once in the Catechism: "In God's sight, it is actually

16 "Das wir den Catechismum so fast treiben und zu treiben beide begeren und bitten, haben wir nicht geringe ursachen. Die weil wir sehen, das leider viel prediger und pfarher hieryn seer seumig sind und verachten beide yhr ampt und diese lere." (WA 30 I: 125,2ff).

17 In this volume, Rasmus Skovgaard Jakobsen and Nina Koefoed outline the impact of the Catechisms on Danish Lutheran confessional culture.

18 "Wer nu hie gehorsam, willig und dienstbar ist und gerne thuet alles, was die ehre belanget, der weis, das er Got gefallen thuet, freud und glueck zu lohn krigt" (WA 30 I: 154,1ff. See also BC: 404/WA 30 I: 151,24f; BC: 405/WA 30 I: 151,32–35).

19 "Gehorchestu yhm, so bistu das liebe kind, verachtestu es aber, so habe auch schande, iamer und hertzleid zu lohn." (WA 30 I: 153,27f).

faith that makes a person holy; it alone serves God, while our works serve people" (BC: 406)[20] In the *Calwer-Lutherausgabe*, this sentence is bracketed as if to acknowledge its exceptional character within the Catechism. Thus, rather than facilitating a break with the oppressive work-righteousness of the Roman Church, *The Large Catechism* is aimed at securing the actual obedience towards authorities in acknowledgment of a common human need for subordination.

4.2. Sin and the Human Need for Subordination

In *The Large Catechism*, Luther emphasizes that even though all humans are equal before God, inter-human relationships are characterized by inequality: "We are indeed all equal in God's sight, but among ourselves it is impossible for there not to be this sort of inequality and proper distinction" (BC: 401).[21] In *A Treatise on Good Works*, Luther claims that the purpose of the fourth commandment is to facilitate the Christian's necessary subordination: "For everyone must be ruled and subject to other human beings" (LW 44: 82).[22] The underlying assumption is the sinful nature of humanity. This condition necessitates the containment and suppression of sin by the law. Therefore, Luther describes the duty of parents to break down a child's will and to teach him to be humble in order that he be able to act against his own depraved nature (LW 44: 86/ WA 6: 255,6ff).

As a consequence, the hierarchical structures of society are established on the basis of a human need for subordination. Luther outlines these hierarchies on the basis of the fourth commandment and focuses on the notion of honor as the proper attitude towards superiors: "Thus these seven commandments teach us how we should exercise ourselves in good works towards human beings, first of all, towards our authorities" (BC: 44).[23] In *The Large Catechism*, Luther describes how God has given authorities great honor, which entails the power and the right to govern.[24] In this way, Luther understands the commandment to honor parents to outline necessary hierarchical relationships in which one rules and the other is ruled over.

20 "Denn fur Got eigentlich der glaube heilig machet und alleine yhm dienet, die wercke aber den leuten." (WA 30 I: 153,18ff).

21 "Sonst sind wir zwar fur Gottes augen alle gleich, aber unter uns kan es on solche ungleicheit und ordenliche unterscheid nicht sein." (WA 30 I: 148,3f).

22 "Dan es musz ein iglicher regiret unnd unterthan werden andern menschen" (WA 6: 252,1f).

23 "Nu szo leren uns diesse sieben gebot, wie wir uns gegen den menschen in gutten wercken uben sollen, und zum ersten gegen unser obirsten" (WA 6: 250,30ff).

24 [...] "Ehre, das ist macht und recht zu regieren [...] " (BC: 409/WA 30 I: 156,10).

4.3. The Hierarchies of the Three Estates as God's Order of Creation

Luther understands society to be divided into certain estates instituted by God in or directly following creation. According to Luther, the human being is guided by God in two ways; inwardly, through the conscience and, outwardly, through the three estates; the church (*ecclesia*), the household (*oeconomia*), and the state (*politia*).[25] In the exposition of the fourth commandment, these two levels intertwine as Luther employs the notion of three estates as a pattern for outlining God's invocation of the conscience in the fourth commandment and unfolds how children are to honor their parents, subjects are to honor their prince, and laymen are to honor the ecclesiastical authorities.

In his various works, Luther refers to the three estates as orders (*Ordnung, ordo, ordination*), hierarchies (*hierarchia*), establishments (*Stifft*), rights (*Recht*), and forms of life (*genus vitae*) and this points to the unsystematic and situational character of Luther's exposition of the created order (Saarinen: 2005). In the *Confession concerning Christ's Supper* from 1528, Luther construes creation to be structured by the three holy orders of priesthood, marriage, and worldly authority (LW 37: 364f./WA 26: 504,30–505,3). Luther elaborates further on these three orders in the exposition of Gen 2:16–17 in *Lectures on Genesis* from 1535. Here, Luther determines the church to be the original order of creation. The creation of Eve leads to the establishment of the household. The state is created as a result of the fall because sin requires containment (LW 1: 103f/WA 42: 79,3ff; cf. WA TR 5: 219,14ff).[26]

In his exposition of the fourth commandment, Luther claims that the relationship between parents and children is the fundamental relationship of obedience in the earthly realm. In the Catechism, Luther states that parents are to be honored because God executes his goodness through them (BC: 404/WA 30 I: 151,10ff). According to Luther, all other kinds of authority emanate from the authority of parents and rule in their place: "For all other authority is derived and developed out of the authority of parents [...]. Thus, all who are called masters stand in the place of parents and must derive from them their power and authority to govern" (BC: 405f).[27] *A Treatise on Good Works* stresses how the

25 The distinction between three created orders is part of the medieval theological tradition and can be found in, for instance, medieval catechetical literature. Furthermore, it mirrors the medieval distinction between *ethica monastica*, *ethica politica*, and *ethica oeconomica* (Saarinen: 2005, 196ff). Oswald Bayer (2007, 111–115) has argued that the notion of three estates is more fundamental to Luther's understanding of society than the teaching of the two kingdoms or realms.

26 As instituted in a postlapsarian situation, the state, strictly speaking, does not belong to the created order. However, as appears from the exposition of the fourth commandment, the *politia* is in some sense grounded in the household (Bayer: 2007, 111–115).

27 "Denn aus der eltern oberkeit fleusset und breitet sich aus alle andere [...]. Also das alle die

commandment teaches the human being to be obedient and obliging toward any kind of authority (LW 44: 80/WA 6: 250,22ff). In this way, the fourth commandment does not only structure the relationship between parents and children but also the obedient relationship to all kinds of earthly authority, secular as well as spiritual.

Accordingly, Luther states that the household relations between a husband and his wife and between the master or the mistress of the house and their servants mirror the relation between parents and children: "What a child owes to father and mother, all members of the household owe them as well" (BC: 406).[28] Luther admonishes the master to show tolerance towards servants and to show mercy, recalling that he himself is subjected to a heavenly master and is in need of God's mercy (LW 44: 98/WA 6: 263,34f). Furthermore, marriage is described as a relation between the husband, who should be obeyed as an authority, and the wife, who should be loved: "a wife ought to be obedient to her husband as her lord, be subject to him, yield to him, keep silent, and agree with him as long as it is not contrary to God. On the other hand, the husband should love his wife" (LW 44: 98).[29]

Moreover, Luther interprets the fourth commandment to encompass obedience towards ecclesial authorities (LW 44: 87/WA 6: 255,18ff). According to Luther, Christians owe ministers or pastoral caretakers a twofold honor, which consists of an obligation to exhibit kindness towards them and to provide for them. In *The Large Catechism*, Luther asserts that the so-called spiritual fathers must reign through the word of God and thus the church is no longer authorized to use force: "For the name of spiritual father belongs only to those who govern and guide us by the Word" (BC: 408).[30]

Instead, Luther ascribes the execution of power in society to secular authority, whom the fourth commandment also commands obedience towards: "The third work of this commandment is to obey secular authority" (LW 44, 91).[31] In *The Large Catechism*, Luther states that secular authority belongs to the so-called *Vater Stand* in the broadest sense of the word (BC: 407/ WA 30 I: 153,30). A prince is not only the father of his children but of all his citizens and subjects and,

man herrn heisset an der eltern stad sind und von yhn krafft und macht zuregiren nemen muessen." (WA 30 I: 152,20f; 152,26f).

28 "Was nu ein kind vater und mutter schuldig ist, sind auch schuldig alle [Ehre und gehorsam gegen herrn und frawen] die yns haus regiment gefasset sind." (WA 30 I: 152,36f). Cf. LW 44: 97/WA 6: 263,5ff.

29 "Hie solt ich auch wol sagen, wie ein weib seinem man, als seinem ubirsten, gehorsam, unterthenig, weichen, schweygen unnd recht lassen sol, wo es nit widder got ist, widderumb der man sein weib lieb haben." (WA 6: 264,10ff).

30 "[D]as heissen allein geistliche veter, die uns durch Gottes wort regieren und furstehen." (WA 30 I: 155,6f.)

31 "Das dritte werck disses gebotis ist der weltlichen obirkeit gehorsam sein." (WA 6: 258,32f).

therefore, is obligated to protect his subjects and punish sin. God upholds his creation by providing food, shelter, and protection through the princes (BC: 407/WA 30 I: 153,32f). *A Treatise on Good Works* summarizes this obligation of secular authority in three works stating that secular authority should prevent gluttony, hinder the use of lavish clothing by which humans seek worldly honor, and prohibit usury (LW 44: 95f/WA 6: 261,23–262,13).[32] Furthermore, secular authority should protect people from the greed of the Roman Church, eliminate prostitution, and handle problems with unruly youths (LW 44: 92ff/WA 6: 261f).

In this way, although not directly referring to three estates, both texts unfold the hierarchical structures of the earthly realm as a created order instituted and sustained by God and defined by relations of honor. The hierarchical relations of this order gain their legitimacy from mirroring and in some sense even acting out the relation between God and the human being.

4.4. The Profanity of the Church and the Sacredness of Everyday Life

It seems that the notion of three estates has two contrasting consequences for Luther's conception of worldly order. On the one hand, the church is understood to be part of the created order of the postlapsarian world and, as such, is counted along with the orders of household and state. In this way, Luther distances himself from any notion of an invisible church promulgated by members of the so-called Radical Reformation and maintains the church as a worldly phenomenon, which is subjected to sin and contains hierarchical relationships. As part of the created order, the church does not correspond to Luther's notion of the heavenly realm but is rather a part of the earthly realm.[33] On the other hand, Luther asserts that all three areas of created life are holy in that they are instituted and ordered by God.[34] This is elaborated in the vocational ethics, whereby Luther maintains that God is honored in the daily life of the believer. In doing so, Luther

32 Cf. the two sermons on usury from 1519 and 1520 (WA 6: 1–8; 36–60) and *On Trade and Usury* from 1524 (WA 15: 279–314).

33 Luther distinguishes between a heavenly and an earthly realm or kingdom in at least three different ways; firstly, in separating between the realms of God and Satan, secondly, in discerning the church from the state, thirdly, in differentiating between the human relationship to God and interpersonal relations (Kolb: 2009, 177). I refer to the latter meaning. For an analysis of Luther's understanding of society as structured in two kingdoms and three estates, see the chapter of Svend Andersen in this volume. Andersen underlines that Luther in his *Confession Concerning Christ's Supper* mentions the office of priesthood rather than the church as such as part of the created order.

34 Cf. Schwanke (2014, 207ff). Ronald F. Thiemann (2014, 169) points to this by employing a notion of sacramental realism claiming that Luther's Christology and Eucharistic theology "'sacralize' the everyday" by maintaining Christ's mediated presence "clothed in the familiar, ordinary and everyday."

broadens the understanding of worship and underlines the sacredness of everyday life as part of God's created order in opposition to the emphasis on monastic life as a way of life pleasing to God (cf. Bayer: 2007, 129). Rather than promoting the secluded life of monks, Luther determines the highest form of worship to be firm faith in God's promises and regard for God as truthful and righteous (LW 31: 350/WA 7: 54,3f). Accordingly, in *A Treatise on Good Works*, Luther accuses the Roman Church of claiming that good works belong in the monastery and maintains that truly good works are performed by authorities who take care of their subjects (LW 44: 99/WA 6: 264,30ff). Likewise, in the Catechism, Luther describes the works of servants in the household as "truly golden works" (BC: 406/WA 30 I: 153,7f). Both aspects are evident in Luther's exposition of the fourth commandment. On the one hand, authorities as such are perceived as part of God's order embodying all of creation and act as representatives of God, who mediate God's will. On the other hand, ecclesial authorities are leveled with all other forms of authority and should not be honored and obeyed at any expense. This will be elaborated in the following section.

4.5. The Relation to God Limits Earthly Obedience

Throughout his works, Luther maintains that the human being is constituted by his relationship to God and that interpersonal relations emanate from this foundational relation. On this basis, Luther asserts the possibility of maintaining a proper relationship with God as a touchstone to the validity of earthly authorities and states that Christians should only honor and obey authorities who refrain from interfering with the honor and obedience towards God. Accordingly, both texts claim that children are only obliged to honor their parents as long as it does not interfere with the first three commandments: "God is to be more highly regarded than parents according to the first three commandments" (LW: 44: 84).[35]

In *A Treatise on Good Works*, Luther intends to justify his own disobedience towards the Roman Church and vehemently opposes the allegation against him that going against specific ecclesial authorities equates a failure to acknowledge any kind of church authority. Thus written in the midst of conflict with the Roman Church, the treatise intensively describes the decline of the church that has left it more secular than secular authority at all. According to Luther, ecclesial authorities fail to meet their obligations to preach and teach, to defend the church against erroneous teachings, to punish sin, and to encourage piety. As the distribution of indulgences and the reigning policy for awarding ecclesial offices go

35 "Dan got ist in den ersten dreyen gebotten hoher zuachtenn den die eltern." (WA 6: 253,2f).

against the first three commandments, Roman clergy has no claim to honor (LW 44: 90f/WA 6: 258,11ff). As a consequence, the fourth commandment has been destroyed, and Luther encourages Christians to act as children of parents who have gone insane (LW 44: 90/WA 6: 257,27f).

Contrary to this firm call for a break with ecclesial injustice, Luther maintains that the injustice of secular authority is of little importance to God. Therefore, Christians are to tolerate unjust authorities. However, obedience should cease whenever the first three commandments are broken. By downplaying the importance of unjust secular authorities, Luther seems to acknowledge the need for some kind of authority to support him in the midst of what led to a tumultuous break with the Roman Church.

5. The Relation of Honor

5.1. A Dual Obligation of Love

Towards the end of *A Treatise on Good Works*, Luther epitomizes the fourth commandment in the two fundamental notions of obedience and care: "But all that has been said of these works is included in these two, obedience and care. Obedience is the duty of subjects, care, of masters, that they be diligent to rule their subjects well, deal kindly with them, and do everything to benefit and help them" (LW 44:99).[36] In this way, a relation of honor entails a dual obligation: Subjects are obliged to obey their superiors and superiors are obliged to care for their subjects in a loving manner and do everything in order to be of use and help to them. This emphasis on love is echoed in *The Large Catechism*, in which Luther states that the fourth commandment concerns the honoring of four kinds of fathers; the actual, biological father, the father of the house, the father of the country, and fathers of the church: "So we have introduced three kinds of fathers in this commandment: fathers by blood, fathers of a household, and fathers of the nation. In addition, there are also spiritual fathers" (BC: 408).[37] Luther refers to the Roman titles of *patres* and *matres familias* and *patres patriae* in order to prove his claim that all kind of authority has a fatherly office and therefore ought to have a fatherly heart towards their subjects. Authorities of all kinds are under a

36 "Alles aber, was gesagt ist von dissen werckenn, ist begriffen in den zweyen, Gehorsam und sorgfeltickeit. Gehorsam gepurt den unterthanen, sorgfeltickeit den uberhern, das sie fleisz haben yhr unterthanen wol zu regiren, lieblich mit yhn handeln, und alles thun, das sie yhn nutzlich und hulfflich sein." (WA 6: 264,16ff). Luther develops his notion of the good prince in *On Secular Authority* from 1523 (WA 11: 245–282).

37 "Also haben wir dreyerley veter ynn diesem gepot furgestellet: des gebluts, ym hause und ym lande, Darueber sind auch noch geistliche veter." (WA 30 I: 155,3f).

special obligation to act out of their fatherly hearts and care for their subjects. Likewise, Christians are to honor authorities as fathers (BC: 405f/WA 30 I: 152,28ff). In thus turning to the notion of love to expound the commandment to honor parents, Luther seems to draw on the tradition that interprets the Decalogue in light of the double commandment of love. This tradition understands the fourth commandment as part of a fulfillment of the love of neighbors. In this way, the hierarchical relations of society become familiarized in the original meaning of the word as they are based on the loving obligation of a father towards his child.[38]

5.2. Honor as a Divine Attribute

In both texts, Luther maintains that honor transcends the commandment's neighborly love interpretation because honor indicates participation in a divine attribute. In the Catechism, Luther asserts that God does not only command children to love their parents but to honor them. He interprets this as a sign that God has installed parents as his earthly representatives: "For God has exalted this estate above all others; indeed, he has set it up in his place on earth" (BC: 403f).[39] According to Luther, this obligation to honor distinguishes parental relationship from that of siblings who are only obliged to love each other: "God has given this estate of father- and motherhood a special position of honor, higher than that of any other estate under it in that he has not only commanded us to love parents but to honor them" (BC: 400f).[40]

Luther distinguishes between the office of superiors, whether parents, pastors, or princes, and the persons who hold the office (Andersen: 2010, 19). God legitimizes the office rather than the person. Consequently, Luther stresses that parents are to be honored due to the will of God and not because of their own efforts or personality. Therefore, even deficient parents deserve honor (BC: 401/WA 30 I: 147,36–148,1). In *A The Treatise on Good Works*, Luther laments the fact that some children are ashamed of their parents because of their poverty or lack of worldly honor. According to Luther, such parents are given by God in order to test the children and their adherence to the commandments (LW 44: 82/WA 6: 251,26ff). In this way, Luther understands honor as an attribute of God in which

38 See Bo Kristian Holm's chapter for an analysis of Luther's and Melanchthon's employment of the father-child metaphor in outlining the human relation to God in justification.

39 "Denn Gott hat diesen stand oben angesetzt, ia an seine stad auff erden gestellet." (WA 30 I: 150,26f).

40 "Diesem vater und mutterstand hat Got sonderlich den preis gegeben fur allen stenden, die unter yhm sind, das er nicht schlechts gepeut die eltern lieb zuhaben sondern zu ehren." (WA 30 I: 147,22ff).

earthly authorities participate when they administer the earthly offices instituted by God. Authorities are God's earthly representatives so that when Christians honor their superiors they ultimately honor God (BC: 401/WA 30 I: 147,34).

5.3. Obedience and Fear

Furthermore, Luther determines honor to be a superordinate term, rising above not only love but also fear. In the Catechism, Luther states that honor includes love, castigation, humility, and timidity: "For it is a much higher thing to honor than to love. Honor includes not only love but also deference, humility, and modesty as shown towards a majesty." (BC: 401,106).[41] In *A Treatise on Good Works,* Luther maintains that honor encompasses both love and fear: "True honor is such a fear mingled with love." (LW 44: 81).[42] As a counter image, Luther describes how parents, out of worldly love, bring up children to honor them with love but without fear. According to Luther, this results in children who seek worldly honor and possessions rather than the honor of God and eternal goods (LW 44: 82f/WA 6: 252,6ff).

However, Luther stresses that God does not want himself or parents to be honored with a loveless fear of punishment, which leads to hatred. Instead, they should be honored with a fear mixed with love and trust, which annihilates any fear of punishment and is instead a fear of disappointing the parents (LW 44: 81/ WA 6: 251,4ff).

In a similar line of thought, Luther distinguishes between honor and blind obedience. In the Catechism as well as in *A Treatise on Good Works*, Luther claims that human beings honor their superiors by obeying and serving them. Accordingly, disobedience is considered to be the greatest of sins. Luther describes how God appreciates and rewards obedience (BC: 405/WA 30 I: 152,9ff). However, Luther does not refer to a notion of blind obedience but rather qualifies obedience with reference to honor. In *The Large Catechism*, Luther stresses that the household should imitate the obedient relationship between a child and its parents. Consequently, "servant and maids should take care not just to obey their masters and mistresses but also to honor them as their own fathers and mothers." (BC: 406/WA 30 I: 152,37–153,2).[43] In this way, Luther opposes honor to any conception of blind obedience and underlines that the Christian does not honor

41 "Denn es ist viel ein hoeher ding Ehren denn Lieben, als das nicht alleine die liebe begreifft sondern auch eine zucht, demut und schewe als gegen einer maiestet." (WA 30 I: 147,27ff).

42 "Ein solche furcht, mit lieb vormischt, ist die rechte ehre." (WA 6: 251,9f).

43 "Daruemb sollen knecht und megde zusehen, das sie yhren herrn und frawen nicht allein gehorsam sein sondern auch ynn ehren halten als yhr eigene veter und muetter." (WA 30 I: 152,37–153,2).

his superiors because of fear of punishment or hope of reward. As opposed to blind obedience, honor originates in a God-given commandment and is not given reluctantly but gladly and cheerfully (BC: 406/ WA 30 I: 153,3 f). Honor is given on the basis of trust and love. In this way, the interpersonal relationships of the earthly hierarchies mirror the relationship between the human being and God insofar as the God-human relationship is characterized by the honor of faith, signaling trust in God based on his preceding promise of salvation. In *On the Freedom of a Christian*, Luther underlines a similar point when stating that works should be done out of a joyful surplus emanating from the relationship to God.

In these descriptions, Luther paraphrases his break with the erroneous understanding of the relationship to God in the Roman Church, which is based on a dismissal of meritorious works done out of a fear of punishment or a wish for reward. Based on his own experiences as a monk, Luther continuously claims that rather than being done out of love of God, meritorious works lead to hatred of God. In this way, Luther asserts that blind obedience, fear of punishment, and hope of reward belong to a mistaken notion of both the human relationship to God as well as the relations between subjects and superiors in the earthly realm.

6. Human Equality and the Hierarchies of Honor

As mentioned above, Luther maintains that all human beings are equal *coram Deo* and are given a share in the common priesthood of all believers through justification. In this way, the renewed interpretation of justification leads to a destruction of any notion of hierarchy in the heavenly realm. At the same time, though, the exposition of the fourth commandment unfolds the statement that in order to contain sin, inequality is necessary in interpersonal relationships. As a result, these relationships are structured within the God-given hierarchies of the earthly realm, which Luther interprets as expressions of the fundamental relation between parents and children. The question is, then, whether the notion of common human equality before God kindles a notion of equality in the Lutheran understanding of society. John Witte Jr. argues along this line when claiming that the egalitarian impulse inherent in the doctrine of justification results in a deconstruction of hierarchy in Luther's view on secular authority and the church institution (Witte: 2002, 106 ff).[44]

44 Likewise underlining the egalitarian consequences of Lutheran theology, Antti Raunio (2001) has argued that Luther's stressing of the Golden Rule, which places the needs of the neighbor at the center of ethics, deteriorates the social rank designating the theological ethics of the Middle Ages.

In this chapter, I have shown how Luther understands the human relationship to God to be marked by a radical asymmetry, which is underlined in the commandment to honor God in faith and hence renounce all human claims to honor. This radical subordination under God is a common human condition that as such evens out all interpersonal differences. However, the relations of honor between authorities and their subjects do not mirror this common submissiveness to God but rather reflect the hierarchical relationship between God and the human being. God sustains his creation through the earthly hierarchies and as representatives of God authorities have a right to be honored. Simultaneously, however, Luther maintains that obedience towards any kind of authority is secondary to the obedience towards God and should be broken if opposing the first three commandments. In this way, although admonished to submit to the earthly hierarchies, Christians are authorized to break with them in consideration of the primary relation that is the relationship to God. In this sense, the radical equality of all human beings *coram Deo*, which is established with Luther's interpretation of justification, could be seen to take precedence over the inequality that sustains the necessary order of earthly hierarchies.

Furthermore, in line with biblical tradition Luther maintains that the true Christian identity is that of the humble servant and continuously asserts that even superiors are subjects in their relation to God. In *On the Freedom of a Christian*, Luther describes how a Christian based on his relationship to God willingly submits to his neighbor even though the Christian is master over all things by virtue of the relation to God. In *Lectures on Romans* from 1515/16, the epitome of the young Luther's *humilitas* theology, the Christian is described as foolish and weak in the eyes of the world although wise and strong *coram Deo* (LW 25: 153f/WA 56: 173,27ff). Luther asserts how this demand for foolishness endangers the prince and other people with authority. They have to show their power and wisdom in order to maintain their status, but by doing so, they act against God. Behind these statements is a well-known biblical conundrum between attaining worldly honor and seeking honor from God (cf. John 5:44.12:43; Matt 6:2ff). Moreover, in acting on behalf of God, superiors could be led to believe that they are equal to God, thus succumbing to what Luther describes as the epitome of sin. However, Luther claims that as God's representative the prince is authorized to employ judgment, glory, and vengeance (LW 25: 444/WA 56: 451,8f). In this way, earthly hierarchies based on honor are legitimized because they act out the created order of God. As such, Luther interprets the commandment to honor parents as an expression of the first commandment to honor God. By referring to authorities as representatives of God and by explicitly distinguishing between the office and the person holding it, Luther asserts the equality of all human beings *coram Deo* even while acknowledging the necessity of earthly hierarchies. Thus, he maintains the *sine qua non* of his Reformation theology, namely, that all honor and glory are due to God: *Soli deo honor et gloria* (e.g. LW 42: 81/WA 2: 130,19).

Bibliography

ANDERSEN, SVEND (2010), Macht aus Liebe: Zur Rekonstruktion einer lutherischen politischen Ethik (TBT 149), Berlin/New York, NY: de Gruyter.

BAYER, OSWALD (1993), Luthers Verständnis des Seins Jesu Christi im Glauben, in: Anja Ghiselli/Kari Kopperi/Rainer Vinke (ed.), Luther und Ontologie. Das Sein Christi im Glauben als strukturierendes Prinzip der Theologie Luthers, LAR 21, Erlangen: Martin Luther Verlag, 94–113.

BAYER, OSWALD (2007), Martin Luthers Theologie: Eine Vergegenwärtigung, 3rd ed., Tübingen: Mohr Siebeck.

EBELING, GERHARD (1993), Luthers Wirklichkeitsverständnis, ZThK 90, 409–424.

HOLM, BO KRISTIAN (2006), Gabe und Geben bei Luther: Das Verhältnis zwischen Reziprozität und reformatorischer Rechtfertigungslehre (TBT 134), Berlin/New York, NY: de Gruyter.

HONECKER, M. (1999), Article "Ehre. Systematisch-theologisch", RGG[4] 2, 1999, 1103–1105.

JOEST, WILFRIED (1967), Ontologie der Person bei Luther, Göttingen: Vandenhoeck & Ruprecht.

JUNTUNEN, SAMMELI (1998), Luther and Metaphysics: What Is the Structure of Being According to Luther?, in: Carl E. Braaten/Robert Jenson (ed.), Union with Christ: The New Finnish Interpretation of Luther, Grand Rapids: W.B. Eerdmans, 129–160.

KAUFMANN, THOMAS (2006), Konfession und Kultur: lutherischer Protestantismus in der zweiten Hälfte des Reformationsjahrhunderts, Tübingen: Mohr Siebeck.

KOLB, ROBERT (2009), Martin Luther: Confessor of the Faith, New York: Oxford University Press.

LANDMESSER, CHRISTOF (2008), Individualität und Sozialität: Perspektiven biblischer Theologie zur Intergenerationalität, in: Friedrich-Otto Scharbau (ed.), Wohlfart und Langes Leben. Luthers Auslegung des 4. Gebots in ihrer aktuellen Bedeutung, Erlangen: Martin-Luther-Verlag, 45–67.

LUTHER, MARTIN (1515–1516), Lectures on Romans (LW 25/WA 56).

LUTHER, MARTIN (1520), A Treatise on Good Works (LW 44, 15–114/WA 6: 202–276).

LUTHER, MARTIN (1520), On The Freedom of a Christian (LW 31: 333–377/WA 7: 12–73).

LUTHER, MARTIN (1525), Against the Heavenly Prophets on the Matter of Images and Sacraments (LW 40: 79–223/WA 18: 37–214).

LUTHER, MARTIN (1525–1526), Lectures on Jonah (LW 19: 35–104/ WA 19: 185–251).

LUTHER, MARTIN (1528), Confession Concerning Christ's Supper (LW 37: 161–372/WA 26: 241–509).

LUTHER, MARTIN (1529), The Large Catechism (BC: 379–480/WA 30 I: 125–238).

LUTHER, MARTIN (1535), Lectures on Galatians, chapters 1–4 (LW 26/WA 40 I).

LUTHER, MARTIN (1535–1545), Lectures on Genesis, chapters 1–5 (LW 1/WA 42: 3–263).

NOWOSADTKO, JUTTA (1994), Betrachtungen über den Erwerb von Unehre: Vom Widerspruch 'moderner' und 'traditionaler' Ehren- und Unehrenkozepte in der frühneuzeitlichen Ständegesellschaft, in: Ludgera Vogt/Arnold Zingerle (ed.), Ehre: Archaische Momente in der Moderne, Frankfurt am Main: Suhrkamp, 230–248.

Peters, Albrecht (1990), Kommentar zu Luthers Katechismen, vol. 1–5, Göttingen: Vandenhoeck & Ruprecht.

Raunio, Antti (2001), Summe des christlichen Lebens, Mainz: Verlag Philipp von Zabern.

Saarinen, Risto (2005), Ethics in Luther's Theology: The Three Orders, in: Risto Saarinen/Jill Kraye (ed.), Moral Philosophy on the Threshold of Modernity, Dordrecht: Springer, 195–215.

Schwanke, Johannes (2014), Luther's Theology of Creation, in: Robert Kolb/Irene Dingel/L'ubomír Batka (ed.), The Oxford Handbook of Martin Luther's Theology, Oxford: Oxford University Press, 201–211.

Taylor, Charles (2007), A Secular Age, Cambridge, MA: Belknap Press of Harvard University Press.

Thiemann, Ronald Frank (2014), The Humble Sublime: Secularity and the Politics of Belief, London: I.B. Tauris.

Witte Jr., John (2002), Law and Protestantism: The Legal Teachings of the Lutheran Reformation, Cambridge: Cambridge University Press.

Candace L. Kohli

The Gift of the Indwelling Spirit

Anthropological Resources in Luther's Robust Pneumatology

1. Introduction

Luther is often seen as the harbinger of the modern individual. In his treatise *The Freedom of a Christian* (1520), Luther theologically defined human personhood according to a binary derived from 2 Cor 4:16: "Though our outer nature is wasting away, our inner nature is being renewed every day." (LW 31: 344/WA 7: 50,8ff). The "inner person" is the seat of human subjectivity from a theological perspective; it is the soul as it relates to God apart from any causal determination from outer works (LW 31: 344/WA 7: 50,15ff). The "outer person" has to do with the body and its "dealings with men" (LW 31: 358/WA 7: 60,2). The outer person conceives of the social and political aspects of the human person. The inner person encapsulates the essence of one's personhood.

Luther sets this anthropological binary within a moral paradox known as the *simul* construct. In faith, the human person is *simul iustus et peccator*, the person is both just and sinner. The inner person is justified passively through faith in Christ as a faith relation – Christ's attributes are attributed to the inner person thereby forensically constituting the person as just. The outer person remains a sinner by virtue of its carnality. Luther thinks this moral determination flows from inner to outer. He says, "Good works do not make a good man, but a good man does good works." (LW 31: 361/WA 7, 61,39f). Therefore, he seems to suggest that any good works the outer person performs towards the neighbor spring spontaneously out of Christ's love in the soul, not from the person's own affections. The outer person in this construction provided a material cause for action towards the neighbor, but Luther's emphasis on human passivity in justification left no way to ontologically root acts of love in the human soul itself. Inner justification before God, then, resulted in a paradox: the inner and outer persons existed in a state of moral incoherence articulated in the *simul* construct.

This essay asks why it might be fruitful to stress the coherence between the inner and outer persons in Luther's theology in spite of Luther's *simul* construct as one model for imagining the Christian in society from Lutheran perspective. Luther's notion of the Holy Spirit provides a conceptual resource for answering this anthropological question.

Luther's emphasis on the inner person made its appearance in Denmark most famously in Søren Kierkegaard's Kantian philosophical conceptualization of the human and the "leap to faith" (Kirkegaard: 1985, 73, 83; 1992, 33, 54).[1] The inner assent to faith – the leap – played on the dialectical incommensurability between the historical – the realm of corporeal experience – and the existential as the inner faith response. Only this hidden, inner act could liberate the human from "nonbeing," the aesthetic and ethical existential stages that gave way to the religious. The leap lifted the human to the realm of the religious, where true being was existentially constituted (Ferreira: 1998, 211, 215). Like Luther's notion of faith in the *Freedom Treatise*, Kierkegaard's "leap" prioritized the inner as the realm of being truly human while paradoxically the outer is as naught.

Lutheran theology in the twentieth century inherited a similarly Kantian approach to Luther's theology that emphasized the inner life of the soul in relation to God over and above the outer person. Karl Holl initiated this turn in 1917 when he isolated the role of the conscience as the heart of Luther's religious innovation (Karl Holl: 1917/1948, 1–110). Holl's approach influenced Gerhard Ebeling's development of the "*coram* relations" as an interpretive grid for Luther's anthropology in the *Disputatio de Homine* (1536) (Ebeling: 1982, 89).[2] The *coram* relations pitted the inner person *in moral relation* to God in faith (*coram Deo*) eschatologically against the (ultimately fleeting) outer person *as moral-ethical actor* in political and social relations temporally (*coram mundo*). Ebeling dealt a death-blow to Lutheran ethics by undermining the teleological relevance of the outer person's moral quality. Nevertheless, his ongoing influence is exemplified in Reinhard Flogaus' view that neighborly love extends from the *relation* to God's love and not from any kind of rehabilitated or reformed human love per se (Flogaus: 1997, 303). In a contemporary context that privileges the inner mental life-world of the human person as relation, the subjective grounds, those onto-

1 Similar privileging of the inner can be seen in Lockean political philosophy and Cartesian metaphysics. John Locke defended religious toleration by elevating the conscience over outward practice (Locke: 2003, 232f). Similarly, Rene Descartes' *ego cogito, ergo sum* posited human ontology on the dualistic basis of rationality alone (Descartes: 2000, 1,7).

2 Holl's elevation of the mind is also evident in Wilfried Joest's emphasis on the change in "self-understanding" as a result of justification, in Ulrich Asendorf's conclusion that justification has a psychological and relational effect only, and in Ian McFarland's constructive anthropology that defines human persons exclusively on the basis of whether or not the human has an internal relation to Christ (Joest: 1967; Asendorf: 1988; McFarland: 2001).

logical conditions in the inner human soul necessary for outer human moral action, remain elusive in Luther's theology (cf. Lindhardt: 1986, 29).[3] As such, the inner and outer person suffer under a theological vacuum that fragments human subjectivity.

The challenge, then, as I see it, is to find a way to identify the subjective grounds for moral action in Luther's theology in a way that makes possible new approaches to the *unity* and *continuity* between the inner and outer persons without undermining Luther's emphasis on human passivity in justification. To do so is to open Luther's theology up to the fullness of human experience in faith as simultaneously an *inner experience* in the mind and conscience that is inseparable from the *embodied experiences* in which faith is realized, challenged, nourished, and practiced (cf. Gregersen: 2014, 175–189). Luther understood the embodied life of faith to be ordered by three social arenas in which a person participates. Luther labeled these arenas church, politics, and the household (*ecclesiasticus, politicus, oeconomicus*), what scholars now call the "three estates." Within these three "estates", the Christian encounters challenges and opportunities to enact and deepen the soul's relation to Christ and the righteousness given over to the Christian in faith. A brief survey of Luther's pastoral writings and letters reflects the everyday realities of sixteenth-century life in which a Christian could practice right action on the basis of sound judgment and choice in faith. Luther addressed the realities of the plague and other illnesses, miscarriage and grief, marriage, education, and even financial choice and economics, all from the perspective of action driven by faith.[4] Without subjectivity for moral agency, Luther lacked the grounds to suggest that faith comes to bear on a Christian's action in response to these realities faced within the three estates in which one exists.

Luther aims to establish precisely these kinds of subjective grounds for moral action in his *Antinomian Disputations* (1537–40). Luther's opponent, the Antinomians led by his former student Johann Agricola, dismissed the ongoing utility of the law in the Christian life on the basis of Luther's own inner-outer anthropological dualism and his doctrinal binary of law and gospel (WA 39 I: 344,30; cf. Kjeldgaard-Pedersen: 1983, 20–25). Agricola's antinomianism created a slew of potential social and theological problems for Luther: civil anarchy and

3 Lindhardt is also critical of the privilege given to the inner person in Luther scholarship. Whereas I look to Luther's medieval theological sources for overcoming this emphasis, Lindhardt seeks to establish Luther's reliance on Renaissance Theology as a path forward.

4 For example, see *On Trade and Usury* (1519): WA 6: 36–60; *Whether One May Flee the Deadly Plague* (1527): LW 43: 119–38/WA 23: 339–379; *Consolation for Women Whose Pregnancies have Not Gone Well* (1542): in Lull/Russell: 2012, 283–285/WA 53: 205–208; *On Marriage Matters* (1530): LW 46: 259–320/WA 30 III: 205–248; *A Sermon on Keeping Children in School* (1530): LW 46: 207–258/WA 30 III: 518–588.

lawlessness, a diminution of the Spirit's trinitarian personhood, and leniency towards moral laxity and depravity (LW 41: 113/WA 50: 600,8). The problem was that Luther threw out the medieval anthropological categories for conceptualizing human action before the law in the way he premised human freedom on total human passivity in *The Freedom of a Christian.* He needed to recover language and categories to more carefully discuss the human action before the law prior and subsequent to justification by divine grace alone.

Medieval theologians borrowed language to talk about this inner-outer interplay from Aristotle but added the nuance that this reciprocal anthropological relation always occurs as part of the human's existence before God. Aristotle's and then Aquinas' term "habituation" (lat: *habitus*, or habit) referred to an active condition in which a person's inner moral virtues (either acquired or divinely bestowed by the Spirit) came to bear on a person's actions towards objects of desire by habituating, or acclimating, oneself to acting virtuously in the face of temptation (Aquinas: ST 1–2.52). The subjective grounds for habituation existed in the soul's faculties or powers; habituation occurred by means of an intellectual and volitional interplay in the soul that directed the person's bodily action towards one's final end. This process is called "moral reasoning" or "moral decision-making."

Luther looked to pneumatology as his resource for discussion moral action. By focusing on the activity of the Holy Spirit in, on, and with the human soul *as a result of* justification, Luther constructed a theological anthropology of the regenerate soul in which the inner and outer persons begin to come back together in ongoing relation to the law after justification.[5] This essay elevates the role of the Spirit in the *Antinomian Disputations* as Luther's *means* for recovering language to discuss the subjective grounds for the inner-outer anthropological unity of the regenerate person. The critical role of the Spirit emerges in the ways Luther relies on the Spirit for discussing human moral reasoning and obedience as an inner-outer interplay. Luther assigns three modal functions to the Spirit as consoling, vivifying, and sanctifying. These modes allow him to reconstruct subjective grounds in the human's inner intellectual and volitional acts that lead to outer obedience to the law, which he understands to be expounded and

5 Luther's "positive" use of the law in the *Antinomian Disputations* perplexed mid-century German scholars who compared it to Melanchthon's *tertius usus legis.* They tried to reconcile Luther's "positive use" conceptually with his earlier conclusions about the accusing function of the law. Ultimately, the consensus became that the *Antinomian Disputations* were an "anomaly" and Luther's law/gospel dichotomy prevailed (cf. Althaus: 1952; Bornkamm: 1963; Ebeling: 1967, 50–68; Elert: 1948; Joest: 1961). Recently, Michael Whiting painted an alternative picture of Luther's understanding of the *tertius usus legis* by examining how Luther's understanding of law developed in proximity to Melanchthon and tracing the influence of these concepts in the English Reformation (2010, 124–145).

modeled in Christ's life. The remainder of this essay examines the role of the Spirit in Luther's anthropology by looking to the systematic requirements for human moral action (sec. 1) and Luther's narrative depiction of human moral reasoning in relation to the Spirit (sec. 2) before proceeding to analyze the Spirit as an anthropological resource (sec. 3).

2. Systematic Requirements for Human Moral Action

The subjective grounds for human moral action as Christian theology systematically conceived it at the turn of the sixteenth century came about as an interplay between the human intellect and will working together to move the body in action. Christian theologians in the three centuries before Luther overlaid these Platonic and Aristotelian structures with Christian theological concepts. Per Aquinas, this way of theorizing about human action is rooted in the *imago Dei*. Like the divine Trinity, the human is the source of its own action. This requires that the human be free in judgment and possess the power to act (Aquinas: ST 1–2, prologue). Judgment is rightly attributed to the intellectual faculties, or acts, of the rational soul. The intellect discerns the good on the basis of God's revealed will and law through its power of reason and judges the value of an object of desire according to this standard. The intellect determines whether an object moves the person towards or away from its telos or end, a contribution of Augustine's Platonism, as either a "lesser good" or a concupiscent desire. The human telos, conceived platonically as the highest good or in its Aristotelian incarnation as happiness, is love of God for God's own sake and eternal union with him. Augustine thought the human is able to judge an action towards or away from an object as good if that object serves as a means to the end of loving God (Augustine, *De trinitate* 15.22, CChr.SL 50 A). The intellect judges an object to be good if loving the object helps the lover to love God.

As to the power to act, Luther's nominalist predecessors followed Aristotle and attributed this power to the volitional faculties or acts. Ockham, for instance, thought the will weighs the dictates of reason regarding the good against the will's own desires and passions. Then the human wills or nills action based on reason's dictates in proximal relation towards (or away from) an end (Ockham: OTh 8, 409, 411; 7, 359; cf. Biel: 2 Sent. d.6 A). Biel thought freedom of the will in conformity with right reason makes possible the love of God above all else; a rational desire proceeds from a free judgment such that the will and intellect freely agree (Biel: 2 Sent. d.30, q.1 H 16–27; 3, d.36, q.1 D 18–28). Agency for moral action occurs when these internal processes proceed to move the body. Morally good action stems from judging and choosing well so that the actions move the entire person – intellect, will, and body – towards God, though movement towards God as merit may come only through divine assistance or acceptance (Ockham: OTh 3, 445, 452–55; Biel: 2 Sent. d.25, N.O.; 4, d.1, q.3, D 15–29. Cf. Adams: 2013, 52–56; 1999, 251–261; 1986). This requires that the intellect and will judge and choose God as its proper end and, simultaneously, which actions move the person towards that end. Aristotelians like Aquinas would add that the person does so consistently and with ease (in habituation) (Aquinas: ST 1–2, q.54, a.4, r.1). Moral evil, or sin, occurs when one of these processes fails. In the rationalist scenario, the intellect errs and judges poorly to determine God's will or an object's contribution to the human's end and, thus, fails to sufficiently guide the will (Aquinas: ST 1–2, q.76, a.1). The voluntarist alternative tends to liberate the will from reason's dictates. Either the will exercised its freedom to nill an action in opposition to reason's dictates or it lacked fortitude to resist its concupiscent desires and was overcome (Ockham: OTh 7, 350–351, OTh 7, 352; Biel: 2 Sent. d.21, q.un C; d.43 q.1 B 6–18).

This systematic structure for human moral action did not come to Luther straightforwardly, but through a dizzying set of additions, clarifications, and alterations set within medieval commentaries on Peter Lombard's discussion of free choice in the *Sentences* (cf. Lombard: 2 Sent. d. 25). Luther inherited Augustine's Platonic theory as it had been modified by Aquinas' seemingly impossible attempt to harmonize Augustine's theory with Aristotle's rational soul concept. Duns Scotus, Ockham, and Ockham's successors, unhappy with these measures, further attempted to reconcile the two through more Augustinian distinctions read alongside their own innovations.

One thread these changes followed had to do with what a human is capable of doing "by nature and apart from grace" (*ex naturalibus*). Augustine distinguished between good works before and after divine grace and, secondarily, of the capacity of good works to merit salvation. He concluded that humans were capable of good works *ex naturalibus*, but never of meritorious good works (Augustine, *De corruptione et gratia*, PL 44: 35f). Aquinas rethought the "by nature alone" question in light of infused grace, which he defined as the charity of the Holy Spirit infused into the soul. He came up with a new notion of the "natural" intellect-reformed-by-grace, which could judge well and control the human will (Janz: 1983, 53). Scotus and then Ockham complicated the will concept. Ockham ascribed the will with the "liberty of indifference," which escalated the priority of the will insofar as the will could will with or nill against reason, should it so desire (Adams: 1999, 19). Ockham's development led Luther to question the viability of this way of theorizing about human action. If the human could judge rightly, he may, in fact, choose against reason's dictates! (cf. *Disputation against Scholastic Theology*, LW 31, 3–15; WA 1: 221–228). But another resource in Augustine had gone relatively untapped that left open possibilities for conceptualizing human action. Augustine predicated true knowledge in the intellect upon proper love of God in the will made possible by the soul's relation to the Holy Spirit (Augustine: *De trinitate* 8.4–5, CChr.SL 50 A). Luther, as we will see, takes advantage of this idea to find subjective grounds for human action that bring the inner and outer persons back together.

3. Moral Reasoning and the Spirit in Luther's 'Christian Youth' Narrative

The systematic demands of theological anthropology and moral action required Luther to conceptualize the regenerate Christian with inner intellectual and volitional acts that lead to outer acts in obedience to the Spirit's and Christ's example of law fulfillment. Luther turned to the art of rhetorical narrative in order to compose a new anthropological image of the regenerate Christian's moral capacity against the propositions of the Antinomians:

> If I, a Christian, still a strong youth, were to fall in love with a beautiful girl or woman, here, unless I were a total tree trunk, I could not help but feel affection toward her, even if I were baptized and justified, and desire to attain her, if it were only permitted by disgrace or another punishment, which I fear. Yet nevertheless, if I am a Christian, the heart and the Spirit in the heart right away exclaim: "Get behind me, Satan! Shut up! No, don't rule, flesh! Be completely silent! You shouldn't thus persuade or incite me to fornication, adultery, passion or to do any other shameful acts against my God, but I will wait until God will give a woman to me whom I will love! Besides, with her I will make an end. I will leave her to her bridegroom and family." These and such words are not man's, but Christ's and the Holy Spirit's, who says in the heart: "Let the girl in peace. I will give you another in due time, whom you will easily love." This Christian, even if he is affected by sexual desire, nevertheless obeys the Spirit, averts by prayer the evil he feels, and prays that he might not enter into temptation. (Sonntag: 2008, 148f/WA 39 I: 500,16–501,6).

Both the inner and the outer person appear in the narrative as the Christian reckons with and acts in response to his temptation. Luther begins and ends with the activity of the outer person who first feels the temptation of lust at the sight of the beautiful girl. The Christian's outer action occurs in a sequence of verbs: obey-avert-pray (*obedit-ne intret-orans*). At the end, Luther depicts the Christian, working together with the Spirit, to resist the temptation in obedience to the Spirit.

The middle portion of the account turns to the Christian's inner acts of moral reasoning as a progression of desire, judgment, and decisive declaration (*cupio-reclamo-expectabo*). These inner acts, however, do not stem from the soul alone, but from the heart (cf. Stolt: 1997, 407) and the indwelling Spirit. Using the third person singular form of the verb *reclamo*, Luther infers a constitution of the inner person made up of a particular relation between the heart and the Spirit inside of or within (*intus)* the heart. This relation leads to collective action signified in the singular verb form; the declarative judgments against the temptation belong simultaneously to the human and to the indwelling Spirit as a single entity. The Christian does not act "by nature alone" apart from grace, as Biel had put it for his Christian *viator* (pilgrim) who worked to assent to love of God by "doing what was in her" (*facere quod in se est*). Rather, Luther's Christian youth acts on the basis of this new inner constitution made up of the soul plus the Spirit as one unit.

When Luther analyzes the content of the inner judgment a second and third time (not quoted here), he turns away from the heart-Spirit complex to the activity of the second and third divine persons. Christ and the Spirit speak the content of the Christian's declaration about the temptation. Now Luther alters the function of the speech away from judgment and intention, which are anthropological categories. Rather, the speech contains a divine command (leave the girl in peace; *Laß das medlein mit friden*) and promise (I will give you another; *dabo tibi aliquam suo tempore, quam facile amabis*) (WA 39 I: 501,2f). This alteration is noteworthy because these divine declarations are not imposed on the Christian from the outside against his will as the accusing law had done. Rather, the divine command and promise form the very basis of what the Christian himself judges and wills for his action. Christ's and the Spirit's declarations become the Christian's own as he employs them in his inner moral decision-making about outer moral actions in collective action with the Spirit. The Spirit makes possible the shared judgment between Christ and the human heart and then, on this basis, the shared action between the righteous inner person and the outer person where the faith relation is realized and practiced.

The ways Luther presents the moral interplay between the inner and outer persons in the Christian youth narrative subtly appropriates the language of scholastic moral philosophies having to do with the Aristotelian rational soul – precisely the moral philosophies Luther is said to have repudiated. Luther was influenced in this regard by Pierre d'Ailly (cf. d'Ailly: 1978, 58–65; Pluta: 1987; Kärkkäinen: 2008; Slotemaker: 2013). Like d'Ailly, Luther spoke in this narrative of the soul's various actions – the acts of knowing or loving – rather than the soul's faculties or powers.[6] The interplay between objects of desire, intellectual

6 Ockham, Biel, and d'Ailly subscribed to the nominalist principle of the substantial unity and simplicity of the soul, but the accidental plurality of the soul's acts. This means they did not divide the soul into distinct faculties such as the intellect and will, but thought the soul to be one entity with acts of knowing/judging and loving/choosing. D'Ailly was engaged in a conversation that tried to improve the Augustinian language in William of Ockham's noetic descriptions of the soul, which d'Ailly and Gregory of Remini feared had swayed too far towards the Aristotelian rational soul to retain its truly trinitarian shape. The way Luther

judgments, and volitions are identifiable in the Christian youth's feelings, deliberations about, and actions towards the pretty girl. When the Christian youth encounters the girl, Luther uses the language of affection, desire, and attainment of the desire (*non possum non affici; ut cuperem eam attingere*) (WA 39 I: 500,18f). The negative declarations (*reclamat [...] non sic me debes impellere*) against the desire coming from the heart and the Spirit in the heart (*cor et Spiritus sanctus intus corde*) echo the deliberations and judgments Pierre d'Ailly ascribed to the soul's intellectual acts (WA 39 I: 500,21.23; d'Ailly: 1978, 61). This interplay between the desire and intellectual acts progress to a volition; the heart and Spirit declare an action (will) in accord with the judgment against the desire (*sed expectabo, donec Deus dederit aliquam, quam amabo*) (WA 39 I: 500,24f). The Christian youth appraises and then decides to act on the divine plan contained in Christ's and the Spirit's words. The Christian's will and intellect worked together in accord with Christ's and the Spirit's commands and promises.

Luther names the activity of moral coherence between the inner intellectual and volitional acts and the outer action in relation to Christ and the Spirit's words "obedience." Obedience and its verb forms, *obedit* and *obediens*, are characterized by a struggle to increase the external expression of inner righteousness and to decrease the remaining sin (or "flesh") that makes possible such temptations as the desire for the pretty girl. The "becoming-obedient-Christian" is in a battle and war against sin and temptation (*in pugnam et militiam adversus reliquias peccatum et tentationes*) and must cut down (*deprecans*, deprecate) temptations all the while praying (*orans*) for God's help (WA 39 I: 500,13.501,4f. Cf. Sonntag: 2008, 164/WA 39 I: 526,5ff).[7]

Obedience is also on an ascending spectrum. Luther measures it according to "the degree to which Christ is raised in us" (Sonntag: 2008, 135/WA 39 I: 356,9f.15f). The more Christ's righteousness takes hold, the more obedient the Christian becomes in his actions. The moral conformity of the outer person to the inner righteous person comes (albeit slowly and imperfectly) by means of hard work in conjunction with the Spirit to elevate and escalate the inner righteous state, or disposition, in actions as the Christian youth is shown to do in Luther's narrative.

The progressive, ascending nature of this obedience echoes the scholastic and nominalist notion of habituation. For Aquinas, for example, habituation referred to the process by which the will came to more easily accord with reason in control

rehabilitates the soul via the Spirit in the *Antinomian Disputations* reflects this influence insofar as Luther describes the soul's acts without naming specific faculties (cf. Kärkkäinen: 2008).

7 "[...] lest you complain that you are utterly forsaken, I will give you my Holy Spirit, who makes you a soldier; he will even produce mighty and unspeakable cries against sin in your heart, so that you thus finally do what you wish." (WA 39 I: 526,5ff).

of the body by "habituating," or acclimating, oneself to virtuous action in the face of a temptation. When it came to the infused virtues, which unlike the acquired virtues Aquinas linked to friendship with God, habituation was always in conjunction with the infusion of the Spirit (Aquinas: ST 1–2.60). Habituation for the nominalist Gregory Biel, on the other hand, was an act of the Christian pilgrim (*viator*) who aimed to merit the infusion of divine grace. Biel thought merit for the infusion of divine grace required the Christian to fight to "do what is in him" (i.e. assent to the good by means of ontological structures unharmed by sin) to love God for God's own sake. Biel thought the *viator* could accomplish love of God through reasonable deductions about the good (Biel: 2 Sent. d. 27 q.1, a.2; d. 28, q.1, a.3). Habituation, then, for Biel allowed for the increase of moral virtue prior to grace through practice much like one learns to more easily play the piano beautifully through repetition, and struggle to acquire and develop skill. Luther threw out this nominalist understanding in his *Disputation against Scholastic Theology* (1518) as a form of pelagianism because he thought it impossible to habituate human nature to love God above all. In Luther's estimation, the command to love God was the one demand upon which all other law fulfillment rested, and yet, paradoxically, the one demand that could only be satisfied by divine grace.

The expression of inner righteousness bestowed by divine grace over outer sin is characteristic of obedience. In this way, obedience functions similarly to habituation save that it is premised exclusively upon the presence of grace signified by the shared action with the Spirit. By overcoming sin, the Christian becomes even more able to battle future sin and overcome temptation. In order to clearly set his discussion of Christian obedience and shared action with the Spirit apart from human merit, Luther makes a critical addition to his narrative. The Christian youth feels temptation "even though he is baptized and justified" (*etiamsi baptizatus sum et iustificatus*) (WA 39 I: 500,19). His doctrine of justification sets his discussion of the moral integrity between the inner and outer persons as obedience squarely within the regenerate person as a revision of the medieval moral philosophies he previously refuted. Luther is not talking about human moral action before the law apart from grace as a form of merit by habituation (a là Biel). Instead, Luther demonstrates the capacities of human nature under the influence of grace, but in such a way that human nature is not lost or diminished precisely because he aims to recover subjective grounds in relation to the Spirit. In order to understand how Luther is able to take this precarious position, it is necessary to examine Luther's dynamic introduction of the Holy Spirit into his discussions of the soul.

4. The Spirit as Anthropological Resource

In Luther's *Antilatomus* and *Wartburgpostille*, the reformer wrote of Christ as *donum*, or gift, to describe the ways Christ's benefits come to the human soul in justification by faith.[8] In the *Antinomian Disputations*, Luther instead spoke of Christ as *donator*, or giver, and the *donum* that Christ gives is the Holy Spirit who comes to dwell in believers' hearts as consoler, vivifier, and sanctifier. This pneumatological turn enabled Luther to relate the regenerate Christian to the law taught by Christ in sanctification (*Heiligung*).[9] The Spirit's three modal functions laid the groundwork for recovering the subjective grounds for moral action of the entire person in a justified state. As consoler, the Spirit works inner contrition and consolation through the gospel. As vivifier, the Spirit recreates the soul and gives it a new will with new affective inclinations. As sanctifier, the Spirit drives the recipient to fulfill the law, to work virtue, and to resist temptation. Each way the Spirit relates to and acts on the Christian brings the imputed righteousness given to the inner person in justification increasingly more to the outer person in formal, actual righteousness (Sonntag: 2008, 48.50,121/WA 39 I: 380,3ff. 383,9. 483,1–4).[10]

Luther orients his discussion of the Spirit as gift in trinitarian terms. The Spirit is given by Christ himself from the Father (Sonntag: 2008, 56/WA 39 I: 389,6). Christ is the immediate *donator* of the Spirit because, Luther clarifies, Christ received the Spirit from the Father as a result of his obedience (Sonntag: 2008, 55/

8 Luther alluded to an Augustinian christological binomial known as Christ as *sacramentum et exemplum* in *Against Latomus* (LW 32, 239; WA 8: 114), the Wartburg Postille sermon *Von der frucht und nutz der auffersteung Christi* (WA 10 I/2: 220,20), and *A Brief Instruction on What to Look for in the Gospels* (LW 35: 118; WA 10 II/1: 9,1) to relate Christ's death and resurrection to the human person in faith. To do this, he often exchanged *sacramentum* with *donum* in order to articulate how Christ's justifying righteousness was given to the inner person. Bo Holm deduced two meanings of *donum* in *Antilatomus. Donum* means, first, the grace by which Christ hides the sinner under his wings (mother hen analogy) and, second, a presence of divine justice in the Christian. The latter meaning presents the inner person as the beginning of a completely just person, which requires the outer person to become like the justice of the inner person (Holm: 2006, 164, 169).

9 In the 1531 *Galatians Lectures*, Luther discusses the two uses of the law (spiritual and civil) but acknowledges that the Christian under grace continues to relate to the law to diminish ongoing sin. He maintains the two uses but begins to recognize another way of relating to the law (LW 26: 5–6/WA 40 I: 43–44). Four years later in the *Genesis Lectures*, Luther identifies three different relations to the law as determined by the *ordo salutis:* before the Fall, after the Fall, and under the New Covenant. The latter guides Adam in the outward act of worship in obedience (LW 1: 108–10; WA 42: 82f). The critical relation between the Spirit and the Christian's obedience to the law emerged in *On Councils and Churches* (1539): (LW 41: 113f/ WA 50: 599,5–600,8).

10 Luther reiterates the same proximal relation between proper and formal righteousness he used in his 1518 sermon *On Two Kinds of Righteousness* (Stjerna: 2016, 9–24/WA 2: 145–152, cf. Holm: 2006, 60).

WA 39 I: 388,2–5). When Christ gives his benefits to the soul by faith in justification, the obedience to the law that Christ gives is tied up with his giving of the Spirit. The Spirit in its role as gift can be connected with obedience because Luther understands the Spirit in its divine nature according to John 16:8; the Spirit is the giver of the law. As such, the Spirit accuses, terrifies, and kills (Sonntag: 2008, 40/WA 39 I: 370,14.371,9). The Spirit as gift, on the other hand, consoles, vivifies, and sanctifies. Luther's formulation of the Spirit as gift is connected to obedience because the Spirit as divine nature in the Trinity is connected to the law.

The Spirit as *consoling* gift works in conjunction with Christ in justification to place the Christian within a regenerate state. The Spirit as lawgiver has already come to the Christian to set the stage for the pronouncements of Christ's benefits in the gospel by accusing the conscience. The consoling Spirit comes along with Christ's gift in order to ready the Christian's heart in contrition to receive Christ's benefits. While Christ makes the inner person just before God,[11] he also gives the Spirit he received from the Father, so the heart is able to receive his benefits in faith. The consoling Spirit not only works contrition but also comforts the contrite heart on the basis of Christ's gift of righteousness (Sonntag: 2008, 41/ WA 39 I: 370,15 f). Because Luther predicates the consoling Spirit's presence and activity on the nearly simultaneous arrival of Christ, the consoling Spirit enables him to theorize about what the Spirit accomplishes in the soul to reestablish subjective grounds for action.

Luther found a volitional resource for the regenerate Christian in the Spirit as *vivifying* gift. If Luther is to identify subjective grounds for action before the law, he requires a way to assert that the human wills or nills in accord with reason's dictates and God's law without succumbing to the doctrine of merit he repudiated twenty years prior. His orientation to the regenerate Christian allows him to

11 The operative modes Luther assigns to the Spirit – consoler, vivifier, and sanctifier – can be seen to divide the Spirit as gift concept in such a way that the Spirit suffuses the entire *sacramentum-exemplum* christological schema Luther adopted from Augustine. Whereas Augustine's schema related Christ's double death to the Christian's double resurrection in faith, Luther's pneumatological twist to the schema relates Christ's life and death to the Christian in faith to expand the metaphor from justification to include sanctification. The operations of the consoling Spirit contribute to the first resurrection of inner renewal while the vivifying and sanctifying Spirit work on the outer person in such a way as to point towards the second resurrection of the body eschatologically and in relation to the law as obedience in sanctification. This remains, however, an implication of the way Luther structures his use of the binomial rather than a proposition in his argument because Luther's inner/outer binary was not precisely parallel to Augustine's mind-body dualism. For Luther, the outer person implied the body along with all of the social and political relations implied in the three estates of church, politics, and household. In that regard, Augustine's double resurrection theme required amendment in order to remain compatible with Luther's anthropology (cf. Bayer: 2009, 349; Iserloh: 1965, 250; Löhrer: 1995, 382; Wolgast: 2014, 402 ff).

correlate the Spirit's role in justification with the Spirit's role in creation.[12] Luther describes the Spirit to "recreate the soul with the law in view and to give [the soul] the will to do it" (Sonntag: 2008, 42/WA 39 I: 373,2ff).[13] The Christian's new will conforms to the law because it is formed by the lawgiver to desire objects deemed good by the law. The Christian's volitional ascent to the law is premised on altered affections. The Christian "begins to hate wholeheartedly[14] everything that offends God's name," "to hate sin," "to love and worship God," and to "find enjoyment in the law rather than burden or accusation" (Sonntag: 2008, 51, 55/WA 39 I: 383,10–13. 388,4f).[15] Since Luther had previously summarized the law in the first commandment – to love God above all else – these new affections provide the basis for Luther's claim that the Spirit drives Christians to "also in this life begin to fulfill the law." The temporal beginnings of law fulfillment lead to the "most joyful and perfect obedience" in the life to come (Sonntag: 2008, 36/WA 39 I: 365,3ff). Just as Luther spoke of Christ's benefits, he could have also spoken in this context of the Spirit's benefits that make possible the Christian's effective relation to the law in a regenerate state such that the inner and outer come back together in proximal relation.

For the Christian's obedience to move beyond the will into action, Luther must also rescue right reason from its erring state. The will's desires must be guided by reason's judgments about God's will. Luther had adopted Ockham's nominalist principle of the liberty of the will, which distinguished God's ordained from God's absolute will (cf. Adams: 1986; 1999). God's absolute will was hidden in eternity. Only God's ordained will could be known by reason, but God's unknowable absolute will could temporarily override God's ordained will. Even if

12 "It is the great consensus of the church that the mystery of the Trinity is set forth here. The Father creates heaven and earth out of nothing through the Son, whom Moses calls the Word. Over these, the Holy Spirit broods. As a hen broods her eggs, keeping them warm in order to hatch her chicks, and, as it were, to bring them to life through heat, so Scripture says that the Holy Spirit brooded, as it were, on the waters to bring to life those substances, which were to be quickened and adorned. For it is the office of the Holy Spirit to make alive." (LW 1: 9/WA 42: 8,23–29).

13 "Deinde affert Spiritum sanctum credentibus in se [...] atque ita recreantur per eam animae ipsorum, datque voluntatem, ut faciant eam, hic spiritus." (WA 39 I: 373,2ff).

14 Luther's decision to maximize the hatred for sin here – wholeheartedly (lat: *ex animo*; from the whole spirit) – should be understood in context of the weakness of will, the half-heartedness, that plagues Gabriel Biel's Christian *viator* (pilgrim), who struggles against mortal sin to elicit delight (love) in God. 'Wholeheartedly' inverts the *viator*'s difficulty with reference to the uniformity and consistency of the regenerate will's affections in loving God above all else and for God's own sake. Luther positions the *Antinomian Disputations* within the nominalist semi-Pelagian controversy against "Occam (*sic*) and the moderns" in the preface to the second disputation. (Sonntag: 2008, 83/WA 39 I: 419,18f; cf. Dieter: 2001; Saarinen: 2011, 108; Oberman: 1963).

15 Enjoyment (lat: *suavem;* agreeable, sweet) is again a terminological reference to the Christian pilgrim, whose aim it was to enjoy and delight in God above all else in the pursuit of merit.

reason were able to correctly discern God's ordained will, which it could not because of sin, there was no way to know for sure that God's ordained will would not be overridden thereby, in Luther's estimation, nullifying reason's dictates.

Luther sets up Christ as teacher of the law and Christ's life as an example of law fulfillment to compensate for this troubled picture of reason and the soul's intellectual acts:

> For to present Christ as example is nothing else than showing how to live in obedience to God and parents and superiors and to be a follower of all good works and virtues, as they are recited by Paul and Peter at the end of almost all their epistles. In both ways, the example of the law is shown to us as it is fulfilled and as it is to be fulfilled. Therefore, the law is not abolished by Christ, but rather firmly established. Should they not teach this way: "My man, Christ fulfilled the law, and now it is certainly appropriate that we follow his footsteps by living piously and saintly; that you not be an adulterer, a thief, a robber, as Christ says to the Pharisee (Luke 10:37): 'Go and do likewise'?" (Sonntag: 2008, 111/WA 39 I: 464,19–465,1).

By presenting Christ as a teacher and example of the law, Luther sidestepped the nominalist problem of the liberty of the divine will for reason. Christ, as divine Word and trinitarian person, both speaks the divine will as law and interprets the specific demands made by the law. This interpretation is encapsulated in his example. Christ summarizes the law according to the double love command to love God and neighbor. In doing so, Luther concludes that "Christ teaches the same thing as the law" (Sonntag: 2008, 110/WA 39 I: 464,5). He demonstrates what this command means in his actions within the three estates and calls for imitation of this example.[16] Christ models how to live a life of obedience to authority in church, politics, and the household out of a love for God and neighbor that is firmly established in the soul. Now Luther can conclude that the Christian is able to "understand what kinds of works and fulfillment is required of [him]" (Sonntag: 2008, 54/WA 39 I: 387,6f) so that "we might become imitators of good works" (Sonntag: 2008, 110/WA 39 I: 464,3). Christ's fulfillment of the law on our behalf in justification rejoins the Christian's mimetic obedience to the law

16 Lindhardt links the *exemplum Christi* in Luther to the genre *De viris illustribus* (the illustrious man), in antiquity and the Renaissance. He shows that the *exemplum* "does not merely mean that one illuminates his representations of something with a number of examples, but rather that the representation of itself is intended to provide examples for imitation." However, after showing the strong likeness between Luther's *exemplum* concept and the Renaissance genre, Lindhardt confusingly concludes that the *exemplum* in Luther "simply signifies that the audience is offered a model into which they may be absorbed and thus find their identity [...], in other words, [Luther] understood Christ to be my lord, as well as the creator of identity for my life." What evidence causes Lindhardt to move from interpreting the *exemplum* in line with the *viris illustribus* as moral example to nothing more than a source of identity (with zero associated action) goes unstated. Cf. Lindhardt (1986, 143f).

as an intellectual resource. Right reason may be unreliable, but recourse to Christ's double love command and example moves reason's errors out of the way.

Together, the Spirit as lawgiver and Christ as teacher of the law form an intellectual resource for the Christian to know the ways the law remains to be fulfilled. Luther identified two ongoing legal demands for the Christian. First, Christ's instruction on the law promulgates moral continuity between the inner and outer selves: the law requires inner purity of heart (*cor*) and chastity and simultaneously forbids the outer, corporeal (*externe, corpore*) antitheses of these attributes in murder or lust (Sonntag: 2008, 54/WA 39 I: 387,12ff). Just as scholastic moral philosophy called for virtuous action out of a virtuous (inner) disposition; so too, Luther elevated coherence between the inner obedient person and the outer action to which that inner state should logically lead. Second, Christ taught the double love command to love God and neighbour (cf. Raunio: 1993). In the Christian youth narrative, Luther modeled these laws as they are fulfilled by the Christian. The Christian acted towards the girl in continuity with his inner judgments and desires. He also loved God and the girl as his neighbor when he recited and chose to act on God's plan for him. When Luther reiterated Christ's command to "go and do likewise," he defended law fulfillment by the human person as a theological and moral possibility, but only after "punishment and reward have lost their meaning or logic" by means of Christ and the Spirit as gift (Holm: 2005, 82).

The Spirit's third modal function, the *sanctifying* Spirit, brings the Christian as an agent of mimetic law fulfillment into relation with Christ's instruction. The sanctifying Spirit is the Spirit who "teaches piety by the law" (Sonntag: 2008, 40/WA 39 I: 371,12f). Luther has already accounted for the intellectual and volitional grounds necessary for human moral reasoning. He found them in Christ's demonstration of the law and in the vivifying Spirit's recreation of the soul, will, and affections. According to medieval moral paradigms, Luther still lacked a mechanism to account for movement between the volitional and intellectual acts as those acts proceed to move the body. As the Christian deliberated over the pretty girl or other objects of desire, how was his new will informed and guided by the intellectual content of God's will contained in Christ's instruction so that he could act?

I contend that the sanctifying Spirit fills this void. Three times in the narrative of the Christian youth obedience to the Spirit involves 'running' to Christ's instruction. Once in the story itself, the Christian wills and acts according to the judgments Luther had attributed to Christ's and the Spirit's command and promise. Then, Luther expands the illustration to "how it happens with all sins" and spiritual sins such as despair and doubt (Sonntag: 2008, 149/WA 39 I: 501,15). In the second explanation – the expansion to 'all sins' – the Christian remembers Christ's words, prays for the Spirit's help, and then obeys. Lastly, the Christian, prompted by the Spirit, runs to Christ who commands, "do not despair." The Spirit moves the Christian to Christ's instruction on the law for both inner and outer actions, as an imperative to love God and neighbor.

The Spirit prompts the Christian to run to Christ's example. Christ's active law obedience in life shows the law "as it is to be fulfilled." Therefore, the Christian ought to "follow his [Christ's] footsteps by living piously and saintly" even though the law is already fulfilled before God spiritually in justification. Like Christ, the Spirit also "teaches piety by the law." So that the sanctifying Spirit and Christ form a double judgment to elicit the "first fruits" of salvation as part of the Christian's increasing obedience; first fruits further extend the call to obedience (Sonntag: 2008, 35/WA 39 I: 363,6f). Part of Christ's instruction, however, also urges the Christian to rely on the Spirit for help to obey the law. Luther depicts Christ himself to say, "'I will give you my Holy Spirit [...], he will produce mighty and unspeakable cries against sin in your heart, so that you finally do what you wish.' But am I not unable? 'Pray that I may hear you, and I will make you able.'" (Sonntag: 2008, 164/WA 39 I: 526,5–8; cf. Staubach: 2011). The sanctifying Spirit and Christ's law come together to guide and aid the Christian's action out of his new will and affections. The sanctifying Spirit repositions Christ's example in temporal proximity to the golden rule. To love God and neighbor involves the integration of the inner and outer persons. Neither form of loving occurs without the complex interplay between the new volitional capacities and affections or the intellectual judgments supplied by Christ and the Spirit.

The gradual reintegration of the inner and outer persons in acts of obedience, then, also serves as a form of assurance of justification in Christ. Obedience to the Spirit becomes its own form of example to the Christian's conscience. This leads Luther, speaking again as the Christian, to realize that "even though I have the occasion, place, and time to fornicate, commit adultery, steal, etc. without any disgrace or punishment, I still do not do it. Here, I experience truly and in myself that the Holy Spirit dwells in my heart and is efficacious" (Sonntag: 2008, 94/WA 39 I: 436,15–437,3). The outer person's obedient acts before the law (modeled after Christ) confirms and affirms the presence of all of Christ's benefits, Christ's righteousness and the Spirit, as they are given to the inner person in justification. To experience new affections and a newly empowered will confirms the Spirit's presence and efficacy in the soul. Because the Spirit only resides in the soul on account of Christ's gift, the experience of obedience in the Spirit corroborates, via the Spirit, that justification in Christ is true and efficacious.

5. Conclusions

Luther made the Spirit work on the regenerate soul to restore subjective grounds for moral action in a way that reaffirms the important coherence between the inner and outer persons. If justification of the inner person resulted in moral incongruence between the righteous inner and still-fleshly-outer persons as is the case in Luther's *simul* construct, then Luther seems to expand the salvation concept in the *Antinomian Disputations* to include sanctification. The completion of salvation as an eschatological event includes the gradual but progressive temporal reintegration of the inner and outer persons enacted by the Spirit in conjunction with the person himself. Thus, anthropology for the regenerate soul looks to human perfection as the divine image. Moral action towards the neighbor does not just spring spontaneously from Christ's love in the heart, but moral action is grounded in the very constitution of human subjectivity after justification and presents an opportunity to practice and expand the efficacy of faith in the soul through obedience in the social realm.

The outer person emerges as a place where the efficacy of Christ's benefits is realized through the inversion of active righteousness over sinful flesh as one model for conceptualizing human social activity in Lutheran perspective. The emergence of active righteousness in the outer person comes to function as a realm of self-referential assurance. The more the Christian overcomes temptation, runs to Christ's instruction on the law, and wills according to it, the more assurance the Christian feels that Christ's gift of the Spirit has truly affected change in the inner person. This model stands in stark contrast to the privilege Kierkegaard and neo-Kantian strains of Lutheran theology give to the inner person to the detriment and disregard of the outer person. In the *Antinomian Disputations,* Luther aims to tie the justification of the inner person before God to actual effects in the outer person in social and political relations. Kierkegaard constituted true human subjectivity (being) on the basis of the inner leap. Such a prioritization of the religious over the aesthetic and ethical is discontinuous from Luther's efforts in opposition to the Antinomians.

This points us towards the critical integrity Luther envisioned between the inner and outer persons. Moral action in obedience to the law in the outer person resulted from changes to the inner person's moral reasoning in relation to Christ's benefits and the gift of the Spirit in justification. With the addition of the Spirit to the gift in the *Antinomian Disputations,* Luther could now discuss not only the Spirit's role in justification and sanctification but also how Christ's gift extends beyond the eschatological fulfillment of justification. Christ's gift, the Spirit, works in and on the human recipient in this temporal life to ground action in the subjective intellectual and volitional processes that lead to obedience. Luther's narrative about the Christian youth demonstrated this emergence in the outer person as the dynamic interplay between inner moral reasoning with Christ and the Spirit and outer action in obedience to the Spirit. Luther developed a model for moral action that sees social action as a location for inner faith to take root and grow, both driving action all the while being reciprocally deepened inside the soul.

The introduction of the Spirit to the soul served Luther's project to defend the law by identifying subjective grounds for action. Pneumatology became a robust resource because Luther was able to show how the indwelling Spirit moves across the anthropological boundary between the inner and outer person – across intellectual judgments, volitional decisions, and corporeal actions – by means of the Spirit's three modal functions. This move had the added benefit of opening up a way to make Christ's instruction on the law effectual for the temporal realm. The consoling-vivifying-sanctifying Spirit recreates the inner person in such a way that the person becomes newly able to direct the outer person's moral actions on the basis of Christ's example. In doing so, the theological concept of the Spirit provides a method to draw the inner and outer persons back together. These modifications aimed at anthropological integrity – one person with two necessarily interactive parts – place human subjectivity in a reciprocal relation between the inner mind and embodied experience in the world. For Luther, the inner self, a self of the heart and conscience, cannot be unproblematically severed from the outer self who acts and responds to the world, who lives out and practices the life of faith in proximity to others. The outer self must correspond to the inner self as a testimony to Christ and the Spirit's presence in the soul.

Bibliography

Adams, Marilyn McCord (1986), The Structure of Ockham's Moral Theory, Franciscan Studies 46, 1–35.

Adams, Marilyn McCord (1999), Ockham on Will, Nature, and Morality, in: Paul Spade (ed.), Cambridge Companion to Ockham, Cambridge: Cambridge University Press, 245–272.

Adams, Marilyn McCord (2013), Genuine Agency, Somehow Shared? The Holy Spirit and Other Gifts, in: Robert Pasnau (ed.), Oxford Studies in Medieval Philosophy, vol. 1, Oxford: Oxford University Press, 23–60.

Althaus, Paul (1952), Gebot und Gesetz: zum Thema "Gesetz und Evangelium", Gütersloh: Bertelsmann.

Aquinas, Thomas (1981), Summa Theologica, Fathers of the Dominican Province, vol. 5, Westminster, MD: Christian Classics.

Augustine (426), De Civitate Dei (CChr.SL 48).

Asendorf, Ulrich (1988), Die Theologie Martin Luthers nach seinen Predigten, Göttingen: Vandenhoeck & Ruprecht.

BAYER, OSWALD (2009), Ethik der Gabe, in: Veronika Hoffmann (ed.), Die Gabe: ein "Urwort" der Theologie?, Frankfurt am Main: Otto Lembeck, 99–124.

BIEL, GREGORY (1973), Collectorium circa quattuor libros Sententiarum, vol. 2, Hanns Rückert/Wilfrid Werbeck (ed.), Tübingen: J.C.B. Mohr (Paul Siebeck).

BORNKAMM, KARIN (1963), Luthers Auslegungen des Galaterbriefs von 1519 und 1531: ein Vergleich (AKG 35), Berlin: Walter de Gruyter.

D'AILLY, PIERRE (1978), Questions on the Books of the Sentences, in: Janine Idziak (ed.), Divine Command Morality: Historical and Contemporary Readings, New York: Edwin Mellon Press, 58–65.

DESCARTES, RENE (2000), Principles of Philosophy, in: Roger Ariew (ed.), Philosophical Essays and Correspondence, Cambridge: Hackett Publishing Co.

DIETER, THEODOR (2001), Der Junge Luther und Aristotles: eine historisch-systematische Untersuchung zum Verhältnis von Theologie und Philosophie (TBT 105), Berlin/New York, NY: de Gruyter.

EBELING, GERHARD (1967), Wort und Glaube, Tübingen: Mohr Siebeck.

EBELING, GERHARD (1982–89), Lutherstudien 2: Disputatio de Homine, vol. 2–3, Tübingen: J.C.B. Mohr (Paul Siebeck).

ELERT, WERNER (1948), Zwischen Gnade und Ungnade, Munich: Evangelischer Presseverband für Bayern.

FERREIRA, M. JAMIE (1998), Faith and the Kierkegaardian Leap, in: Alastair Hannay/ Gordon D. Marino (ed.), The Cambridge Companion to Kierkegaard, Cambridge: Cambridge University Press, 207–234.

FLOGAUS, REINHARD (1997), Theosis bei Palamas und Luther: ein Beitrag zum ökumenischen Gespräch (FSÖTh 78), Göttingen: Vandenhoeck & Ruprecht.

GREGERSEN, NIELS HENRIK (2014), Incarnate vs. Discarnate Protestantism: Martin Luther and the Disembodiment of Faith, in: Carl-Henric Grenholm/Göran Gunner (ed.), Justification in a Post-Christian Society, Eugene, OR: Pickwick Publications, 173–191.

HOLL, KARL (1948), Gesammelte Aufsätze Zur Kirchengeschichte, vol. 1, 7th ed., Tübingen: J.C.B. Mohr (Paul Siebeck).

HOLM, BO KRISTIAN (2005), Luther's Theology of the Gift, in: Niels Henrik Gregersen et al. (ed.), The Gift of Grace: The Future of Lutheran Theology, Minneapolis, MN: Fortress Press, 78–86.

HOLM, BO KRISTIAN (2006), Gabe und Geben bei Luther: Das Verhältnis zwischen Reziproität und reformatorischer Rechtfertigungslehre (TBT 134), Berlin/New York, NY: de Gruyter.

ISERLOH, ERWIN (1965), Sacramentum et Exemplum: ein augustinisches Thema lutherischer Theologie, in: Erwin Iserloh/Konrad Repgen (ed.), Reformata Reformanda: Festgabe für Hubert Jedin zum 17. Juni 1965, Münster: Aschendorff, 247–264.

JANZ, DENIS (1983), Luther and Late Medieval Thomism: A Study in Theological Anthropology, Waterloo, ON: Wilfried Laurier University Press.

JOEST, WILFRIED (1961), Gesetz und Freiheit: Das Problem des Tertius usus legus bei Luther und die neutestamentlische Parainese, Göttingen: Vandenhoeck & Ruprecht.

JOEST, WILFRIED (1967), Ontologie der Person bei Luther, Göttingen: Vandenhoeck & Ruprecht.

KIERKEGAARD, SØREN (1985), Philosophical Fragments, Howard Hong/Edna Hong (trans.), Princeton: Princeton University Press.

Kierkegaard, Søren (1992), Concluding Unscientific Postscript to the Philosophical Fragments, trans. Howard Hong/Edna Hong, Princeton, NJ: Princeton University Press.

Kärkkäinen, Pekka (2005), Luthers trinitarische Theologie des Heiligen Geistes (VIEG 208), Mainz: Verlag Philipp von Zabern.

Kärkkäinen, Pekka (2008), Interpretations of the Psychological Analogy from Aquinas to Biel, in: Pekka Kärkkäinen (ed.), Trinitarian Theology in the Medieval West, Helsinki: Luther-Agricola Society, 256–279.

Lindhardt, Jan (1986), Martin Luther: Knowledge and Mediation in the Renaissance, Lewiston, NY: Edwin Mellon Press.

Locke, John (2003), A Letter Concerning Toleration, in: Ian Shapiro (ed.), Two Treatises of Government and a Letter Concerning Toleration, New Haven, CT: Yale University Press.

Lombard, Peter (2008), The Sentences, Book 2: On Creation, trans. Guilio Silano, Toronto: Pontifical Institute of Mediaeval Studies.

Lull, Timothy F./William R. Russell (ed.) (2012), Martin Luther's Basic Theological Writings, 3rd ed., Minneapolis, MN: Fortress Press.

Luther, Martin (1518), Sermon on Two Kinds of Righteousness (Stjerna: 2016, 9–24/WA 2: 145–152).

Luther, Martin (1520), The Freedom of a Christian [Latin version] (LW 31: 343–377/WA 7: 49–73).

Luther, Martin (1521), Against Latomus (LW 32: 137–260/WA 8: 43–128)

Luther, Martin (1535–1545), Lectures on Genesis (LW 1–8/WA 42–44).

Luther, Martin (1537–1540), Theses and Disputations Against the Antinomians (Sonntag: 2008/WA 39 I: 342–584).

Löhrer, Magnus (1995), Das augustinische Binom "Sacramentum et Exemplum" und die Unterscheidung des Christlichen bei G. Ebeling und E. Jüngel, in: Elmar Salmann (ed.), Mysterium Christi: Symbolgegenwart und theologische Bedeutung: Festschrift für Basil Struder, Rome: Pontificio Ateneo S. Anselmo, 377–403.

McFardland, Ian (2001), Difference and Identity: A Theological Anthropology, Cleveland, OH: Pilgrim Press.

Oberman, Heiko A. (1963), The Harvest of Medieval Theology: Gabriel Biel and Late Medieval Nominalism, Cambridge, MA: Harvard University Press.

Ockham, William (1967–86), Opera theologica, G. Gál (ed.), vol. 1–10, St. Bonaventure, NY: Franciscan Institute Publications.

Peura, Simo (1998), Christ as Favor and Gift: The Challenge of Luther's Understanding of Justification, in: Carl Braaten/Robert Jenson (ed.), Union with Christ: the New Finnish Interpretation of Luther, Grand Rapids, MI: William B. Eerdmans, 42–69.

Pluta, Olaf (1987), Die philosophische Psychologie des Peter von Ailly, Amsterdam: Verlag B.R. Grüner.

Raunio, Aniti (1993), Summe des christlichen Lebens: Die "Goldene Regel" als Gesetz der Liebe in der Theologie Martin Luthers von 1510–1527, Helsinki: University of Helsinki.

Saarinen, Risto (1987), Ipsa dilectio deus est: Zur Wirkungsgeschichte von 1. Sent. Dist. 17 des Petrus Lombardus bei Martin Luther, in: Tuomo Mannermaa (ed.), Thesaurus Lutheri, Helsinki: Luther-Agricola Society, 185–204.

Saarinen, Risto (2005), God and the Gift: An Ecumenical Theology of Giving, Collegeville, MN: Liturgical Press.

SAARINEN, RISTO (2007), Gunst und Gabe. Melanchthon, Luther und die existentielle Anwendung von Senecas "Über die Wohltaten", in: Johannes Brosseder/Markus Wriedt (ed.), "Kein Anlass zur Verwerfung!": Studien zur Hermeneutik des ökumenischen Gesprächs: Festschrift für Otto Hermann Pesch, Frankfurt am Main: Otto Lembeck, 184–197.

SAARINEN, RISTO (2011), Weakness of Will in Renaissance and Reformation Thought, Oxford: Oxford University Press.

SLOTEMAKER, JOHN (2013), Reading Augustine in the Fourteenth Century: Gregory of Remini and Pierre d'Ailly on the Imago Trinitatis, Studia Patristica 69, 345–357.

SONNTAG, HOLGER (ed.) (2008), Only the Decalogue is Eternal: Martin Luther's Complete Antinomian Theses and Disputations, Minneapolis, MN: Lutheran Press.

STAUBACH, NIKOLAUS (2011), Die Meditation im spirituellen Reformprogramm der Devotio Moderna, in: Karl Enenkel/Walter Melion (ed.), Meditatio: Refashioning the Self: Theory and Practice in Late Medieval and Early Modern Intellectual Culture, Leiden/Boston, MA: Brill, 181–208.

STJERNA, KIRSI I. (ed.) (2016), The Annotated Luther, vol. 2: Word and Faith, Minneapolis, MN: Fortress Press.

STOLT, BIRGIT (1997), Herzlich lieb habe ich dich, Herr, meine Stärke (Ps. 18:2), in: Oswald Bayer/Robert Jenson/Simo Knuuttila (ed.), Caritas Dei: Beiträge zum Verständnis Luthers und der gegenwärtigen Ökumene, Helsinki: Luther-Agricola Society, 405–421.

WHITING, MICHAEL (2010), Luther in English: the Influence of His Theology of Law and Gospel on Early English Evangelicals (1525–35), Eugene, OR: Pickwick Publications.

WOLGAST, EIKE (2014), Luther's Treatment of Political and Social Life, in: L'ubomír Batka/Irene Dingel/Robert Kolb (ed.), The Oxford Handbook of Martin Luther's Theology, Oxford: Oxford University Press, 397–413.

Thomas Kaufmann

Lutheran Academic Culture in Early Modernity – Some Remarks

1. Introduction

It is widely known that the Reformation originated within the University of Wittenberg. The first debates on faith and grace, the indulgences, man's free will, and the limits of scholastic scholarship were rooted within the academic space of a newly founded university.[1] The flaw of a rich tradition in a place in the middle of nowhere, Wittenberg,[2] favored the efforts to give the place a profile and to make it well-known. It is very unlikely that one of the famous universities of the time would have worked as a starting point for the Lutheran Reformation (Schöffler: 1936).

Luther and his colleagues, such as Andreas Rudolf Bodenstein, named Karlstadt,[3] the later enemy, used disputation and argumentation in spoken and written words as crucial intellectual and rhetorical skills. By means of spectacular public disputations, the reformers adopted academic events for academic and public purposes starting in the summer of 1519 in Leipzig (Schubert: 2008; Hein: 2011).[4] The printing press used by academic publishers helped to ensure Luther's

1 The classical study on the impact of the university on the Reformation is: Bauer (1928). For further reading, see Kaufmann (1997a); Kaufmann: 2010); Hammerstein (1969); Hammerstein (1994); Schindling (1994); Oehmig (1995); Lück (1998); Rupieper (2002); Berg (2002); Hennen (2013); Kohnle (2013). For the university in the process of the beginning of the Reformation see Kruse (2002). For the intellectual and cultural preconditions see Grossmann (1975).

2 Cf. Luther's famous dictum: "Wir sitzen alhie Wittenbergae nur in einem schindeleich [i.e. Schindanger; graveyard for the damned] testante Domino Mellerstadt [the first rector of the university in Wittenberg Martin Pollich of Mellerstadt or his son Valentin]. Wittenbergenses sunt in termino civilitatis; si paulo longius progressi fuissent, in mediam barbariam venissent." (WA TR 2: 669,11 ff, no. 2800b).

3 For all questions on Karlstadt in the mirror of older and recent research tradition see Keßler (2014). A critical edition of Karlstadt's works and letters supervised by me appears currently in an electronic (hosted by the HAB in Wolfenbüttel) and a printed version, published by the *Verein für Reformationsgeschichte* in its series QRFG.

4 For all aspects of contemporary disputations and the academic culture of debate see Traninger (2012).

religious leadership before the public (Gössner: 2006; Reske: 2015; Pettegree: 2015; Kaufmann: 2017). Due to the political commitment of the Ernestine territorial state, the university also functioned as a legal sphere. Universities protected their faculty members from the infringements of canonical law and papal power (Friedensburg: 1917; Friedensburg: 1926; Lück: 2004). Without the university, I would argue, the Reformation would not have taken place.[5]

Outside Ernestine Saxony, the early urban reformation movements tended to develop institutions similar to universities. Huldrych Zwingli's "Prophezei" (Nabholz: 1939; Brecht: 1992), his famous use of academic disputation to introduce the reformation in Zurich (Moeller: 2011), the lectures on the Bible given by the Strasbourg reformers to public audiences in the Imperial city (Schindling: 1977, 27f.), or the Genevan Academy (Lewis: 1994) – these were all cultural inventions derived from academic traditions. In many cases, the introduction of the Reformation was connected with building up or reorganizing institutions of higher education (Benrath: 1966; Benrath: 1970; Oberman: 1984; Kittelson: 1990). In both its beginnings and also in its continuation, the Reformation and the university were closely intertwined.

2. Academic Culture in Reformation Church and Society

Academic culture had a significant impact on church and society during the tumultuous initial years of the Reformation and during the establishment of new organizational structures when Lutheran confessional churches where developed. The voids that resulted from the abolition of canon law were in some practical respects filled by the academic staff serving the Prince Elector, who had occupied and inherited the legal rights of the bishops (Sprengler-Ruppenthal: 2004; Kreiker: 1997; Sichelschmidt: 1995; Wolgast: 2015; Friedrich: 2008; Frassek: 2005; Arend/Dörner: 2015). In the context of the early visitations, which began in Ernestine Saxony as early as the early 1520s (Peters: 2003; Schneider-Ludorff: 2014), the government representatives were academic persons, that is professors of law, theology and, in some cases, even professors of arts. The *Instructions for the Visitors of Parish Pastors in Electoral Saxony* (LW 40: 269–320/CR 26: 49–96/WA 26: 195–240), a kind of handbook of what pastors were required to teach and people to believe, was written by several theologians at the University of Wittenberg. The *Examen Ordinandorum*, which defined the knowledge and the confessional state of a person preparing for ordination, was composed by Philip Melanchthon, an unordained, academic official (MSA 6: 168–259; see on Mel-

5 In my Habilitationsschrift (Kaufmann: 1997a, 11) I have summarized this thesis in the sentence: "Ohne Universität keine Reformation."

anchthon Scheible: 2016). When Luther's and other reformers' attacks against the sacrament of consecration created a gap of institutional legitimacy, Bugenhagen, Luther, and in some cases other members of theological faculties in Lutheran territories temporarily oversaw ordinations (Krarup: 2007; Wendebourg: 2007). Without the professors, especially the professors of theology, I surmise, Lutheran confessionalization would not have taken place.[6]

Compared with the role professors of theology played in late-medieval or early-modern Roman Catholic universities, the importance of these learned actors in Lutheranism increased enormously. In the Lutheran confessional territorial states, professors of theology became a multi-functional academic and governmental elite. In many cases, members of this group compiled church orders, wrote catechisms, or composed liturgies. Many of the professors of theology also held high clerical positions as preachers at the court, superintendents, or members of the consistory. In the numerous conflicts on doctrinal issues that churned up in Lutheranism between the Interim and the Formula of Concord, especially within the Empire, professors of theology played a crucial part.

Lutheran professors of theology acquired a new professional habitus. Some of their key duties were censoring books, normally for books printed within a certain geographical domain (Hasse: 2000; Hasse: 2014), providing an expert opinion on doctrines and practices of all kinds, and they had jurisdiction over marriage matters, for instance impediment and divorce.[7] In some of the Lutheran territories, these responsibilities fell to consistories made up of jurists and theologians, in others cases, by the faculties of theology. In contrast to the social setting of the late-medieval church when noblemen held the leading positions within the ecclesiastical or monastic hierarchies, bourgeois people occupied the key functions of the territorial regime in Lutheranism (Moeller: 1972 is still inspiring). The rise of learned people, the elevation of academic experts (Rexroth: 2008) in late medieval society, in a certain respect, was maintained and perfected in Lutheranism. Lutheran Confessional Culture was rooted in late-medieval urban and bourgeois culture. The learned elite supported the princes and became the leading social group in the future history of Protestantism. Although formally the princes dominated the Lutheran church government and occupied the episcopal laws, the cultural guidance of bourgeois academic tradition is undeniable.

---

6 In my book on university and confessionalization (Kaufmann: 1997a, 605), I have summarized this in the thesis: "Ohne Theologieprofessoren keine Konfessionalisierung!"

7 Cf. for the faculty of theology at the university of Wittenberg: Brecht (2005). For Leipzig: Gössner (2003a); Gössner (2003b). Further perspectives in Kaufmann (2006b, 323–363; 2006c).

Statistics illustrate the important role universities played in Lutheran confessional culture (Asche: 2001; Eulenburg: 1904). Around 1600, there were eleven Lutheran universities with approximately 2,500 matriculated students. By comparison, there were only six Catholic universities with 400 students and two reformed universities (Heidelberg and the quasi-university high school of Herborn) with approximately 280 students. Within Lutheranism, the universities were the decisive institutions for promoting the process of confessionalization and for implementing a confessional culture.[8] For the German Lutheran territorial states, the universities were critical for instructing the trained staff, which was needed for public and clerical services. Anytime the Reformation was introduced in a territory without a university, a new one was founded. For example, in 1527, the Landgrave of Hesse founded the University of Marburg (Schneider-Ludorff: 2006); Duke Albrecht of Prussia constituted the University of Königsberg in 1544 (Kaufmann: 2001b; Moeller: 2001; Kaufmann: 2001a); in 1558 and 1576, Jena (Kaufmann: 2006a) and Helmstedt (Mager: 1986; also the webpage http://uni-helmstedt.hab.de/, seen 09.03.2017) began their work. In other territorial states that became Lutheran, existing universities were rebuilt and reformed. These included Rostock, Greifswald, Tübingen, Heidelberg, Leipzig or Frankfurt/Oder, which in most cases had been centers of anti-reformation resistance in the early 1520s. The reform measures applied at these institutions were, in many cases, based on the Wittenberg model.[9]

The function of the universities in Lutheran Germany was rooted in the princes' duty to ensure the spiritual well-being of people in his realm. He was obligated to improve true knowledge of the holy word, to help educate pastors to preach the gospel, and to enable people to distinguish between true and false doctrines. For the second generation of Lutheran academics who were impressed by Melanchthon, universities were heavenly plants, or as Simon Pauli in Rostock put it, "quasi paradisus dei,"[10] almost God's paradise.

---

8 For my concept of Lutheran confessional culture see Kaufmann (2016) (with further bibliographical references).

9 In the mirror of Melanchthon's influence, this has been stressed in the classical study of Hartfelder (1889).

10 "Sunt Academiae, puram Evangelii doctrinam, honestas leges, artem medicam, Philosophiam & linguam propagantes, quasi Paradisus DEI, unde coelestes plantae, semen verbi divini, virtutis, honestatis, & publici commodi spargantes & disseminantes, in diversa & quidem multa loca, transferuntur." (Pauli 1575, 78vf). Concerning Pauli, see Kaufmann (1995a).

3. Lutheran Changes to Medieval Universities

Although Lutheran Universities still accommodated the four faculties of the traditional Parisian model, students were no longer to graduate from the faculty of arts before being allowed to enter the lectures and disputations of the theological faculty (Grane: 1987; Grane: 1990). Students' reports that we have from the late-sixteenth century onwards (Kaufmann: 1997a, 354ff) document that prospective pastors normally shared lectures and teaching sessions of both faculties. The decision to apply for a position as a pastor did not come at the beginning of the studies, but in many cases at its end. During the sixteenth and the seventeenth centuries, academic studies were concluded with entrance exams for the pastorate, not final exams (Kaufmann: 1997a, 209ff with reference to different territories and cities).

The boundaries between the faculty of theology and the faculty of arts were fluid – for the teachers as well as for the students. Before one entered into a position as a well-paid professor in the faculty of theology, he normally had to teach several years in the by far less prestigious faculty of arts.[11]

Comprehensive differences in knowledge between a student in theology and one in arts at Lutheran universities during the entire confessional age are difficult to determine. All students, not just theologians, were required to have language skills in the three "classical" ancient languages. The normative sources describing the best course of study (Kaufmann: 1997a, 256ff; Nieden: 2006; Kang: 2001; Selderhuis/Wriedt: 2006) also indicate that all students at a Lutheran university had to be well educated in biblical and catechetical topics. In the later seventeenth century, the linguistical and catechetical knowledge of those who started their studies at the university had increased. During the late-sixteenth and seventeenth centuries, academic theology developed and became a sophisticated science, making it increasingly problematic for students to switch between both faculties.[12] However, in the late sixteenth and early seventeenth centuries, the gap between the "normal" Lutheran students and the prospective pastors was defined purely by knowledge of the *Examen Ordinandorum.* Usually in Lutheranism the superintendents or the consistories examined the candidates. The candidates wanting to be ordained and to apply for a pastor's position were required to pass an exam on Melanchthon's *Examen.* In Lutheran academic culture, all students of Lutheran universities received a far-reaching religious or theological educa-

11 For all the questions that deal with symbolic distinctions and hierarchical attitudes in the university as a specific cultural space, see Füssel (2006).

12 For the state of discussion between theology and philosophy in the late sixteenth and early seventeenth centuries, see Friedrich (2004). See also: Sparn (1976); Stegmann (2006); Elkar (2015, 98f.105ff) (respecting the transformation of theology by introducing the analytical method).

tion that differed very little from the knowledge of "professional" theologians entering a parish.

Melanchthon's 1545 statutes of the faculty of theology in Wittenberg (Friedensburg: 1926, 261–265; CR 10: 1001–1008) established a model of theological education that later became common in most other Lutheran universities inside and outside Germany (Frank/Treu: 2001). Although normative sources of this kind do not reflect the educational realities as such, they represent a frame of what was or was supposed to be common. In this Wittenberg model, the colleagues of the theological faculty were part of the "ministerium evangelii" (ministry of the gospel); the "studia doctrinae coelestis" were dealing with a "praecipuus cultus dei," a special form of divine service.

4. The Theological Knowledge

Theological studies focused on biblical texts and the Creeds of the ancient church (the Apostolicum, the Nicenum, the Athanasianum);[13] the "consensus" of true doctrine in the Catholic Church across time was – so the statutes assume – included in the Augsburg Confession. In Wittenberg, professors of theology were required to give lectures on Old and New Testament texts. The books of *Romans, the Gospel of John*, the *Psalms, Genesis,* and *Isaiah* were to be treated regularly. One lecture on the Nicene Creed (cf. Hasse: 1996) was meant to provide a comprehensive interpretation of the entire doctrine ("integra doctrina"). Apart from the Bible and the Creeds, Augustine's treatise *De spiritu et litera* was to be regularly taught. The theological education at Lutheran universities aimed to teach students that the doctrine of the Lutheran church was rooted in the consensus of the ancient church, at least in its purer parts.

The 1545 statutes of the faculty of theology in Wittenberg required its members to concentrate their teaching on valuable content. The teaching staff of the faculty was committed to caring for a student library, to give seminars in Greek and Hebrew, and to tend to students' social and moral behavior. Studying at a Lutheran university was synonymous with entering an academic world focused on the true doctrine, its foundation in the Holy Bible, and the tradition of the church and its consequences for ethical attitudes. The Pietist critique that early modern Lutheran theological studies focused too much on dogmatics does not really fit in the picture depicted by students' reports, faculty statutes, and lecture timetables, at least up to the syncretistic quarrels over Georg Calixt's

13 The role of the ancient confessions seems to be derived from their reception in the 1580 Book of Concord.

theology (Staemmler: 1963; Ritschl: 1927; Böttigheimer: 1996, 53–68; in relation to Köningsberg, Kaufmann: 1995b; Moldaenke: 1909, 65).

The basic texts to instruct both "professional" theologians and Lutheran academics were Melanchthon's *Loci theologici*,[14] Luther's *Small Catechism*, the *Augsburg Confession*, or one of the widely-held catechetical summaries in Latin by David Chytraeus, Jakob Heerbrand or Matthias Hafenreffer – to name only the most frequently reprinted works (Ohlemacher: 2010; on catechetical literature in general, Bast: 1997; Strauss: 1978). As far as I can determine, most of the young men joining a Lutheran institution of higher education were familiar with central elements of Lutheran confessional theology and had a solid foundation in biblical topics. Johann Jakob Schütz, the early leader of the radical Pietists in Frankfurt, was disappointed with Lutheranism because he was taught Konrad Diederich's highly sophisticated and polemical catechism (Deppermann: 2003, 56–58). Schütz's viewpoint was characteristic of the mental disposition of a young man educated at a Lutheran university.

5. Popular Effects of Lutheran Academic Reforms

Lutheran confessional culture connected academic religious knowledge with the everyday life of common Christian men and women. The pious middle-class people from whom most Lutheran pastors descended took up the confessional knowledge that had been elaborated on and cultivated in the academic context (Schorn-Schütte: 1996). They adopted it in their daily life. Transfer processes between the university and popular culture make comprehensible the rich tradition of, for instance, casual poetry (Garber: 2010) – especially in Latin, biographical writings, so-called "Selbstzeugnisse" (von Greyerz: 2007; von Greyerz: 2013), or phenomena such as biblical mottos on nearly every house and in a variety of languages,[15] especially in northern Germany. The central figure of transmission between the academic and popular contexts was the pastor, the representative of academic knowledge and learned culture even in the village (Seidel/Spehr: 2013).

The period leading up to the 1580s can be seen as the initial phase of Lutheran confessional culture. It took approximately two generations or approximately 50 years after the introduction of the Reformation in a territorial state like Brandenburg or Mecklenburg before university educated Lutheran pastors were

14 Concerning the role of *Loci theologici* within different study programs, see the remarks in Kaufmann (1997b, 185–190). Instructive as well: Stegmann (2006,130ff); Filser (2001, 398ff).

15 See the volumes of the project "Deutsche Inschriften," supported by the Union of German academies of sciences (http://www.inschriften.net, seen 09.03.2017).

regularly installed in nearly every parish (Kaufmann: 1997a, 336ff; 2006, 313ff; Schorn-Schütte: 1996, esp. 512f). In most territories, the first generation of Lutheran pastors were former priests. In many cases, these priests simply married their housekeeper, legitimized their children, took up some elements of Lutheran doctrine, and stayed in their parish. In Ernestine Saxony, only around 25% of the first generation pastors after the Reformation had an academic education (Karant-Nunn: 1979, 15). The average was higher in Franconia, reaching close to 50% (Cramer: 1990, 25ff). The rate of educated pastors in the cities was higher than in the villages both before and after the Reformation. Between the introduction of the Reformation in 1549 (Wolgast: 1995) and 1580, less than the half of the pastors in Mecklenburg had attended a university at all. Twenty years later, around 1600, however, this situation has changed fundamentally. Now, more than 75% of pastors had attended university.[16] Although it appears that these changes occurred later in Mecklenburg, we can be sure that the professionalization process for educated churchmen that took place here is similar to many other Lutheran countries.

The amount of time prospective pastors spent at the university differs significantly. In some territories, such as Wurttemberg, a period of three years was common even in the sixteenth century. Here, professors of theology held the exams, not the leading clergymen. In other territories, a large number of candidates stayed at the university no longer than one or two years, typically depending on their financial resources.[17] Surprisingly, this educational structure was not fundamentally altered by the Thirty Years War. While the Lutheran pastor was established as an identity marker of confessional attitudes during the war, in many cases he became a target of hostile soldiers.[18]

In many cases, Lutheran pastors came from non-academic, urban, middle-class social backgrounds. The pastorate was a position for social mobility.[19]

16 For Mecklenburg cf. Kaufmann (1997a). Research has been conducted for different regions in the Holy Roman Empire some examples: Vogler (1976, 57) has shown for Palatine in 1590 that 85% of the pastors had studied at university; in 1605 it was 90 % and in 1619, 94 %. In Zweibrücken, the proportion of educated pastors increased between 1555 and 1580 from 30 % up to 70 %, and in Sponheim from 22% up to 80% (Vogler: 1976, 78). In Kitzingen not more than one third of academically educated pastors over the century can be proved (Weyrauch: 1982, 296). Around about 1600, 97 % of the pastors had graduated university (Weyrauch: 1982, 300). Even in England, the change in the education of the priests has not been finished earlier than 1600 (O'Day: 1979, 2ff).

17 For the education of the pastors in Württemberg, see Brecht (1969). For the following period, Hasselhorn (1958). Statistical material on the duration of university studies from different territories and countries is collected in Kaufmann (1997a, 346ff.)

18 See Kaufmann (1998, 102ff). Interesting texts of an autobiographical character, many of them from evangelical pastors, are to be found in von Krusenstjern (1997); cf. Autenrieth (2000).

19 See for all questions on the social-history of Protestant clergy in general Schorn-Schütte (1996); Kaufmann (1997a, 349ff) (on Mecklenburg); see also Schorn-Schütte/Dixon (2003).

Academic education at Lutheran universities more or less enabled talented young men from non-academic families to climb into higher classes. In the late-seventeenth and early-eighteenth centuries, the rate of self-recruitment, that is, the portion of pastor's sons themselves becoming pastors, was approximately 33 %. However, it is necessary to emphasize that more than 60 % of the pastors also strove for other professions. Some of them ascended to jobs in governmental administration or to academic positions in higher faculties.[20] All over the Old Empire, the urban middle-classes represented the social background of Lutheran pastors. From a sociological view, Lutheran confessional academic culture was a bourgeois phenomenon.

It is commonplace that the Reformation influenced the development of early modern state building.[21] This is true for the protestant monarchies in Scandinavia and England as well as for the Lutheran territorial states in- and outside of the Holy Roman Empire. The universities helped to stabilize this process. The academic actors stood in close relations to the princes and their administrations. A high percentage of the students at each university came from the prevailing territory. In many cases, the students who wanted to earn a position in a certain country had to study at its university. Apart from the famous Saxon universities in Leipzig and Wittenberg, which always had a large number of non-Saxon students, many other German Lutheran universities predominantly educated students from their own region. The number of pastors coming from "abroad," that is, from outside the country in which they earned employment, was approximately 20 %. In Mecklenburg and the Palatine this was a bit higher (25 %) and, in Brandenburg, a bit lower (15 %) (Kaufmann: 1997a, 333ff). Sometimes prestigious academic teachers attracted students from outside a territory and were responsible for regional exchanges. The number of pastors with an academic degree was quite small, approximately 20 %. Most of those educated clerics served in urban parishes. Lutheran confessional culture has intensified the relationship between the people and their region. From this perspective, German regional identity building or even provinciality was strengthened by Lutheranism.

One of the best-known *lieux de memoire* of German Lutheranism is the "Pfarrhaus," the pastor's household (Schorn-Schütte: 2013). The "Pfarrhaus" is regarded as an island of urban and learned culture within the uncivilized sea of a

---

20 On the role of Protestant theologians and their sons in the intellectual history of eighteenth-century Germany, especially in literature, see Schöne (1968). In relation to the history of philosophy, see Büttgen (2009).

21 This aspect was emphasized in the discussion on confessionalization from the 1980s onwards; a summation of the results can be seen in Kaufmann (2007). The recent discussion seems to deconstruct the concept of confessionalization and to dissolve the connections between state-building processes and early modern religion, e.g.: Pietsch/Stollberg-Rilinger (2013).

rude, quasi-pagan rural society.[22] The pastor's housewife and his children were sometimes seen as co-missionaries who helped the pastor to develop Christian standards and to cultivate an ethos of forgiveness and mercy. Even if some aspects of this picture are of doubtful merit, I assume that a Lutheran pastor within rural society was normally a kind of foreigner[23] and that the members of his family were too. The pastor's household was the breeding ground of education in the rural world. The pastor himself often taught young boys while his wife taught the girls. Here, students had access to books, music practice, and were introduced to a number of educational topics, even agricultural ones.

The German word "Kopfarbeit" (head work) was coined by the Lutheran preacher Johannes Mathesius to convince his parishioners, who consisted mostly of miners, that reading books and preparing sermons constituted "work."[24] We have several examples that common parish people were not willing to support the building of a study – in German: "Studierstube" – for their pastors, because they did not accept that he was "working" at all.[25] Although many pastors were obliged to do agricultural work for large parts of their income, they felt different because they were educated. The academic Lutheran culture was seen as necessary for preaching duties, in some sense it erected cultural barriers. On the other hand, the pastor as a representative of higher urban culture could help his parishioners when certain knowledge was needed. Thus, the pastor's household was a bubbling source of cultural innovation. Many poets, scientists, famous politicians up to the highest positions in recent Germany came from pastor's households, a productive place even for those who turned their back on it.

In conclusion, Lutheran confessional culture depended to a certain degree on academically-educated representatives. The central role Scripture played within the religious-cultural framework of Lutheranism was accompanied by interpretation and adoption. In the context of the Holy Roman Empire, confessional competition was notorious and omnipresent. Lutheranism in itself was divided; proponents of different interpretations of the true doctrine fought against each other. The political structure of German territorialism favored this development. Well-educated pastors meant to guarantee – at least within the boundaries of a certain territorial space – that the true doctrine was unambiguous. Their edu-

22 See Aschenbrenner (2015). Interesting in a more popular approach, Eichel (2012); see also the literature mentioned in footnote 16 above.

23 This is also the scope of Rublack (1989). Concerning the role of the pastor's wife is still important: Schorn-Schütte (1991).

24 "Denn wer fleissig studieret / lernet / lehret / regieret / der arbeitet mit dem Kopff / Munde und Henden / und wird jhm offt vciel sewrer / denn einem Handwercksmanne oder Bergmann." Cit. after Münch (1992, 359).

25 Different sources and examples concerning conflicts between a pastor and his parishioners regarding his "higher education" are mentioned in Kaufmann (1997a, esp. 341 ff).

cation was intended to enable them to defend the simple truth of the gospel against competing interpretations. The inner-confessional tensions that characterized early modern Lutheranism within the Holy Roman Empire produced a specific form of academically-based Lutheran confessional culture.

As far as I can see, in the Scandinavian Lutheran countries, these inner-confessional tensions were successfully limited. Has this favored or promoted different forms of Lutheran confessional culture? Probably yes – a question interesting enough to provoke further research.

Bibliography

Arend, Sabine/Döner, Gerald (ed.) (2015), Ordnungen für die Kirche – Wirkungen auf die Welt (SMHR 84), Tübingen: Mohr Siebeck.

Asche, Matthias (2001), Frequenzeinbrüche und Reformen – Die deutschen Universitäten in den 1520er bis 1560er Jahren zwischen Reformation und Humanistischen Neuanfang, in: Walther Ludwig (ed.), Die Musen im Reformationszeitalter (Schriften der Stiftung Luthergedenkstätten in Sachsen-Anhalt 1), Leipzig: Evangelische Verlagsanstalt, 53–96.

Aschenbrenner, Cord (2015), Das evangelische Pfarrhaus: 300 Jahre Glaube, Geist und Macht: Eine Familiengeschichte, Munich: Siedler Verlag.

Autenrieth, Bernd (2000), Samuel Gerlach, Feldprediger, Hofprediger, Prälat (1609–1683). Ein schwäbischer Pfarrer zwischen Mecklenburg, Holstein, Danzig und Württemberg (Lebendige Vergangenheit 21), Stuttgart: Kohlhammer.

Bast, Robert J. (1997), Honor Your Fathers: Catechisms and the Emergence of a Patriarchal Ideology in Germany, 1400–1600 (SMRT 63), Leiden/Boston, MA: Brill.

Bauer, Karl (1928), Die Wittenberger Universitätstheologie und die Anfänge der Deutschen Reformation, Tübingen: Mohr Siebeck.

Benrath, Gustav Adolf (1966), Die Universität der Reformationszeit, ARG 57, 32–51.

Benrath, Gustav Adolf (1970), Die deutsche evangelische Universität der Reformationszeit, in: Hellmuth Rössler/Günther Franz (ed.), Universität und Gelehrtenstand 1400–1800, Limburg: Starke, 63–83.

Berg, Gunnar (ed.) (2002), Emporium: 500 Jahre Universität Halle-Wittenberg: Landesausstellung Sachsen-Anhalt, Katalog zur Ausstellung, Halle: Fliegenkopf.

Böttigheimer, Christof (1996), Zwischen Polemik und Irenik. Die Theologie der einen Kirche bei Georg Calixt (Studien zur Systematischen Theologie und Ethik 7), Münster: Lit.

Brecht, Martin (1969), Herkunft und Ausbildung der protestantischen Geistlichen des Herzogtums Württemberg im 16. Jahrhundert, in: ZKG 80, 163–175.

Brecht, Martin (1992), Die Reform des Wittenberger Horengottesdienstes und die Entstehung der Zürcher Prophezei, in: Heiko A. Oberman/ Ernst A. Saxer/Alfred Schindler/ Heinzpeter Stucki (ed.), Reformiertes Erbe: Festschrift Gottfried W. Locher (Zwingliana 19/1), Zurich: Theologischer Verlag, 49–62.

BRECHT, MARTIN (2005), Die Consilien der Theologischen Fakultät der Universität Wittenberg, in: Irene Dingel/Günther Wartenberg (ed.), Die Theologische Fakultät Wittenberg 1502 bis 1602 (LStRLO 5), Leipzig: Evangelische Verlagsanstalt, 201–222.

BÜTTGEN, PHILIPPE (2009), L'Oeuvre des Fils: La question pastorale en philosophie allemande (1560–1810), unpublished Higher Doctoral Thesis, Université de Paris-Sorbonne IV.

CRAMER, MAX-ADOLF (1990), Die ersten evangelischen Pfarrer in Badisch und Württembergisch Franken (Veröffentlichungen des Vereins für die Kirchengeschichte Badens 44), Karlsruhe: Verl. Evang. Presseverb. für Baden.

DEPPERMANN, ANDREAS (2003), Johann Jakob Schütz und die Anfänge des Pietismus (BHTh 119) Tübingen: Mohr Siebeck.

EICHEL, CHRISTINE (2012), Das deutsche Pfarrhaus: Hort des Geistes und der Macht, Cologne: Quadriga.

ELKAR, TIM CHRISTIAN (2015), Leben und Lehre: Dogmatische Perspektiven auf lutherische Orthodoxie und Pietismus: Studien zu Gerhard, König, Spener und Freylinghausen, Frankfurt am Main: Peter Lang.

EULENBURG, FRANZ (1904), Die Frequenz der deutschen Universitäten von ihrer Gründung bis zur Gegenwart (Abhandlungen der Königlich-Sächsischen Gesellschaft der Wissenschaften zu Leipzig XXIV/2), Leipzig: Teubner.

FILSER, HUBERT (2001), Dogma, Dogmen, Dogmatik: Eine Untersuchung zur Begründung und zur Entstehungsgeschichte einer theologischen Disziplin von der Reformation bis zur Spätaufklärung (Studien zur systematischen Theologie und Ethik 28), Münster: Lit.

FITOS, STEPHAN (2000), Zensur als Mißerfolg: Die Verbreitung indizierter Deutscher Druckschriften der Zweiten Hälfte des 16. Jahrhunderts, Frankfurt am Main: Peter Lang.

FRANK, GÜNTER/MARTIN TREU (ed.) (2001), Melanchthon und Europa, vol. 1: Skandinavien und Mitteleuropa (Melanchthonschriften der Stadt Bretten 6/1) Stuttgart: frommann-holzboog.

FRASSEK, RALF (2005), Eherecht und Ehegerichtsbarkeit in der Reformationszeit (JusEccl 78), Tübingen: Mohr Siebeck.

FRIEDENSBURG, WALTER (1917), Geschichte der Universität Wittenberg, Halle: Niemeyer.

FRIEDENSBURG, WALTER (1926), Urkundenbuch der Universität Wittenberg Teil 1 (1502–1611) (Geschichtsquellen der Provinz Sachsen und des Freistaates Anhalt, N.R. 3), Magdeburg: Die historische Kommission.

FRIEDRICH, MARKUS (2004), Die Grenzen der Vernunft: Theologie, Philosophie und Gelehrte Konflikte am Beispiel des Helmstedter Hofmannstreits und seiner Wirkungen auf das Luthertum um 1600, Göttingen: Vandenhoeck & Ruprecht.

FRIEDRICH, WOLFGANG (2008), Territorialstaat und Reichsjustiz (JusEccl 83), Tübingen: Mohr Siebeck.

FÜSSEL, MARIAN (2006), Gelehrtenkultur als Symbolische Praxis, Darmstadt: Wissenschaftliche Buchgesellschaft.

GARBER, KLAUS (2010), "Gelegenheitsdichtung", in: Andreas Keller et al. (ed.), Theorie und Praxis der Kasualdichtung in der Frühen Neuzeit, Amsterdam/New York, NY: Rodopi, 33–37.

GERMAN, MARTIN (1994), Die reformierte Stiftsbibliothek am Großmünster Zürich im 16. Jahrhundert (Beiträge zum Buch- und Bibliothekswesen 34), Wiesbaden: Harrassowitz.

GRANE, LEIF (1987), Studia humanitatis und Theologie an den Universitäten Wittenberg und Kopenhagen im 16. Jahrhundert: Komparative Überlegungen, in: Gundolf Keil/ Bernd Moeller/Winfried Trusen (ed.), Der Humanismus und die oberen Fakultäten (Mitteilung XIV der Kommission für Humanismusforschung), Weinheim: Acta Humaniora, VCH, 65–114.

GRANE, LEIF (1990), Teaching the People: The Education of the Clergy and the Instruction of the People in the Danish Reformation Church, in: Grane/Hørby: 1990, 164–184.

GRANE, LEIF/KAI HØRBY (ed.) (1990), Die dänische Reformation vor ihrem internationalen Hintergrund (FKDG 46), Göttingen: Vandenhoeck & Ruprecht.

GROSSMANN, MARIA (1975), Humanism in Wittenberg 1485–1517 (Bibliotheca humanistica et reformatorica 11), Nieuwkoop.

GÖSSNER, ANDREAS (2003a), Konkordienluthertum und Regionale Identität: Fallanalyse der Theologischen Fakultät Leipzig zu innerkirchlichen Streitigkeiten in Iglau (Mähren) im Jahr 1582: Mit einem Quellenanhang, in: Michael Beyer/Andreas Gössner/Günther Wartenberg (ed.), Kirche und Regionalbewusstsein in Sachsen im 16. Jahrhundert (Leipziger Studien zur Erforschung von Regionalbezogenen Identifikationsprozessen 10) Leipzig: Leipziger Universitätsverlag, 43–78.

GÖSSNER, ANDREAS (2003b), Die Gutachten der Theologischen Fakultät Leipzig von 1540 bis 1670, in: Michael Beyer/Andreas Gössner/Günther Wartenberg (ed.), Kirche und Regionalbewusstsein in Sachsen im 16. Jahrhundert (Leipziger Studien zur Erforschung von Regionalbezogenen Identifikationsprozessen 10), Leipzig: Leipziger Universitätsverlag, 189–262.

GÖSSNER, ANDREAS (2006), Die Anfänge des Buchdrucks für universitäre Zwecke am Beispiel Wittenbergs, in: Enno Bünz (ed.), Bücher, Drucker, Bibliotheken in Mitteldeutschland: Neue Forschungen zur Kommunikations- und Mediengeschichte um 1500, Leipzig: Leipziger Universitätsverlag, 133–152.

HAMMERSTEIN, NOTKER (1994), Universitäten und Reformation, HZ 258, 339–358.

HAMMERSTEIN, NOTKER (1996), Handbuch der deutschen Bildungsgeschichte, vol. 1: 15. – 17. Jahrhundert, Munich: C.H. Beck.

HASSE, HANS-PETER (ed.) (1996), Philipp Melanchthon: Enaratio secundae tertiaeque partis Symboli Nicaeni (1550) (QFRG 649, Gütersloh: Gütersloher Verlagshaus.

HASSE, HANS-PETER (2000), Zensur theologischer Bücher in Kursachsen im konfessionellen Zeitalter (AKThG 5), Leipzig: Evangelische Verlagsanstalt.

HASSE, HANS-PETER (2014), Article “Zensur”, in: Volker Leppin/Gury Schneider-Ludorf. (ed.), Das Luther-Lexikon, Regensburg: Verlag Bückle & Böhm, 784–785.

HASSELHORN, MARTIN (1958), Der altwürttembergische Pfarrstand im 18. Jahrhundert (Veröffentlichungen der Kommission für Geschichtliche Landeskunde in Baden-Württemberg, Reihe B: Forschungen 6), Stuttgart: Kohlhammer.

HARTFELDER, KARL (1889), Philipp Melanchthon als Praeceptor Germaniae (Monumenta Germaniae paedagogica 19,) Berlin: A. Hofmann & Comp.

HEIN, MARKUS/ARMIN KOHLE (ed.) (2011), Die Leipziger Disputation 1519 (Herbergen der Christenheit Sonderband 18), Leipzig: Evangelische Verlagsanstalt.

HENNEN, INSA C. (2013), Reformation und Stadtentwicklung: Einwohner und Nachbarschaften, in: Heiner Lück/Enno Bünz et al. (ed.), Das Ernestinische Wittenberg: Stadt und Bewohner (Wittenberg-Forschungen 2/1), Petersberg: Imhof, 33–76.

KANG, CHI-WON (2001), Frömmigkeit und Gelehrsamkeit: Die Reform des Theologiestudiums im lutherischen Pietismus des 17. und frühen 18. Jahrhunderts (Kirchengeschichtliche Monographien 7), Gießen/Basel: Brunnen.

KARANT-NUNN, SUSAN (1979), Luther's Pastors: The Reformation in the Ernestine Countryside (Transactions of the American Philosophical Society 69, Part 8), Philadelphia, PA: American Philosophical Society.

KAUFMANN, THOMAS (1995a), Article "Simon Pauli", in: Sabine Pettke (ed.), Biographisches Lexikon für Mecklenburg, Vol 1, Rostock: Schmidt-Römhild, 175–180.

KAUFMANN, THOMAS (1995b), Königsberger Theologieprofessoren im 17. Jahrhundert, in: Dieter Rauschning/Donata von Nerée (ed.), Die Albertus-Universität zu Königsberg und ihre Professoren (Jahrbuch der Albertus-Universität zu Königsberg 29), Berlin: Duncker und Humblot, 49–86.

KAUFMANN, THOMAS (1997a), Universität und lutherische Konfessionalisierung (QFRG 66) Gütersloh: Gütersloher Verlagshaus.

KAUFMANN, THOMAS (1997b), Martin Chemnitz (1522–1586): Zur Wirkungsgeschichte der theologischen Loci, in: Heinz Scheible (ed.), Melanchthon in seinen Schülern (Wolfenbütteler Forschungen 73), Wiesbaden: Harrassowitz, 183–253.

KAUFMANN, THOMAS (1998), Dreißigjähriger Krieg und Westfälischer Friede: Kirchengeschichtliche Studien zur lutherischen Konfessionskultur (BHTh 104) Tübingen: Mohr Siebeck.

KAUFMANN, THOMAS (2001a), Article "Königsberg", in: RGG[4] 4, 2001, 1584–1586.

KAUFMANN, THOMAS (2001b), Theologische Auseinandersetzungen an der Universität Königsberg im 16. und 17. Jahrhundert, in: Klaus Garber/Manfred Komorowski/Axel E. Walter (ed.), Kulturgeschichte Ostpreußens in der Frühen Neuzeit (Frühe Neuzeit 56), Tübingen: Niemeyer, 243–318.

KAUFMANN, THOMAS (2002), Tholucks Sicht auf den Rationalismus und seine "Vorgeschichte", ZThK 99, 45–75.

KAUFMANN, THOMAS (2006a), Die Anfänge der Theologischen Fakultät Jena im Kontext der "Innerlutherischen" Kontroversen zwischen 1548 und 1561, in: Volker Leppin/Georg Schmidt/Sabine Wefers (ed.), Johann Friedrich I. – der Lutherische Kurfürst (SVRG 204), Gütersloh: Gütersloher Verlagshaus, 209–258.

KAUFMANN, THOMAS (2006b), Konfession und Kultur: Lutherischer Protestantismus in der Zweiten Hälfte des Reformationsjahrhunderts (SuR NR 29), Tübingen: Mohr Siebeck.

KAUFMANN, THOMAS (2006c), Religions- und konfessionskulturelle Konflikte in der Nachbarschaft: Einige Beobachtungen zum 16. und 17. Jahrhundert, in: Georg Pfleiderer/Ekkehard W. Stegemann (ed.), Religion und Respekt (Christentum und Kultur 5), Zurich: Theologischer Verlag, 139–172.

KAUFMANN, THOMAS (2007), Article "Konfessionalisierung" in: Friedrich Jaeger et al. (ed.), Enzyklopädie der Neuzeit, vol. 6, Darmstadt: Wissenschaftliche Buchgesellschaft, 1053–1070.

KAUFMANN, THOMAS (2010), Théologie, Univerité, Societé. Quelques remarques sur le premier Protestantisme du point de vue de l'Histoire de l'Église, in: Philippe Büttgen/Christophe Duhamelle (ed.), Religion ou Confession: Un Bilan Franco-Allemand sur l'Époque Moderne (XVIe–XVIIIe siècles), Paris: Éditions de la MSH, 461–484.

KAUFMANN, THOMAS (2016), What is Lutheran Confessional Culture?, in: Per Ingesman (ed.), Religion as an Agent of Change (Brill's Series in Church History and Religious Culture 72), Leiden/Boston, MA: Brill, 127–148.

KAUFMANN, THOMAS (2017), Von der Handschrift zum Druck – einige Beobachtungen zum Frühen Luther, in: Thomas Kaufmann/Elmar Mittler (ed.), Reformation und Buch. Akteure und Strategien frühreformatorischer Druckerzeugnisse, Wiesbaden: Harrasowitz Verlag, 9–36.

KESSLER, MARTIN (2014), Das Karlstadt-Bild in der Forschung (BHTh 174), Tübingen: Mohr Siebeck.

KITTELSON, JAMES M. (1990), Learning and Education: Phase Two of the Reformation, in: Grane/Hørby: 1990, 149–163.

KOHNLE, ARMIN (2013), Die Wittenberger Theologische Fakultät in der Reformationszeit Probleme – Themen – Perspektiven, in: Heiner Lück/Enno Bünz et al. (ed.), Das Ernestinische Wittenberg: Stadt und Bewohner (Wittenberg-Forschungen 2/1), Petersberg: Imhof, 201–212.

KRARUP, MARTIN (2007), Ordination in Wittenberg: Die Einsetzung in das kirchliche Amt in Kursachsen zur Zeit der Reformation (BHTh 141), Tübingen: Mohr Siebeck.

KRUSE, JENS-MARTIN (2002), Universitätstheologie und Kirchenreform. Die Anfänge der Reformation in Wittenberg 1516–1522 (VIEG 187), Mainz: Philipp von Zabern.

KREIKER, SEBASTIAN (1997), Armut, Schule, Obrigkeit: Armenversorgung und Schulwesen in den evangelischen Kirchenordnungen des 16. Jahrhunderts (Religion in der Geschichte 59), Bielefeld: Verlag für Regionalgeschichte.

LEWIS, GILLIAN (1994), The Geneva Academy, in: Andrew Pettegree/Alastair Duke /Gillian Lewis (ed.), Calvinism in Europe 1540–1620, Cambridge: Cambridge University Press, 35–63.

LÜCK, HEINER (ed.) (1998), Martin Luther und seine Universität, Cologne: Böhlau.

LÜCK, HEINER (2004), Article "Wittenberg", in: TRE 36, 2004, 232–243.

MAGER, INGE (1986), Article "Helmstedt", in: TRE 15, 1986, 35–39.

MOELLER, BERND (1972), Pfarrer als Bürger (Göttinger Universitätsreden 56), Göttingen: Vandenhoeck & Ruprecht.

MOELLER, BERND (2001), Die Universität Königsberg als Gründung der Reformation, in: Bernd Moeller, Luther-Rezeption: Kirchenhistorische Aufsätze zur Reformationsgeschichte (ed. by Johannes Schilling), Göttingen: Vandenhoeck & Ruprecht, 182–191.

MOELLER, BERND (2011), Zwinglis Disputationen: Studien zur Kirchengründung in den Städten der frühen Reformation, Göttingen: Vandenhoeck& Ruprecht.

MOLDAENKE, THEODOR (1909), Christian Dreier und der synkretistische Streit im Herzogtum Preußen (Schriften der Synodalkommission für ostpreußische Kirchengeschichte Heft 6), Königsberg: Emil Rautenberg.

MÜNCH, PAUL (1992), Lebensformen in der Frühen Neuzeit 1500 bis 1800, Frankfurt am Main/Berlin: Ullstein.

NABHOLZ, HANS (1939), Zürichs höhere Schulen von der Reformation bis zur Gründung der Universität, 1525–1833, in: Ernst Gagliardi/Hans Nabholz/Jean Stroh (ed.) (1938), Die Züricher Schule seit der Regeneration, Teil 3, Die Universität Zürich von 1833–1933 und ihre Vorläufer: Festschrift zur Jahrhundertsfeier, Zurich, Verlag der Erziehungsdirektion, 3–164.

NIEDEN, MARCEL (2006), Die Erfindung des Theologen. Wittenberger Anweisungen zum Theologiestudium im Zeitalter von Reformation und Konfessionalisierung (SuR NR 28), Tübingen: Mohr Siebeck.

OBERMAN, HEIKO A. (1984), University and Society in the Threshold of Modern Times: The German Connection, in: James M. Kittelson/Pamela Transue (ed.), Rebirth, Reform and Resilience: Universitites in Transition 1300–1700, Columbus, OH: Ohio State University Press, 19–41.

O'DAY, ROSEMARY (1979), The English Clergy: The Emergence and Consolidation of a Profession 1558–1642, Leicester: Leicester University Press.

OEHMIG, STEFAN (ed.) (1995), 700 Jahre Wittenberg: Stadt Universität Reformation, Cologne: Böhlau.

OHLEMACHER, ANDREAS (2010), Lateinische Katechetik der frühen lutherischen Orthodoxie (FKDG 100), Göttingen: Vandenhoeck & Ruprecht.

PAULI, SIMON (1575), Dispositio in partes orationis rhetoricae, et brevis textus enarratio evangeliorum, Magdeburg: Kirchner, Rostock University Library Fl 3358 (VD 16 P 992).

PETERS, CHRISTIAN/FRIEDRICH KRAUSE (2003), Article "Visitation", TRE 35, 2003, 151–163.

PETTEGREE, ANDREW (2015), Brand Luther: 1517, Printing, and the Making of the Reformation, New York, NY: Penguin Press.

PIETSCH, ANDREAS/BARBARA STOLLBERG-RILINGER (ed.) (2013), Konfessionelle Ambiguität. Uneindeutigkeit und Verstellung als religiöse Praxis in der Frühen Neuzeit (SVRG 214), Gütersloh: Gütersloher Verlagshaus.

RESKE, CHRISTOPH (2015), Die Anfänge des Buchdrucks im vorreformatorischen Wittenberg, in: Stefan Oehmig (ed.), Buchdruck und Buchkultur im Wittenberg der Reformationszeit, Leipzig: Evangelische Verlagsanstalt, 35–70.

REXROTH, FRANK (2008), Expertenweisheit. Die Kritik an den Studierten und die Utopie einer geheilten Gesellschaft im Späten Mittelalter (Freiburger Mediävistische Vorträge 1), Basel: Schwabe.

RITSCHL, OTTO (1927), Dogmengeschichte des Protestantismus, vol. IV, Göttingen: Vandenhoeck & Ruprecht.

RUBLACK, HANS-CHRISTOPH (1989), "Der wolgeplagte Priester": Zum Selbstverständnis lutherischer Geistlichkeit im Zeitalter der Orthodoxie, ZHF 16, 1–30.

RUPIEPER, HERMANN-JOSEF (ed.) (2002), Beiträge zur Geschichte der Martin-Luther-Universität Halle-Wittenberg 1502–2002, Halle: mdv.

SCHEIBLE, HEINZ (2016), Melanchthon: Eine Biographie, 2nd ed., Munich: C.H.Beck.

SCHINDLING, ANTON (1977), Humanistische Hochschule und freie Reichsstadt: Gymnasium und Akademie in Straßburg 1538–1621 (VIEG 77), Wiesbaden: Steiner.

SCHINDLING, ANTON (1994), Bildung und Wissenschaft in der Frühen Neuzeit 1650–1800 (Encyklopädie deutscher Geschichte 30), Munich: Oldenbourg.

SCHNEIDER-LUDORF, GURY (2006), Der fürstliche Reformator: Theologische Aspekte im Wirken Philipps von Hessen von der Homberger Synode bis zum Interim, Leipzig: Evangelische Verlagsanstalt.

SCHNEIDER-LUDORF, GURY (2014), Article "Visitationen", in: Volker Leppin/Gury Schneider-Ludorf. (ed.), Das Luther-Lexikon, Regensburg: Verlag Bückle & Böhm, 725–726.

SCHORN-SCHÜTTE, LUISE (1991), "Gefährtin" und "Mitregentin": Zur Sozialgeschichte der evangelischen Pfarrfrau in der frühen Neuzeit, in: Heide Wunder/Christina Vanja (ed.), Wandel der Geschlechterbeziehung zu Beginn der Neuzeit, Frankfurt am Main: Suhrkamp, 109–153.

SCHORN-SCHÜTTE, LUISE(1996), Evangelische Geistlichkeit in der Frühneuzeit (QFRG 82), Gütersloh: Gütersloher Verlagshaus.

SCHORN-SCHÜTTE, LUISE (2013), Das ganze Haus. Evangelische Pfarrhäuser im 16. und 17. Jahrhundert, in: Seidel/Spehr: 2013, 37–53.

SCHORN-SCHÜTTE, LUISE/SCOTT DIXON (ed.) (2003), The Protestant Clergy of Early Modern Europe, Houndsmills/New York, NY: Palgrave.

SCHÖFFLER, HERBERT (1936), Die Reformation: Eine Einführung in die Geistesgeschichte der deutschen Neuzeit, Bochum: Pöppinghaus.

SCHÖNE, ALBRECHT (1968), Säkularisation als sprachbildende Kraft, 2nd ed., Göttingen: Vandenhoeck & Ruprecht.

SCHUBERT, ANSELM (2008), Libertas Disputandi: Luther und die Leipziger Disputation als akademisches Streitgespräch, ZThK 105, 411–442.

SEIDEL, THOMAS A./CHRISTOPHER SPEHR (ed.) (2013), Das evangelische Pfarrhaus: Mythos und Wirklichkeit, Leipzig: Evangelische Verlagsanstalt.

SELDERHUIS, HERMANN J./MARKUS WRIEDT (ed.) (2006), Bildung und Konfession. Theologenausbildung im Zeitalter der Konfessionalisierung (SuR NR 27), Tübingen: Mohr Siebeck.

SICHELSCHMIDT, KARLA (1995), Recht aus christlicher Liebe oder obrigkeitlicher Gesetzesbefahl? (JusEcc 49), Tübingen: Mohr Siebeck.

SPARN, WALTER (1976), Wiederkehr der Metaphysik (Calwer theologische Monographien 4), Stuttgart: Calwer.

SPRENGLER-RUPPENTHAL, ANNELIESE (2004), Das kanonische Recht in Kirchenordnungen des 16. Jahrhunderts: Eine Dokumentation, in: Anneliese Spengler-Ruppenthal, Gesammelte Aufsätze zu den Kirchenordnungen des 16. Jahrhunderts (JusEcc 74), Tübingen: Mohr Siebeck, 298–373.

Staemmler, Heinz (1963), Der Kampf der kursächsischen Theologen gegen den Helmstedter Synkretismus, unpublished Doctoral Dissertation, Martin-Luther-Universität Halle-Wittenberg.

STEGMANN, ANDREAS (2006), Johann Friedrich König: Seine theologia positiva acroamatica (1664) im Rahmen des frühneuzeitlichen Theologiestudiums (BHTh 137), Tübingen: Mohr Siebeck.

STRAUSS, GERALD (1978), Luther's House of Learning: Indoctrination of the Young in the German Reformation, Baltimore, MD: The Johns Hopkins University Press.

THOLUCK, AUGUST (1853), Das akademische Leben des 17. Jahrhunderts: Vorgeschichte des Rationalismus Erster Theil, 1. Abt., Halle: Eduard Anton.

TRANIGER, ANITA (2012), Disputation, Deklamation, Dialog: Medien und Gattungen europäischer Wissensverhandlungen zwischen Scholastik und Humanismus (Text und Kontext 33), Stuttgart: Franz Steiner.

VOGLER, BERNHARD (1976), Le clergé protestante rhénan ou siècle de la réform 1555–1619, Association du publications prés les universités de Strasbourg, Paris: Ophrys.

VON GREYERZ, KASPAR (ed.), (2007), Selbstzeugnisse in der Frühen Neuzeit (Schriften des Historischen Kollegs 68), Munich: Oldenbourg.

von Greyerz, Kaspar (2013), Von Menschen, die glauben, schreiben und wissen, Göttingen: Vandenhoeck & Ruprecht.

von Krusenstjern, Benigna (1997), Selbstzeugnisse der Zeit des Dreißigjährigen Krieges: Beschreibendes Verzeichnis (Selbstzeugnisse der Neuzeit 6), Berlin: Akademie-Verlag.

Wendebourg, Dorothea (2007), Martin Luthers frühe Ordinationen, in: Stefan Ehrenpreis/Ute Lotz-Heumann/Olaf Mörke/Luise Schorn-Schütte (ed.), Wege der Neuzeit. Festschrift für Heinz Schilling, (Historische Forschungen 85), Berlin: Duncker und Humblot, 97–115.

Weyrauch, Erdmann (1982), Informationen zum Sozialprofil der evangelischen Geistlichen Kitzingens im 16. Jahrhundert, in: Ingrid Batori/Erdmann Weyrauch. (ed.), Die bürgerliche Elite der Stadt Kitzingen (Spätmittelalter und frühe Neuzeit 11), Stuttgart: Klett-Cotta, 291–312.

Wolgast, Eike (1995), Die Reformation in Mecklenburg (Veröffentlichungen der Historischen Kommission für Mecklenburg Heft 8), Rostock: Schmidt-Römhild.

Wolgast, Eike (2015), Die Einführung der Reformation und das Schicksal der Klöster im Reich und in Europa (QFRG 89), 2nd ed., Gütersloh: Gütersloher Verlagshaus.

Mattias Skat Sommer

Three Estates and Three Uses of the Law in Niels Hemmingsen's *Liffsens Vey*

1. Theological Theory and Confessional Politics: The Case of the Three Estates

A key task in theological ethics has always been to articulate a perspective of human action in the world. This chapter explores how this view was established in sixteenth century Lutheran Reformation theology with the book *Liffsens Vey* (The Way of Life), written by the Danish reformer Niels Hemmingsen (1513–1600) in 1570.[1] The point of departure is the recent observation in Luther scholarship that the so-called teaching of the three estates was Martin Luther's attempt to propose a theological solution to the problem of human action (Stegmann: 2014, 377–385; Saarinen: 2005, 210.213). Some thirty years ago, Reinhard Schwarz pointed out that the teaching of the three estates played an important role in the 1562 opus magnum of Niels Hemmingsen, *De lege naturae* (Schwarz: 1984, 85ff). According to Schwarz' interpretation of *De lege naturae*, the three estates remained a rather abstract concept, having no connection to social institutions.[2] However, Hemmingsen formulated his version of the estates teaching in both *De lege naturae* and in *Liffsens Vey*, which gives it a different tone. Based on the observation that Hemmingsen was a key figure in the Danish post-Reformation Lutheran adaption of society, the present chapter argues that the theological complex "the three estates" played another role in Hemmingsen than in Luther.

Today Hemmingsen is mainly known because of his immense contributions to the foundation of early modern Danish-Norwegian jurisprudence and to the

1 Throughout the chapter, I quote the first English translation of *Liffsens Vey*, printed in 1578 in Elizabethan London. The original wording in Hemmingsen's Danish edition is maintained in the footnotes. In case of uncertain wordings or insufficient translation, I consulted the 1574 Latin edition because this is the source of the English translation.

2 "Die naturrechtliche Theorie hat bei Hemmingsen ihre Grenzen darin, daß sie mit einem allgemeinen Gottesbegriff arbeitet und die Institutionen des gesellschaftlichen Lebens kaum in den Blick bekommt." Schwarz (1984, 87).

evolution of a Lutheran theory of the natural law (Ingesman: 2010, 15 ff; Scattola: 1999, 77–86; Tamm: 1983). Studies by legal historians have shown that Hemmingsen exemplifies the intertwining of politics and religions that was dominant in early modern European history and which is normally termed "confessionalization". The urgent question of his theological character, however, has still not been answered sufficiently despite Reinhard Schwarz's demonstration that Hemmingsen shared Luther's three estates doctrine. Two major twentieth century studies were somewhat reluctant in their characterization of his theology: he was labelled either a Melanchthonian Calvinist (Barnekow: 1940) or a Calvinist Melanchthonian (Madsen: 1946). In both cases, the judgement is based on an alleged departure from Luther and on Hemmingsen's strong emphasis on believers' sanctification and man's moral abilities, indicating that Luther's theology could not include such doctrines. Recent Luther research has demonstrated that this kind of interpretation is highly misleading: Luther in fact did include considerations on human morality in his theology, however only in the backdrop of the doctrine of justification (Työrinoja: 2002). And exactly the three estates constitute a crucial locus of human agency and morality in Luther's thought (Saarinen: 2005).

By exploring this theology, the present chapter amplifies these two approaches by linking Hemmingsen to the early modern confessionalization process. I suggest that Hemmingsen's reception of the Lutheran three estates teaching should be seen in the context of his role of a political adviser to the Danish rulers. As it will be shown, Hemmingsen did not restrict himself to reproducing Luther's teaching, but combined this with Melanchthonian elements. With regards to his version of the teaching of the three estates, he sought to cohesively combine his two masters' opinions. Like Luther, Hemmingsen used the three estates as a framework for conceptualizing theological ethics, but added to this the notion of the three uses of the law (*triplex usus legis*), which played a central role in the ethics of Melanchthon since the 1535 edition of the *Loci communes.*[3] By combining the two traditions, Hemmingsen's social theology obtains an original character: it is a clear example of a sixteenth-century reception of Luther's teaching outside the Saxon heartland of the Reformation on the one hand, but on the other, it has distinctive features that can only be fully understood in the context of Hemmingsen's role in the royal confessionalization efforts within the early modern Danish-Norwegian kingdom. To integrate this aspect of Hemmingsen's activities into the discussion might shed new light on his theology

3 Although Luther occasionally used the language of the third use of the law, e.g. in the *Christmas Postil* from 1522 (WA 10 I 1: 456,8–458,11), it does not correspond to the systematic discussion of the law's proper uses in Melanchthon and Hemmingsen.

while eschewing the futile discussion of his more or less "Calvinist-Melanchthonian" thinking.

The first part of the chapter contextualizes Hemmingsen's biography and is followed by an account of the ethical traditions of the Wittenberg reformers that formed the background of Hemmingsen's version of the three estates. The last part is devoted to an in-depth study of the chapter on the law in *Liffsens Vey*, in which the teaching of the three estates is introduced.

2. Niels Hemmingsen in Confessional Denmark and Europe

Niels Hemmingsen was born in 1513 on the island Lolland in the Baltic Sea.[4] He grew up in humble circumstances, but was eventually sent for schooling in the chapter of Roskilde, the most important bishopric in late medieval Denmark, where a great part of the canons was in favor of ecclesiastical reform. Having been taught Greek at the chapter of Lund (present-day Sweden), the Danish archbishopric, Hemmingsen went to Wittenberg in the mid-1530s. During Hemmingsen's years at the Ernestine capital, the Lutheran Reformation consolidated itself and refined its doctrines. After Luther's and Melanchthon's efforts to cultivate discipline in the late 1520s and Johannes Bugenhagen's work as a legal-theological adviser to courts and magistrates in the Empire and beyond, the Saxon ecclesiastical model was spread around northern Europe (Sommer: 2017b; Rasmussen: 2013). In 1537, Christian III (r. 1534–1559) was crowned the king of Denmark and Norway after successfully bringing the civil war to an end in the prior year. He introduced a church ordinance drafted by Bugenhagen, installed superintendents to replace the old bishops, and reopened the University of Copenhagen (founded in 1479) with new statutes modelled after the Wittenberg Leucorea. Over the years, the king banned other confessions from his realm, and thus, gradually established a Lutheran monoconfessional religious culture, which, however, was different from Lutheranism developed in the German lands (Grell: 2016).

In Wittenberg Luther lectured on Genesis between 1535 and 1545 although he was interrupted by diplomatic work, ecumenical negotiations, and the outbreak of plague. Hemmingsen likely attended Luther's lectures, in which Luther developed his mature thought on the three estates. In 1539, Luther published his *On the Councils and the Church* in which he accused the Roman-Catholic church and its pope of being the Antichrist and constructed human hierarchies above the divine hierarchies and "masks" (*larven*) of house, city, and church as "true remedies against the devil" (LW 41: 177 f/WA 50: 652,7–653,3). In the same years

4 On Hemmingsen's biography, cf. Lausten (2013).

Melanchthon published his second edition of the *Loci* (1535), in which he developed the three uses of the law in contrast to the first edition of 1521 (cf. CR 21: 405f). Between the publication of the first and the second edition, Johannes Agricola, the Eisleben reformer, rejected the place of the Mosaic law in Christian religion much to Melanchthon's and Luther's chagrin.

In the early 1540s, Hemmingsen obtained a master's degree in philosophy, after which he returned to Denmark to take a position as professor of Greek philology and dialectics in Copenhagen. After defending twenty-four theses on the Eucharist in 1553, he became a bachelor of theology and accepted the position of the second theological chair, thus rising in the academic ranks. In 1557, Hemmingsen again defended a number of theses on the Eucharist, upon which a doctorate was conferred on him and he was made *primus theologicus*, the primary university professor of theology. In the same year, the king appointed him as a canon in the chapter of Roskilde, which provided him with a considerable income. The poor boy raised on the edge of the realm was now a member of the Danish elite.

During the reign of Frederik II (r. 1559–1588), Christian III's son, Hemmingsen actively helped to shape the confessional policy and polity of the Danish-Norwegian dual monarchy that avoided the growing split between Gnesio-Lutherans and Philippists in the German lands (cf. Lockhart: 2004, 63–100; Wallmann: 2012, 91–94; Koch: 1992). In 1561, the king demanded a national confession, which was promulgated in the *Confessio et Ordinatio Ecclesiarum Danicarum*. This confession reflected the emerging confessional conflicts between different Protestant groups in Europe and, especially, the emergence of so-called *Corpora Doctrinae* in imperial territories beginning in Leipzig in 1560.[5] After the Augsburg religious peace in 1555, allegiance to the Augsburg Confession was crucial for the Lutheran princes in the Empire. Questions pertaining to the edition of the confession, and to other Protestant theologies that espoused different views of the Eucharist were urgent. These questions might have led Frederik, inspired by August of Saxony (r. 1553–1586), a frontline fighter for the cause of Lutheranism and the king's brother-in-law, to order the publication of a steadfast doctrinal text that could function to mark the dual monarchy as a true Lutheran realm. It is very likely that Hemmingsen was instructed to do so on behalf of the king. However, the 1561 attempt failed, and another confession-like text, the so-called Foreign Articles was published in 1569 (Rørdam II, 126–134). Hemmingsen probably also authored its 25 articles on matters religious. In order to dispel rebellion and disorder, foreigners were to submit to the theology pre-

5 On the Danish 1561 confession, cf. Kornerup (1953, XV–LXXII). On the various *Corpora Doctrinae*, cf. Dingel (2012).

sented in the Foreign Articles and to take oaths before receiving a residence permit. If they refused to do so, they were to be expelled from the realm.

Faced with the confessional developments in Europe, alleged accordance with the Augsburg Confession was not sufficient. Moreover, Hemmingsen assisted Frederik in providing a new matrimonial legislation in the 1580s, and his Danish language publications aimed at instructing the people in Christian and virtuous living. Thus Hemmingsen in *Liffsens Vey* presented to his readers that "which is behouefull for them to knowe, beleeue, or doe, which desire to be made partakers of eternall saluation" (Hemmingsen: 1578, D1v).[6] As a professor in Copenhagen for almost forty years, he influenced the second and third generation of Reformation theologians in Denmark; some of his students even stood behind translations into Danish of his Latin works (Fink-Jensen: 2011). Therefore, Hemmingsen was an important player in the post-Reformation ecclesiastical policy of the dual monarchy, granting decisive assistance to the royal strategies for confessionalization.

Hemmingsen was also an international figure. His Latin corpus comprising some eighty-five titles was printed throughout Europe. This corpus was also published in the vernacular, along with some of his Danish works, including *Liffsens Vey*. Beginning in 1569 and peaking around ten years later, printers in epicenters of the book industry like Geneva, Basel, and London published Hemmingsen for the non-Lutheran market. Scholars, clergymen, nobles, and princes from all over Europe became acquainted with his works. He corresponded with leading figures in the republic of letters, again crossing confessional boundaries. Hemmingsen was commended throughout Europe as a learned and pious scholar (Sommer: 2017a).

Why, then, did the king suspend Hemmingsen from his position in Copenhagen in the summer of 1579, only allowing him to keep his canonry at Roskilde? Hemmingsen's suspension was likely the result of European politics and of uncertainty about the exact confessional basis of the dual Scandinavian monarchy. As previously mentioned, the religious peace of Augsburg gave legal protections to adherents of the Augsburg Confession without specifying the edition of the confession to which people were required to ascribe. Furthermore, no Danish consensus regarding the edition of the Augsburg Confession in force existed (Glebe-Møller: 2014, 216). The Danish Church Ordinance of 1537 mentions the following books as useful for the clergy: "sacra Biblia," "Postillas Lutheri," "Apologiam Philippi," "Locos communes," "minore catechismo Lutheri," "informationis visitatorum Saxoniae," and finally the Church Ordinance itself, "hujus nostrae ordinationis" (KiO, 136). Even if "Apologiam Philippi" necessa-

6 Cf. Hemmingsen (1570, A2r): "som er fornøden at vide/ tro oc giøre/ alle de som Salighed haffue vil."

rily includes the Augsburg Confession it is still not clear which edition is applied by the Danish Church Ordinance. When Hemmingsen declared that he was in accordance with the confession by maintaining that Christ in the Eucharist displays (*exhibere*) his true body and his true blood (Hemmingsen: 1576/1867–1868, 310), he was not following the invariata art. 10 (BC 44/BSELK 104, 8–11), but rather the variata editions, in which Melanchthon stresses the "vere exhibeantur" (CR 26: 357). August had recently dismissed some of his professors on grounds of false Eucharist teachings, and these professors had all invoked Hemmingsens's books in their defense. Through the Electress Anna, August informed his brother-in-law of the indirect accusation of the Danish professor, whom Frederik was compelled to remove from Copenhagen. He was not motivated by some presentation of non-Lutheran doctrine, but rather had the Augsburg religious peace in mind. Discussions about the correct interpretation of the Eucharist were just as, or maybe even more, political than theological. Faced with political pressure from his Saxon relatives, the king had no choice but to suspend his *primus theologicus* and have him relocated to his canonry in Roskilde, where he stayed until his death in 1600. In the course of events, Hemmingsen was drawn into a royal family drama, and paid the price with his position. Even if he contributed actively to establish a Lutheran culture, ironically it was only after his suspension that the precise confessional foundation of the Danish-Norwegian realm was determined. From circa 1580 onwards, there can be no doubt that *Confessio Augustana* meant the *invariata* in a Danish context. Before Hemmingsen, this was not the case.[7]

7 Cf., e.g., Frederik II's missive to the episcopacy, 26 June 1574, regarding "goed endrectighed udi religionen oc lerdommen" (sound concord in matters religious and doctrinal). The king explicitly prohibits "nye unøttige disputatser" (futile disputes on 'new' matters), admonishing the clergy to teach and preach only according to "dend augsborgiske confession" – yet not specifying the edition of the confession. For the missive, cf. Secher I, 582f. As a contrast, Frederik's son and successor Christian IV (1588–1648) in a 1624 ordinance concerning Jesuits and other Roman-Catholic clergy, states that our Christian confession "anno 1530 til Augsborg af voris religions forvanter er overgifven och nu udi disse vore lande och riger, Gud vere lofvet, høris och underholdis" (has been presented at Augsburg anno 1530 by the allies in our religion, and is now in these our territories, thank God, being heard and observed), cf. Secher II, 148. The explicit formulation "anno 1530," never used by Frederik II, inevitably refers to the invariata. In 1672, Christian IV's grandson Christian V (1670–1699) introduced a ban on German books concerning foreign religion that were contrary to "den rette Augsburgiske Confessions Troe oc Religion" (i. e. the faith and religion of the rightful Augsburg confession), and four years after in the ordinance on foreign religion, the Augsburg Confession is phrased as "den ypperste skat," which must be kept "reen oc uforfalsket" (i. e. the most upstanding treasure to be kept pure and authentic), cf. Rørdam III, 494.502. According to Christian V's DL of 1683, the confessional basis of the king's territories is, besides the Bible, the ancient creeds, and Luther's Small Catechism, "den Uforandrede et tusind fem hundrede og tredive overgiven Augsburgiske Bekiendelse" – the unaltered Augsburg Confession, presented in 1530, cf. Secher (1891, 204f [DL 2-1-1]).

3. Ethical Thinking in Luther and Melanchthon

Following the end of the Peasants' Wars in central Germany and the emergence of divergent Reformation theologies, the Wittenberg theologians became aware of the intimate connection between "theology" and "social formation" and that theological discourse can have unintended social consequences. Therefore, they recognized the necessity to outline a framework for conceptualizing order using theological language. This led to a period of institutionalization in the Saxon Reformation. In 1526, Luther published his *German Mass* (LW 53: 333–354/ WA 19: 72–113). In 1526 and 1527, visitations organized by the Electoral court were performed. In 1528, the Saxon *Instruction for Visitors* (LW 40: 269–320/ CR 26: 49–96/WA 26: 195–240) was published by the group of theologians in Wittenberg. Finally in 1529, Luther published his two catechisms (BC 379–480.347–375/WA 30 I: 125–238.243–425). In the same years, the Wittenberg theologians were challenged by the teachings of Agricola and others, which compelled them to formulate doctrine in a "legal" and "ordained" framework. The late 1520s display, therefore, a condensation of texts, doctrines, and acts, through which an early Lutheran understanding of order was established (Michel: 2014; Wolgast: 1977). This is the context of two important texts by Martin Luther that place moral agency on the Reformation agenda, namely the *Confession* from the treatise on the Eucharist (1528; LW 37: 364f/WA 26: 504:30–505,28), and the lectures on Genesis (1535–1545; LW 1–8/WA 42–44). These texts hint at the paramount role the teaching of the three estates would come to play as a discourse on good order in the mature theology of Luther.[8] Because Luther's teaching of the three estates has been accounted for in depth elsewhere in this volume, I will limit myself to focus on the ethical thinking of Melanchthon, based on his elucidations on the nature of the law primarily in the 1553 German edition of the *Commonplaces*, the *Heubtartikel*. In contrast to previous German translations of the *Loci* done by Justus Jonas, Melanchthon undertook this translation himself, shaping it in a direction towards catechetical exposition and consolation within an educational context.[9]

Melanchthon taught that human obedience towards the law cannot lead to salvation, which equally cannot be obtained by works. So what is then, he asked for himself, the use of the law? The answer is that there are three uses (Melanchthon: 1553/2002, 228,8f). The first use is the civil law, which serves the purpose of disciplining the limbs of a person: the tongue should not speak

8 On the three estates in Luther's theology, cf. Saarinen (2005), and the contributions of Svend Andersen and Hans-Martin Gutmann to this volume.

9 It is worth paying attention to the fact that Melanchthon in his own words wrote the exposition of the law in the German *Loci* for the instruction of children (Melanchthon: 1553/2002, 234,3). Cf. on the various *Loci* editions Junghans (2011).

heretically or tell lies; the hands should not kill or steal others' property – in overall terms, the body should not conduct itself in an indecent manner.[10]

The second use of the law is, so Melanchthon's words, "der furnemist," the most distinguished, i.e. the sermon of wrath, in which God accuses the heart, frightens it, and leads it to anxiety (cf. Rom 4:15). Because God is just, he allows the law in its second use to point to the Gospel.[11] However, in order that man grasps the message of the Gospel, God has created him in such a state that he is able to perceive it.[12] Hence man has insight into God's own wisdom, but given that human nature is full of doubt after the fall, even if God by creation has installed the ability to perceive the law in it, he can only know God's wisdom in mediated forms, of which the Decalogue is primary.[13] But how can this take place, how is the teaching of the Decalogue and the grace freely offered, expressing God's ordained will, implemented? According to Melanchthon's understanding, God in Paradise instituted the office of preaching to secure the proclamation of the divine ordination. By concentrating on divine ordination and offices established by God in creation, Melanchthon here bore a resemblance to Luther's theology in the lectures on Genesis and elsewhere. However, Melanchthon did not recur on the three estates teaching of Luther; in his edition of Justus Menius' 1547 treatise on the right to resistance, conceived in the light of the Schmalkaldic War's menaces to the Protestant cause in the Empire, Melanchthon erased any mentioning of a three estates teaching (Peterson: 1990). The two Wittenberg reformers agreed that God cannot be known outside his revelation, expressed in external forms. Melanchthon, nevertheless, goes one step further than Luther by stressing that God would keep this high doctrine in his churches (Melanchthon: 1553/2002, 230,33).

The third use of the law pertains only to the holy, i.e. the believers that are reborn through God's word and the Holy Spirit. God sends his law to the heart of those. Nonetheless, the regenerated should carry out daily spiritual exercises in penitence, the more so because they are mere human beings, continuing to carry

---

10 "[...] das man die eusserlichen glidmasß in zucht halde nach allen geboten von eusserlichen werken, alß nemlich das die zung nicht lesterlithe von gott rede, das die hende nicht todschlagen, nicht fremde gutter zu sich zihen, das der leib keine eusserliche unzucht treib, das die zung nicht lugen rede etc." (Melanchthon: 1553/2002, 228,11–14).

11 As a consequence of the human heart being cast into anxiety due to the Law *uso secundo*, the Gospel has a pastoral function, namely that men "durch das evangelium widerumb getröst, bekert und selig warden." (Melanchthon: 1553/2002, 229,8).

12 "[...] hatt ehr [sc. God] erkantnus seines gesetz in unser natur geschaffen." (Melanchthon: 1553/2002, 229,24f).

13 "Und uber das [sc. the light implanted in man by God in creation] hatt ehr offentlich mit grossen wunderwerken die zehen gepott verkundigt, damit sie nicht verleschen sollten, dweil menschlich vernunnft in diser zerstorten natur voll zweifels ist." (Melanchthon: 1553/2002, 230,3ff).

feebleness and sin with them (Melanchthon: 1553/2002, 233,15–18). Again, the preaching of the divine Word has an edifying function, as it, together with contemplation of the punishment on others or on oneself, assists in pointing out the nature of the human being, also that one installed in the renati.

In conclusion, Melanchthon summarized the law's function: it proclaims what is right and what is sinful according to God, so that sin can be punished, the wicked be converted, and the converts grow in devoutness. For this purpose, God has given the church the ability to know his eternal law according to his will in the form of the Decalogue, or the moral law. The church is assigned the task of preserving this expression of the divine will.[14] Not rejecting the impact of the fall on man, Melanchthon set forth a somewhat more optimistic anthropology than Luther. He supposed that the Christian in fact is able to live consistently with God's will. The decisive factor is, however, that it is only possible in an "ordained setting," i. e. where the Decalogue is preached by someone rightfully holding the office of minister. Then, Melanchthon sketched a small theory of human development since creation, asking why the Decalogue is actually necessary given that persons were created with intellect that enables them to understand the moral law. Naturally, the fall is crucial. When sin came into the world, the light of human intellect faded away so that God had to spell out the moral law in the Decalogue and in the proclamation of the churches through public and splendid preaching. In Melanchthon, the human person has minimal powers, but major obligations. God gives the moral law, or natural law in order to instruct persons to honor God, to abstain from harming others, and to share all things with the brethren.

Luther's estates teaching and Melanchthon's teaching on the law both grounded morality in the created order. The two reformers further agreed on the grounds of God's authority conveyed in creation and in structures of human life, man can act in a way pleasant to God. This is what one interpreter has called "theological action" in Luther (Saarinen: 2005, 210f), and, I would add, in Melanchthon, too. The rather depressing findings of the Saxon visitations in the late 1520s encouraged and possibly even compelled the Wittenberg theologians to sketch their thoughts on human action, reflected in the abundant discourse on order in the Wittenberg writings. Luther divided his understanding of human action into three estates within which humans works of love towards neighbor, church, and political authorities please God. Alternatively, Melanchthon focused

14 "Und in summa: Gott hatt erkantnus seines ewigen und unwandelbaren gesetz, das man nennet Lex Moralis oder zehen gebott, seiner kirchen geben und will, das es darinn erhalden werde, das man gottlich zeugnis habe, was recht und was sund sey, und das mann fur und fur in disem leben sund in allen menschen straff, in den unbekerten, das sie bekert werden, und in den berkerten, das gottes forcht in yhnen sterker werde etc." (Melanchthon: 1553/2002, 233,23–28).

on the church as it conserved and distributed God's ordained will and as it modeled temporal structures by proclaiming the Decalogue in public. Bearing the similarities and differences between the reformers in mind, we are now able to analyze Hemmingsen's somewhat centrist position.

4. Hemmingsen's Integration of Lutheran and Melanchthonian Thought

Like Melanchthon's *Heubtartikel*, *Liffsens Vey*, the Way of Life, was published for the instruction of lay persons and divided into standard topics. The biblical term "way" is Hemmingsen's preferred metaphor for describing the human situation in the world (Madsen: 1946, 91–94). Hence, *Liffsens Vey* is an outline of the paths man wanders with God through life. The biblical books, especially the New Testament epistles, the gospels, and the wisdom literature are the main sources, but Hemmingsen also draws on general adages, moral examples, and fables as did his other Renaissance humanists of his day.

Hemmingsen begins his chapter on the law with considerations on the law's content (i.e. to love God and the neighbor). He also defends the law against interpretive variances, whether these varieties be rejection of the law altogether or maintenance of the possibility of human law fulfillment by works. Hemmingsen thereby outlines a theological model of order and disorder. Because the law is God's gift, it expresses the divine will regarding social structure. At the same time, efforts to appraise the law in a different manner are seen as diabolical attempts to turn order into disorder. In the rest of the folios considering the law, Hemmingsen utilizes the teaching of the three estates and the three uses to discuss the regulation of earthly order. Generally, the social order outlined by God's law are regulated by the correct uses of the law. Like Melanchthon, Hemmingsen counts three such uses: external, internal, and spiritual. Here, Luther's teaching of the three estates is applied directly in the first use, but also plays a minor, but important role within the two other uses, especially the third use.

In its first, external use, the law teaches "by discipline to gouerne ỷ people, that in outward honesti of manners, they might liue quietly, according to the Law" (Hemmingsen: 1578, G4r). Indeed, Hemmingsen's original words are more specific than the English "liue quietly." A better translation is: "The external use of the law is that it shall govern men, so that they live a good outward life among each other [...] and so that they behave themselves in their outward customs and dealings according to the Law."[15] Hemmingsen emphatically underlines the

15 "Louens vduortis Brug er/ at hun skal regere Mennisken/ at de føre it gaat vduortis leffnit iblant huer andre [...] oc at mand skicker sine vduortis seder oc omgengelse effter Louen."

'social' dimension of the external use left unclear in Denham's English translation: the law governs relations between people, not just the individual. It is possible to interpret this as the sum of governing the people by discipline; the discipline, therefore, is a discipline towards sociality. This is an important point: discipline, according to Hemmingsen, is not to be completed for its own sake, but has as its object the common good, i. e. regulating the inter-human relations. This assumption is reinforced by the following paragraphs when Hemmingsen adopts the estates teaching, equally framing it in reciprocal terms. The external Law, which Hemmingsen calls *Moralis*, can only be practiced within the appointed places of the three estates.

Primarily, *Moralis* applies to the office of parents in each and every household in which they instruct their children to live a decent life in outward discipline. To this end, Hemmingsen assigns to the parents five methods: doctrine, i. e. the catechism, consisting of the Decalogue, the Lord's Prayer, the symbols of faith, and the teaching on baptism and the Eucharist.[16] As soon as the children are able to speak and to comprehend, they should memorize and recite the contents of the catechism every morning and every evening.

The second method is that of example. Parents turn the words of moral instruction into deeds when their way of life is performed in front of their children. Parents living an immoral life are "learning backward" that which they "learned forward" to their children through speech (Hemmingsen: 1570, D5r). It follows that the household is the primary estate. When parents live an immoral life before their children, they cause many evil incidents in the two other estates (Hemmingsen: 1578, G4v/Hemmingsen: 1570, D5r). If children are to be brought up to be obedient and loyal in a larger social setting, then it is all the more important that obedience and morality begin in the household.

The third method is that of parents using gentle words with their children, a method not discussed thoroughly by Hemmingsen. When the use of gentle words is insufficient, however, parents are to employ the fourth method of critical words, warning and threatening them with the punishment of disobedience. If all other methods should fail, they have no choice but to use the fifth and last

---

(Hemmingsen: 1570, D3v). To be sure, Nicholas Denham's dependence on Anders Vedel's Latin translation disturbs the understanding of Hemmingsen's own text. Vedel and Denham are combining the two sequences quoted from the Danish text into one, i. e. "Vsus legis externus est, vt disciplina regat homines, vt in externa honestate morum, inuicem pacifice iuxta legem viuant" (Hemmingsen: 1574, 71f), and "THE EXTERNAL, (or outward) VSE of the Law, is, by discipline to gouerne ẏ people, that in outward honesti of manners, they might live queietly, according to the Law" (Hemmingsen: 1578, G4r).

16 Hemmingsen (1570, D4v). Denham, following Vedel's "Catechismi singulas partes" (Hemmingsen: 1574, 73), does not follow Hemmingsen's specification of "doctrine" corresponding to the contents of Martin Luther's Small Catechism, but summarizes it as "all the partes of the Christian instruction" (Hemmingsen: 1578, G4v).

parental remedy: the rod. In the cases of swearing, lying, theft, fist fights, and improper speech, the rod is the best means of correction. Hemmingsen finds Scriptural evidence in Sir 30:1 ("He who loves his son will whip him often, so that he may rejoice at the way he turns out") and in Prov 23:13 ("Do not withhold discipline from your children; if you beat them with a rod, they will not die"). To strengthen his argument further, he narrates a moral story about a young man sentenced to death for a heinous, but unspecified crime. At the place of execution, the young man cried to the crowds: "Thinke not (O ye beeholders) this tormentor to haue brought me to this so infaimous a kinde of punishment, but rather mine owne Mother." (Hemmingsen: 1578, H1r).[17] The background of the son's accusation of his mother is that she had brought him up with too much affection, forgetting to punish his trespassing. Hemmingsen uses the story to stress his point that parents should raise their children according to the moral law. In this context, he also repeats that the good work of parents makes it easier for children to show obedience to state and church authorities once they become adults.

External discipline is also enjoined to public authorities following Paul's explanation in Rom 13:1–7 that rulers are servants of God, instituted in the earthly realm to promote goodness and punish wickedness. These are moral categories. The king is conceived as a *Custos utriusque tabulae*, the guardian of both tables of the law in order to encourage God's honor among men, specifically with regard to the outward person. Thus, Hemmingsen understood the spiritual welfare of subjects as a royal matter. With this point Hemmingsen also justifies his own involvement in the Danish royal confessionalist politics since the 1560s through a theological argument. Political authorities lead the way in this effort by functioning as a mirror for their subjects. Authorities become examples in whom their subjects can see how to behave properly in this world according to the Decalogue.[18] Consequently, the laws promulgated by political authorities should be consistent with God's law, which authorities are charged to protect. Therefore, every violation of divine law according to the law, whether it is blasphemy, idolatry, swearing, curses, perjuries, disdain for God's Word, disobedience, homicide, adultery, etc. If authorities fail to punish transgressions of the divine law, they themselves fall under God's wrath. Technically speaking, this is a clear

17 Cf. Hemmingsen (1570, D6r): "det er icke Bødelen/ men det er min Moder som mig leder til denne slemme Død."

18 Hemmingsen (1570, D7r): "at hand kand være sine vndersaate som en Spegel hour vdi mand kand see/ huorlunde mand skal skicke sig i Verden/ effter Guds Low." Vedel and Denham have a simpler formulation than Hemmingsen himself: "[...] vt sit exemplar & speculum, in quo subditi bene viuentes, intueri possint" (Hemmingsen: 1574, 75), and "that hee may be a patterne, and a glasse, into which his subiects liuing godly may looke into" (Hemmingsen: 1578, H1v), omitting to translate "skicke sig i Verden" (i. e. to behave properly in this world).

example of a post-Reformation attempt to turn sins into crime by a magisterial assumption of pre-Reformation ecclesiastical jurisdiction (Bossy: 1985, 116–140). As one legal example, Hemmingsen tells his readers about a man who had killed seven men. When this man was accused of seven homicides at court, he answered that he killed only one. The authorities, having failed to penalize his misdeed, were responsible for the other six killings (Hemmingsen: 1578, H2r/ Hemmingsen: 1570, D7v). Had they followed divine law, there would have been only one homicide. The story serves as an example of the moral obligation of the authorities: they are not only to punish crimes as such, but are to punish them because they are given a divine mandate to do so.

The final paragraph concerning the external use of the law is devoted to the third estate, the ministers of the divine Word. When preaching law, the ministers are responsible for promoting outward discipline in their congregations. In admonishing their audience, the ministers should not distinguish between high or low social status. All persons are capable of blasphemy and immoral living, but nevertheless, Hemmingsen complains (paraphrasing Juvenal) that many ministers punish the dove and pardon the raven.[19] The preacher should regard God's glory and man's salvation higher than his own life and security, and thus be willing to lose his head, following John the Baptist's example.

Hemmingsen discusses the internal use of the law only briefly in 3 ½ folios. Here, Hemmingsen initially contrasts the internal use of law with the outward use. Whereas the outward use pertained to human act and speech, the internal use is concerned with one's heart and consciousness, which is to be tried before God's court on the Day of Judgement. If one is found to have been obedient and observant to the law in every scenario, then he has direct access to God's blessing. However, no one except Christ has lived up to this lofty requirement. Therefore, God can only keep his promise by helping persons through the Gospel. Hence the internal use of the law is activated when one meditates on particular commands of the law and examines for himself whether or not he has observed them in his way of life. Realizing how often he has been disobedient to God's law, he will find himself inevitably struck by God's wrath and revenge. Consequently, there are only two possible solutions: either desperation and eternal death or the mercy

19 "Her finder mand mange som strafe Duerne oc lade Raffnene fare." (Hemmingsen: 1570, E1r). Denham represents the passage in verse, following Vedel: "The rauening Crow, is pardoned still: The simple Dooue, susteynes much yll." (Hemmingsen: 1578, H3r). Cf. Hemmingsen: 1574, 78: "Dat veniam coruis, vexat censura columbas"). Hemmingsen himself does not make it clear that he refers to a proverb; Vedel and Denham insert, however, a "poëtae" and a "verse of the Poet," respectively, before depicting the proverb. All three editions conceal that Hemmingsen quotes Juvenal's (first and early second centuries AD) *Satires*, 2.63: "dat ueniam coruis, uexat censura columbas." Most likely, Hemmingsen has Erasmus, *Adag.* 2473 (ASD II/5: 333,120–334,131) in mind.

seat of Jesus Christ the reconciler (Hemmingsen: 1578, H4r/Hemmingsen: 1570, E3v). Therefore, the second use of the law, in close agreement with Melanchthon and Luther, points toward the Gospel, in order to communicate God's salvific intentions towards man. In doing so, the second use of the law also points towards faith as the mode for man's reception of God's gift of salvation.

The third use of the law applies only to the faithful who are regenerated in faith. Obviously, this requires that the moral guidelines stipulated in Hemmingsen's discussion of the first use of the law be valid for all people, Christians and non-Christians alike. However, throughout Hemmingsen's treatment of the spiritual use of the law, the moral teaching of the law for Christians seems to equate with the first use of the law. Criticizing Antinomism Hemmingsen maintains that "because the man that is borne anew, would shew obedience unto God, he looketh againe into the lawe, and setteth the same as an infallible rule before him, that he may vnderstand, what hee shoulde doe, and what hee should leaue vndone, in ỷ right seruing of God." (Hemmingsen: 1578, I1rf).[20] Although the exact content of the law is not revealed, Hemmingsen is certain that it can be derived from exposition of the first use of the law.[21] Here, Hemmingsen suggests along with Luther and Melanchthon that God's will is expressed in social structures. Therefore, Hemmingsen shows that true service of God through obedience to the law comes by way of observing and retaining social structures.

Elsewhere, Hemmingsen holds that a Christian's obedience to the law is proof of one's faith in God, to which God has added a promise of reward (Hemmingsen: 1578, I1v.I2r/Hemmingsen: 1570, E6r.E6v). Hemmingsen returns to the metaphorical imagery of father and child that he used to describe the household duties under the first use of the law in order to depict Christian obedience. The sinner is like a disobedient child disinherited by his father because of his disobedience. After the child plead to be restored to the father's favor, the father felt pity on the child and restored him. Nevertheless, the child forgot his father's command, relapsed into old habits, and took advantage of the father's affection and goodness. Hemmingsen then asks, is it not fair that the father resorts to extreme justice?

---

20 Cf. Hemmingsen (1570, E5rf): "Effterdi nu den som troer/ vil være Gud lydig/ saa tager hand Guds Low for sig paa ny/ oc haffuer hende som en vis Regel/ paa det mand giøre oc lade skal/ saa viit som Guds dyrckelse ved kommer."

21 Hemmingsen's conclusion of the part on the third use resembles of the linguistic forms in the part on the first use: "[...] it becommeth all those which beleeue in Christe, to set the Lawe of GOD before them, as the glasse of their liues, according unto which, they should direct al their doings [...]" (Hemmingsen: 1578, K1v); "at de som tro paa Jesum Christum/ skulle sette sig Guds Low for til it liffs Spegel/ effte huilcket de skulle skicke deris leffnit" (Hemmingsen: 1570, F4r).

There is a certain ambiguity regarding the priority of grace or the Christian's observation of the law in its third use in Hemmingsen's account of the father-child metaphor and the father's use of extreme justice. If the third use is substantively equivalent to the first use, where does this leave Hemmingsen's rejection of works righteousness and the second use of the law for one's self-knowledge as a law breaker in need of God's grace? To be sure, Hemmingsen does not answer this question, although he hints at a possible solution to the problem. By faith, he says, one receives Christ and the forgiveness of sins as a gift. This is not an invitation to sin, but an admonition to keep the gift in the human heart and, in renewed obedience, to use the gift to renounce the devil and his works. I would argue that the three estates are implicitly contained within this new obedience. As Luther argued in *On the Councils and the Church*, to live within the estates is a true remedy against the devil (LW 41: 177/WA 50: 652,18 ff). Formally, this can be interpreted as equivalent to the function of the third use of the law in Melanchthon's understanding. That is, the third use of the law aids the Christian's daily penitence (Melanchthon: 1553/2002, 233,16 f). Therefore, perhaps the question about the priority of grace or law obedience in Hemmingsen is not the most appropriate question here. Rather, Hemmingsen's insistence on the law's enduring authority for the regenerate correlates with another commonplace, namely, sanctification. By living out this new obedience, Christians are sanctified by the work of the Holy Spirit. In fact, Hemmingsen designates the Christian's faith to be the temple of the Holy Spirit, who not only gives faith through the gospel message and thereby regenerates the person, but also elevates the Christian to gratitude towards God such that the Christian gains greater reverence for God's will over all earthly things.[22] Here, the heritage of both Luther and Melanchthon is fruitfully combined by Hemmingsen. The law is an incentive in the life of a Christian, caused by the Holy Spirit, and works with efficacy to allow the regenerate to yield the fruits of faith in works of love. It is implicit that these fruits are harvested with the three estates, namely, when love unfolds between the different agents within the estates.

Bearing in mind Hemmingsen's activities in assisting the kings' shaping of a Lutheran confessional society, it seems adequate to propose that *Liffsens Vey* is a theological legitimation of the political process. While Luther and Melanchthon were driven to construct coherent social theologies and doctrines of the law by the growing institutionalization of the Wittenberg Reformation in the later 1520s, Hemmingsen actively used the imagery of household, govern-

22 "Huor denne Tro er vis oc vden Hychlerj/ der er den hellig=Aands tempel/ som baade forarbeider Troen vdi Menniskens hierte/ naar mand hører det salige Euangelium/ oc igenføder ocsaa Mennisket/ oc opuecker det/ til Tacknemmelighed mod Gud/ sa at Mennisket tager sig for at ville være Gud lydig oc mere acte hans vilie/ end alt det vdi Verden er/ ihuor gaat oc kiert det være kand." (Hemmingsen: 1570, E5rf).

ment, and church, and the parent-child relation as a metaphorical grid to theologically form the post-Reformation Danish-Norwegian society. Also, he used this theological foundation to develop a society that was characterized by an intense confessionalization process. The divine law is moral instruction and implementation of God's ordained will in the social structures. As it is revealed in social structures, the law becomes a principle that guides the creation of a Christian society.

5. Conclusion

This chapter has demonstrated that Luther and Melanchthon agreed that morality was given by God in creation. However, they disagreed about the outer moral structures within which persons exist. While Luther conceived of the three estates, Melanchthon reckoned instead with three uses of the law. Niels Hemmingsen, a student of both reformers, combined their approaches, and eventually concluded that the three estates are the locations of true living for faithful Christians. By agreeing with both Wittenberg reformers that the law is a moral guide for the Christian, Hemmingsen adopted a mediating position, in which the three estates are the locations in which Christians live according to the third use of the law.

Hemmingsen's writings and political efforts under Frederik II is a clear example of an attempt to describe human action in the world by smoothly unifying theology, ethics, and jurisprudence. Therefore, his defense and high esteem of the law was a welcomed ideological support for the Danish-Norwegian monarchs' confessional politics, in which Hemmingsen himself, as already shown, played an important part as royal theological and legal adviser. In order to secure a Lutheran religious culture, the population needed to have "Lutheran" morals. Hemmingsen sought to provide such a mentality by combining Lutheran and Melanchthonian thought. Assisting the kings in their attempts to establish a Lutheran culture, he became a key figure in the early modern confessionalization of the dual monarchy of Denmark-Norway insofar as he offered a theological motivation for the royal politics in the three estates, with their paternal imagery and focus on the household.[23]

23 For their insigtful questions and comments, I am grateful to the audience at the 2015 meeting of the Sixteenth Century Society Conference in Vancouver, and to professor Mathias Schmoeckel, Bonn.

Bibliography

BARNEKOW, KJELL (1940), Niels Hemmingsens teologiske åskadning: En dogmhistorisk studie, Lund: C.W.K. Gleerup.

BOSSY, JOHN (1985), Christianity in the West 1400–1700, Oxford: Oxford University Press.

DINGEL, IRENE (2012), Melanchthon and the Establishment of Confessional Norms, in: Irene Dingel et al., Philip Melanchthon: Theologian in Classroom, Confession, and Controversy (R5AS 7), Göttingen: Vandenhoeck & Ruprecht.

ERASMUS OF ROTTERDAM (1500–1536/1981), Opera Omnia Desiderii Erasmi Roterodami, Ordinis Secundi, Tomus Quintus: Adagiorum Chilias Tertia, ed. Felix Heinimann/ Emanuel Kienzle, Amsterdam/Oxford: North-Holland Publishing Company.

FINK-JENSEN, MORTEN (2011), Printing and Preaching After the Reformation: A Danish Pastor and his Audiences, in: Charlotte Appel/Morten Fink-Jensen (ed.), Religious Reading in the Lutheran North: Studies in Early Modern Scandinavian Book Culture, Newcastle upon Tyne: Cambridge Scholars Publishing, 15–47.

GLEBE-MØLLER, JENS (2014), Omkring suspensionen af Niels Hemmingsen i 1576, KHS, 209–219.

GRELL, OLE PETER (2016), The Reformation in Denmark, Norway and Iceland, in: Jens E. Olesen/E. I. Kouri (ed.), The Cambridge History of Scandinavia, vol. II, Cambridge: Cambridge University Press, 44–59.

HEMMINGSEN, NIELS (1570), Liffsens Vey: Det er/ En vis oc Christelig Vnderuisning, Copenhagen: Laurents Benedicht. The Royal Library, Copenhagen, Hielmst. 491 8vo (LN 921).

HEMMINGSEN, NIELS (1574), Via vitae: Christiana et Orthodoxa Institutio Complectens Praecipva Christianae Relligionis capita, trans. Anders Sørensen Vedel, Leipzig: Andreas Schneider. Bayerische Staatsbibliothek, Munich, Dogm. 493 w (VD16 H 1861).

HEMMINGSEN, NIELS (1576/1867–1868), Retractio D. Nicolai Hemmingii, qva errorem in Syntagmate nuper editio de Cœna Domini revocavit, ed. Holger Frederik Rørdam, KHS 2/IV, 309–310.

HEMMINGSEN, NIELS (1578), The VVay of lyfe, A Christian, and Catholique Institution Comprehending Principal Points of Christian Religion, trans. Nicholas Denham, London: Richard Jones. Bodleian Library, University of Oxford, reel 569:10 (STC 13068).

INGESMAN, PER (2010), Skriften, Loven og Sværdet: Mosaisk lovs indflydelse på dansk retsudvikling efter reformationen, Kritik 195, 12–20.

JUNGHANS, HELMAR (2011), Philipp Melanchthons Loci Theologici als Lehrbuch Während Seiner Lebenszeit, in: Irene Dingel/Armin Kohnle (ed.), Philipp Melanchthon: Lehrer Deutschlands, Reformator Europas, LStRLO 13, Leipzig: Evangelische Verlagsanstalt, 153–161.

KOCH, ERNST (1992), Auseinandersetzungen um die Autorität von Philipp Melanchthon und Martin Luther in Kursachsen im Vorfeld der Konkordienformel von 1577, LuJ 59, 128–159.

KORNERUP, BJØRN (ed.) (1953), Confessio et Ordinatio Ecclesiarum Danicarum anno MDLXI conscriptae: Den danske Kirkes Lærebekendelse og Kirkeordinans af Aar 1561, Copenhagen: G.E.C. Gad.

LAUSTEN, MARTIN SCHWARZ (2013), Niels Hemmingsen: Storhed og Fald, Copenhagen: Anis.

LOCKHART, PAUL DOUGLAS (2004), Frederik II and the Protestant Cause: Denmark's Role in the Wars of Religion, 1559–1596 (The Northern World 10), Leiden/Boston, MA: Brill.

LUTHER, MARTIN (1522), Epistle at New Year's Day (Gal 3:23–29) (WA 10 I 1: 449–503).

LUTHER, MARTIN (1528), Confession Concerning Christ's Supper (LW 37: 161–372/WA 26: 261–509).

LUTHER, MARTIN (1529), The Small Catechism (BC 347–375/WA 30 I: 243–425).

LUTHER, MARTIN (1529), The Large Catechism (BC 379–480/ WA 30 I: 125–238).

LUTHER, MARTIN (1535–1545), Lectures on Genesis (LW 1–8/WA 42–44).

LUTHER, MARTIN (1539), On the Councils and the Church (LW 41/WA 50: 509–653).

MADSEN, ERIK MUNCH (1946), Niels Hemmingsens Etik: En idehistorisk Studie, Copenhagen: G.E.C. Gads Forlag.

MELANCHTHON, PHILIPP (1530), Confessio Augustana (BC 30–105/BSELK 84–225).

MELANCHTHON, PHILIPP (1535), Loci Communes Theologici Recens Collecti & Recogniti (CR 21: 253–560).

MELANCHTHON, PHILIPP (1542), Confessio Fidei [...] Ex variata Editione Wittembergensi a. 1540. recusa, et cum Editione Mel. principe a. 1531., ac variatis Editionibus Wittembergensibus annorum 1531. et 1541–1542 collata (CR 26: 350–416).

MELANCHTHON, PHILIPP (1553/2002), Heubtartikel Christlicher Lere, ed. Ralf Jenett/Johannes Schilling, Leipzig: Evangelische Verlagsanstalt.

MELANCHTHON, PHILIPP/MARTIN LUTHER et al. (1528), Instructions for the Visitors of Parish Pastors in Electoral Saxony (LW 40: 269–320/CR 26: 49–96/WA 26: 195–240).

MICHEL, STEFAN (2014), Der "Unterricht der Visitatoren" (1528) – Die erste Kirchenordnung der von Wittenberg ausgehenden Reformation?, in: Irene Dingel/Armin Kohnle (ed.), Gute Ordnung: Ordnungsmodelle und Ordnungsvorstellungen in der Reformationszeit (LStRLO 25), Leipzig: Evangelische Verlagsanstalt, 153–167.

PETERSON, LUTHER D. (1990), Justus Menius, Philipp Melanchthon, and the 1547 Treatise, *Von der Notwehr Unterricht*, ARG 81, 138–157.

RASMUSSEN, TARALD (2013), The Early Modern Pastor between Ideal and Reality, LuJ 80, 197–219.

SAARINEN, RISTO (2005), Ethics in Luther's Theology: The Three Orders, in: Risto Saarinen/Jill Kraye (ed.), Moral Philosophy on the Threshold of Modernity, Dordrecht: Springer, 195–215.

SCATTOLA, MERIO (1999), Das Naturrecht vor dem Naturrecht: Zur Geschichte des "ius naturae" im 16. Jahrhundert (Frühe Neuzeit 52), Tübingen: Max Niemeyer Verlag.

SCHWARZ, REINHARD (1984), Ecclesia, oeconomia, politia: Sozialgeschichtliche und fundamentalethische Aspekte der protestantischen Drei-Stände-Theorie, in: Horst Renz/Friedrich Wilhelm Graf (ed.), Protestantismus und Neuzeit (Troeltsch-Studien 3), Gütersloh: Gütersloher Verlagshaus Gerd Mohn, 78–88.

SECHER, V.A. (ed.) (1891), Kong Christian den Femtis Danske Lov, Copenhagen: G.E.C. Gad.

SOMMER, MATTIAS SKAT (2017a), Niels Hemmingsen and the Construction of a Seventeenth-Century Protestant Memory, JEMC 4/1, 135–160.

SOMMER, MATTIAS SKAT (2017b), Visitations, in: Mark A. Lamport (ed.), Encyclopedia of Martin Luther and the Reformation, Lanham, MD: Rowman & Littlefield Publishers, 799–800.

STEGMANN, ANDREAS (2014), Luthers Auffassung vom christlichen Leben (BHTh 175), Tübingen: Mohr Siebeck.

TAMM, DITLEV (1983), Nolo falcem in alienam messem mittere: Der dänische Theologe Niels Hemmingsen (1513–1600) aus juristischer Sicht, in: Karl Kroeschell (ed.), Gerichtslauben-Vorträge: Freiburger Festkolloquium zum 75. Geburtstag von Hans Thieme, Sigmaringen: Jan Thorbecke, 47–56.

TYÖRINOJA, REIJO (2002), Opus theologicum: Luther and Medieval Theories of Action, NZSTh 44/2, 119–153.

WALLMANN, JOHANNES (2012), Kirchengeschichte Deutschlands seit der Reformation, 7th ed., Tübingen: Mohr Siebeck.

WOLGAST, EIKE (1977), Die Wittenberger Theologie und die Politik der evangelischen Stände: Studien zur Luthers Gutachten in politischen Fragen, QFRG 47, Gütersloh: Gütersloher Verlagshaus Gerd Mohn.

Svend Andersen

Two Kingdoms, Three Estates, and Natural Law[1]

1. Introduction

There is dispute concerning the relation between Luther's theories about the two kingdoms and the three estates. Did he change his mind, or are the two concepts compatible? And as theoretical frameworks for understanding social life, how do they fit into his version of natural law theory?

After having proposed an answer to these questions, this chapter will present and analyze one of the main works in Danish Lutheran ethics: Niels Hemmingsen's *De lege naturae*, 1562. In the terminology of Charles Taylor, Hemmingsen's work is seen as a transformation on the level of theory as distinct from social imaginary. But as Hemmingsen was also involved in concrete legislation, his theory of natural law is closely connected to the formation of a Lutheran social imaginary. As a side issue, a possible similarity between the latter concept and "confessional culture" is briefly discussed. In order to trace the development up to the limit of the period covered in this volume, the natural law theory of eighteenth-century Danish playwright and learned person Ludvig Holberg is presented.

2. Two Kingdoms, Three Estates and Natural Law in Luther

In his introduction to Luther's theology, German Luther scholar Oswald Bayer makes the following statement: "Luther's own testimony shows that the teaching about the three estates carries much greater weight for him than the teaching about the two realms of God." (Bayer: 2008, 124). Of course, this is more of an interpretation than a statement of fact. Accordingly, it is open to discussion, amongst other things in light of Luther's emphasis of the fact that no one since the days of the apostles has distinguished so finely between spiritual and

1 Thanks to Robert Stern for linguistic improvement of the text and useful comments.

worldly.[2] In the present context it is however not Luther's self-understanding that is of interest, but rather the thought content of the two doctrines concerning social reality.[3]

2.1. The Two Kingdoms Doctrine

The two kingdoms doctrine is a distinction between two entirely different ways in which God "reigns over" human beings; that is, two ways in which he determines the conditions for their lives and still works in order to fulfill their aims. Concerning common, created human life, God reigns as creator through political government – secular authority ("weltliche Obrigkeit") – with the aim of suppressing the evil caused by sin and thereby creating the conditions for peaceful existence. This is what Luther understands by the worldly kingdom ("weltliches Regiment").

By contrast, the spiritual kingdom ("geistliches Regiment") does not aim at the maintenance of created human life, but rather at the salvation of human beings. Here God is working through the Gospel, his word about Christ and His justifying work. In contrast to the worldly realm, the human exercise of power is inadmissible in the spiritual sphere.

Seen from the viewpoint of humans, this distinction between God's two "regiments" means that profane life has gained a certain independence in relation to religion and the church – and vice versa: political power is to be kept apart from anything having to do with the preaching of the Gospel.[4]

2 Namely in the 1526 *Whether Soldiers, too, Can Be Saved* (LW 46: 95/WA 19: 625,15 ff). Actually, here Luther only emphasizes his praise of secular authority.

3 Methodically speaking, I take Luther's texts to express thoughts in the sense of presentations of theoretical issues, use of concepts and the undertaking of arguments. In my opinion, Luther's texts should be treated the same way as philosophical ones. In my interpretation I focus on the meaning inherent in the texts themselves, leaving aside the historical origin of Luther's concepts. When we are dealing with theories about social and political issues, it is, of course, necessary to take into account the actual conditions to which Luther relates his thoughts. However, my approach is not historical, so I just presuppose the basic socio-political facts. Hence methodically the following differs from both Charles Taylor's "social imaginary" approach, and Thomas Kaufmann's idea of "confessional culture." As the labels show, the two procedures differ, as Taylor is dealing with perceptions of socio-political reality, whereas Kaufmann is occupied with perceptions and practices formed by confessional Christianity. However, the two overlap in so far as a confessional culture of course also relates to the socio-political realm. Common to the two approaches is a kind of holism in that theories and beliefs are treated as embedded in a variety of concrete practices, habits, texts etc. See Taylor (2007, 158 ff) and Kaufmann (2006, 9).

4 The main text, of course, is *On Secular Authority* (LW 45: 81–129/WA 11: 245–280).

As I have pointed out several times previously, the distinction between spiritual and worldly does not equal a "separation of religion from politics" (Andersen: 2010). In the case of Christianity, religion according to Luther encompasses more than faith, namely neighborly love. Neighborly love based in justifying faith so to speak sends the Christian believer into worldly reality, where (s) he has to work for the best of his/her fellow human beings, either by directly exercising political-legal power as ruler, or by supporting the political order as subject, depending on one's office or calling.

It is very important to notice that Luther did not retain his clear distinction between spiritual and worldly. As is well-known, in connection with the organization of evangelical churches he was forced to make use of the princes and other worldly authorities as "emergency bishops." And by what I regard as an irony of history, this emergency regime became the prevailing form of church government in Lutheran churches, including in Denmark. The theological-legal rationale for this is the thesis about the princes as *praecipua membra ecclesiae* ("finest members of the church").[5]

2.2. The Doctrine about the Three Estates

Luther's doctrine about the three estates is formally speaking a development of Aristotle's distinction between *oeconomia* and *politia*, in that Luther adds *ecclesia* to these two.[6] He formulates the distinction at various places, but in my opinion the most important one is in the 1528 treatise *Confession Concerning the Lord's Supper*, in which he both explains his view of the Eucharist, and gives a comprehensive account of his understanding of Christianity, structured after the three parts of the confession. In the following, I will go into this text in some detail in order to get hold of the argument concerning the three estates.

In connection with the second article of faith and the doctrine of justification, Luther emphasizes that humans are justified through Christ alone. He there rejects the idea of free will and condemns the Pelagians. Thirdly, he rejects "all orders, rules, monasteries, and trusts" ("alle orden, Regel, Klöster, stift"). His justification is that within these contexts things are thought that transgress

5 In Melanchthon the thesis reads in German translation: "[I]n jeder Gemeinde müssen die angesehendsten Glieder darin den übrigen vorangehen und den anderen helfen, daß die Kirche reformiert wird. Die Fürsten und anderen Beamten sollen angesehene Glieder der Kirche sein. Also ist es nötig, daß sie die Reform einleiten und unterstützen." (Melanchthon: 1997, 205).

6 It seems that in medieval teaching a tripartite version of Aristotle's practical philosophy was presented in that his ethics was counted as one element besides *oeconomia* and *politia*. According to Schwarz (1984), this *ethical* tripartition was united with the *social* division into clergy, nobility and "working people" to define the Lutheran doctrine of the three estates.

Scripture and that imply that these "human inventions" can contribute to salvation. After this rejection of the Catholic meaning of the monasteries and the other institutions, Luther remarks that they actually could be converted into useful educational institutions. Hence, the problem-context for the "doctrine" is the question about Christian practice and its institutional framework.

Accordingly, Luther next turns to "the holy orders and right trusts" ("die heiligen orden und rechte stiffte von Gott eingesetzt"): the office of preacher, matrimony and secular authority. These orders or estates are embraced by God's word and commandments, and this makes them holy. Elsewhere Luther refers to the three entities as *ecclesia*, *oeconomia* and *politia*, but according to our context the first mentioned is not the church strictly speaking, but rather the office or function of preaching. This he elaborates by saying that pastors serve the word of God, preach and communicate the sacraments. To the office of preacher Luther also counts the administration of the common fund and the sextons. To my mind, it is important to notice that Luther here introduces the so-called three estates as a contrast to institutions that, according to Catholic doctrine, are a means to human salvation.

Luther then mentions Christian love as a factor situated above the three orders, consisting of all kinds of beneficence. But even though love issues in "good, holy works" ("gute, heilige werck"), the orders are not roads to blessedness. For it is necessary to distinguish clearly between blessedness and holiness: we only become blessed through Christ, but we may become holy both through faith and through divine orders.[7] And, as Luther adds, the godless also have many holy things.

In connection with the third article of faith, Luther attributes to the Holy Spirit the ability to let humans acquire the salvific work of Christ. This the Spirit achieves in both an internal and an external way. The former takes place through faith and other spiritual gifts, whereas the latter takes place through the Gospel and the sacraments. These three entities Luther also calls divine orders, and in

7 Luther also uses the terminology of divine orders in the 1535 *Greater Commentary on Galatians:* "You have often heard from me that civil and domestic ordinances are divine, because God Himself has established and approved them, as He has the sun, the moon, and other creatures. Therefore an argument based on an ordinance of God or on creatures is valid so long as it is used properly." (LW 26: 296/WA 40 I: 460, 22–25). The second sentence mirrors the context which is a commentary on the verse "Brothers and sisters, I give an example from daily life: once a person's will has been ratified, no one adds to it or annuls it." (Gal 3:15). Luther's point is that a covenant or testament belongs to the household or the polity, and as they are divine orders, one can draw conclusions about divine matters from them. Hence, *oeconomia* and *politia* are put in line with sun, moon and all creation. Risto Saarinen (2005) takes Luther's formulation here and at other places as an indication that his "doctrine" of three estates is influenced by the distinction between *potentia Dei absoluta* and *ordinata* found in late medieval thinkers as, for example, Occam.

this connection he, of course, mentions the church. It is, he says, a spiritual body, the head of which is Christ, not bishops or priests.

The church in the sense of the third article of faith Luther does not characterize as a divine order, but rather as the spiritual kingdom of Christ. This means, I think, that the office of priesthood as one of the three estates has to be rated among what has been called the visible church, i. e. the church as the totality of those external means through which the Spirit brings about the acquirement of faith and hence justification and blessedness. In the terminology of the two kingdoms doctrine, one may say that Luther rates the office of preacher or the visible church among the worldly. But it would probably be more precise to call the church an external order (LW 37: 364f/WA 26: 504f). Luther presents a similar argument in his *Sermon on Baptism* from 1519. He claims that as also a baptized Christian is still a sinner, his/her life contains suffering. Against those who wish to avoid this, Luther points at three estates ("stend") instituted by God for exercising suffering: the marital, the clerical, and that of temporal rule ("ehelich," "geistlich," "regierend"). But here he still seems to attribute religious orders to the spiritual estate (LW 35: 39.41/WA 2: 734; 736).

Another important text is Luther's *Lectures on Genesis*, in which he introduces the doctrine of the three estates at several places. One is his commentary on the story of the Fall. In a very free interpretation, he understands the tree in the Garden of Eden as a place given to Adam for worship of God, i. e. as a temple or a church. The household is only introduced after the creation of Eve, and the political is only necessary after the Fall (LW 1: 104/WA 42: 79,7–14). Here the church is clearly an order of creation and not specifically Christian. As Bayer (2008, 123) formulates it: "Every human being belongs as a human being – which is what defines one as a human – to the church, because it is an order of creation."[8]

8 In *Exposition of Psalm 127, for the Christians at Riga in Livonia* (1527) Luther interprets the two half-verses "Unless the Lord builds the house, those who build it labor in vain" and "Unless the Lord guards the city, the guard keeps watch in vain" (Ps 127:1) as dealing with *oeconomia* and *politia* respectively. His point is that the welfare of the household and the "state" depends on both the effort of humans and God's support (LW 45: 328–331/WA 15: 370,3–373,17). In *On the Councils and the Church* (1539) Luther refers to the distinction made in Ps 127 between household and city which he now calls "corporeal regiments," and to which he adds the third estate: "Then follows the third, God's own home and city, that is, the church, which must obtain people from the home and protection and defense from the city." (LW 41: 177/WA 50: 652,15ff). Interestingly, Luther mentions the three "hierarchies" in a context where he discusses the use of the school, which is neither part of the house nor of the city. This means that the "estates" are not institutions, for the school would be such on its own. Instead, Luther is thinking of three different frameworks for human activity: "living aright and resisting the devil" (LW 41: 177/WA 50: 652,19f). Another important point is that Luther in this late work uses the terminology of the two kingdoms doctrine: in connection with the city or the land he mentions the rulers as "weltlich regiment" ("secular government"), and the church he calls a

I now want to take a look at some of the other statements Luther makes on the three estates in the Genesis lecture. At some points, Luther simply makes clear the difference in function between the three estates in a way very similar to the distinction drawn concerning the two kingdoms. He also points to some structural differences, such as the one between equality and inequality. Using the distinction between arithmetic and geometrical proportion known from the Aristotelian concept of justice, Luther makes clear that whereas there is equality in *ecclesia*, in *politia* there necessarily has to be inequality (LW 3: 130f/WA 42: 641,1–13). But this is quite on a par with the difference Luther makes when dealing with the spiritual-secular distinction.

However, an important characteristic of the presentation of the three estates in the Genesis lecture consists in Luther placing ecclesia at the first rank, giving the two others a subordinate role. Thus using the terminology of "hierarchies" ("These, then, are the three hierarchies we often inculcate, namely, the household, the government, and the priesthood."), Luther makes clear that the church is above (supra) the two others (LW 5: 139/WA 43: 524,22–27). In fact, not only is the church or the priestly office superior to the two others, but also these latter – particularly politia – ultimately have the function of serving the church. All the estates are instituted with the aim of fighting sin (and Satan; LW 3: 279/WA 43: 74,37–75,4), but besides fulfilling this in an external, corporeal sense, the political ruler contributes to fighting sin in a spiritual way: "For if the church is to be preserved, there must be some pious prince to provide quarters for it and grant it room and peace, so that the doctrine and the Word of God can be spread." (LW 4: 89/WA 43: 199, 6–8). Actually, the role of serving the church is due to both the other estates: "For God has no concern for the state and the household except for the sake of the church." (LW 7: 349/WA 44: 559,17f).[9] If one compares the statements Luther makes about the three estates in the *Confession* and the

"Regiment, wo [...] der Heilige Geist regirt" ("rule and government [... where] the Holy Spirit reigns") (LW 41: 177/WA 50: 652,24.30). This exactly equals the terminology of *On Secular Authority*. By the way: Luther's use of the term "hierarchy" points at other possible influences than the Aristotelian ethics mentioned above. According to Wilhelm Maurer (1970), in late medieval literature, a threefold structure is emphasized in presentations of the Decalogue, particularly the fourth commandment. And this tripartition can be seen as inspired by Pseudo-Dionysios the Areopagite's thoughts about angelic hierarchies. I owe this information to Mattias Skat Sommer. Luise Schorn-Schütte (1998) also points at the tripartition of Aristotelian ethics and the Dionysian hierarchy speculation as preconditions for Luther's thinking about the three estates. She further mentions an important function of the "doctrine": in connection with the establishment of Evangelical city churches, the clergy obtained a new legitimacy in relation to the worldly magistrate.

9 In his 1529 treatise *On War Against the Turks* Luther accuses Moslems of practicing lies, murder, and adultery, which ruins the three estates: "As I said, lies destroy the spiritual estate; murder, the temporal; disregard of marriage, the estate of matrimony" (LW 46:182/WA 30 II: 127,13f).

Genesis Lectures respectively, I find it obvious that he does not formulate a consistent "theory" about the three entities *oeconomia*, *politia*, and *ecclesia*. If, on the other hand, one concentrates on the version in the *Confession*, there does not seem to be a contradiction in relation to the version in the *Genesis Lectures*, but rather a relationship of supplementation. The duality of oeconomia and politia can be seen as a differentiation of the concept of the secular/worldly. And when Luther places *ecclesia* on a par with the two other entities, that can be understood as concerning the church as an organization, cf. what is said above about the *Confession*.

However, things are not as simple as that. In the *Genesis Lectures* Luther clearly subordinates the two "worldly" estates under the church. And he even defends a unification of political and ecclesial leadership in the case of the patriarch Jacob: "Jacob is the teacher in the church and the political magistrate" (LW 5: 159/ WA 43: 538,7 f). This is clearly not compatible with the claim, made in the treatise on secular authority that worldly power should be kept apart from spiritual matters. Luther's line of thought in the Genesis lectures can be seen as a further development of the position he was forced to adopt when facing the challenge of organizing evangelical churches.

According to Ulrich Assendorf, not only should the doctrines about the two kingdoms and the three estates be seen in combination with each other, but in the end the latter doctrine should be regarded as the more important one:

> Erst aus der Zusammenfassung beider läßt sich erkennen, was Luther eigentlich mit seiner Neuordnung des weltlichen und kirchlichen Lebens gewollt hat. Nicht zuletzt läßt sich das latente dualistische Mißverständnis – wie die spätere geradezu perfekte Kanonisierung der Utopie vermuten läßt – von den Hierarchien her als unhaltbar erweisen. (Assendorf: 1998, 475).

Assendorf regards the doctrine of the two kingdoms as a transitory stage ("Durchgangsstufe") in Luther's social teaching. This may be plausible in a purely historical sense at the most.[10] But if one asks the further question, how a Lutheran understanding of social life could be reconstructed today, the two kingdoms distinction between the spiritual and secular could be more convincing than the intertwinement of church, household and commonwealth. I will return to this claim in the end.

10 From a purely historical point of view, one could speculate that Luther's discourse on the three estates is strengthened from about the 1520s compared to the two kingdoms doctrine because of his experiences with the antinomians and the radical interpretation of Evangelical thinking manifested in the peasants' war. However, my interest is not so much historical as systematic.

2.3. Natural Law

What now interests me is how a third "doctrine" of Luther's, viz. the one about natural law, relates to the two others. First of all, we must realize that Luther does actually adopt the traditional doctrine of natural law, even if he gives it his own shape.

As to the basic normative concept, for Luther there is only one law in the sense of God's will for human behavior. And as regards its true intention, law does not have the character of a collection of precepts or prohibitions. Thus Luther writes in his Preface to Paul's Letter to the Romans (1546):

> The little word "law" you must here not take in human fashion as a teaching about what works are to be done or not done. That is the way with human laws; a law is fulfilled by works, even though there is no heart in the doing of them. But God judges according to what is in the depths of the heart. For this reason, his law too makes its demands on the inmost heart; it cannot be satisfied with works, but rather punishes as hypocrisy and lies the works not done from the bottom of the heart [...] If, now, there is no willing pleasure in the good, then the inmost heart is not set on the law of God. Then, too, there is surely sin, and God's wrath is deserved, even though outwardly there seem to be many good deeds and and honorable life (LW 35: 366/WA DB 7: 3,20ff.5,1ff.5ff).[11]

Now, as a matter of fact, human beings do not obey the law according to its intention: "Hence all men are called liars in Psalm 116[:11], because no one keeps or can keep God's law from the bottom of the heart. For everyone finds in himself displeasure in what is good and pleasure in what is bad." (LW 35: 366/WA DB 7: 5,3ff).

It is because of sin that law appears as commandments which humans either compel themselves to obey, or are forced to by others, not least by the political authorities. What we are talking about here is the law in its so-called first or political use. In addition, the discrepancy between the human "heart" and the law's intention can evoke acknowledgment of one's sin. And this is the second, theological use of the law. Even if the ethical and legal actions of the human sinner are not based on his/her heart, nevertheless the heart possesses some knowledge concerning right and wrong. Luther adheres to the traditional theological interpretation of Rom 2:14: "When Gentiles, who do not possess the law, do instinctively what the law requires, these, though not having the law, are a law to themselves." The passage is the *locus classicus* of the theological doctrine about *lex naturalis:* non-Jews, who do not have the Mosaic Torah, nevertheless have knowledge of the law, because they as creatures have the law inscribed in their hearts (Lehmann: 2015).

11 Luther also emphasizes in his 1519 *Lecture on Galatians* that the law is one and according to its intention is fulfilled with a "joyful heart" (LW 27: 349f.355/WA 2: 576. 580).

Luther expounds his understanding of natural law theory in two treatises about the way Christians should behave in relation to Mosaic Law, namely the 1525 *Against the Heavenly Prophets in the Matters of Images and Sacraments* (LW 40: 79–223/WA 18: 62–125.134–214) and the 1527 *Ein unterrichtung wie sich die Christen ynn Mosen sollen schicken, gepredigt durch Mart. Luther* (WA 24: 2–16). His main point is that the many precepts of the Old Testament basically are to be regarded as positive law – as "the Saxon code of law for the Jews" ("der Juden Sachsenspiegel") –, but that some of the Mosaic norms, primarily those of the Decalogue, are universally valid, because they express natural law. In Luther's view, the latter is summarized in the Golden Rule: "Do to others what you want others to do to you!" The rule is formulated in the Sermon on the Mount (Matt 7:12) in a way corresponding to the Commandment of Neighborly Love. For that reason, Luther in some contexts treats the Golden Rule as equivalent to the Christian love commandment.

In his analysis of the Golden Rule as natural law, Luther emphasizes that every human being has a basic knowledge about right acting in him/herself so that one does not need written rules or authorities. There is so to speak a moral conscience inherent in human self-relation. And this conscience contains both an emotional and a rational component. As to the very content of the rule, Luther rejects an understanding of it as a rule of reciprocity or return. The rule does not say, he claims, that if the other does this or that, I ought to repay him or her. The meaning is the opposite: when I act towards the other, I ought to do what I would wish done to me, if I were in the other's position (cf. *Sermon on the Mount*, LW 21: 239f/ WA 32: 498). As I have pointed out elsewhere, Luther understands the Golden Rule as a rule of role-exchange (cf. Andersen: 2017).

Now one could very well expect that Luther would connect his theory of natural law with the doctrine of the three estates: in both cases, we have to do with creation-based conditions to which humans are submitted, whether they are Christians or not. However, as far as I can see, Luther does not make this connection.[12] As mentioned, he regards the Decalogue as a good summary of natural law, and hence one gets an impression of his concrete understanding of that law from his interpretations of the ten commandments – or rather the last seven – for example in the Large Catechism. However, one has to be conscious of the fact that Luther in this work does not primarily interpret the commandments as natural law, but rather as evident examples of the way Christians are supposed to show neighborly love concretely.

12 It should be mentioned that Luther in his *Genesis Lectures*, dealing with the Abraham-Sarah story characterizes marriage as springing from the "sources of natural law" (LW 4: 210) (ex fontibus iuris naturae, WA 43: 292,38–293,1). See also Assendorf (1998, 456).

As far as I can see, Luther does not interpret the Decalogue against the background of the doctrine of the three estates, which also would have made sense. At any rate, one could say that the first three commandments belong to ecclesia, whereas the fourth relates to oeconomia. On the other hand, when it comes to politia it is hard to see that this estate is the main subject of commandments five to ten. According to Luther, the fourth commandment precisely deals with both oeconomia and politica, whereas the remaining commandments are about various other basic relations within worldly life.

In this connection, the seventh commandment in particular deserves mentioning. This norm according to Luther is not only about theft in a narrow sense, but importantly deals with a number of economic transactions. Luther here criticizes several types of misconduct, corresponding to his objections in his 1524 treatise on usury (*Trade and Usury*, LW 45: 245–310/WA 15: 293–322). Apparently, it is not of great importance for Luther that economic life takes place within *oeconomia* – which of course is also not always the case! Actually, the separation of economy from *oeconomia* – as well as the differentiation of the functions of *oeconomia* – are, in my opinion, significant features in the development into modernity.

In contrast to the doctrine of the three estates, the two kingdoms doctrine has a clear connection to natural law theory. In an appendix to the treatise on secular authority, Luther discusses the role of the Christian prince as law enforcer. Actually, the prince should judge the quarreling parties according to the "law of love" ("Gesetz der Liebe"). However, it may happen that the quarreling parties do not accept being judged according to Christian law, and for such a situation Luther gives this advice:

> If neither party is a Christian, or if one of them is unwilling to be judged by the law of love, then you may have them call in some other judge, and tell the obstinate one that they are acting contrary to God and natural law, even if they obtain a strict judgement in terms of human law. For nature teaches – as does love – that I should do as I would be done by [Luke 6:31]. Therefore, I cannot strip another of his possessions, no matter how clear a right I have, so long as I am unwilling myself to be stripped of my goods. Rather, just as I would that another, in such circumstances, should relinquish his rights in my favor, even so should I relinquish my rights. (LW 45: 128f/WA 11: 279,16–24).

Thus, vis-à-vis non-Christian subjects, a Christian prince can refer to natural law in the shape of the Golden Rule, which apparently for Luther is an ethico-legal norm about which Christians and non-Christians can reach consensus – mind you: within the worldly realm. As will be explained at the end of the article, this role of natural law in connection with the distinction between the spiritual and worldly seems to be of much more relevance in a contemporary context than the three estates doctrine.

3. Natural Law and Three Estates in Niels Hemmingsen

In the following, I shall take a look at how the Lutheran problem complex treated above appears in the thought of Danish theologian Niels Hemmingsen. Without going into details as to the historical context, I want to point at the importance of the fact that Hemmingsen presupposes a realized Lutheran state with a prince's church.[13] Before turning to Hemmingsen's version of Lutheran natural law theory, it is useful to briefly mention an important shift in natural law thinking within the Reformation.

Luther's understanding of natural law – as summarized in the Golden Rule – differs significantly from the natural-law theory of Thomas Aquinas. Even if Aquinas mentions the Golden Rule, two other features of his view are more important: First, he thinks of natural law as a systematic body of norms with one highest self-evident principle: "the good is to be sought and done, evil to be avoided" (*bonum est faciendum et prosequendum, et malum vitandum*). Second, Thomas purports to see a correspondence between norms derived from the first principle and "inclinationes naturales" (natural inclinations), e.g. self-preservation. Among the more specific norms of natural law, Aquinas mentions to "know truths about God" and "living in society" (Summa Theologiae I–II, q 94 a 2, in Gilby: 1966, 76–83).

Remarkably, Melanchthon in his version of natural law theory is more in accordance with Aquinas than with Luther. Melanchthon likewise adopts an Aristotelian concept of practical reason and hence regards natural law as a set of principles from which more specific norms can be logically deduced. Unlike Aquinas however, he does not deal with those inclinations humans have in common with animal, as he regards them as mere "affectus naturales" (natural affections). So natural law for Melanchthon basically consists of the fundamental principles specific for human life. In the first edition of his Loci Communes these principles are: (1) God is to be honored; (2) Because we are born into human societies, no one should be hurt; (3) Human society requires that we use all things in common.[14]

In his exposition of natural law, Melanchthon complains that no one until now has given a satisfactory presentation of the theory, which is strange in light of the fact that "natural" implies that the norms should be deduced by the syllogistic method of reason.[15]

---

13 For the bibliographical and historical context of Hemmingsen's work, see Mattias Skat Sommer's contribution to this volume.

14 "Deus colendum est. Quia nascimur in quandam vitae societatem, nemo laedendus est. Poscit humana societas, ut omnibus rebus communiter utamur." (Melanchthon: 1521/1997, 104).

15 "[...] a rationis humanae methodo earum formulas colligi per naturalem syllogismum." (Melanchthon: 1521/1997, 100f).

In his work, *De lege naturae* from 1562,[16] Hemmingsen refers to the methodological remarks of his Wittenberg teacher. Even if Melanchthon like many poets and philosophers has written sensibly about the basis of law (i.e. moral philosophy), nobody has really shown the way to progress in this kind of art. Hemmingsen, then, undertakes to present natural law in a methodical way similar to Euclid's Geometry (Hemmingsen: 1991, 18–21).[17]

Hemmingsen dedicates his book to Erik Krabbe (1510–1564), counselor of the realm, who endeavored to collect the various Danish laws into one comprehensive law book. The dedication gives Hemmingsen the opportunity to reflect on the very role of law. In his view, it is the law that binds together a commonwealth, a house and a society (*respublica, domus, societas*). And the law does so because its essence is justice: "without the law, the norm of justice, the polity cannot use its parts."[18] Hemmingsen seems to presuppose that the law can best fulfill its cohesive function, if the various laws are united such as Krabbe attempted. It is really important, Hemmingsen claims, that the Danish province laws should be collected into a *systema juris Danici* (law system of Denmark). And they would obtain real unity if regarded as hypotheses derived from natural law. Hemmingsen's natural law theory can thus be seen as an important part of the restructuring of law, which was common to Denmark and the other Lutheran principalities after the abandonment of canon law.[19]

According to Hemmingsen, natural law is also the law of God as God is the creator of nature, and hence he like Luther refers to Paul's statement about the pagans' knowledge of the law. Hemmingsen's interpretation is to the effect that God has given human nature a light that – even though because of the Fall darkened by vices – still retains sparks that can be excited through cogitation (*cogitatio*; Hemmingsen: 1991,16). Hemmingsen uses another metaphor: nature contains seeds of the just (*semina justi*) and the faculty of judgment (*judicium*) that enables humans to prefer the just and the honest (*justa et honesta*) to the unjust and the disgraceful (*injustis et turpidus*; Hemmingsen: 1991, 12).

These seeds or sparks are the natural knowledge (*notitia naturalis*) of the basic difference between the honest and the disgraceful. Despite the depravity of humans, the sparks can be inflamed through good upbringing and the practice of honesty (Hemmingsen: 1993, 290). Hemmingsen's concern is so to speak to carry out these practices on the theoretical level. He wants to bring to light those normative principles which the mentioned seeds or sparks contain, and to for-

16 The full title of the work is *De lege naturae apodictica methodus, concinnata per Nicolaum Hemmingium.* I have used the bilingual edition mentioned in the bibliography. Reference is made to the paragraph-numbering in this edition.

17 Hemmingsen's preoccupation with method is typical of his time, cf. Scattola (1999, 78).

18 "Civitas sine lege, Justiciae Norma, suis partibus [...] uti non potest." (Hemmingsen: 1991, 3).

19 On this process see Witte (2002, 70ff).

mulate, with the help of logical deduction, the fundamental ethical and legal norms. In that endeavor, it will become clear how far human reason can proceed in ethical and legal insight. In any case, however, it is clear that nobody can reach true wisdom and blessedness under the guidance of nature alone (Hemmingsen: 1991, 29). However, even if Hemmingsen regards natural law as given by God, he restricts his outline so as to refrain from using theological statements.[20]

Hemmingsen applies the conceptual apparatus of philosophical theories of knowledge and action to the moral subject that in Luther are more freely described with metaphors such as "heart" and others. Actually the heart according to Hemmingsen is to be understood as designating the inner faculties of the mind (*animae vires interiores*): *intellectio*, *affectio* and *voluntas* (Hemmingsen: 1992, 152).[21] Hemmingsen's definition of natural law reads:

> The law of nature is certain knowledge of the principles of cognition and action divinely imprinted in the human mind, and of the conclusions following these principles and corresponding to the proper destination of man. These conclusions, following necessarily from the principles, are established by reason for the governance of human life in order for humans to cognize, choose and do what is right, and avoid the opposite. As both witness and judge of all this, conscience is given humans in a divine way. (Hemmingsen: 1991, 39).

Hemmingsen himself calls this a broad definition (*definitio plenior*), and in fact, it is not very specific as to the content of natural law. But still a number of important elements are touched upon:

The definition emphasizes that natural law consists of rationally known principles for action and norms deducible from the principles. Elsewhere Hemmingsen talks about evident axioms (Hemmingsen: 1992, 15; Hemmingsen: 1993, 175).

Natural law is related to the destination or goal (*finis*) of human life; Hemmingsen at several places makes clear that the norms of natural law aim at directing humans to their goal, both individually and collectively. And the ultimate goal is God.[22] Conscience plays an important role in the epistemology of natural law. It is a God-given faculty that both discerns the right action, motivates

20 One could speculate that Hemmingsen thereby is taking the first step in the direction of the secularization of natural law, thinking of the latter as expressed in the dictum of Grotius that natural law would be "etsi Deus non daretur" (even if there is no God). Actually, Hemmingsen is by some regarded as a forerunner of Grotius, which however is repudiated by Tamm (1983).

21 I refrain from going into the details of Hemmingsen's moral epistemology and deontic logic (to use contemporary terminology). To a large extent, he adopts classical theory and methodology.

22 According to Scattola (1999, 86), the points 1 and 2 are characteristic of Hemmingsen's approach as he does not derive the concrete norms from innate principles, but rather from the goal of human life, i. e. in the line of Aristotelian teleology.

to act correspondingly, and judges actions (Hemmingsen: 1993, 169ff). Even if no specific norm is mentioned, there is a hint that natural law contains a basic distinction between right and wrong (*recta – contraria*). In the concluding section of the book, he in a similar way makes clear that the basic knowledge of natural law is the distinction between the decent and the disgraceful (*honestus – turpis*; Hemmingsen: 1993, 225). This corresponds to what has been said above about the inborn seeds of light. Hemmingsen's elaboration of the more specific norms of natural law is structured according to three topics: the distinction between a practical and a spiritual form of life, the Decalogue, and the virtues.

In dealing with one of the two forms of life (*genera vitae*), the practical, Hemmingsen presupposes the doctrine of the three estates: "This form of life is triple: economic, political, and spiritual."[23] Two things are interesting here: even though he adopts the Aristotelean distinction between theoretical and practical life, Hemmingsen places the spiritual within the latter.[24] And in connection with the spiritual he does not mention the church at all.

The aim of all three forms of life is self-conservation through one's own actions directed towards God as the final goal. As to the life-form of *oeconomi*a, its aim is the conservation of the family and the house through economic acts (*actiones oeconomicae*; Hemmingsen: 1992, 123). These acts have to be just in the sense that all members of oeconomia render each other their due service, so that sweet harmony (*dulcissima harmonia*) is secured in the home. All acts by spouses, parents, children, etc. that contribute to this harmony are commanded by natural law. The specific norms can both be philosophically derived, and found in the fourth and sixth commandment of the Decalogue.

The goal of the political life-form is "the tranquil and peaceful state of polities through political actions" (Hemmingsen: 1992, 131). As is the case in *oeconomia*, the ideal of political life is harmony marked by justice. Again, all concrete norms and arrangements serving this goal are derivable from natural law. For example, the hierarchical order of rulers and subordinates is required by nature. As God is also the ultimate goal of political life, nothing can take place that conflicts with God. This puts limits both to the actions of rulers and to those of subjects. The latter are not allowed to obey if rulers require ungodly behavior (Hemmingsen: 1992, 149). Hemmingsen mentions the concept magistratus anypeuthynos, a magistrate accountable to nobody. The concept is used by Aristotle to characterize tyranny (1997: 1295 a, 22), but Hemmingsen emphasizes that also a magistrate of this kind can give laws in accordance with natural law. His aim is

23 "Est autem hoc vitae genus triplex: oeconomicum, politicum, et spiritualis." (Hemmingsen: 1992, 123)

24 The theoretical form of life is constituted by contemplation and exploration of truth, which takes place in the sciences and arts (Hemmingsen: 1992, 119).

the opposite of defending tyranny, viz. to picture political rule as legitimized by natural law.[25]

The actions pertaining to spiritual life are knowing, worshipping, fearing and glorifying God. These actions are commanded by natural law and thus not specific to Christians. Hemmingsen explicitly states that they are performed by pagans (*ethnici*; Hemmingsen: 1992, 168). Thus, even if Hemmingsen operates with a trichotomy resembling that of Luther's doctrine of the three estates, he can hardly be said to adhere to that doctrine. The *vita spiritualis* of Hemmingsen is not Luther's *ecclesia!* The reason for this divergence is probably that Hemmingsen only wants to make assertions that reason can extract from natural law. They have to be universal and cannot comprise the specific Christian spirituality that unfolds in the Church. Reason is only able to apprehend that God is to be worshipped!

Directly following the presentation of the three forms of life, we find Hemmingsen's account of the Decalogue. It is true, he says, that the Ten Commandments are called "lex Dei" (God's law), but actually they are a summary of natural law (*Lex Naturae epitome*; Hemmingsen: 1992, 166). Here then Hemmingsen is following Luther, and it is obvious for him that the first tablet is about spiritual life, in that it commands that God is to be worshipped and celebrated (*Deum colendum et celebrandum esse*; Hemmingsen: 1992, 166). In his exposition of the Decalogue, Hemmingsen applies his strict deductive method. In relation to every commandment, he starts with a principle of natural law, from which he by way of syllogism deduces the commandment in question. For example, the major premise of the fourth commandment reads: "Everything that preserves the economic and political status belongs to natural law." The minor premises imply that the fulfilling of their obligations by parents, authorities, children, and subjects contribute to preserving the economic and political status. And from this, it can be concluded that the fourth commandment follows from natural law (Hemmingsen: 1992, 154).

Correspondingly with the sixth commandment: According to natural law, everything that violates decency (honestas) in the economic and political state is prohibited. But now "loose connections" contradict decency, hence the sixth commandment follows from natural law (Hemmingsen: 1992, 156). In examining the commandment more closely, Hemmingsen presents a number of arguments against polygamy, one of which says that if the husband does not want his wife to marry more than one man, he should himself be satisfied with one wife! This statement follows from the well-known natural law rule: *Nemo faciat alii quod sibi nolit fieri* ("Nobody should do to others, what one would not have done to

25 This is pointed out by Glebe-Møller (1979, 47), who remarks that Hemmingsen's political theory is far away from the *rex legibus solutus* principle of absolutism.

oneself"). Remarkably, then, Hemmingsen like Luther emphasizes the Golden Rule, but this rule he only puts forward as one premise among others, not as the summary of natural law. In contrast, the whole second tablet in his opinion can be derived from the commandment of neighborly love, not in the specific Christian, but in a natural sense.[26]

Hemmingsen thus integrates the doctrine of the three estates into his exposition of the Decalogue in such a way that each of the commandments five to ten are about both *oeconomia* and *politia.* As mentioned, the first three commandments according to him are about spiritual life. And the fourth commandment says the essential things about the two "worldly" forms of life. There is no trace of a two kingdoms doctrine in *De lege naturae*, which I, as indicated, suppose can be explained by the fact that Hemmingsen presupposes an organization of the state-church relation that disregards Luther's distinction between the spiritual and worldly.

The third issue, in relation to which Hemmingsen more concretely develops his natural law theory, is the virtue ethics of classical philosophy. Among the virtues, Hemmingsen attaches particular significance to justice. Within the complex content of this virtue, we find three fundamental norms: 1) Nobody is allowed to hurt others. 2) Everybody should receive his/her due. 3) Everything should be subordinated to common utility. The second norm is, of course, equivalent to the classical definition of justice: *suum cuique tribuere* (Hemmingsen: 1993, 175–177).

According to Hemmingsen the concept of law (*jus*) too has to be understood from justice (*justitia*, τὸ δίκαιον). He distinguishes between three forms of law: *jus naturale*, *jus gentium*, and *jus civile.* The first, nature-based law probably is to be regarded as natural law specified into concrete but nonetheless universal principles of law. *Jus gentium* is the law which the peoples actually follow, and which implies reverence to God, religion and mother country. And finally, civil law, of course, is the particular law established by individual peoples, i. e. positive law. But for all kinds of law, it is a requirement that they can be shown to be derived from the axioms of nature (Hemmingsen: 1993, 196).

Hemmingsen's approach to natural law, then, is significantly different from Luther's. The reformer so to speak looks at natural law from the perspective of Christian faith: a Christian knows that also non-Christians have some knowledge of God's law, wherefore he or she can appeal to ethical and legal knowledge in people even if they do not want to be judged according to neighborly love. Hemmingsen takes the standpoint of natural law itself, and expounds its content on the basis of the universal "sparks" of light in the human mind. Accordingly, he almost exclusively draws on ancient sources, both philosophical and poetic.

26 "[...] ex Lege Dilectionis proximi, quae naturalis est" (Hemmingsen: 1992, 192).

Whereas *Liffsens Vey* (1570) according to the presentation by Mattias Skat Sommer in this volume can be seen as an expression of a Danish confessional culture, this is hardly the case with *De lege naturae* – for obvious reasons. The two components of "Konfessionskultur" – confession and culture – each express themselves in various degrees, depending on e.g. the kind of text in question. Now, a treatise on natural law almost by definition pretends to be independent of specific confessional and cultural features.

As already indicated, Hemmingsen's perspective on natural law – expounding it on purely rational grounds – can be seen as a step in the direction of secularization in the sense of emancipation from religious premises. However, if one adopts Charles Taylor's concept of the secular – belief in God is one option among many – then Hemmingsen is not a secular thinker at all. He still presupposes "a society in which it was virtually impossible not to believe in God" (Taylor: 2007, 3). The "social imaginary" of which his treatise is the theoretical counterpart must be characterized as pre-modern.[27]

As to the distinction between the three estates, I would claim that Hemmingsen is using it as a structuring tool for his exposition of natural law, rather than presenting a proper theory about the three. Obviously, there is nothing specifically "Lutheran" to presupposing the Aristotelean distinction between oeconomia and politia when dealing with social life. And as we have seen, the identity of the third "estate" is not quite clear. In Luther himself, it can both be ecclesia in the strict sense of the Christian church – and the universal institution of worshipping God. Hemmingsen seems to distribute these two meanings to *Liffsens Vey* and *De lege naturae* respectively.[28]

4. Holberg: Natural Law without Three Estates Doctrine?

Niels Hemmingsen's ethical and legal thinking can, as indicated, be seen as one step in the direction of a secularization of natural law, i.e. a way of thought that takes its point of departure in the rational part of the theory, formulating the normativity known to universal human reason. Ludvig Holberg (1684–1754), Danish scholar and playwright, can be regarded as a thinker who presupposes

27 Taylor's (2007, 171) definition of "social imaginary" reads: "[T]he ways in which [people] imagine their social existence, how they fit together with others, how things go on between them and their fellows, the expectations which are normally met, and the deeper normative notions and images which underlie these expectations."

28 An indication that Hemmingsen does not strongly advocate a three estates doctrine is the already mentioned fact that he, besides the spiritual aspect of the practical life form, operates with a theoretical genus vitae, placing the arts and sciences within the latter. Seemingly, social life is already too complex and differentiated as to be contained within three "estates."

that further steps on the way of secularisation have been taken. His *Introduction til Naturens- og Folkerettens kundskab* (i. e. "Introduction to the knowledge of the law of nature and peoples") from 1716 is based upon an already developed Protestant natural law theory: *Uddragen af de fornemste juristers besynderlig Grotii, Pufendorfs og Thomasii skrifter* (i. e. "Extracted from the most prominent jurists' works, particularly Grotius', Pufendorf's and Thomasius'"). The latter two – Samuel Pufendorf (1632–94) and Christian Thomasius (1655–1728) – are the main representatives of Lutheran natural law theory.[29] Apart from these Holberg can further – unlike Hemmingsen – presuppose a unified Danish legislation in the shape of Christian V's *Danish Code* from 1683. The following presentation is based upon Holberg's second work on natural law: *Naturens og Folke-Rettens Kundskab.*

In the preface, Holberg briefly touches upon the history of ethics and natural law thinking. After the "barbaric" times of Scholasticism, the great Lutheran Reformation cultivated moral insight with Melanchthon as the first of the Protestants to deal with the matter of natural law (Holberg: 1969, 56). Holberg thus does not seem to be aware of Luther's own natural law thinking. Among the modern natural law theorists Holberg mentions Grotius and Hobbes; of the latter, he says that his works are regarded as godless and misshapen. In contrast, the system of Pufendorf is praised as the best and most perfect. A closer look at Holberg's book reveals that he very closely follows Pufendorf's shorter treatise *De officio hominis et civis juxta legem naturalem libri duo* (1673/1758). Because of its impact on Holberg's view, I shall mention a few major points in Pufendorf's theory.

According to Pufendorf, the most fundamental prescription of natural law is this: "Every human being must according to his capability protect and serve sociality." (Pufendorf: 1673/2001, 64). Even if all humans are able to know the norms of natural law thanks to reason, Pufendorf emphasizes that human nature is corrupted (Pufendorf: 1673/2001, 36). This can be regarded as a specific Lutheran feature implying a rejection of the idea that natural law is based on a common human inclination.[30] In Pufendorf, the basic insight concerning natural law is that God has created human beings for social life. As far as I can see, there is no trace of a three estates doctrine in Pufendorf. In his view, earthly human life is structured differently. Basically, one has to distinguish between two conditions (statuses): the natural and the social. In the state of nature, humans are endowed

29 Important local predecessors of Holberg with regard to natural law theory were Heinrich Weghorst (1653–1722) and Christian Reitzer (1665–1736). The latter, having studied with Thomasius in Halle, was a follower of Pufendorf, whom he introduced to Holberg. For the positions held by Weghorst and Reitzer see Jensen (2016).

30 This is the main thesis in Saastamoinen (1995), a very careful and convincing analysis of Pufendorf's theory.

with the noble right not to be subordinated to anybody but God, which equals natural freedom. The state of nature comprises three relations: to God, to oneself, and to others. The institution of marriage does not belong to the state of nature, but is rather a product of human convention (Pufendorf: 1673/2001, 142–147).

Following Pufendorf, Holberg divides his book into two parts, the first containing some theory of action, the basic definitions of natural law, and a presentation of humans' obligations in relation to God, self, and others. The second part deals with family and the state.

Natural law originates from the capacity defining humans' specific status in relation to "tongueless beasts": their rational soul and their intellect. This latter contains a light, thanks to which we can recognize natural rightness, i.e. the difference between good and evil. Conscience is part of this light. To the rational soul also belongs the will in the sense of the ability to choose and do the right. Holberg retains the traditional thought – also emphasized by Pufendorf – that natural law has its deepest origin in God: "Every rational soul can know that the same who has created all things, also has given the natural laws." (Holberg: 1969, 74).

As to the content of natural law, Holberg, unlike Hemmingsen, adopts the traditional view of the Golden Rule as its summary: "that great commandment of nature; namely: That you must not do to another that which you do not want to befall yourself." (Holberg: 1969, 78). However, Holberg's own (or Pufendorf's), more specific definition reads:

> The groundwork of natural law is that every human, as far as he is concerned, must support equal interaction and society, wherefrom follows that whatever generally helps such interaction and association is commanded by natural law, and what contradicts it is forbidden by that same natural law. In this general law all other commandments are contained. (Holberg: 1969, 80).

As in Hemmingsen and Pufendorf, the essential goal of natural law is the conservation of human sociality.

As indicated, Holberg begins the concrete exposition of the content of natural law with humans' obligation towards themselves and the neighbor. The most important of the latter is not to harm, and then first follows the obligation to contribute to the benefit and utility of the other. That Holberg is thinking on the conditions of modernity becomes clear from his emphasis on self-estimation, the foundation of which is:

> [h]uman nature; for in that word human being there is thought to be some dignity, and it is the strongest argument against those who despise others: I am a human being like yourself; and as human nature is granted all humans in the same degree, it follows that everybody must respect a human being as someone who by nature is like oneself (Holberg: 1969, 112).

Remarkably, Holberg in this grounding first part discusses in detail such concepts as pact, oath, property, value, money, and contract. These highly economic concepts he treats without any reference to oeconomia in the sense of the three estates doctrine.

Holberg opens the second part with a treatment of marriage, but note as the introduction for an exposition of "the nature and origin of human rule." Marriage, after all, is the institution, "wherefrom the families have their origin, and likewise out of which cities and governments are erected" (Holberg: 1969, 249). In the more detailed account of marriage and parenthood, the concept of contract plays an essential role. Spouses are principally equal partners who have entered into a contract with the main goal of procreating. As this does not presuppose a life-long relation, the latter cannot be ordered by natural law but is a specific Christian commandment. Holberg refers to Pufendorf who, following natural law, attributes to the children an equal standing with their parents. They too are contract partners in that they – in a counterfactual way – are supposed to have given their consent to the authority of the parents!

The basic idea about equal and free individuals entering into contracts is also at the foundation of Holberg's understanding of "cities" and republics. The latter concept here does not mean a non-monarchical form of government, but rather the original *res publica.*

Even if Holberg regards the ideas of Thomas Hobbes as "ungodly and malformed," in the end, he agrees with the understanding of the origin of political order:

> The right reason why societies and cities are constituted is the fear one human has for the evil of the other, and therefore the first humans have subordinated themselves to laws and authorities who could protect the weak against the strong, and punish evil that was previously rampant, for if law and order did not exist, one human would – as the saying goes – swallow up the other (Holberg: 1969, 284).

Holberg retains the Lutheran thought that the political order is given by God, though only in the weak meaning that God is the origin of natural law. Actually, contract theory marks a significant breach with the Lutheran idea of the institution of government as an order of creation. Holberg does not see human beings as placed in politia as an order of creation. On the contrary, humans are created in a state of nature, which they only leave by concluding a double social contract: partly to enter into community in the first place, and partly to establish an authority that can sustain law and order. This latter contract can issue in both aristocracy and democracy as form of government. Holberg however prefers monarchy, and his understanding of absolutism is modern in the sense that he interprets its introduction in Denmark in 1660 as being based upon a contract between the king and the people.[31]

All in all, Holberg develops the theory of natural law without connection to a doctrine of three estates. One could say that the very concept of estate in the sense of a given social framework is now problematized, in that humans for Holberg are created free, and themselves provide through contracts those institutions – including marriage and state – that frame their social lives. Institutions are only God-given in the very indirect sense that God is the originator of natural law, on the basis of which humans themselves establish the social framework.[32]

5. Conclusion

The foregoing seems to indicate that the conceptual complexity of the two kingdoms doctrine, the doctrine of three estates, and natural law theory, serves different purposes in different contexts.

In Luther, the two kingdoms doctrine is a distinction between two forms of divine action in relation to human life: sustaining ordinary life (worldly) and bringing salvation (spiritual). The distinction means that the corresponding "logics" on the human side may not be mixed: the freedom of the Gospel cannot be transposed to worldly affairs, and worldly power may not intrude spiritual matters. The discourse of the three estates, on the other hand, emphasizes the

31 This interpretation is sometimes called "opinion-based absolutism" (opionsstyret enevælde). According to some scholars the defense of absolutism by Danish theologian N. F.S. Grundtvig (1783–1872) is inspired by Holberg. Holberg in a way defended this version of absolutism against Montesquieu, who in the opening chapters of *De l'ésprit des lois* deals with the different forms of government: republicanism, monarchy, and despotism. Republicanism can have the shape of either democracy or aristocracy, and according to their nature and principles, the two require virtue and modesty respectively. Virtue in the case of democracy means both patriotism and love for equality. Monarchy – law-based sole reign – functions without virtue in that ambition and striving for honor suffices as motivation for political action. Finally, despotism is defined as sole reign without constraining laws; here fear is the crucial motivation. (Montesquieu: 1759, part one, books 1–3; 1998). Holberg first formulated his critique in his Danish *Epistles* and later published it in French (Holberg: 1753). He rejects the connection Montesquieu makes between the principle of a given form of government, and its motivating virtue – or the lack of the same. For Holberg, it is not the form that determines the success of government, but rather the properties of the reigning persons. Hence, a subject in an (absolutist) monarchy can "love his fatherland and his king as well as a republican can." (Holberg: 1753, Ep. 514). For the appropriateness of Holberg's critique in the context of political thinking around 1789, see Østergård (1995).

32 A relation with the concrete social conditions in Denmark at that time can probably be seen in the fact that the natural law and human rights thinking represented by Holberg is an important basis of ideas for the agricultural reforms of the eighteenth century. For this issue see Løgstrup (2015).

similarity between human actions in relation to the two kingdoms: both of these are frameworks ordained by God so that the church is placed in line with the two worldly orders *oeconomia* and *politia*. As to natural law, one of its functions is to afford a normative foundation for worldly life that also non-Christians can endorse.

In Hemmingsen's theory of natural law, the distinction between the two kingdoms plays no role. The reason for this could be that Hemmingsen presupposes a political order with the church integrated under royal rule. This integration seems to be legitimated by the doctrine of three estates. And natural law is not so much a conflict-solving platform for consensus, but rather a theoretical tool for harmonizing the law of the Lutheran polity. According to Thomas Kaufmann Lutheran confessional culture, in the beginning, was characterized by a conservative tendency centered on the concept of orders: "For God had given this world a good order; the three estates, the *status politicus*, the *status oeconomicus* and the *status ecclesiasticus* provided for that."[33] Hemmingsen's combination of natural law theory and three estates doctrine can be seen as an expression of this feature of Lutheran confessional culture.

Holberg substitutes the idea of given orders for human social life with the modern distinction between the state of nature and the state of society. Even if God is still the author of natural law, the idea of the social contract opens a space for human freedom and endeavor, which can be seen both in the interpretation of absolutism and in the actual social reforms. At the level of theory, Holberg expresses some features belonging to the social imaginary of modernity. Whereas according to premodern imaginary humans were embedded in a given order – both social and cosmic – the modern imaginary sees humans as rational agents co-operating for mutual benefit. According to Charles Taylor, modern natural law theory is a crucial counterpart to this imaginary (Taylor: 2007, 159–171). Holberg's account of natural law can be seen as a manifestation of this shift to modernity.

All in all, our conceptual complex is subject to development in the sense that the two kingdoms doctrine is abandoned at first because social and political reality is defined by the Lutheran prince church-state. In Hemmingsen, we see a version of natural law theory with this state as its precondition and connected to the doctrine of the three estates. In a next step – the one of modernity – natural law theory is developed in such a way that also the doctrine of the three estates is abandoned. If one is allowed to raise the question about the possibility of a contemporary Lutheran social thinking, I would say that it should re-discover

33 "Denn Gott hatte dieser Welt eine gute Ordnung gegeben; die drei Stände, der status politicus, der status oeconomicus und der status ecclesiasticus, gewährleisteten diese." (Kaufmann: 2006, 22).

and reformulate the doctrine of two regiments and connect it with a contemporary version of natural law theory.

Bibliography

ANDERSEN, SVEND (2010), Macht aus Liebe: Zur Rekonstruktion einer lutherischen politischen Ethik (TBT 149), Berlin, New York: de Gruyter.

ANDERSEN, SVEND (2017), The Golden Rule: An Anthropological Universal?, in: Eve-Marie Becker/Jan Dietrich/Bo Kristian Holm (ed.), "What is Human?" Theological Encounters with Anthropology, Göttingen: Vandenhoeck & Ruprecht, 171–195.

ARISTOTLE (1977), Politics, trans. H. Rackham, (Loeb Classical Library 264), Cambridge, MA/London: Heinemann.

ASSENDORF, ULRICH (1998), Lectura in Biblia: Luthers Genesisvorlesung (1535–1545), FSÖTh 87, Göttingen: Vandenhoeck & Ruprecht.

BAYER, OSWALD (2008), Martin Luther's Theology: A Contemporary Interpretation, Grand Rapids, MI: William B. Eerdmans.

GILBY, THOMAS (ed.) (1966), Law and Political Theory (1a2æ. 90–97) (St Thomas Aquinas Summa Theologiæ vol. 28), London/New York, NY: Eyre & Spottiswoode/McGraw-Hill Book Company.

GLEBE-MØLLER, JENS (1979), Socialetiske aspekter af Niels Hemmingsens forfatterskab, KHS, 7–56.

GLEBE-MØLLER, JENS (2014), Omkring suspensionen af Niels Hemmingsen i 1576, KHS, 209–219.

HEMMINGSEN, NIELS (1562/1991), Om Naturens Lov 1562, 1. Part, trans. Richard Mott, Copenhagen: Forlaget Øresund.

HEMMINGSEN, NIELS (1562/1992), Om Naturens Lov 1562, 2. Part, trans. Richard Mott, Copenhagen: Forlaget Øresund.

HEMMINGSEN, NIELS (1562/1993), 3. Part, trans. Richard Mott, Copenhagen: Forlaget Øresund.

HOLBERG, LUDVIG (1751/1969), Naturens og Folke-Rettens Kundskab, in: F.J. Billeskov Jansen (ed.), Værker i tolv bind: Digteren, Historikeren, Juristen, Vismanden, vol. 1, Copenhagen: Rosenkilde og Bagger, 41–423.

HOLBERG, LUDVIG (1753), Remarques sur quelques positions qui se trouvent dans L'Esprit des loix, Copenhagen: Otto Christoph Wentzel.

HOLBERG, LUDVIG (1754), Epistler, Befattende Adskillige Historiske, Politiske, Metaphysiske, Moralske, Philosophiske, Item Skiemtsomme Materier, Copenhagen: s.n.

JENSEN, MADS LANGBALLE (2016), Contests about Natural Law in Early Enlightenment Copenhagen, History of European Ideas 42, 1027–1041.

KAUFMANN, THOMAS (2006), Konfession und Kultur: Lutherischer Protestantismus in der Zweiten Hälfte des Reformationsjahrhunderts, SuR.NR 29, Tübingen: Mohr Siebeck.

LEHMANN, ROLAND M. (2015), Luthers Naturrechtsverständnis, ZEvKR 60, 369–408.

LUTHER, MARTIN (1519), The Holy and Blessed Sacrament of Baptism (LW 35: 29–43/WA 2: 727–737).

LUTHER, MARTIN (1522), Preface to Paul's Letter to the Romans (LW 35: 365–380/WA DB 7: 2–27).

LUTHER, MARTIN (1523), On Secular Authority (LW 45: 81–129/WA 11: 245–280).

LUTHER, MARTIN (1524), Trade and Usury (LW 45: 245–310/WA 15: 293–322).

LUTHER, MARTIN (1524), Ein unterrichtung wie sich die Christen ynn Mosen sollen schicken, gepredigt durch Mart. Luther (WA 24: 2–16)

LUTHER, MARTIN (1525) Against the Heavenly Prophets in the Matters of Images and Sacraments (LW 40: 79–223/WA 18: 62–125.134–214)

LUTHER, MARTIN (1526), Whether Soldiers, Too, Can Be Saved (LW 46: 93–137/WA 19: 623–662).

LUTHER, MARTIN (1527), Exposition of Psalm 127, for the Christians at Riga in Livonia (LW 45: 317–337/WA 15, 360–378).

LUTHER, MARTIN (1528), Confession Concerning Christ's Supper (LW 37: 161–372/WA 26: 261–509).

LUTHER, MARTIN (1529), On War Against the Turk (LW 46: 161–205/WA 30 II: 107–148).

LUTHER, MARTIN (1531/1535), Lectures on Galatians (LW 26–27/WA 40 I–40 II).

LUTHER, MARTIN (1532), Commentary on the Sermon on the Mount (LW 21: 3–294/WA 32: 299–544).

LUTHER, MARTIN (1535–1545), Lectures on Genesis (LW 1–8/WA 42–44).

LUTHER, MARTIN (1539), On the Councils and the Church (LW 41/WA 50: 509–653).

LØGSTRUP, BIRGIT (2015), Bondens frisættelse: De danske landboreformer 1750–1810, Copenhagen: Gad.

MAURER, WILHELM (1970), Luthers Lehre von den drei Hierarchien und ihr Mittelalterlicher Hintergrund, München: Verlag der Bayerischen Akademie der Wissenschaften.

MELANCHTHON, PHILIPP (1521/1997), Loci communes: Lateinisch-Deutsch, trans. H.G. Pöhlmann, 2nd ed., Gütersloh: Gütersloher Verlagshaus.

MELANCHTHON, PHILIPP (1997), Melanchthon deutsch, vol. 2: Theologie und Kirchenpolitik, Leipzig: Evangelische Verlagsanstalt.

MONTESQUIEU (1759), De L'ésprit des Lois, Copenhagen: Philibert.

MONTESQUIEU (1998), Om lovenes ånd, Copenhagen: Gad.

PUFENDORF, SAMUEL (1673/1758), DE OFFICIO HOMINIS ET CIVIS JUXTA LEGEM NATURALEM, LIBRI DUO, LONDON: W. Thurlbourn & J. Woodyer.

PUFENDORF, SAMUEL (1673/2001), Om de mänskliga och medborgerliga plikterna enligt naturrätten, trans. Birger Bergh, Stockholm: City University Press.

SAARINEN, RISTO (2005), Ethics in Luther's Theology: The Three Orders, in: J.Kraye/Risto Sarinen (ed.), Moral Philosophy on the Threshold of Modernity, Dordrecht: Springer.

SAASTAMOINEN, KARI (1995), The Morality of the Fallen Man: Samuel Pufendorf on Natural Law, Helsinki: SHS.

SCATOLLA, MERIO (1999), Das Naturrecht vor dem Naturrecht: Zur Geschichte des "ius naturae" im 16. Jahrhundert(Frühe Neuzeit 52), Tübingen: Niemeyer.

SCHORN-SCHÜTTE, LUISE (1998), Die Drei-Stände-Lehre im reformatorischen Umbruch, in: Bernd Moeller (ed.), Die Frühe Reformation in Deutschland als Umbruch (SVRG 199), Gütersloh: Gütersloher Verlagshaus, 435–461.

SCHWARZ, REINHARD (1984), Ecclesia, oeconomia, politia: Sozialgeschichtliche und fundamentalethische Aspekte der protestantischen Drei-Stände-Theorie, in: H. Renz/

F. W. Graf (ed.), Protestantismus und Neuzeit (Troeltsch-Studien 3), Gütersloh: Gütersloher Verlagshaus.

TAMM, DITLEV (1983), Nolo falcem in alienam messem mittere: Der dänische Theologe Niels Hemmingsen (1513–1600) aus juristischer Sicht, in: Karl Kroeschell (ed.), Gerichtslauben-Vorträge: Freiburger Festkolloquium zum 75. Geburtstag von Hans Thieme, Sigmaringen: Jan Thorbecke, 47–56.

TAYLOR, CHARLES (2007), A Secular Age, Cambridge, MA/ London: The Belknap Press of Harvard University Press.

WITTE JR., JOHN (2002), Law and Protestantism: The Legal Teachings of the Lutheran Reformation, Cambridge: Cambridge University Press.

ØSTERGÅRD, UFFE (1995), "Republican Revolution or Absolutist Reform?", in: G. M. Schwab/J. R. Jeanneney (ed.), The French Revolution of 1789 and Its Impact, Westport, CT: Greenwood Press, 22–56.

Gorm Harste

A Culture of Sovereignty

The Constitutionalization of a Danish Mythology

1. Introduction

The present chapter depicts how the Reformation developed after its preliminary stage in the sixteenth century. Confessional conflicts escalated into military competition and its "reason of state." A French conceptualization framed by Jean Bodin compromised the centrist Catholic view of social organization and a more decentrist Calvinistic view. The hypothesis of this chapter is that Bodin probably followed a Lutheran interpretation of social organization and, therefore, his ideas became extremely useful to Danish state-builders. Nowhere else was absolutist sovereignty constitutionalized in such a penetrating top-down and bottom-up form as the Danish monarchy. The key framework of loyalty and obedience established then still survives today.

The main theme of Immanuel Kant's social and political philosophy develops from his counterposition of reason and nature (Kant: 1790/1974). He likened this distinction to the difference between peace and war, but differentiated it from good and evil. Evil is part of reason. Kant's hope for an eternal peace was that the realities of war became so complex that war was only possible if states copied innovations and, in particular, organizational, legal, and political reforms from each other and thereby actually converged. Hence, the subjects of the state can have whatever moral they will as long as they remain loyal to their duties: "the state itself needs a society of devils" (Kant: 1795/1977; Höffe: 1988; Harste: 2009). This promise lay embedded into past narratives about the future of a free autonomous and sovereign morality somehow differentiated from those particular forms. The narratives began to develop and take shape during the Reformation three centuries before. However, in the sixteenth century, the potential of this new form of rule of law in modern states was severely contested because it was born alongside other narratives about the religious form of social and political order. Subjective faith was about to become autonomous, however, in contrast to a form that remained insecure and without any certainty, such as modern state security (Schrimm-Heinz: 1991; Schrimm-Heinz: 1992). Hence, conflicts about social forms escalated to unprecedented levels. Early modern state-building took place in the midst of these conflicts. However, there is no simple road that leads from a Catholic unified Christianity into a sovereign, unified nation-state. Such a narrative is mythological; other narratives do not confirm it.

In Heinz Schilling's study of confessionalization and state-building, he argues, on the one hand, that a second reformation of political protest occurred after the initial Lutheran years and, on the other hand, that this political protest involved a theological, not to say semantic, specification (Schilling: 1981). Thomas Kaufmann has also affirmed this description of a double phase of the Reformation. He articulated this as a second phase of confessional culture, in which the symbolic codes of confessions found a context in the practices, institutionalized rituals, and meanings of a larger political context themselves (Kaufmann: 2006; 2009, 26, 702–709).

The present analysis takes its departure from Schilling's idea (Schilling: 1981, 36; 2009) that we have to distinguish between settings, in which the theological specification was sharpened in a critical contestation to state-building, and those settings in which the early modern reason of state was affirmed and authorized by those religious foundations. Schilling refers to Poland, the Netherlands, and, of course, to the mixed state- and "Stadt"-constructions in the German Empire. Not to mention what happened in Habsburg Empire where the Counter-Reformation occurred, the Reformation, however, led to a different, unique state formation. In the two Nordic Empires of the Danish monarchy and the Swedish monarchy, Protestantism supplied religious authorization to constitutionalize the state in legal, organizational, and political ways (Stolleis: 1990; Jespersen: 1989, 222; Jespersen: 1984; Lindegren: 1984; Knudsen: 2000; Ingesman: 2000). Hence, the religiously authorized constitutionalization actually occurred earlier than the typical narrative about a war-driven constitutionalization that is usually discussed (Gustafsson: 1994). However, this later structural coupling between war, state-organization, and religion must be studied in accordance with the path-dependencies of institutional history formed in the sixteenth century. More than in British state-formation, this structural coupling would reform and transform the goal and purpose of state-building in the seventeenth century. And yet, state-building was not only empowered by its own Nordic religious reformation, but also because the Nordic state formation created a *reason of state* in accordance and cooperation with French trans-confessional state formation.

In France, religious wars led to a compromise between the decentrist strand of the "Reformists" and the more centrist Catholics. In 1576, Jean Bodin theoretically described this compromise well, and his ideas were later implemented by Armand Richelieu and Baptiste Colbert. Bodin's compromise was imported to the Danish monarchy as constitutive for absolutism where it was given a particularly Lutheran form. In this sense, the Danish state-formation became the *exempli gratia* of the line between the Reformation and modern absolutist state-building; paradoxically, this state also eventually developed into a democratic state in which monarchical sovereignty was replaced by the absolute sovereignty of the people. Hence, my thesis does not conform to the so-called Tilly-thesis that "war makes states and states make war" (Tilly: 1992), since the form of the religious authorization was decisive for the invention of a new modern organization of states, albeit this modern form was rarely known to the inventors themselves, if at all.

According to a short formula established in article 16 of Philip Melanchthon's Augsburg Confession from 1530 ("Von Policey und weltlichen regiment"), the government ("Oberkeit") was not politically questioned by any kind of natural and divine law. On the contrary, it was to be confirmed:

> Concerning public order and secular government it is taught that all political authority, orderly government, laws, and good order in the world are created and instituted by God and that Christians may without sin exercise political authority; be princes and judges; pass sentences and administer justice according to imperial and other existing laws; punish evildoers with the sword; wage just wars; serve as soldiers; buy and sell; take required oaths; possess property; be married; etc.
>
> Condemned here are the Anabaptists who teach that none of the things indicated above is Christian.
>
> Also condemned are those who teach that Christian perfection means physically leaving house and home, spouse and child, and refraining from the above-mentioned activities. In fact, the only true perfection is true fear of God and true faith in God. For the gospel teaches an internal, eternal reality and righteousness of the heart, not an external, temporal one. The gospel does not overthrow secular government, public order, and marriage but instead intends that a person keep all this as a true order of God and demonstrate in these walks of life Christian love and true good works according to each person's calling. Christians, therefore, are obliged to be subject to political authority and to obey its commands and laws in all that may be done without sin. But if a command of the political authority cannot be followed without sin, one must obey God rather than any human beings (Acts 5[:29]). (BC 48.50/BSELK 110.112).

Divine law actually constituted government; it did not question government. According to the classic Augustinian and Lutheran "two regiments" doctrine, the theological authorization of power was simply immanently embedded in this form (Quillet: 1972). The modern concept "state" is certainly not adequate to describe this form of "upper hand" or "superiority" in what at that time most often was conceived as "government" and "res publica" (Koselleck et al.: 1990; Luhmann: 1989a; 1995). Rather, the reformulation in Article 16 found a form in between the papal eternal regiment and the emperor's earthly temporal regiment

(Franklin: 1973). It constituted new forms, a Reformation. But it did not in itself constitute revolutionized modern states built upon a military revolution of navies, fortifications, taxation, tax administration, legal regulation of military finances perhaps a hundred times larger than the construction of power organized before – measured in social, material and temporal complexities of manpower, equipment and finance (Harste: 2014).

According to Luther (1525), obedience to God and ruler meant that "the will is bound"; this was a rejection of the will's freedom. Yet free will is committed will. Today, following Fredrick the Great's criticism of d'Holbach's mechanicism and Kant's *Critique of Practical Reason*, we could conclude with Kant in *Religion within the Limits of Bare Reason* to have a priori knowledge that Luther in his claim for obedient faith established a series of logical, pragmatic and ontological failures, albeit faith is accepted as sinful (Kant: 1794/1977). Indispensably, the will has to will itself, which is a general condition of reason and reasoning in language and not of faith (Allison: 1990, 147). However, to both Luther and Kant transcendent commitment is central, but more than faith, reason is committed beyond earthly desires. Such a pure philosophical statement demands further elaboration and opens itself up to both disobedience in thought and faith like the level of such civil servant obedience to external behavior discussed in Kant's famous article "An Answer to the Question: What is Enlightenment?" (Langer: 1986). However, the point in this chapter is different.

As Erasmus from Rotterdam attested in his 1524 *On Free Will* and his forecasts in the 1515 *Against War* and the 1517 *Complaint of Peace*, in Luther's own day religious wars and the corresponding escalation of armament were already becoming the unintended, but most probable consequences of absolute religious confessions opposed to each other. Erasmus and Luther's quarrel imagined the Catholic and Lutheran positions as they developed after 1517. Erasmus was right. His nightmares became reality, at first with the 1522 Knights' Revolt, and Luther too was shocked by the bloody German Peasant Wars in Southwest Germany in 1524 and 1525. As Kant later described, however, organization for war also paved the way for peace. Escalation risked the "horror of hell"; but with its increasingly complex organization, law, education, welfare, and even democracy also emerged as its consequences. Eventually, neither Catholics nor Lutherans turned out to be angels or devils.

In this chapter, I will examine first how the co-evolution of Reformation and "la raison d'État" developed in the sixteenth century, with reason of state as the answer to the Reformation quarrels. Second, I will briefly reconstruct the development of the French religious wars in order to establish a general model about absolutist state-building using Jean Bodin's theory of sovereign power as an apparently Lutheran construction. Third, Bodin's notion of sovereign power seems influenced by Lutheran doctrines about obedience in centers and in peripheral administration. Fourth, this idea of absolute sovereign rule by the divine grace became constitutive in the Danish monarchy as both top-down and bottom-up reform. In this way, the Danish state was organized in such a way that it could reorganize and – as a result – expect citizen loyalty even during inflated reform and "reorganization fever."

2. The Co-Evolution of Reformation and Militarily Revolutionized "Reason of State"

If we examine the co-evolution of state and religion in the sixteenth century, we observe on the one hand the Reformation's impact on the institutionalized Catholic form of a theological self-description of the church as a center for rituals and faith (Luhmann: 1977; 1990). If this line of analysis is isolated from sociology, the widely used concept of "secularization" narrows the analysis of a theological revolution of religion. In this vein, such a narrative isolates theology to a specifically differentiated conception, which misunderstands how religion established a far wider constitution of early modernity. From Talcott Parsons to Niklas Luhmann, such a differentiation is what German sociologists explain this kind of differentiation as a sub-differentiation or *Ausdifferenzierung* that is part of a wider structural coupling to other sub-differentiated forms in, for example, law, war, finance, and organization (Parsons: 1971, 35–49; 1978; Luhmann: 1989c).

On the other hand, the evil underbelly of the beauty-painted image is seldom analyzed in its structural couplings between political science, historical sociology, or in theology (exceptions are Bonney: 1991 and van Creveld: 1999, 170ff). Beyond any observable vision in the early sixteenth century, the diabolic "cunning of reason" (Hegel) is that this century witnessed a still more accelerated military revolution, which completely transformed the goal and focus of state power (and financial power). The power of the sword dramatically transformed the proper constitution of political organization. Certainly, Niccolò Machiavelli describes too simplistic a vision of this development in *The Art of War* (*L'arte della Guerra*, 1521). In Luther's introduction to his 1520 *Address to the Nobility of the German Nation*, he indicates some vague, but developing intuitions that "we must realize that in this matter we are not dealing with men, but with the princes of hell [that] could fill the world with war and bloodshed" (LW 44: 125/WA 6: 408,7ff). Luther's reform competitor, Erasmus of Rotterdam, alone was far more aware of both the risks and possibilities embedded into the conflict of confessional cultures. He tried to describe how the will to reason and to believe in an undogmatic way without ontological, pragmatic, and temporal fallacies could constitutionalize diplomacy and cooperation (Halkin: 1987; Zweig: 1934/2015).

In this sense, Erasmus preceded a Kantian mindset by centuries (Koskenniemi: 2006; Heerikhuizen: 2008). Erasmus's idea was useful for diplomacy, but Luther's idea was useful for state-building, especially in places like the Nordic states.

For a brief overview of the last 500 years of the reform period and the 500 years preceding it, see table 1.

Nine phases of transformed constitutionalism	**Forms of legitimacy**	**Forms of state power**
1054–1494	Catholic coordination and synchronization of inclusion and excommunication.	Corpus spiritus of the Church; church law.
1494–1529	Early Lutheran Reformation in Germany. Luther's (1523) *On Secular Authority*; Erasmus's (1517) *Complaint of Peace.*	Danish massacre of Swedish aristocrats in Stockholm 1522; The military revolution of cannons and powder; German Peasant Wars 1525; Danish "Count's Feud" (1534–1536).
1529–1555	The Augsburg Confession, Schmalkaldic War, *Landfriede* (Peace of Augsburg).	Consolidation.
1555–1618	Lutheran rule of estate, establishment of rule in parishes.	Military armament, first and second Danish-Swedish wars; early central administration.
1618–1660	Noble councils.	Contested military reforms, Thirty Years War, Denmark partly conquered 1627, 1643–1645, 1657–1660.
1660–1722	Absolute constitution, divine rule.	Military and organizational revolution in Denmark.
1722–1815	Triumph of absolutist rule, reform fever.	Tax reforms, extremely armed military state.
1815–2001	From Lutheran absolutism to democratic welfare state and Rechtsstaat.	Stabilized frame of ministerial rule.
2001–	Rule of law shrinking; Lutheran work ethics of obedience, Calvinist work ethics of discipline.	Reconstitutionalized state of exception.

Table 1. Legitimacy and power context for the Danish monarchy

3. French Lessons of Trans-confessionalism: Jean Bodin and the Constitution of Sovereignty

Lutheranism had a lasting impact on French social, philosophical, and theological thought. Luther was frequently discussed in the mid-sixteenth-century France (Calvin, Beza, Budé), yet the important point is that Luther understood the form of faith to be unconditionally separated from the organizational form of the institution. Human beings should not be judged by their acts, but according to their faith. Thus, their acts alone were subject to worldly power because guilt, sin, piety, innocence, shame, and honor transcended earthly life. Inclusion into eternal recognition was distinct from inclusion in earthly life.

Niklas Luhmann's analysis of the abstraction process in the inclusion of membership focuses the "take-off" (Luhmann: 1997, 565; 2000) of the self-description in organizational systems. This narrows the sought after take-off to what French historian Barnard Barbiche (1987) calls the "organizational revolution." Michael Stolleis, in *Staat und Staatsräson in der Frühen Neuzeit* (1990) has argued that all along with major developments of state power, new ethics of civil servants emerged at the individual and corporate level, including the level of the elite estates nearest to the princes.

The focus is limited to seek transformations in between Claude Seyssel's *Monarchie de la France* (1516) and Niccolò Machiavelli's more famous *Il principe* (1513) on the one hand and the *Anti-Machiavel* of Fredrick the Great (1738) on the other. Since mid-sixteenth century, Anti-Machiavellism named the extreme endeavor to find social, legal, political, and organizational communication codes beyond those of cynicism and despotism (Meinicke: 1924/1963; Thuau: 2000). Those efforts were less about rude and cruel destructive powers of annihilation than about the social might of enabling synchronization and disciplined coordination inside a framework of loyalty that was no longer indebted to a catholic semantic of a common *corpus spiritus.* However, the goal was not simply to replace cynicism with a secular form of *esprit de corps* or military *corporate spirit.* We should not directly use later modern ideas of central and local (Gustafsson: 1994), or centralization and decentralization, albeit such ideas could be observed in the central perspective. The central perspective did not come in use before the gardens of Versailles, which depicted a new territorial form of the state (Mukerji: 1997; Harste: 2013a).

Barbiche (1987) points towards a separation between legal and organizational power that should have taken place at the end of the sixteenth century under Henri IV. With Luhmann's systems theory and Gadamer's hermeneutics, we can observe how codes of organization as "systems" began reflexively as a re-entering of self-organization in order to code organization in Jean Bodin's famous 1,100-

pages-long *Les six livres de la republique* from 1576 (Gadamer: 1975, 158). This masterpiece owes its reputation to its description of perpetual monarchical sovereignty. The point is about “membership.” Indeed, Bodin began the revolution with his description of the magistrates in their positions as commissioned officers with perpetual tasks. The officer was modeled according to the idea of Jesus and thus became conceptualized as an eternal Christ (Kantorowicz: 1957; Luhmann: 1977, 273ff; Harste: 2001). Like the King’s two bodies, as temporal Jesus and eternal Christ, the same distinction was valid for his officers; they were to become included members of a political body or corporate spirit, yet their earthly life remained excluded. Bodin’s analysis was meant to ascribe new functions to the monarch, his estate, and the hierarchical estate society in which this new form of monarchical estate should place itself as the highest estate. This distinction between temporal commission and eternal office was restrained to the aftermath.[1] Yet it became decisive for those descriptions of the civil servants in the immediate environment of the Huguenot positions, who mediated Bodin’s reconstitution of the monarchy along with the Huguenot leader, the king of Navarre since 1572 and king of France after 1594.

Since the late fifteenth century, the king’s staff in France was undoubtedly the biggest among European monarchies. Because the estate established as staff, with functions, salaries, and positions, Roland Mousnier was able to account for the weight of the dynastic administration as it was retained and delegated. In the early sixteenth century, the officers were nominated and patrimonialized into positions; they were not employed in the later sense of delimited employment. They did not have a certain job, an office as a place for working with tasks, and they did not have delimited budgets, nor an administratively recognized education. Nevertheless, Mousnier found about 7–8,000 nominated officials altogether for the year 1515 when Francis I came into power. However, François I marks a turning point in the symbolization of government: He certainly symbolically authorized rule and conquered, so to say, quite a few rituals and symbols that were previously monopolized by the church, for example, the procession fête de Dieu (Jouanna: 1991; 1996, 11; Elwood: 1999).

It was a period when all kinds of symbols and concepts were “essentially contested” – to use the famous and useful conceptualization of Gallie and Wil-

1 “An officer is the public person who has an ordinary charge defined by law. The holder of a commission is the public person who has an extraordinary charge defined in the terms of the commission.” (Bodin: 1576/1583/1961, 372). In the Roman military, this concept of permanency had some significance, but it remained a weak point and a problem for the stabilization of Roman administration. It is, indeed, a very Christian invention formed by the Western Catholic church, where it became very different from the still clientilist Orthodox Byzantine church that later heavily influenced Russian clientilism from the Tsar regime to Stalin and Putin (cf. Thornhill: 2011, 327ff; Foucault: 2004, 159).

liam Connolly (1983). Remember, these were the years when Seyssel's, Machiavelli's, Erasmus', Luther's and Calvin's writings were written and published. The New World was discovered (Bonne: 2007). The world, its symbols, concepts, its organizations, and social orders were adrift (Wilentz: 1999). Amazing new powerful symbols began to emerge, such as the statues of Justitia, which depicted a hybrid between a half-naked innocent Virgin (Maria), a warrior with a sword, and a balance between justice and injustice, virtue and vice. Religion, military, and justice were about to find new, public forms (Robert: 1993). The hybrid statues of Justitia indeed expressed this essential confusion of concepts and figures.

Yet in between those forms – early Reformation and early Enlightenment – there was a kind of organizational revolution. This particular revolution initially began with Machiavelli and Claude de Seyssel both of whom wrote about the form of power in 1515 (Bonne: 2007). This was the year Charles V of the Holy Empire and Francois I of France inherited their dynastic authoritative positions. However, these were still positions rooted in the household. It was not until Jean Bodin, and later, Duc de Sully, and even Axel Oxenstierna, that we see another form of organized power, which Alexis de Tocqueville (1856/1988, 299–312) calls "an administrative revolution" and Barbiche (1987) calls an "organizational revolution" (Bourdieu: 2004). It was not only French but, in particular, it spread to Lutheran state-formations, such as the Danish monarchy.

My central point is that this revolution is based in the Reformation. Certainly, in 1520 Luther observed a form of equality between households and between individuals, reading the Bible or facing God. He even used this form to constitute a foundational principle. After 1530 and the Augsburg Confession, this equality was still able to form an abstract constitutive principle of natural law and even positive law, but this was not so easily accomplished when power was organized into early modern states. There is no direct causal link from Luther to the modern state. Rather, the modern state emerged as unintended consequence of the religious quarrels that began in Luther's time. They were probably the result of stubbornness on both sides, which both used theological interpretations of concretely opposed interests.

The modernized estates and social orders began to be dominated by a more abstract, yet extremely contested, form. The function of this new form required new kinds of conceptual distinctions, which consolidated persons and functions into a new form of estate all the while excluding the old dynastic forms of patronage that were familiar and trusted. It is possible to identify a transformation of a social form, a temporal form, and a form of matter. Certainly, families were still important and unavoidable, but more significant were the organizational merits of those who could master new skills of law, of complex military logistics, and diplomatic skills of negotiation. This shift led to jealousy and conflict when a new estate was granted older privileges. In the loosely coupled staff of appointed entrusted men, Francis I could count only about 7–8,000 loose employees in 1515, whereas Henri II could count about 25,000 and Henri IV about 46,000 with something like guaranteed employment (Chaunu: 1977, 37).

A more important factor for authorization was temporal permanence. The royal estate authorized above the earthly estates began to signify stability and even eternity. "Absolute power" was less power over things or subjects, but a temporal power connected to eternity as permanence, that is, a power understood to be able to derogate from privileges according to its own necessities and reasons. Botero's "ragion di stato" (1589) was combined with Bodin's construction of a unitary form of sovereign power maintained by a new body of commissars with permanent powers. If the monarchy in the form of a king could survive the death of the king, so could the official as commissar; the function of the commission, the tasks, was still to be implemented even if the individual in charge died, and the juridical person in charge did not die under these circumstances (Luhmann: 1989b, 253ff). Bodin's authorization of this distinction was that Jesus could die, but Christ survive. The souls, the functions, and the eternal order survived despite their earthly contingencies (Bodin: 1576/1583/1961, 372–392). Thus, a number of eternal virtues developed as invisible arcane virtues (Luhmann: 1989d).

At the heart of the French Wars of Religion were Catholic centrism and Reformist decentrism (Jouanna: 1989; 1996, 288–339). At the same time, the estates organizing the dynastic power and the military regiments grew to unprecedented sizes. When we recall that the idea of full-time employees was inconceivable before Jean Bodin's conceptualization of the differences between temporary commissars and perpetual officers[2] in *Les six livres de la République* (1576/1583/1961, 372–389), the shift from temporary nomination to permanently employed constituted a self-accelerated organizational revolution. This paved the way for new notions of a "reason of state." However, the question that developed over the next 150 years was if the "ragion di stato" (Botero) was "Machiavellistic" or if it was possible to constitute a reason of state according to "Anti-Machiavellistic" natural and divine law?

Fundamental to Bodin's notion of constitutionalization was his description of a state-administrated with such precision that it received an entirely legal form. Afterwards, Botero, in distinction to Machiavelli, claimed that decisions, ac-

2 The devil is in the details: Bodin's explanation begins with a description between green, yellow and red sealing wax. This triple distinction is well known today in traffic lights, yellow is only for temporary letters, whereas green and red is for permanent authorizations (Bodin: 1576/1583/1961, 375).

cording to the reason of state, should obtain authorization from the people (Botero: 1589/2014; Thuau: 2000; Meinecke: 1924/1963).

In France, absolutism came to rule (Jouanna: 2013). However, it was always a severely moderated absolutism with independent (in principle "sovereign") courts and with provincial and general estate assemblies (Descimon et al: 2000; Cosandey/Descimon: 2002; Bordes: 1972). Today, Bodin certainly is most famous for his description of monarchial sovereignty in book II, chapter one – often, the only chapter read by wider audiences. The Danish monarchy imported a large range of ideas and reforms from French absolutist rule. One example is the formula for the perpetual power of the monarch in the Danish KL (Stolleis 1990), especially §§ 1–7, 17, 25 and 26. This formula explicitly fused the notion of perpetual power with a late-Lutheran/Melanchthonian Protestant notion of rule by means of ecclesiastically organized religion and divinely given law. Thus, in distinction to French constitutionalism, no constitutionalist mindset was able to transcend such a form of absolute rule. Monarchical power became sovereign and was only later replaced by the people's sovereignty represented by parliament. This notion was summarized in the parliamentary self-description of "no one above or beside the parliament" (by Viggo Hørup in the late nineteenth century, cf. Friisberg: 2006). I frame this initial description in Table 2 and then go on to explain the motives behind it.

	Machiavellism	**Anti-Machiavellism**
Secular state-building	Military revolution; "necessitas" of a cynical "state of exception," ("Machtstaat," "Macht is Acht"). Despotic law. Management mindset.	Non-confessional abstract *Raison d'État* with a minimum of natural law (Richelieu). Moderated absolutism. Power mediatized by law: Secular law.
Authorized state legitimacy	Religious and theological authorizing a unitarian power state. Danish full absolutism. Loyalty is a duty. Power mediatized by law: Confessional culture of law.	A constitutionalization of a Rule of law ("Rechtsstaat") to come, which replaces "rights to rebel." Chancellor D'Aguesseau's separation of powers. Kantian mindset.

Table 2. The co-evolution of Reformation and Military Revolution: Consequences for constitutionalization of state-building

4. The Devoted Officers and Citizens

From beginning to end, Bodin seems to some extent to frame his analysis in his *Les six livres de la Rḗpublique* according to Lutheran doctrine. The first book begins with a phrase that states the orders: "A Republic is a right to govern several households [menages]" (Bodin: 1576/1583/1961, 1; Friedeburg: 2016: 359).

Moreover, the concluding chapter imagines an almost cabbalistic figure of the future permanent sovereign monarchy as a form which resolves the conflicts in the French religious wars (Bodin: 1576/1583/1961, 1056). However, what some call Bodin's cabbalism also appears in an earlier form, which Bodin depicts (1576/1583/1961, 662). The adjoint somewhat cabbalist idea probably functions to explain how the order of nature or natural law conforms to the later conclusion, depicted, from the original, in figure 1.

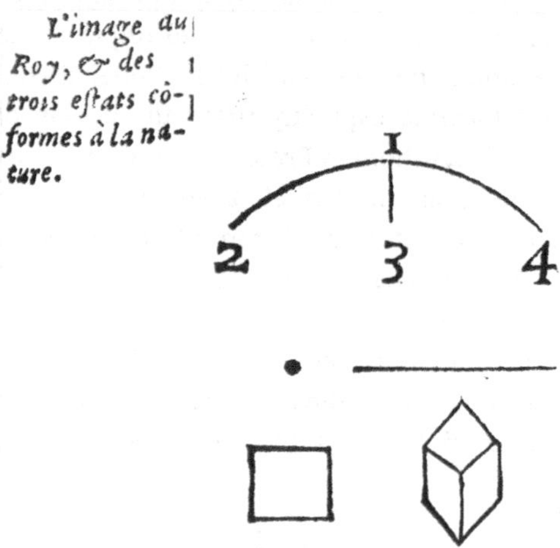

Figure 1. Jean Bodin's picture of the estate of the estates (Bodin: 1576/1583/1961, 1056)

The permanent eternal order re-enters into the temporal orders. This permanent and sovereign hierarchical order is present in the form of the monarchical estate as a kind of estate of the estates. It fits perfectly well into the transition of the king's household into an upper estate. The king's household is reordered in order to organize and re-organize safety and security into a permanent, certified, and authorized sovereign. The form of this sovereign lies somewhere in between papal and imperial regimes, but simultaneously distinct from both. Among the three temporal orders, first, of course, we have the clerical order. In theology, it is debated whether this is somewhat paradoxical. Why should the estate of the king's household be above the clerical order? Yet Luther's doctrine is that everyone is equal before God and in interpretations of the holy word. In fact, Luther's entire rebellion against the Catholic Church is grounded in dismantling the hierarchy of the church; no one in the church is above the commoners. The *oikos* of economy shows that order is earthly and counts for the household, including noble households. Therefore, the polity takes two forms, the local and regional polity, estate assemblies and judicial bodies, whereas the sovereign power withholds an upper hand, as if an eternal natural order is embodied in the three bodies.

My point is not to offer any theological solution to the complex and much-discussed issue, whether the richly debated importance of the bipartite doctrine or the doctrine of the three orders for Luther or in later Lutheran theology (Bayer: 2007, 110–138, 281–296). Luther's temperament was uncompromising; but many other authors who were inspired by Luther, such as Melanchthon, sought compromise. Bodin's book attempted a compromise between centralist substantialism and decentralist symbolically-disciplined delegation of powers and competences.

Most certainly, there is a difference between Bodin's compromise, on the one hand, and the way, for example, Colbert's later co-opted local servants for the French monarchy and the Danish monarchy co-opted Luther's *Small Catechism* for school education. In France, this later form was widespread after Napoleon, but in a thoroughly secular form of historical, geographical, literary, and mathematical education.

This picture, or *Fürstenspiegel*, is contemporary to at least four forms of professionalization of the orders. These four forms were authorized as permanent orders: the civil servants, the officers of the crown, the ennobled judges ("la noblesse de robe"), and in Lutheran countries, the pastors as local representatives of the king. In this sense, the permanent natural law re-entered into local estates and established order, obligation, and duty from the top down. Loyalty functioned in the opposite direction, from bottom up, as a devoted privilege to serve the king and thereby God, the gospels, and the true order of the world. In Lutheran countries, every pupil was required to read Luther's *Small Catechism.* Thus, the state was organized in order to certify particular forms of obedience, duty, and loyalty, which followed. To clean the house, to build a moral soul in a strong body, from the children to the households, and from households to parishes and towns, and from those localities to the lands, every body and everybody were obliged and authorized to be loyal citizens of the monarchical state. The French monarchy, in particular with the Paulette beginning in 1604, demanded that the local elites and estates be members of the French estate and buy shares as a contribution to French finances. In the short-term, this served a financial purpose, but in the long-term, it had a territorial and political rationale (Harste: 2013a; 2013b). By contrast, the Lutheran monarchies demanded that the souls of the parishes adjoin and obey the king as head of justice and the foremost member of the church – and the state.

Still today, the Danish mythology of "sovereignty" has only half-heartedly escaped this pre-Enlightenment and post-Reformation formation at the political or popular levels, in mass media narratives, or in Danish legal thought (Petersen: 2016). Indeed, Martin Luther's early linguistic disenchantment of eternal ideas embedded in political power still requires an enlightenment in the so-called modern state tradition. Furthermore, this deconstruction is extremely important to an enlightenment of a post-national European constitutionalization (Habermas: 2005a; 2005b; Brunkhorst: 2014; Thornhill: 2011; Kjær: 2014)

Bodin's famous definition, "Sovereignty is that absolute and perpetual power vested in a commonwealth" (Bodin: 1576/1583/1961, 122), has its strength less in the old idea of *potestas absoluta* as it does in the idea of permanency. This is bolstered by the fact that the content of permanence is shown in a theory of permanent magistrates, regardless whether the referent is "officers" or "commissars." The lawgiver is sovereign because he can refer to two kinds of magistrates, those who judge for him, the "officers" and those who command for him, the "commissars." Thus, the sovereign presents what Bodin calls "the state" as a unified state; and he can govern because his government is executed. In fact, Bodin elaborates an early notion of the bureaucracy needed by the sovereign:

> After the sovereign, the magistrate is the chief personage in the commonwealth, for upon him the sovereign devolves his authority and his power of commanding obedience. We must therefore consider what obedience is due from the magistrate to the prince, since this is his first duty. Unlike the sovereign who knows no superior, but sees all his subjects obedient to his power, or the private citizen who has no official right to use compulsion against anyone, the magistrate is many personages of different quality, bearing, appearance, and mode of action in one. (Bodin: 1576/1583/1961, 409)

Now, why should the magistrates obey the sovereign? Aren't they just networks of more or less trustworthy ("fidele") persons, more or less loyal? Bodin's point is that they do not only have to obey the laws, they are also bound by a natural divine law. Why do they take part in a natural divine law? Because they receive a completely new status as perpetual parts of the monarchical estate from it. Here, Bodin uses a current distinction between ordinary juridical officers and commanding commissars as "extraordinary appointed king's men" (Bodin: 1576/1583/1961, book III, chap. II).

In the Empire of the Danish Monarchy, which included Norway, Iceland, present-day Southern Sweden, and the duchies of Schleswig and Holstein, in principle every parish and citizen could and should be included in this order of a total state. After some quarrel with for instance the Danish Erasmus scholar Poul Helgesen (1485–1534) in the 1530s, everyone was to be loyal, and it was not conceivable that anyone reasonable could have other ideas. Accordingly, it was also contested whether some more Calvinist notions of discontent were to be found in Danish theologian and philosopher Niels Hemmingsen's philosophy of a natural order. This discussion is not completely settled (Stybe: 1975, 105–111; contributions by Sommer and Andersen in the present volume). My point is a bit different, however, and concerns the rationalities of state power.

The emerging Danish-Norwegian power state ("Machtstaat") soon underwent the evolution and revolution of military competition. As with the inter-Catholic military conflicts between the Habsburg and French dynasties, the Protestant Danish and Swedish dynasties conflicted. They developed even larger armies with even greater numbers of armaments, from navies to fortifications, cannons, and musketeers to still more permanent administrations, taxation specifications, complex finances, and symbols, like quarrels over the inherited heraldic of two or three crowns. This form of competition between military states certainly formed a revolution of military, organization, and finance. It demanded a politically reformed symbolic order (Roberts: 1973; Downing: 1992; Ertman: 1997). It was expressed in state architecture, not only in Kronborg (Prince Hamlet's palace from 1570) but all over the country with small palaces or mansions of the king's counts and vice-counts ("Lensmænd"). The Scandinavian countries were able to profit from the sale of timber and grain to the Dutch navy, in particular after 1609, and the Dutch soon demonstrated that they could pay through their even more revolutionary, organized self-referential finance system (Harste: 2014; Israel: 1998, 616–619; Stasavage: 2011, 150–154).

If this converged multiplex of reforms and revolutions took place from 1560–1660 (Roberts: 1955/1995), a phase of triumphant absolutism developed from the 1660s all the way up to the end of Napoleon's empire. This was when the Danish monarchy – probably because of severe military constraints – copied Bodin's constitutional form of power, sovereignty, and organization into the Danish KL of 1665 (Stolleis: 1990). However, here too, we can briefly distinguish a first phase of over-integrated power from a second phase of functional differentiation and separation of power. The rule of Louis XIV was copied directly into Danish state reforms of taxation, territorial rule, measurement of the quality and quantity of landed production and economy ("Hartkornskatter"); about every corner of this was seen beforehand in Colbert's instructions to his commissioners (later intendants and prefects). Yet French absolutism always met resistance and moderation not to mention de facto separation of powers with strong provincial estates and regional courts ("les parlements"). After 1661, a part of the rights to supplications, such federal resistance and moderation were not found in the Danish heartland; and the absolute rule never implemented as strongly in Norway and the Duchies. In fact, neither Danish nor French absolutism were despotically defined as rule without law; on the contrary, absolute rule established a range of huge legal reforms. Only under Louis XIV and Colbert were they sufficiently integrated into the executive organization in order to successfully avoid rebellion against taxation.

5. The Absolute Sovereign "Rule by the Grace of God in the Danish Monarchy"

Long before the 1665 KL and the 1683 DL, quite a few Danish theologians and lawyers traveled to the German Empire, the United Kingdom, and France to study (Stybe: 1975: 133–155). In the spectacular reform, or constitutive "revolution," around 1660, Hans Wandahl drafted *Jus Regium* as a theological defense of absolutism instituted by God. At the same time, the German lawyer Johann Friedrich Horn published a very similar dissertation in Denmark. Horn's dissertation argued that the monarchy was constituted before any contractual tradition was established. This resembles a theme in Bodin's books. Following Bodin, some arguments for monarchy took the kings of ancient Israel, Saul, David, and Solomon, as the starting point of the monarchical "divinely privileged authority." Gabriel Knudsen Akelaye brought the so-called Tacitism, which is particularly important for the doctrine of absolutism as arcane *Geheimverwaltung*. Moreover, he wrote a dissertation about Tacitus' *Germania* (Thuau: 2000; Stolleis: 1990). Jesper Brochmand wrote about the political aspects of Luther's teachings in *Systema universæ theologica* (1633), probably inspired by Armand Richelieu, whose thoughts on the "raison d'état" and natural law were widely disseminated after his rise to power in 1624, culminating in the *Testament Politique* (1638); Rasmus Vinding studied in Paris and wrote about the foundation of monarchy as heritage in a book from 1640. Even before this, two Germans, Henrik Ernst (1634) and Henning Arnisæus, lectured in Sorø. Arnisæus defended his Bodinian dissertation *De jure majestatis* and Ernst defended his dissertation about the absolute nature of the king as supreme judge.

The first to import Jean Bodin's trans-confessional political sociology of law to the Danish Empire was Christoffer Dybvad, who in 1615 argued for Bodin's catalog of seven monarchical privileges. The last and most decisive author was, of course, Peter Schumacher (ennobled as Griffenfeld) who studied Bodin carefully in Leiden (Olden-Jørgensen: 1999, 46) and finally, backed by the king's secretary Christoffer Gabel, wrote KL in 1665, declaring the king's semantic institution by the Grace of God.

After this indeed unique constitution of absolutism, the more substantial DL (1683) took several years to compile. Not the least, the Danish monarchy organized a territorial reform, also inspired by Richelieu and, in particular, Louis XIVs first Controller Jean-Baptiste Colbert's very important *Instructions* issued in 1664 as *Mémoire pour messieurs les maitres des requêtes comissaires départis dans les provinces.* This reform – or revolution – instituted the central administration as control of the provincial administration, and this carried the substance of absolute rule (Harste 2003). Without a doubt, absolutism was far more penetrating in Denmark – the central part of the monarchial empire – than it ever was in France, perhaps until the much later Napoleon legacy of prefects and departments (Burdeau: 1994, 81–87; Rosanvallon: 1990, 101–106).

On the one hand, in a widespread European (military) competitive reform fever during a two hundred year period, the Danish monarchy imported about every possible important reform from France – often helped by Holsteinian, Hanoverian and Prussian experts. On the other hand, the monarchy did not separate its powers according to French or Prussian enlightened standards. The Danish monarchy was an outstanding example of unmodified absolutism (Ertman: 1997, 306–311). The reforms concerned the *maître des requêtes* (a Danish expression with French words), the Grain taxes land measurements ("Hartkornskatter"), the departmental reforms ("amter," "amtmænd") and, as mentioned, the very constitution of absolute rule (Pedersen: 1998; Jørgensen/Westrup: 1982; Ladewig Petersen: 1984; Lind: 2000; Knudsen: 2003).

Yet courts were not – and probably never were – separated from the central administration (Dübeck: 1993; Christensen: 2002). Between the time that the Danish central administration was formed in Copenhagen and got delegated representatives in the provinces and the early 1960s, the administration essentially changed only once. That moment of change came in the years directly following 1809 and 1848 by means of a budget-restricting Prussian departmentalization (from collegial administration to individual resorts). As such, the legacy of a centralized eternal sovereign form of power was not challenged. Power remained in Copenhagen, unified and undivided into the relatively huge capital – particularly after 1864. Moreover, the heritage monarchy has the longest track record in Europe. The system of those narratives turned into an almost indispensable self-referential mythology of sovereignty (Harste: 1998).

After the eighteenth-century reform fever, some stabilization followed. This certainly was the case in the Danish kingdom. In 1960, the departmental structure of Danish central administration underwent a major revision. In order to do the reforms well, the Administrative Commission of 1960 wrote a report about the history of ministerial reforms (Petersen: 1962). The report concluded that only incremental mushroom evolution, but no administrative reforms followed the reforms of 1809 and 1849 when Danish central administration copied the famous Prussian reforms of Karl von Stein and Karl von Hardenberg (Koselleck: 1975; Winter: 1931).

When we analyze the numerous (eighty-five) Danish reports on power today, the so-called *Magtudredningen*, it should be possible to discover an equally critical picture of democratic power as in the corresponding *Maktutredning* in Sweden and Norway reflected. Though expected, this is not actually the case (Harste: 2004; Knudsen: 2003). Almost all of the reports depict the Danish state as a legally and democratically well-ordered state – to use the conceptual framework of the Kantian ideal state (Langer: 1986). This beauty-panting is expected because, as Bourdieu describes the paradox (1994, 97 ff), the state establishes a political science of the state to describe and reflect upon the state, and not surprisingly, the state is formed in such a way that it is presupposed to have legitimacy. The historical organization and form of the state remain undisputed. With this form already given, democracy can decide upon (less) important matters (Poggi: 1978, 1–15).

However, such a positive result also appears because the Danish state never separated powers. This is also depicted in the Danish reports on power (Christensen: 2002). The Danish state can decentralize exactly because its local civil servants continue to codify their behavior according to central agendas (Pallesen: 2001). Public law ("Offentlighedsloven"; Knudsen: 2003) has no consequences and, although celebrated as a particular Danish law, it only is retained because of demands from Brussels – before it was severely reduced in 2014.

6. The Dark Shadows of Dialectic Enlightenment

It is difficult to avoid discussing a perspective suggested by this 500-year review of European state-building history and the Danish position in this long history. Due to early inspiration from the Reformation and the events leading up to it, since the time of the Danish church rule (bishop Absalon in the twelfth century), the Danish monarchy adequately formed itself according to a number of modern ideas about symbolism and power. After the first two phases of Reformation, however, the power structures of rule transformed what was already underway, as seen in Machiavelli. The military revolution of cannons, navies, and fortifications implied a complete revolution in state organization and state finance.

Thus, the Lutheran symbolic world – the form of the estates and the separation between a worldly order and a heavenly order – had to transform itself. The symbolic order was useful for power-building in the Danish monarchy. In addition, French ideas of compromise and moderation, reuniting centralization and decentralization, as depicted by Jean Bodin were extremely useful to the Danish almost coup d'État in 1660–1661. The ideas were also useful for the Danish monarchy's constitutionalization of absolutist rule for a period that formally ended in 1849, but in practice did not end until 1901. Absolutist rule was partly reconstituted as a "state of exception" (Agamben: 2005) with still less moderation since the September 11 attacks. Fukuyama's hopes about "getting to Denmark" (Fukuyama: 2011, 431–434) began to vanish.

How is this reconstitutionalization of total rule into the soul of the citizen and in grossly obedient research institutes and governmental civil servants possible?

How is it possible that a population with the highest work frequency in the world – because so many women are included full time into the workforce – accepts being repeatedly told that it does not work enough, until the moment of complete psychological and physical fatigue, traumatization, and burn out from stress (Prætorius: 2013; Weber: 1920/1972)? The chapter has followed two lines of argumentation. The first argument is that the Danish state and its citizens have been subject to a military competition of wars and rearmament. Although almost every other European state has endured such developments, the Danish state had to provide both an army and a navy to an incomparable degree, the results of which appear, for example, in the level of taxation accepted by the population.

The second line is that Lutheranism transformed into a doctrine of natural law and duties that compelled citizens to obey and have faith, trust, and confidence in the monarchy's rule. For hundreds of years after the constitutionalization of absolute rule, state reforms repeatedly committed the population to "committed obedience" and to "readapt to readaption" as the very form of personal ontology and devotion to work (Knudsen: 2000; Ingesman: 2000; Andersen: 2008). More than a Dutch Calvinist and Prussian pietistic disciplinary revolution (Gorski 2003), Danish citizens long ago accepted a Lutheran, or we may call it post-Lutheran, a spirit of corporate work and an inclusive, egalitarian form of welfare before God (Petersen 2016). This unites a form of neo-liberal neo-Calvinism (Jessen: 2015; Harste: 2003) with a neo-Catholic communitarian corporate spirit of commitment. The social democracy strengthened this post-Marxist cult of labor and barely succeeded to offer any alternative. Confederalist constitutionalism alone came out of Brussels along with very specific, protected citizens' rights. However, neo-national and neo-liberalism – both strongly affected by the Danish dismissal of the Maastricht Treaty in 1992 – have de-constitutionalized European politics, its Kantian Mindset, and its possible constitutionalist forms of protecting a civilized lifeworld, which in the sense of Luther and Kant could have had a faith to believe in itself and have trust into its own judgement.

7. Conclusion: A Danish Secularization?

This chapter investigated a number of related questions. How do forms of coding and interpretation develop within the different theological legacies of the Eucharist about centralization and decentralization? How do legacies of sovereignty differ? And how do imaginaries of European constitutionalization differ? Does constitutional law emerge as a permanently, completely unchangeable concept as, for instance, in the very notion of sovereignty? Which form of authorization makes this form permanent, contingent or subject to a community of interpreters?

In order to grasp how the form of Lutheran theology shaped modern society, we must first observe the impact of Lutheranism upon the projects to reform power as the legal organization of the states. Second, we must observe how functionally differentiated and Universalist systems of inclusion and exclusion got their start. This eventually decisive modern transformation could only emerge when the function of systems was distinguished from their organization. If law, education, art, research, and religion should become free to code only on behalf of their own self-reference and self-description, their form of organization would become separated from their functions (Luhmann: 1997). Religion should be clearly distinguished from church, but so too with art from organizations of art, education from schools, politics from parliaments, research from universities. Hence, the organization of professional membership was to be subject to one form of decisions, whereas decisions add codes about the functions in order to distinguish their validity from the organizational form. This transition took place long before Kant's major writings and probably did so in the early Enlightenment. This conceptual distinction between administration and function paved the way for a separation of powers and constitutes what "secularization" should be.

Certainly, however, sovereignty happened to be founded in mythology. The reality is that states copied each other and learned about reforms and innovations from each other. Eventually, they converged their forms, constitutions, organizations, and, in particular, their functions.

Indeed, this, too, was what Enlightenment was about. God had to become a principle of universal coding. The very earliest form of such coding is probably seen in the writings on will formation by Boétie, *Discours de la Servitude volontaire* from 1548, with a later philosophical milestone in Marcel Mersenne's *L'usage de la raison* (1622). The post-Jansenist French lawyer, legal philosopher, and chancellor Henri-Francois d'Aguesseau offered a final form in his *l'institution du droit publique* (1727). He, before Montesquieu, constituted the separation of powers. European states developed as a dynamic form of synchronization of organizations and functions. The hermeneutic "spirit of law" (Montesquieu) and mindset constitutionalized in the shadows of those evolutions.

Hence, the constitutional problem of Europe must allow for such a sufficiently abstract political, organizational, and legal integration between those confessional cultures such that Europe can enter a post-confessional phase. In such a phase, it is decisive to observe the historical learning processes about compromises and convergences and, eventually, coordination procedures. Moreover, a Rousseauian and Kantian political and reasonable distance – in a kind of veil of ignorance (Rawls) – is decisive to post-confessional replacements such as the big narratives of nationalism, communism, and neoliberalism. Yet after the Napoleonic Wars, the Nordic countries developed welfare – often imitated from Prussia – in the contingent shelter from the huge wars of the twentieth century. In distinction to the Finnish experience, the Nordic countries eventually did so with the result that it became difficult to find their interpretation of their European legacies in preference to their own mythological stories of self-determination and sovereignty.

Bibliography

AGAMBEN, GIORGIO (2005), State of Exception, Chicago: Chicago University Press.

ALLISON, HENRY (1990), Kant's Theory of Freedom, Cambridge: Cambridge University Press.

ANDERSEN, NIELS ÅKERSTRØM (2008), The world as Will and Adaptation: The Intercursive Coupling of Citizen Contracts, Critical Discourse Studies, 5/1: 75–89.

BARBICHE, BERNARD (1987), Une révolution administrative, in: A. Stegman (ed.), Pouvoir et Institutions en Europe au XVIème Siècle, Paris: Vrin, 97–106.

BAYER, OSWALD (2007), Luthers Theologie: Eine Vergegenwärtigung, Tübingen: Mohr Siebeck.

BODIN, JEAN (1576/1583/1961), Les Six Livres de la République, Aalen: Scientia.

BOÉTIE, ETIENNE LA (1548/2013), Discours de la Servitude Volontaire, Paris: Mille et une nuits.

BONNEY, RICHARD (1991), The European Dynastic States 1494–1660, New Jersey: Oxford University Press.

BONNE, REBECCA ARD (2007), War, Domination, and the Monarchy of France: Charles Seyssel and the Language of Politics in the Renaissance (Brill's Studies in Intellectual History 156), Leiden/Boston, MA: Brill.

BORDES, MAURICE (1972), L'administration Provinciale & Municipale en France au XVIIIe Siècle, Paris: SEDES.

BOTERO, GIOVANNI (1589/2014), De la Raison d'État, Paris: Gallimard.

BURDEAU, FRANÇOIS (1994), Histoire de l'administration française. Du 18e au 20e siècle, Paris: Montchrestien.

BOURDIEU, PIERRE (2004), From the King's House to the Reason of State, Constellations, 11/1, 16–36.

BRUNKHORST, HAUKE (2014), Critical Theory of Legal Revolutions: An Evolutionary Perspective, London: Bloomsbury.

CHAUNU, PIERRE (1977), L'Etat, in: F. Braudel/E. Labrousse (ed.), Histoire Économique et Sociale en France, vol. 1, Paris: PUF, 162–166.

COSANDEY, FANNY/ROBERT DESCIMON (2002), L'absolutisme en France, Paris: Seuil.

CHRISTENSEN JENS PETER (2002), Domstolene: Den tredje statsmagt, Aarhus: Magtudredningen.

CONNOLLY, WILLIAM (1983). The Terms of Political Discourse, New Jersey: Princeton University Press.

Creveld, Martin van (1999), The Rise and Decline of the State, Cambridge: Cambridge University Press.

Descimon, Robert et al. (2000), La Longue Durée de l'État, Paris: Seuil.

Downing, Brian (1992) The Military Revolution and Political Change. Origins of Democracy and Autocracy in Early Modern Europe, New Jersey: Princeton University Press.

Dübeck, Inger (1993), Hvornår blev Danmark en retsstat?, in: Helle Blomquist/Per Ingesman (ed.), Forvaltningshistorisk antologi, Copenhagen: Jurist- og Økonomforbundets Forlag, 99–114.

Elwood, Christopher (1999), The Body Broken: The Calvinist Doctrine of the Eucharist and the Symbolization of Power in Sixteenth-Century France, Oxford: Oxford University Press.

Erasmus of Rotterdam (1517/1968), Die Klage des Friedens, der von allen Völkern verstoßen und vernichtet Wurde, Darmstadt: Wissenschaftlicher Buchgesellschaft.

Erasmus of Rotterdam (1524/1991), La Diatribe sur le Libre Arbitre, in: Oevres choisies, Paris: Librarie Générale Francaise.

Ertman, Thomas (1997), Birth of the Leviathan. Building States and Regimes in Medieval and Early Modern Europe, Cambridge: Cambridge University Press.

Franklin, Julian (1973), Jean Bodin and the Rise of Absolutist Theory, Cambridge: Cambridge University Press.

Foucault, Michel (2004), Sécurité, Territoire, Population, Paris: Gallimard.

Friedeburg, Robert von (2016), Luther's Legacy: The Thirty Years War and the Modern Notion of "State" in the Empire, 1530s to 1790s, Cambridge: Cambridge University Press.

Friisberg, Claus (2006), Ingen over og ingen ved siden af Folketinget, Varde: Vestjysk Kulturforlag.

Fukuyama, Francis (2011), The Origins of Political Order, London: Profile Books.

Frédéric Le Grand (1738/1788), Anti-Machiavel ou examen du Prince de Machiavel, in: Oevres Posthumes, T. 6, Berlin.

Gadamer, Hans-Georg (1975), Wahrheit und Methode, Tübingen: J.C.B Mohr (Paul Siebeck).

Gorski, Philip (2003), The Disciplinary Revolution, Chicago: University of Chicago Press.

Gustafsson, Harald (1994), Political Interaction in the Old Regime: Central Power and Local Society in the Eighteenth-Century Nordic States, Lund: Studentlitteratur.

Habermas, Jürgen (2005a), Die Grenze zwischen Glauben und Wissen. Zur Wirkungsgeschichte und aktuellen Bedeutung von Kants Religionsphilosophie, in: Zwischen Naturalismus und Religion: Philosophische Aufsätze, Frankfurt am Main: Suhrkamp, 216–257.

Habermas, Jürgen (2005b), The Kantian Project of the Constitutionalization of International Law: Does It Still Have a Chance?, in: M. Escamilla/M. Saavedra (ed.), Law and Justice in a Global Society, Universidad de Granada: International Association for Philosophy of Law, 115–126.

Halkin, Leon (1987), Erasme, Paris: Fayard.

Harste, Gorm (1998), Mytologien om dansk suverænitet, in: Anders Berg-Sørensen/Morten Greve (ed.), Staten, det er … Stat og politik – historisk, politiologisk og sociologisk, Roskilde: Roskilde Universitetsforlag, 212–238.

HARSTE, GORM (2001), Jean Bodin om suverænitet, stat og centraladministration, Distinktion 2, 35–52.

HARSTE, GORM (2003), Arbejdssamfundet: Weber og Durkheim om arbejdsetik og samarbejdsetik, Økonomi og Politik 76/1, 53–66.

HARSTE, GORM (2004), Magtudredningens magt: I enevældens skygge?, GRUS 71, 45–68.

HARSTE, GORM (2009), Kant's Theory of European Integration, Jahrbuch für Recht und Ethik 17, 53–84.

HARSTE, GORM (2013a), The Improbable European State: Its Ideals Observed with Social Systems Theory, in: Robert Egnell/Peter Halden (ed.), New Agendas in Statebuilding, London: Routledge, 95–121.

HARSTE, GORM (2013b), The Big, Large and Huge Case of State-Building: Studying Structural Couplings at the Macro Level, in: Alberto Febbrajo/Gorm Harste (ed.), Law and Intersystemic Communication: Understanding 'Structural Coupling', London: Ashgate, 67–96.

HARSTE, GORM (2014), From War to Financial Crisis, Nordicum-Mediterraneum 9/3, 1–19.

HEERIKHUIZEN, ANNEMARIE VAN (2008), How God Disappeared from Europe: Visions of a United Europe from Erasmus to Kant, The European Legacy 13/4: 401–411.

HÖFFE, OTTFRIED (1988), Der Staat braucht selbst ein Volk von Teufeln, Stuttgart: Reclam.

INGESMAN, PER (2000), Kirke, stat og samfund i historisk perspektiv, in: Knudsen: 2000, 65–86.

ISRAEL, JONATHAN (1998), The Dutch Republic. Its Rise, Greatness, and Fall 1477–1806, Oxford: Clarendon Press.

JESSEN, MATHIAS HEIN (2015), Sovereign Bodies: Constitution and Construction of State, Subject and Corporation, unpublished PhD thesis, Aarhus University.

JESPERSEN, KNUD (1989), Danmarks historie: Tiden 1648–1730, Copenhagen: Gyldendal.

JESPERSEN, LEON (1984), 1600-tallets danske magtstat, in: Ladewig Petersen: 1984, 9–40.

JOUANNA, ARLETTE (1989), Le devoir de révolte, Paris: Fayard.

JOUANNA, ARLETTE (1991), Des 'Gros et Gras' au 'Gens D'honneur", in: Guy Chaussinand-Nogaret et al., Histoire des élites en France, Paris: Tallandier, 17–144.

JOUANNA, ARLETTE (1996), La France du XVIe Siècle, 1483–1598, Paris: PUF.

JOUANNA, ARLETTE (2013), Le Pouvoir Absolu: Naissance de l'imaginaire politique de la royauté, Paris: Gallimard.

JØRGENSEN, FRANK/MORTEN WESTRUP (1982), Dansk centraladministration i tiden indtil 1848, Copenhagen: Dansk Historisk Fællesforening.

KANT, IMMANUEL (1790/1974), Kritik der Urteilskraft, Werkausgabe X, Frankfurt am Main: Suhrkamp.

KANT, IMMANUEL (1794/1977), Religion Innerhalb der Blossen Vernunft, Werkausgabe VIII, Frankfurt am Main: Suhrkamp.

KANT, IMMANUEL (1795/1977), Zum ewigen Frieden, Werkausgabe IX, Frankfurt am Main: Suhrkamp.

KANTOROWICZ, ERNST (1957), The King's Two Bodies: A Study of Medieval Political Theology, New Jersey: Princeton University Press.

KAUFMANN, THOMAS (2006), Konfession und Kultur: Lutherischer Protestantismus in der zweiten Hälfte des Reformationsjahrhunderts, SuR.NR 29, Tübingen: Mohr Siebeck.

KAUFMANN, THOMAS (2009), Geschichte der Reformation, Frankfurt am Main/Leipzig: Verlag der Weltreligionen.

KJÆR, POUL (2014), Constitutionalism in the Global Realm, London: Routledge.

KOSKENNIEMI, MARTII (2006), Constitutionalism as a Mindset: Reflections on Kantian Themes about International Law and Globalization, Theoretical Inquiries in Law 8/1, 9–36.

KOSELLECK, REINHART (1975). Preussen Zwischen Reform und Revolution, Stuttgart: Klett-Cotta.

KOSELLECK, REINHART et al. (1990), Article "Staat und Souveränität", GGB 6, 1990, 1–155.

KNUDSEN, TIM (ed.) (2000), Den nordiske protestantisme og velfærdsstaten, Aarhus: Aarhus University Press.

KNUDSEN, TIM (2003), Offentlighed i det offentlige: Om historiens magt, Aarhus: Aarhus University Press.

LADEWIG PETERSEN, ERLING (1984) (ed.), Magtstaten i Norden i 1600-tallet og dens sociale konsekvenser, Odense: Odense Universitetsforlag.

LANGER, CLAUDIA (1986), Reform nach Prinzipien: Untersuchungen zur Politischen Theorie Immanuel Kants, Stuttgart: Klett-Cotta.

LIND, GUNNAR (2000), Den heroiske tid? Administrationen under den tidlige enevælde 1660–1720, in: Ditlev Tamm (ed.), Dansk Forvaltningshistorie, vol. 1, Copenhagen: Jurist- og Økonomforbundets Forlag, 159–226.

LINDEGREN, JAN (1984), Den svenska militärstaten 1560–1720, in: Ladewig Petersen: 1984, 99–130.

LUHMANN, NIKLAS (1977), Funktion der Religion, Frankfurt am Main: Suhrkamp.

LUHMANN, NIKLAS (1989a), Staat und Staatsräson im Übergang von traditionaler Herrschaft zu moderner Politik, in: Gesellschaftsstruktur und Semantik, vol. 3, Frankfurt am Main: Suhrkamp, 65–148.

LUHMANN, NIKLAS (1989b), Individuum, Individualität, Individualismus, in: Gesellschaftsstruktur und Semantik, vol. 3, Frankfurt am Main: Suhrkamp, 149–258.

LUHMANN, NIKLAS (1989c), Die Ausdifferenzierung der Religion, in: Gesellschaftsstruktur und Semantik, vol. 3, Frankfurt am Main: Suhrkamp, 259–357.

LUHMANN, NIKLAS (1989d), Geheimnis, Zeit und Ewigkeit, in: Niklas Luhmann/Peter Fuchs, Reden und Schweigen, Frankfurt am Main: Suhrkamp, 101–137.

LUHMANN, NIKLAS (1990), Die Weisung Gottes als Form der Freiheit, in: Soziologische Aufklärung, vol. 5, Opladen: Westdeutscher Verlag, 77–94.

LUHMANN, NIKLAS (1995), Metamorphosen des Staates, in: Gesellschaftsstruktur und Semantik vol. 4, Frankfurt am Main: Suhrkamp, 101–137.

LUHMANN, NIKLAS (1997), Die Gesellschaft der Gesellschaft, vol. 1–2, Frankfurt am Main: Suhrkamp.

LUHMANN, NIKLAS (2000), Die Politik der Gesellschaft, Frankfurt am Main: Suhrkamp.

LUTHER, MARTIN (1520), To the Christian Nobility of the German Nation Concerning the Reform of the Christian Nation (LW 44: 123–217/WA 6: 404–469).

LUTHER, MARTIN (1523), On Secular Authority (LW 45: 81–129/WA 11: 245–280).

LUTHER, MARTIN (1525), The Bondage of the Will (LW 33: 15–295/WA 18: 600–787).

MEINICKE, FRIEDRICH (1924/1963), Die Idee der Staatsräson in der Neueren Geschichte, München: Oldenbourg Verlag.

MELANCHTHON, PHILIPP (1530), Confessio Augustana (BC 30–105/BSELK 84–225).

MUKERJI, CHANDRA (1997), Territorial Ambitions and the Gardens of Versailles, Cambridge: Cambridge University Press.

Olden-Jørgensen, Sebastian (1999), Kun navnet er tilbage, Copenhagen: Gad.
Pallesen, Carsten (2001), Objectum Fidei: Luthers nadverlære i systemteoretisk belysning, DTT 64, 16–44.
Pedersen, Karl Peder (1998), Enevældens amtmænd, Copenhagen: Jurist- og Økonomforbundets Forlag.
Petersen, Jørn Henrik (2016), Fra Luther til konkurrencestaten, Odense: University Press of Southern Denmark.
Petersen, Niels (1962), Oversigt over centraladministrationens udvikling siden 1848, Copenhagen: Administrationsudvalget.
Parsons, Talcott (1971), The System of Modern Societies, Englewood Cliffs: Prentice-Hall.
Parsons, Talcott (1978), Christianity, in: Talcott Parsons, Action Theory and the Human Condition, New York: Prentice-Hall, 173–212.
Poggi, Gianfranco (1978), The Development of the Modern State, Stanford: Stanford University Press.
Prætorius, Nadja (2013), Den etiske udfordring i en global tid, Copenhagen: Dansk Psykologisk Forlag.
Quillet, Jeaninne (1972), Les clefs du pouvoir au moyen âge, Paris: Flammarion.
Robert, Christian-Nils (1993), La Justice: Vertu, Courtisane et Bourreau, Genève: Georg.
Roberts, Michael (1955/1995), The Military Revolution 1560–1660, in: Clifford Rogers (ed.), The Military Revolution Debate, Boulder, CO: Westview Press, 13–35.
Roberts, Michael (1973), Gustavus Adolphus, London: Longman.
Rosanvallon, Pierre (1990), L'État en France de 1789 à nos jours, Paris: Seuil.
Schilling, Heinz (1981), Konfessionskonflikt und Staatsbildung, QFRG 48, Gütersloh: Gütersloher Verlagshaus.
Schilling, Heinz (2009), The Confessionalization of European Churches and Societies: An Engine for Modernizing and for Social and Cultural Change, NTT 110, 3–22.
Schrimm-Heinz, Andrea (1991), Gewissheit und Sicherheit vol. I, ABG 34, 123–213.
Schrimm-Heinz, Andrea (1992), Gewissheit und Sicherheit vol. II, ABG 35, 115–213.
Schumacher, Peder (1665), Kongeloven, from http://www.danmarkshistorien.dk/leksikon-og-kilder/vis/materiale/kongeloven-1665/ (seen 27.02.2017).
Stasavage, David (2011), States of Credit, Princeton: Princeton University Press.
Stolleis, Michael (1990), Staat und Staatsräson in der Frühen Neuzeit, Frankfurt am Main: Suhrkamp.
Stybe, Svend (1975), Fra folkevækkelse til enevælde af Guds nåde: Den danske reformations idéhistorie, Copenhagen: Berlingske Leksikonbibliotek.
Thornhill, Chris (2011), A Sociology of Constitutions: Constitutions and State Legitimacy in Historical-Sociological Perspective, Cambridge: Cambridge University Press.
Thuau, Etienne (2000), Raison d'État et pensée politique à l'époque de Richelieu, Paris: Albin Michel.
Tilly, Charles (1992), Coercion, Capital, and the European States, AD 992–1992, Oxford: Blackwell.
Tocqueville, Alexis (1856/1988), L'ancien Régime et la Révolution, Paris: Flammarion.
Weber, Max (1920/1972), Die protestantische Ethik, Tübingen: J.C.B. Mohr (Paul Siebeck).
Wilentz, Sean (ed.) (1999), Rites of Power, Philadelphia: University of Pennsylvania.

Winter, Georg (ed.) (1931), Die Reorganisation des Preussischen Staates unter Stein und Hardenberg, vol. 1, Leipzig: Verlag Hirzel.

Zweig, Stefan (1934/2015), Erasmus of Rotterdam, London: Random House Plunkett Press.

Rasmus Skovgaard Jakobsen

The Burden of the Highborn

The Nobility and Lutheranism in Late Sixteenth-Century Denmark

1. A Noble Altar

The Danish National Museum collection features a private house and traveling altar from the noble couple, Herluf Trolle (1516–1565) and Birgitte Gøye (1511–1574). The altar shows the couple kneeling in front of a relief of the Holy Family, consisting of St Anna, her three daughters (one of them is the Virgin Mary), their husbands and a number of children. The Catholic motif has puzzled scholars because Trolle and Gøye were not Catholic. Instead the couple stood out as some of the most Lutheran, of the Danish nobility in the sixteenth century. Traditionally, scholars agree that the Catholic theme must have roots in Trolle and Gøye's hope for an heir – a hope that was never fulfilled (Bolvig: 1999, 23–14).

In my estimation, the traditional interpretation of the altar is incomplete, as it is too bound to the personal story of its two noble owners. In this chapter I will study the background for the motif on Trolle and Gøye's alter in the time period from 1559–1596. Seen through the noble death sermons of the period, I will look at the relationship of the nobility to Evangelical Lutheranism and how it affected the values and virtues of the nobility as a group. The period not only witnessed the formation of the new Lutheran confession in Denmark, but was also a phase of negotiation and formation for the role of the Lutheran magistrate. Through the role of the magistrate, the nobility could access the new dominant Lutheran worldview and legitimize its power by performing the responsibilities given to the magistrate as an institution. This chapter is thus a story of power, but to refine the story I will refer throughout to Pierre Bourdieu's theory of capital and practice to provide a broader perspective (Bourdieu: 1977, 159–197). For Bourdieu, power is not just about domination over others. The battle of power is just as much a battle of capital, legitimation, and acceptance. This perspective is especially important when one studies the nobility, a social group that traditionally has been seen as particularly hungry for power.

2. Methodological Frame

The study will be conducted with a concentration on the members of the Council of the Realm (Rigsrådet) in the time periode of 1559–1596. That is to say the Council of the Realm under King Frederik II (1534–1588) and the regency of his son Christian IV (1577–1648). The Council members were part of the Danish high nobility and thus some of the richest and most politically influential nobels in the Danish Kingdom.

The main source material for the study is noble death sermons and material artefacts found in churches affiliated with the nobility. The sermons and material artefacts concentrated on the ideal of the nobility and, as such, their factual value must often be taken lightly. But at the same time the sources illuminate the way the nobility negotiated their new role as magistrate after the Danish Reformation in 1536. Martin Luther had not made much room for the nobility in his religious theory of society – there was no noble estate in his teaching on the three orders.

Through the death sermons and the material artefacts, the nobility developed their association with the right to power and legitimacy of authority of the new confession. Their problem was Martin Luther had only granted power and legitimacy to the prince – not to the nobility. It is in this light that we must approach the death sermons and material artefacts. These sources reflect the nobility's attempts to be inscribed into what Pierre Bourdieu would call the social, cultural, and symbolic capital of the prince. As we will see, this inscription demanded that the nobility not only had to think in a Lutheran way, but also to act as a Lutheran was supposed to do. Thus, the Lutheran confession actually influenced the physical actions of the nobility.

3. Previous Research

Previous research in the Danish Reformation has not focused very much on the impact of the Reformation on the nobility. Charlotte Appel and Morten Fink-Jensen (2013) briefly touched on the subject of the Reformation in their major work on Danish school history prior to 1780. The topic of the Reformation's impact on the nobility has also not been broached within research on the nobility. Instead, the focus has been on the vanity of the nobility after the Reformation (Bang: 1897; Gjellerup: 1873) and, later, on political, economic, military, and social approach.[1] Noble religion and faith has not been a separate field of research in Danish noble history. This lacuna is peculiar because the group played a central role in the Danish Reformation, initially as opponents and later on as

1 For a short summary of the Danish history of noble research, see Lind (2014).

staunch supporters of the Lutheran Reformation in Denmark. Internationally, the field has gotten more attention. In Sweden, Peter Ullgren has published the book *Lantadel* (2004) in which he describes the patriarchal system that formed early modern noble-farmer relations in Sweden. He examines the relations between social groups, but not the origin of these relations. In Germany, where the link between Reformation and nobility is more evident, there have been some studies on the subject. But because of the Augsburg Peace of 1555 and the power held by the local princes, German historians have studied these princes more than the nobility, missing the impact of the Reformation on the elite as a whole (Jendorff: 2015; Gehrt/von der Osten-Sacken: 2015). In the Anglo-Saxon world, there have been some studies in the piety and beliefs of the nobility. For example, the book by Felicity Heal and Clive Holmes *The Gentry in England and Wales 1500–1700* (1994) attempts to give a full picture of the landed gentry in England and Wales, including two chapters on piety, belief, and the church. Still, the focus is more on the personal religion of the gentry than how religion formed the noble ideal through a confessional culture.

Thomas Kaufmann's concept of *confessional culture* frames this chapter. The theory emphasizes that Lutheran Denmark was not the same as Lutheran Sweden or Germany. Instead the Danish confessional culture was formed by local concerns, thus making room for a uniquely Danish understanding of the Lutheran magistrate. Kaufmann stresses that religion was present in all layers of culture and is an important point for historical analysis (Kaufmann: 2006, 10). Therefore, the main goal of the chapter is to introduce religion as an inescapable object for analysis in Danish nobility research. Religion played just as important a part of noble identity as politics, wars, and economy. A second aim is to contribute to an international research discussion on how confessional culture formed the ideal, mentality, and activity of a social group in an early modern Lutheran society.

4. The Historical Context

The Lutheran Reformation eliminated the late medieval theory of society, based on the societal division in *oratores, laboratores,* and *bellatores* (Duby: 1978). Instead Lutheranism offered a new social theory based on Luther's three orders of society (household, church, and government). The theory of the three orders was widely distributed in Denmark through preaching in the parish churches, the educational system, and religious books such as Luther's two catechisms (Appel/Fink-Jensen: 2013, 45.89). However, the dissemination of Luther's works left no place for the nobility and threatened the religious legitimation the group had enjoyed in the Middle Ages. As I will show, practice differed from the Lutheran worldview, but in Luther's point of view, the nobility constituted a household under the same conditions as the household of a peasant or merchant.

The Danish government, the Crown, in Reformation era Denmark (roughly 1536–1660), consisted of the king together with the noble members of the Council of the Realm. This structure contrasts with the pre-Reformation government, which consisted of the king, the nobility, and the Catholic bishops. It also differs from the period of absolutism after 1660, when the king alone, at least in theory, comprised the government. In Danish historiography, the time period from 1536 to 1660 is often named the "Reign of the Aristocracy" (Adelsvældet). The suitability of this title is debatable, but it indicates how the Danish government built on a consensus between the upper nobility and the king. This worked well until the middle of the reign of king Christian IV, when the council and the king no longer trusted each other and the king began to act in general independence from the council (Lockhart: 2007, 155–169).

The extent of power the ordinary nobility possessed under the Reign of the Aristocracy remains unclear. However, it is possible to assert that the council-members themselves wielded significant power through their position in the council and the offices given to them by the king. The Danish nobility only represented 0,2–0,3 % of the entire population. Including women and children, the noble population consisted of about 2.000–3.000 individuals, of which approximately 700–800 were members of the upper echelons of the nobility. By contrast, European nobility made up on average somewhere around 1–2 % of the population (Rasmussen: 2002, 135; Hansen: 1964, 240). Even though the number of Danish nobles was very low, they dominated not only political life, but also agricultural and economical life. The development has in recent Danish history been named the "process of aristocratization" (*Aristokratiseringsprocessen*). Through the process, where the lesser gentry lost their rights and titles as nobles, the majority of the remaining group of nobles gained extreme wealth and political power (Ingesman: 2001, 244). From the beginning of the sixteenth century, the group began coining noble last names like Rosenkrantz and Gyldenstierne,[2] taking long and expensive educations and, in doing so, distancing themselves from the rest of society. The group was thus increasingly aware of the collective ideal of the nobility in the 1500s (Helk: 1987, 9f; Netterstrøm: 2012, 12).

The development of the noble ideas and the nobility's monopoly on political power meant that membership of the Council was more or less unofficially passed along through noble families during this period. The upper nobility's monopoly over the state administration was a fairly new development. Up until the Reformation, the upper nobility had competed with high ranking members of

2 In the medieval period the last name of a noble would normally be the name of his father, for instance Otte Nielsen, d. 1477 (Otte Niels*son*), instead of Otte Rosenkrantz.

the clergy for seats in the Council of the Realm and offices in the royal administration. Sometimes this even resulted in armed conflict between the two groups (Ingesman: 2001; Netterstrøm: 2012).

The process of aristocratization, the removal of the clergy from political positions after 1536, and the creation of the centralized state all influenced the nobility. After the Reformation, the king gained control over former church lands, which increased the power of the crown dramatically. The nobility, in turn, were reduced to small players in the political game. Although the king gained new material power through annexation of church lands etc., after the Reformation, the Crown nevertheless still depended upon the nobility's presence at the local level. After 1660 the nobility lost great part of its inherited power, but before this, the second half of sixteenth century in Denmark was a time of crisis, negotiation, and formation. To substantiate royal power over the country, the king needed an alliance with a local power namely, the nobility. Therefore, the Crown was prepared to inscribe the nobility into the powers assigned to the Lutheran magistrate (Jespersen: 2007, 63–87). This is why the king began granting official juridical rights over their peasants, ownership of churches, own noble law courts, etc. to the nobility as early as 1536.[3]

5. The Source Material: Death Sermons as Media of Negotiation

The main source material of the present chapter is noble death sermons.[4] The sermons were intended as devotional writings, but their nature was to inscribe the particular noble into an Lutheran framework. The Protestant death sermons originated because of the need to explain to the congregation how to both to live and die as a Lutheran Christian and, thus, to require salvation (Holst: 1999, 281–286; Jacobsen: 2015, 1–11). Inspiration was found partly in the sermons given by Martin Luther, Johannes Bugenhagen (1485–1558), and Philip Melanchthon (1497–1560) and partly from an older tradition from antiquity (Holst: 1999, 284f). The published sermons began with a preface (often a small sermon in itself) addressed to the bereaved and which set the theme of the sermon. The sermon itself came next and included a chosen passage, chapter or book from the Bible. This was followed by a biography of the deceased. This biographical conclusion was meant to be an exemplum on how to live and die in the correct manner. Some death sermons from this time placed the biography prior to the

3 *Hals- og håndsret, patronatsret, birkeret.* For more on the legal rights of the nobility, see Lerdam (2004).

4 The sermons were written in Danish and all translations are done by me.

sermon, but the structure outlined here was the most common (Jacobsen: 2015, 3–11).

Between 1565 and 1800 557 death sermons were published in Denmark. The majority of these date to the period leading up to 1660. 73 % of the surviving sermons are noble. This stands in contrast to Germany, where only 34 % are noble (Holst: 1999, 281). Twenty-six death sermons have been handed down from Frederik II's Council of the Realm and these constitutes the written source material of this chapter. The sermons were intended to speak first and foremost to other nobles, but we know that also parish pastors and even the burghers owned and read them (Appel: 2001, 749f).

The death sermons were normative. This means that they emphasized a role and ideal for the nobility that might not have existed, but rather presented a theoretical understanding for the shape and function of the group. The sermons should consequently be seen to reveal the ongoing negotiation of the ideal of the nobility. Next to the nobility, there were at least two other actors in creation of the noble ideal in sixteenth century Denmark. As mentioned above, Martin Luther and Lutheranism had not made much room for the nobility in the social ordering of society. But in the sixteenth century this ordering was still only a theological construction that was just beginning to take shape in the Danish society. Instead, the Crown adopted a very liberal approach to the nobility both on a national and local level. On the national level high ranking nobles had an important voice in political matters through their membership of the Council of the Realm. At the local level, the king confirmed rights of the nobility that had been unofficial before the Reformation. The king also granted lucrative state offices to the nobility, such as lordships of royal fiefs (*lensmandsskab*). The Crown, thus, bestowed power on the nobility at both a local and a national level. We could say then that the Crown had access to what Bourdieu would define as the political and economic capital – a capital that the nobility sought to attain. Besides the nobility the Crown was thus an actor in the negotiation of the noble ideal.

Another actor was the clergy. This estate had lost most of its secular powers after the Reformation and was now dependent on a friendly secular authority. Since the nobility in both juridical terms and in praxis was often "the best of the parish" (Bay: 2001, 297), he/she had authority over the physical church after the Reformation. But on the other hand, as administrators of the ecclesial institution, the clergy had access to the symbolic capital and the legitimation of authority that the nobility desired. Consequently, numerous death sermons reveal the clergy to mount several demands to the nobility just after thanking them for their friendship and economic support. These demands had to be met if the nobility wanted access to the symbolic capital and legitimation that only the clergy could grant. Bishop Peder Vinstrup (1549–1614), for example, listed no less than nine virtues that the nobility had to follow. If they did not, then "unhappiness and plague" (Vinstrup: 1594, C8v) would engulf the country.

To summarize, at least two other actors existed in addition to the nobility in the negotiation of the noble ideal. Through the roles Lutheranism had ascribed to the king and clergy, they became able to grant the nobility a legitimate right to perform power. But to be granted this, the nobility had to accept the rules and hierarchies in the conceptual framework of the Lutheran Confession. If not accepting these rules, which Pierre Bourdieu calls the *doxa* or the unspoken rules of a given social field, the two other actors would not export their capitals to the nobility (Bourdieu: 1977,159–170). In the following section I will turn to the content of the *doxa*.

6. The Lutheran Virtues

6.1. The Noble Encounter with Lutheran Ideas

When discussing in what way the Reformation influenced the Danish nobility, the first question that arises is how the nobility encountered the new religious ideas and thoughts of the century. The first generations of nobility actually met Martin Luther, Philip Melanchthon, and other reformers face to face. For example, we know that Herluf Trolle, Jørgen Rosenkrantz (1523–1596), and Johan Friis (1494–1570) studied in Wittenberg in the time of Luther and Melanchthon (Colding: 1979–1984/2017; Rosenkrantz: 1590/1750; Vedel: 1571)

Leading Danish theologians were also in contact with the nobility. Sometimes nobles and scholars had studied together and sometimes the aristocracy had sponsored the works and educations of the learned. Herluf Trolle studied with the famous Danish theologians Niels Hemmingsen (1513–1600) and Peder Palladius (1503–1560). Both theologians were also in contact with other high ranking members of the Danish nobility, such as Frands Brockenhuus (1518–1569) and Mette Rosenkrantz (1533–1588) (Glebe-Møller: 1979–1984/2017; Rockstroh: 1933–1934/2017; Bruun: 199–1934/2017). Whereas the theological networks of the noblemen was very international, it seems that the female network often were more regional. This was probably due to the fact that the single most used international language of scholars was Latin, and normally Latin was not taught to females (Andersen: 1971, 91–99).

The generations after the deaths of Luther and Melanchthon encountered the Lutheran Reformation mainly through education. Luther's catechisms were especially popular. Both sexes became acquainted with these texts throughout their years of study. Noble boys and girls were raised in a life of devotion and piety. There were two ways for noble children to encounter Lutheranism: Through private tutoring or by studying under professors from the public Latin schools.[5] The latter was only available to boys. Sources for these private tutors only exist after the year 1600, but they all seem to follow the educational structure found in the Danish Church Ordinance from 1537/1539 (KiO, 157). The sources after 1600 can therefore exemplify how the private teaching of the nobility took place.

In 1650, the private tutor Basilius Chemnitz wrote *Bibliotheca Rothkirchiana Eqvestris.* The work is a summary of the daily education of the nobleman Wenzel Rothkirch (1597–1655) and his wife Kirsten Reedtz's (1610–1646) many children. In it, Chemnitz explains that each day consisted of three lessons. The boys and girls were educated separately. Each lesson began with singing a hymn followed by a prayer. Almost the entire school day for the boys consisted of lessons in Latin. Therefore, to practice Latin and "To truly recognize and acknowledge God" (Chemnitz: 1971/1650, 129), they read parts of Martin Luther's Latin and German catechism every morning and evening. Like the boys, the girls also studied Luther's catechism, however only the German version.

Even though private tutors at the estates educated most noble children, some noble boys also went to the public Latin schools. Sources dating to before 1600 testify to these institutions. Like private tutors, the schools focused on Luther's catechisms, which taught the children Latin while also instilling in them right faith. The first year syllabus from the Latin school in Aalborg (which at least twelve noble boys attended between 1536–1660) indicates that the first year of study included Luther's Latin catechism among other topics. In the second to third year syllabi, the students had to study the Wittenberg Catechism, dating from 1571 (Andersen: 1971, 38–52, 65f).

Because of the educational emphasis on central pieces of Lutheran theology, it is possible to argue that the Lutheran worldview helped to shape the way that the Danish nobility understood their position in the world. The main source to this self-understanding was the catechism. Noble boys and girls went through both the Small and the Large Catechism every week. As if this was not enough, virtually all male members of the upper nobility went on yearlong travels to Germany, Italy, and France. In France and Italy, they studied how to become the perfect aristocrat, but in Germany they studied theology (Helk: 1987, 10). Thus the nobility as a social unit might have been the most learned Lutheran group in all of the Danish-Norwegian Realm.

5 Can be compared with a secondary school or high school.

6.2. What Did the Nobility Learn from Luther?

Much can be said about the influence of Luther's catechisms on society, but other chapters in this book deal with that subject. Therefore, the present chapter will only give attention to the ideal role of the magistrate – it was the role of the magistrate that the Danish nobility tried to monopolize as a distinctly noble attribute.

Luther ordered society based on the fourth commandment: Thou shalt honor thy father and thy mother as described in his two Catechisms from 1529. The commandment engages the inter-human relations and deals with the authority in the temporal kingdom. Luther argues that all authority in the world originates from this commandment. Authority was required because the fall of Adam and Eve had brought sin into the temporal kingdom and that sin had to be controlled. Thus to obey the authorities meant to honor God and consequently do good works: "if you do your daily household chores, that is better than the holiness and austere life of all the monks" (BC 406/WA 30 I: 153,15f). The authorities were instituted by God and, hence, masks of Him, *larvae Dei:* "It must therefore be impressed on young people that they revere their parents as God's representatives." (BC 401/WA 30 I: 147,23f). The authority of the magistrate was constructed on the base of the authority of the housefather and mother: "Thus all who are called masters stand in the place of parents and must derive from them their power and authority to govern." (BC 406/WA 30 I: 152,26f).

Luther's conception of the role of the mother and father was not just applied to the master and mistress of the household, but also to the national authorities. He claimed, "[f]or all other authority is derived and developed out of the authority of parents" (BC 405/WA 30 I: 152,20f). Just as the institutions of the fathers and mothers of the household were masks of God (and thus deserved to be honored like Christians had to honor God), likewise the institution of the magistrate was a mask of God. The magistrate was the father of society and society was his household. Because the institution of the magistrate was sanctioned by God, honoring the magistrate was the same as doing good works. Even if they "go too far" (BC 401/WA 30 I: 148,11), subjects were called to honor and obey the magistrate. Thus, honor was the central element for Luther when he dealt with the relation between the subjects and the institution of the magistrate. Patience and humility to the institution were also present as key duties for the subjects.[6]

However, it was not only the children, servants and subordinates that had a responsibility. The father, or the magistrate, had duties to fulfil towards the greater noble household. Thus, the last part of the section about the fourth commandment deals with the responsibility of the parents and the temporal

6 See also the chapter by Sasja Emilie Mathiasen Stopa in the present volume.

authorities. Magistrates and parents had been given the right to rule over different aspects of the temporal world. But to justifiably claim this right, they had to fulfill various duties. One of the most important obligations for a magistrate was righteousness: "Therefore do not imagine that the parental office is a matter of your pleasure and whim. It is a strict commandment and injunction of God, who holds you accountable for it" (BC 409/WA 30 I: 156,14–17). The authorities were not to abuse their subjects. Instead, it was the duty of the authorities to try to instill the Christian faith in their subjects. That was a very important duty, so important that the magistrate could lose God's support if he/she did not fulfill this responsibility: "Therefore let all people know that it is their chief duty [...] at the risk of losing divine [if they do not try to fulfil their duty]" (BC 410/WA 30 I: 156,32 f).

As we will see in the next part of the chapter, the nobility understood themselves as local magistrates. As such, they were very well aware of the duties that Luther had placed on the subjects of the greater noble household. But they were also aware of their own responsibilities towards their subjects.

7. The Duties of the Magistrate as a Central Part of the Noble Ideal

7.1. The Magistrate as a Noble Ideal

Since the nobility was well-rehearsed in Lutheran theology and social teaching, it is fruitful to study to what extent this affected the noble ideal and how it formed the everyday activities of the group. To study how the nobility performed a self-image as Lutheran magistrates, this section will analyze chosen death sermons of the members of the Council of the Realm. In the next section, I will investigate whether this ideal influenced the physical actions of the nobility. As I sketched above, the Lutheran magistrate was chosen by God and, therefore, had the right to be honored by his/hers subjects. At the same time, the magistrate was obligated to be a pious Christian and an example to his/her subjects. Parts of the magistrate's authority, therefore, rested on his/her performance of piety. The nobility had to prove that they had the symbolic capital to legitimize their power over their subjects. If they could not do this, they would not be accepted as a legitimate magisterial power according to Lutheran beliefs.

Niels Kaas' (1535–1594) death sermon by bishop Peder Vinstrup from 1594 demonstrates how symbolic capital can create and legitimize economic and political capital. God has blessed the country by "giving a clever and very wise magistrate, by which Council and Government Churches / School / and Police is kept." These pious men are "paid" by God, both in "the temporal world and later in the Eternal Realm" (Vinstrup: 1594, A4v). Vinstrup proceeds to explain why the authorities are so wealthy. He refers to the Psalms of David and argued that all the great characters in the Old Testament, such as Abraham, David, Solomon etc., were rich because they were more pious than others, "the LOrd's Blessing makes Rich without trouble" (Vinstrup: 1594, 105). Then, why are not all pious men wealthy? To this question Vinstrup answers that only the finest of the finest can handle being both rich and pious (Vinstrup: 1594, E8v). Piety is an important element for the authorities. For Vinstrup piety could be inherited "Just as [...] they [sc. the pious] follow in the footsteps of their God-fearing and Honorable Parents: So also, he [sc. Christ] says, will the Offspring of the impious / inherit the same conditions as their Parents before them." (Vinstrup: 1594, G5v).

If the nobility wanted to be perceived as just parents of society they had to act piously; they had to generate symbolic capital to be accepted. If not, they had no right to hold authority in the temporal world. This was not an original invention. According to Luther, wealth and piety were inheritable: "where there are fine, old families who prosper and have many children, it is certainly because some of them were brought up well and honored their parents" (BC 405/WA 30 I: 152,5ff). Because piety was inheritable, the children of the rich were by definition born pious themselves. Since the wealthiest people in the temporal world were the nobility, they were also by definition the most pious and thus the best candidates to hold authority in the temporal world. Through this kind of socio-cultural worldview, different forms of capital could according to the death sermons be inherited down through the generations of the nobility.

If a magistrate did not possess the proper characteristics, such as piety and setting a good example for his/hers subjects, God's wrath would create chaos in the temporal world and all kinds of disasters would ensue: "the People shall bully [each other] / the one over the other / and everyone over his Neighbor / And the Young shall be proud towards the Old [that is to say, not heed their advice] / and a contemptuous Man against an honorable [Man]" (Vinstrup: 1594, C8r).

7.2. Good Works as Proof of Noble Faith

Besides branding magistrates as unusually pious individuals, the death sermons also describe at least three ideal behaviors of the Lutheran magistrate. All three ways are based on the ideal of the Lutheran authority of the parents and their duty to promote and support the Protestant faith and common good of society. The practical ideal was not contrived out of thin air: Central Lutheran theologians and jurists had been discussing the responsibilities of the magistrate since Martin Luther himself (Witte: 2002, 15ff).

The nobility attended especially to education, care for the poor and support of the church. In theory, these obligations were the responsibility of the prince, but in practice support of the nobles was welcome. These three welfare institutions were the responsibility of the church in Catholic times and, as such, the nobility took over aspects of these obligations at least on a local level.[7]

According to the sermons, education was perhaps the most important thing for the nobility to support. In his *On the Councils and the Church* from 1539 Martin Luther describes the significance of education as "second in importance only to the church" (LW 41: 176/WA 50: 652,1). Without basic skills such as reading and writing it was not possible to read the Bible and thus the Word of God. So education was one of the most important things to promote as a noble magistrate. The noble magistrate should "promote GOd's Teaching and Honor among Humans" (Gødissøn: 1597, A3r) and "the Christian Church cannot hold sway for long, if no one is being trained in Academic studies and the Holy Scripture" (Wad: 1893, xviii). Economic support to the educational system could thus generate symbolic capital and liken the role of magistrate to the donator.

Furthermore, the noble support of educational institutions and individuals was essential for the early modern Danish educational system. The Danish church ordinance of 1539 established one Latin school in every market town, but it was quickly evident that the finances did not support the obligations. Consequently, teachers at the schools were poorly paid and did not stay for long. To have pre-university schools was not a new thing. Before the Reformation many a noble boy and girl had been educated in the Cathedral schools or monasteries, but it was a new thing that the government established an official network of schools in the Realm.

The noble support of education can be split in two groups. The first group was the economic support to public institutions that educated the young. In a sermon written by Anders Sørensen Vedel at the death of Johan Friis, it is specified that he often gave to the schools and other educational developments. He has "not saved neither Goods nor Penny / to promote Schoolchildren with" (Vedel: 1571, L7v). Friis is also said to have given 300 rix-dollars (*Rigsdaler*) to the school and the poor in Odense and he supported twelve students at the University of Copenhagen. We cannot prove this support, but that is not the essential part. What is important is the public perception in early modern Denmark. The noble magistrate had not only rights, he also had paternal duties: "In all manners did he [sc. Johan Friis] promote and improve schools like a Father," writes Niels Hemmingsen (Vedel: 1571, L7v).[8]

7 For the role of the nobility in the creation of a concrete welfare institution, see Ørnbjerg (2011).
8 One of the greatest school benefactors was Herluf Trolle and Birgitte Gøye. In 1565 they

The other way the nobility supported the educational system in Denmark was through their very important role as benefactors of the training of individual scholars. This could be done in two ways. The first was by giving direct grants to scholars. We know that Birgitte Gøye, Peder Oxe (1520–1575), Jørgen Rosenkrantz, and others supported the educational travels of young scholars (Helk: 1987, 16). However, the main way for the nobility to support young scholars was indirect. By hiring scholars as private tutors *(præceptores)* for the compulsory Grand Tour of the noble boys, the nobility not only educated their own kin, but also gave the tutors the possibility of further studies at the universities they visited. This way, the private tutor also got educated according to the most modern standards. The nobility thus played a key part in creating a modern and internationally-oriented Danish academic elite (Helk: 1987, 13–24).

Care for the poor was another welfare institution that the nobility supported as one of the magistrate's duties. Many manors had established or at least supported a local hospital or poor house close to their main estate.[9] These were situated close to the local church that the particular nobleman or noblewoman either had rights over or believed to have rights over. Also the death sermons often deal with poor relief of some sort. Poor relief is always mentioned when the religious qualities of a nobleman or noblewoman are discussed. Usually the noble would donate a sum of money, when lying on their deathbed. For instance, Jørgen Rosenkrantz donated 600 pence of corn and founded a grant for poor people in his parish: "And he did this so that the poor Farmer with his Wife and Children would be able to keep up [with their rent] / and not be impoverished and go bust." (Gødissøn: 1597, G2r).

One of the nobles that tended most dutifully to the poor was Pernille Gøye (1550–1589). On her deathbed, she is said to have donated 300 rix-dollars to the poor and the year she died, she reduced the annual rent of her tenants by 50 %. But her greatest magisterial deed was her yearly "Charity alms and [donating] rather [large] Sums of Money" (Madsen: 1590, K2vf). In her death sermon, the author bishop Mogens Madsen (1527–1611) describes her yearly alms as a performance worthy of a true noble magistrate. The reason for this was not the amount she gave, but that she gave her alms in secret – only the local parish priest knew who had given it. Thus, he praised her saying, "This was what Christ taught / when he punished the Jews [...] that gave their charity alms on [for their own] praise." (Madsen: 1590, K3vf).

Gøye's donations and kindness to the poor definitely generated symbolic capital, but her secrecy about it did not give her access to that capital. However,

founded the free noble school of Herlufsholm. It was the first Danish private school that was directly inspired by Lutheran ideals (Andersen 1971: 44f).

9 See http://www.danskeherregaarde.dk (seen: 27.02.2017).

Madsen's emphasis on her religious qualities and the sociocultural noble inheritance of capital staged her husband, Hak Holgersen Ulfstand (1535–1594), to inherit Gøye's symbolic capital.

As with education, care for the poor was one of the ways that the Lutheran virtues of setting a good example for the public and helping and supporting one's subjects was performed in practice. The more one wanted to be perceived by the population as a legitimate magistrate, the more one had to support the poor. This way economic capital could be converted into symbolic capital. There is only one example in the source material where a noble does not give alms to the poor on his deathbed, and that is in the case of Niels Kaas. Bishop Peder Vinstrup tries to move attention away from this neglect by arguing that Kaas "no longer wanted to deal with Worldly matters" (Vinstrup: 1594, B6v). Furthermore, Vinstrup argued that it was not Kaas's fault, it was actually the people around him that had forgotten to remind him that he was expected to donate to the poor, the church, and educational institutions (Vinstrup: 1594, B6rf). In this respect, Kaas did not act according to *doxa*. The error was apparently so grand that Vinstrup mentioned it in the death sermon and highlighted several times that Kaas was worthy of the role as magistrate despite this minor forgetfulness on his part.

Individual care for the poor was not a new thing; it existed very much in the Middle Ages, but the form had changed with the Reformation. In medieval times, one gave support to the poor to gain sacred capital that could be used in the afterlife.[10] Traces of this process were likely also present after 1536, but the form had changed. After the Reformation, the nobility gave money to the poor because it was a duty of the caring and loving magistrate – it was a central part of the magisterial duty to support the common good in society. To act as a magistrate who cared for the poor was thus a legitimation of the nobility's right to power.[11]

Church support was the third way the nobility could communicate their positioning as Lutheran as magistrates. Some nobles rebuilt the medieval church to match the new religion (for instance Svindinge church that was built to match its owner's leanings towards Philippism), but the most common act was to donate objects. The chancel arch in Ålsø church declares that the noble couple Thomas Fasti (1538–1600) and Christence Bryske (1545–1611) donated to the church. Their gifts included important Lutheran objects such as an altar and a pulpit, but also investments in church pews, a tower, and a porch. By inscribing Fasti's and Bryske's donations to the church on the chancel arch (beautifully painted with the couple's coats of arms held by angels), the local congregation would always be aware of what the couple had done for the church and the religious welfare of its congregation. This way, Fasti and Bryske fulfilled the role as magistrates and thus

10 For more on this subject, see Bisgaard (1988).
11 For more on this subject, see Jürgensen (2011).

legitimated themselves as a local noble magistrate. Their flow of economic capital to the church was converted into symbolic capital that could be exchanged to legitimate their social, cultural, and political capital in both local and national society.

The nobility sponsored high alters, pulpits, epitaphs, burial chambers, pews, and other items in the churches. This was not a new thing. Nobles also had a presence especially in the abbey churches in the late Middle Ages. To make sure that people did not forget who had sponsored the art in the churches, the nobles made sure to write their names or coat of arms on the donations. However, the difference after the Reformation in 1536 was that now the nobility also became a group of magistrates. Martin Luther's showdown with indulgences had changed the view of the donation. The noble donations were, at least in theory, no longer for their own sake. Now it was for the common good of the people. By performing according to the Lutheran *doxa*, that confession helped legitimize the power of the nobility in society.

A modern analysis of the heightened presence of the nobility in the parish churches would emphasize political power as the main motivation (Bay: 2001, 298f). But this was not the way the nobles themselves branded their presence in the church room. Instead, they branded their gifts for "the honor of God, decoration of the church, and themselves to eternal remembrance" (ibid., 298). The death sermons reveal that the eternal remembrance of a nobleman or noblewoman had nothing to do with a person's nobility, but instead was linked to the noble person's God-given authority as a father of society. The people should:

> thank God who has given us for a while these Instruments of Grace and Honor of his. [We should] not only raise Monuments and Memorials for them / after the old Roman ways / or [just] adorn their Graves with Death writings / But speak of their Name / Virtue and works / with a honest remembrance / that God / whose Instruments they have been / therefore can be honored / [and] others can be attracted and cultivated in Virtue and competences so that they may reach their course. (Gødissøn: 1596, A4v).

The branding of the nobility as God's chosen authorities and examples to the people is clearly reflected in this quote. Noble monuments, epitaphs, death writings, and other church donations were donated to the churches to decorate it with art for the sake of the people and to the glory of God. And the reason that the nobles put their names, coat of arms, and pictures on the art is because they were God's chosen magistrates, fathers of society, and thus holders of symbolic capital.

8. Concluding Remarks

If we return to Herluf Trolle's and Birgitte Gøyes' traveling altar several possible interpretations exist for their choice of the motif of the Holy Family. The first could be an economic perspective. The reason Trolle and Gøye had not changed the altar might have been that it simply was cheaper to reuse a Catholic image it than to buy a new traveling altar. After all, the nature of a traveling altar is to be private, so only a few would see the supposedly Catholic theme. Another interpretation could be that Trolle and Gøye kept the old motif for nostalgic reasons. The Holy Family was a well-known subject matter that had been popular through the entire Middle Ages.

There is also the possibility that the motif was retained because the Lutheran worldview was a fundamental part of the noble ideal. Lutheranism was the basic framework, the social imaginary, of all social groups in sixteenth-century Denmark. All authority in sixteenth-century Denmark was rooted in Lutheranism and also the authority of the nobility. To be legitimized as an authority, the nobility had to act according to the Lutheran confession. That meant that they had to prove their religiosity – their symbolic capital. It was not enough to say that you were a Lutheran magistrate; you also had to act like one.

I have shown that the key element in the authority-subject relationship was reciprocity. On the one hand, the nobility claimed the supremacy over their subjects in a given field of interest. But on the other hand, the nobility had to gain symbolic capital that could legitimize their right as magistrates. The nobility's authority was, thus, not secured in the time period after the Reformation. Instead, their authority was up for negotiation. The group had to act according to the new social rules of post-Reformation Denmark, the *doxa* of Lutheranism. Martin Luther conceived authorities as the masks of God and, therefore, the nobility had to fulfil this expectation in their actions. To be a mask of God meant to be pious, more pious than the rest of the population, because the magistrate had to be an example to his/her subjects. The question was how to prove one's piety and, by it, to legitimize the noble person's magisterial role under the new religion? How to negotiate yourself into being accepted as a legitimate actor in the social field? The noble's answer was through donations and support of welfare institutions. Good works revealed the noble's faith to the people and created the symbolic capital that was needed to legitimate his/her magisterial authority. It was a point of negotiation for the nobility. A true Lutheran magistrate was responsible for the welfare of the population, thus the nobility supported the schools, the poor, and the churches, just as Martin Luther had written in his two catechisms that the true magistrate should do. Power was not given to the magistrate for their arbitrary will, instead it was a strict command and injunction of God (BC 409f/WA 30 I: 156). It was not supposed to be pleasurable to be a rich magistrate. Instead, it was the burden of the highborn. Herluf Trolle touched on this topic in his death sermon: "Aye, do we want the sweet things, we also have to include the sour" (Wad: 1893, xxii).

Through donations and welfare support (and especially the branding of one's donations) the nobility communicated their faith and piety to the world and thus legitimized their right to the role as magistrate. According to the death sermons, the nobles' donations were proof of their piety and faith, but also proof of their fulfilment of their responsibilities as magistrates. If we see Herluf Trolle and Birgitte Gøye's altar in this context, we do not see a noble couple praying to a Catholic saint. Instead they pray to the Lutheran ordering of the world, the responsibility of the magistrate, and the burden of the nobility, the burden of the highborn.

Bibliography

Andersen, Birte (1971), Adelig opfostring, Copenhagen: G.E.C Gad.

Appel, Charlotte (2001), Læsning og bogmarked, vol. 1–2, Copenhagen: Museum Tusculanum Press.

Appel, Charlotte/Morten Fink-Jensen (2013), Da læreren holdt skole (Dansk Skolehistorie 1), Aarhus: Aarhus University Press.

Bang, Gustav (1897), Den gamle Adels Forfald, Copenhagen: Gyldendal.

Bay, Ole (2001), Den danske adel og kirken efter reformationen (1536–1660), in: Per Ingesman/Jens Villiam Jensen, Riget, Magten og Æren, Aarhus: Aarhus University Press, 286–313.

Bisgaard, Lars (1988), Tjenesteideal og fromhedsideal, Aarhus: Arusia.

Bolvig, Axel (1999), Fru Birgittes kunst, Skalk 1, 20–27.

Bourdieu, Pierre (1977), Outline of a Theory of Practice (Cambridge Studies in Social and Cultural Anthropology 16), Cambridge: Cambridge University Press.

Bruun, Henry (1933–1934/2017), Article "Mette Rosenkrantz", DBL, http://denstoredanske.dk/Dansk_Biografisk_Leksikon/Landbrug,_skovbrug_og_gartneri/Godsejer/Mette_Rosenkrantz (seen 01.03.2017).

Chemnitz, Basilius (1650/1971), Bibliotheca Rothkirchiana Equvestris, reproduced in: Andersen: 1971, 124–137.

Duby, Georges (1978), Les trois ordres ou L'imaginaire du féodalisme, Paris: Gallimard.

Gehrt, Daniel/Vera von der Osten-Sacken (2015), Fürstinnen und Konfession (VIEG 104), Göttingen: Vandenhoeck & Ruprecht.

Gjellerup, S.M. (1873), Nogle Bemærkninger om Samfundsforholdene, især Opdragelsen, hos den danske Adel, HT 4/IV, 1–42.

Glebe-Møller, Jens (1979–1984/2017), Article "Niels Hemmingsen", DBL, http://denstoredanske.dk/Dansk_Biografisk_Leksikon/Kirke_og_tro/Teolog/Niels_Hemmingsen (seen 01.03.2017).

Gødissøn, Jens (1597), Den XC. Dauids Psalme/ som kaldis Mose Guds Mands Bøn/ Udlagt og forklaret vdi en Liigpredicken/ i Hornslet Kircke paa vor Herris Himmelfarts Dag/ som vaar den 20. Maij 1596, Copenhagen: Vingaard (LN 661).

Hansen, Svend Aage (1964), Adelsvældens grundlag, Copenhagen: G.E.C. Gad.

Heal, Felicity/Clive Holmes (1994), The Gentry in England and Wales, 1500–1700, Stanford, CA: Stanford University Press.

Helk, Vello (1987), Dansk-Norske Studierejser, vol. 1, Odense: Odense Universitetsforlag.

Hens, H.A./Paul Colding (1979–1984/2017), Article "Herluf Trolle", DBL, http://denstoredanske.dk/Dansk_Biografisk_Leksikon/Samfund,_jura_og_politik/Myndigheder_og_politisk_styre/Rigsr%C3%A5d/Herluf_Trolle (seen 01.03.2017).

Holst, Elisabet (1999), Kvindedyd og kvindedød i danske ligprædikener 1570–1700, in: Flemming Lundgreen-Nielsen/Hanne Ruus (ed.), Svøbt i mår, vol. 1, Copenhagen: C.A. Reitzel, 281–325.

Ingesman, Per (2001), Milicia contra Ecclesiam? in: Per Ingesman/Jens Villiam Jensen (ed.), Riget, Magten og Æren, Aarhus: Aarhus University Press, 243–274.

Jacobsen, Grethe (2015), Danske ligprædikener 1565–1610, HT 115/1, 1–36.

Jendorff, Alexander (2015), Heroen oder Verräter des Gotteswortes?, in: LuJ 82, 106–148.

Jürgensen, Martin Wangsgaard (2011), Changing Interiors, unpublished higher doctoral dissertation, University of Copenhagen.

Jespersen, Mikkel L. (2007), Administration og statsdannelse i Danmark 1400–1660, Den Jyske Historiker 116, 63–87.

Kaufmann, Thomas (2006), Konfession und Kultur: Lutherischer Protestantismus in der zweiten Hälfte des Reformationsjahrhunderts (SuR NR 29), Tübingen: Mohr Siebeck.

Lerdam, Henrik (2004), Birk, lov og ret, Copenhagen: Museum Tusculanum Press..

Lind, Gunner (2014), Adelsvældens grundlag 50 år efter, HT 114/2, 492–502.

Lockhart, Paul D. (2007), Denmark, 1513–1660: The Rise and Decline of a Renaissance Monarchy, Oxford: Oxford University Press.

Luther, Martin (1529), The Small Catechism (BC 347–375/WA 30 I: 243–425).

Luther, Martin (1539), On the Councils and the Church (LW 41/WA 50: 509–653).

Madsen, Mogens (1590), En Predicken af det elluffte Capitel i S. Hansis Euangelio Predicket i [...]Pernille Gyøes Begraffuelse i Gennerup Kircke i Skaane den 5. Octobris Anno etc. 1589, Copenhagen: Vingaard (LN 1124).

Netterstrøm, Jeppe B. (2012), Fejde og magt i senmiddelalderen, Auning: Landbohistorisk Selskab.

Rasmussen, Carsten Porskrog (2002), Nyere tid, in: Steen Busck/Henning Poulsen (ed.), Danmarks historie – i grundtræk, Aarhus: Aarhus Universitetsforlag.

Rockstroh, K.C. (1933–1934/2017), Article "Frands Brockenhuus", DBL, http://denstoredanske.dk/Dansk_Biografisk_Leksikon/Samfund,_jura_og_politik/Myndigheder_og_politisk_styre/Lensmand/Frands_Brockenhuus (seen 01.03.2017).

Rosenkrantz, Jørgen (1590/1750), Jørgen Rosenkrandses til Rosenholm Levnets Løb, DM 1/IV, 193–207.

Ullgren, Peter (2004), Lantadel: Adliga godsägare i Östergötland och Skäne vid 1600talets slut, Lund: Sisyfos Förlag.

VEDEL, ANDERS SØRENSEN (1571), En Predicken som skeede vdi Erlig Velbyrdig oc Gudfryctig mands/ salige Johan Friisis begraffuelse vdi Kiøbenhaffn/ den nittende dag Decembris/ Aar effter Guds byrd 1570, Copenhagen: Laurentz Benedicht (LN 1617).

VINSTRUP, PEDER (1594), Ligpredicken som i Erlige/ Velbyrdige oc Salige Herris Niels Kaasis [...] Begraffuelse bleff sørgelige holdit i Vor Frue Kircke i Kiøbenhaffn den IX. Søndag efter Trinitatis, som vaar den 28. Julii Anno 1594, Copenhagen: Vingaard (LN 1640).

WAD, GUSTAV (1893), Breve til og fra Herluf Trolle og Birgitte Gjøe, vol. 1, Copenhagen: Thaning og Appel.

ØRNBJERG, JAKOB (2011), Da den lokale Fattigforsorg i Aalborg blev Statsreguleret, Siden Saxo 2/28, 16–25.

Laura Katrine Skinnebach

Family Matters

The Formation of the Early Lutheran Devotional Household

1. Introduction: Spritualization of *Oeconomia*

Luther's doctrine of the three estates – *ecclesia, oeconomia*, and *politia* – newly defined *oeconomia* as household and marriage. Although the three estates were fundamentally interlaced, Luther regarded the household as particularly important because it sustained, developed, and provided the other estates (Wolgast: 2014, 402). The household was, according to Luther, a divine institution protected by the fourth commandment.[1]

Correspondingly, the household was inseparably intertwined with religious conduct. The household was regarded as the primary setting for teaching and practicing the words of the gospel. Luther described the religious household and the responsibility of parents in particular by using the ecclesiastical hierarchy as metaphor and model:

> Most certainly fathers and mothers are apostles, bishops, and priests to their children, for it is they who make them acquainted with the gospel. In short, there is no greater or nobler authority on earth than that of parents over their children, for this authority is both spiritual and temporal (LW 45: 46/WA 10 II: 301,23–27).

The metaphor establishes the authority and responsibility of parenthood as the mediating link between the spiritual and temporal. This was further emphasized in Luther's great lectures on Genesis (LW 1–8/WA 42–44) in which the Old Testament patriarchs and matriarchs were set forth as virtuous *exempla* for the household members. The lecture firmly links earthly living with the word of God: the practice of everyday life is an enactment of the biblical narratives (Strohl:

1 All the estates are divinely instituted as Luther underlines in the passage: "We are saved through Christ alone; but we become holy both through this faith and through these divine foundations and orders." (LW 37: 365/WA 26: 505,18ff).

2014, 373). Through the practice of parental authority and teaching, the household was spiritualized (Walsham: 2014b; Finch: 2007, 200).

Luther's writings on *oeconomia* manifests a firm conviction that a Christian life is a life ultimately governed in every detail by faith in God the Father, and that to live in Christ is fundamentally a *family matter*.

As scholars have argued, Reformation theology and practice interacted with wider cultures into which it was infused (Scribner: 2001; Marshall: 2002; Dietz: 2014). One should thus be mindful of sharp periodization and characteristics – medieval/modern, sacred/secular, Catholic/Lutheran – categories that mainly serve as principles of regulation, differentiation, occlusion and reification (Davis: 2002). Luther attempted to cultivate and propagate the domestic sphere as devotional "space," but the ideal of a devout family was not a new invention. The visual and devotional motif of the *Holy family* stands forth as a substantial example of medieval family ideals. However, Luther's conception of the household and its significance in the practice and dissemination of devotional values seems more systematic (Webb: 2005, 27–47; Blatt/Renevey/Whitehead: 2005, 195–250; Hanawalt/Kobialka: 2000).[2]

The appropriation and absorption of new religious and devotional practices and religious imagination into the very fabric of household conduct was a gradual process, but primed by and idealized in the domestic teaching of the catechism and especially the practice of the household manuals or table of duties (Appel: 2001; Pleijel: 1970). Aiding that process – or parallel to it – was the concurrent transformation and appropriation of material culture as a result of theological, devotional, social and political changes (Hamling/Richardson: 2010, 3ff). These transformations materialized not only in domestic settings, but also in other social and religious spaces in which the new Lutheran ideals were practiced, negotiated, and diffused.

With reference to Charles Taylor and in concert with the methodological framework of the present volume, the pious household can be understood as a "social imaginary," carried in, but also instrumentalized through words, pictures, music, practices, sermons, and spaces (Taylor: 2007, 171).[3] The chapter illustrates how the fundamental instrumentality of images and texts was explicated in early Lutheran devotional books and images, and investigates how the "social imaginary" of the pious household was represented in visual objects and devotional texts that may have influenced and encouraged a reinforcement of the spiritual household. The strengthened emphasis on household comes to the fore in two types of material in particular that will form the core of the present investigation: epitaphs that often depict whole families and thus il-

2 Changes in material culture were greatly affected by changes in production and consumption.

3 For a further presentation of the concept, see the introduction to the present volume.

lustrate ideas and ideals about household and devotional books (catechism, prayer books, and psalm books) used – often collectively – in the domestic sphere. These material signs of the integration of Lutheran ideals into household practice, sheds light on the dynamic formation of a Lutheran household and devout family habitus.

2. Material Objects and the Shaping of Social Imaginaries

In recent years, art historians and archaeologist have increasingly focused on how material and sensory objects – images, books, house wear, technological tools, etc. – serve as instruments that form and transform our perception of the world (Appadurai: 1986; Gaimster/Gilchrist: 2003; Findlen: 2013, 3–27; Jørgensen: 2015). The material culture of the early Lutheran period was extremely complex, combining old material with new and "reflect the patterns of belief and behaviour of the people who created and consumed (...)" these objects (Walsham: 2016, 570). Art Historian Caroline A. Jones (2006, 5–49, esp. 8) has stated that our senses are connected to the sensory tools we make; these tools then instrumentalize our senses. Media and material objects extend the bodily sensorium while at the same time it functions as a prism through which we perceive the world. Material transformations ultimately lead to transformations in our perception and commemoration. Objects surrounding us affect and configure our perception of the world; they form and transform our 'social imaginaries'. From a visual culture perspective, art historian Marx W. Wartofsky has argued that representations are in some sense heuristic and didactic because they teach us to see and guide our vision (Wartofsky: 1979, 276). Along the same lines David Morgan proposes an approach to religion that

> [...] attends to belief as an embodied epistemology, the sensuous and material routines that produce an integrated (and culturally particular) sense of self, community, and cosmos. It is not only to systematic theology or sacred philosophy that we look to learn this, but to the lived world of belief. In particular to forms of materiality which organize the world. (Morgan: 2010, 8).

On this basis, devout perception may be understood as a cultural construct developed in accord with sensory objects. Materiality and mentality go hand in hand, even – or perhaps especially – in times of transition. This interaction between interiority and exteriority was to a large extent acknowledged and explicated and debated in both Medieval and Lutheran texts. The didactic potential of material objects, images and texts in particular were often described in theology as well as communicated in devotional books and the objects themselves. It was generally agreed that texts and images could aid the internalisation and memory of devotional ideals and practices and that perceptible matter could potentially affect the inner sentiments of the soul.

In his prologue to the rhymed Danish translation of *Oeconomia* from 1571, originally written by Johann Mathesius, Rasmus Hansen Reravius explicitly states that this manual is useful to all members of the household, but only if it is *practiced*, not just read, but diligently stored ("met flid at giemme") forever in memory. The housefather is specifically instructed to use the manual to "[…] feel and learn/ And hold as a mirror before himself/ How he should rule […]." (Mathesius: 1571, A2v).[4] Reravius' *Tables of Duties (Hus Taffle)* translated and published in Danish 1572 from a German work by Matthias Weber, was consciously written in rhymed verses because, as Reravius states in the dedication of the volume to Peder Hanssøn, Mayor of Varberg, ordinary folk prefer to read ryhmed verses and they stick to memory and remain there much better than ordinary speech (Weber: 1572, 4v–5v; Fink-Jensen: 2011, 42).[5] A later edition of the volume (from 1634) commences with a short verse written as if the *Manual* speaks about itself and addresses the reader. The very first verse underlines the importance of *practice* for those who wishes to perform their duties with honor with a reference to the epistle of St James (1:22): "be aware of my rules / and observe them with diligence / and be not merely the hearer of the words/ as James states / but also the doer." (Weber: 1634)[6] Living a true Christian life was not at matter of words and reading alone, but also internalization, memory and *doing* (Fink-Jensen 2011; Laugerud; 2017, forthcoming)

In line with this, individuals who were not able to read were encouraged to use images as devotional aids. The devotional and didactic importance of images was explicated by Luther in the prologue to his fully illustrated *Passional, Om vaar Herris død oc Pine oc om Billede*, published in 1522 as part of his Prayer Book, and it was repeated in Danish translations and adaptations by the work of Rasmus Hansen Reravius and Christian Pedersen (both illustrated). In his adaptation *On the death and suffering of our Lord and on Image*, Christiern Pedersen states that Christ always spoke in parables so that simple folk could more easily feel and remember his words and sermons and, as a result, be liberated from evil, eternal death, and suffering. Thus, Pedersen reasons that it is good to have stories from the Old and New Testaments printed and painted in the books. Furthermore, it is

4 "[…] kand dette mercke oc lære/ Oc som en Spegel haffue for sig/ Huor hand sig skal regere […]"

5 "Effterdi at Menige mand vil gierne læse Rim, de henge ocsaa bedre ved Hukommelsen oc ere lættere at beholde, end anden slæt tale." (LN 1608,8, Karen Brahe's Library A.6-1. The Royal Library. Copenhagen).

6 "Saa skalt du derfor mine Regle acte / Met alt flittighed dem betracte / Vær icke aleniste ordenes høere / Som jacob siger / men ocsaa giørere." (4, 76, 8, 618, The Royal Library, Copenhagen).

> useful to paint such images in living rooms, houses and lodgings, accompanied by some written words, so that one may have the words of God everywhere, and wonderful deeds before the eyes wherever one turns, and use them as examples [...] It would also be very good and useful if lay folk had images from the Old and the New Testament in their living rooms, houses and lodgings, and in their books, and call it the Bible and Gospel of the lay, because one cannot teach or educate the words of God and wonderful works enough to the ordinary and simple commoners, unless one preached, spoke, wrote and taught them at all hours. It is useful and suitable for every man to read, speak, paint, hear, feel, reflect and remember the wonderful works of God and his word and learning of all of his heart (Pedersen: 1531, A2r–A3v).[7]

The ideal of Luther was a household permeated with didactic guidelines, biblical stories, and educational examples, aimed at aiding memory and religious education. This view on devotional and didactic potential of visual objects was however, not a novelty, but firmly embedded in medieval theology and practice (Laugerud: 2017 forthcoming).

An example of how images could be used as devotional aids is found in Hans Thomesen's (1532–1573) richly illustrated book of hymns and prayers from 1569 (*Den danske Psalmebog met mange christelige Psalmer*). It became the official hymn book until 1699. The example in question is Niels Hemmingsen's hymn on "The daily use of the Cross" (*Christi Kaarssis daglige Brug*) supplied with an illustration of the cross (Thomesen: 1569, 81r). In the center of the cross stands the word faith. Humility, obedience, patience, and love are written on each of the cross arms respectively (Ill. 1). Hemmingsen's hymn begins on the next page with the following words:

7 "Der vaare oc vel gaat ath man lede prente eller male nogre historier aff det gamble testamente i samme bøger / Ath de kunde diss beder i hwkome Gudz store underlige gerninger som ham giorde de gamble forfedre / Det vaare oc vel nøtthelight at mand lode male de i stuer / hwss oc herbere / oc lode der scriffue nogle Gudz ord hoss / ath mand kunde diss bedre alle vegne haffwe Gudz ord / och underlige gerninger faar øgen / chuort mand vende sig eller saage om sig / Oc toge saa gaat eksempel der aff [...] Det vaare oc gantske gaat oc nøtteligt at ligfolk lode male historier aff det Gamble oc Ny testamente i deris stwer hwss oc herberge / Oc i deris bøger / oc kallede det ligfolkis Biblie oc Testamente / Thi man kan icke formegt laere sige eller underuise den menige enfoldige almwe aff Gudz ord oc underlige gerninger / En dog ath man predickede larde sadge screffue och underuisde dem det baade aarle och sille [...] Thi er det endelig nøtteligt oc tilbørligt / at huert menniske læser taler / maler hører / merker / besinder oc i hwkommer aff alt sit hierte Gudz vnderlige velgerninger oc hans ord oc lerdom / Oc de gode loffte som han haffuer oss loffuit oc til sagd / Oc ath huer gør all sin flit der til i alle maade / at han kan stedsse see Gudz vnderlige velgerninger sig baade malne oc screffne."

pine oc Død. 81.

Hand ſtyre oc regære oſſ alleſammen/
At wi hannem frycte oc elſke/ Amen.

IX.

Chriſti Kaarſſis daglige
Brug.

Kierlighed.

Lydactighed.

Troen

Taalmodighed.

Ydmyghed.

D. Ni

Ill. 1

Those wishing to adorn the cross of Christ
And enjoy from it eternal blessing
He should decorate it with five precious gems
And never forget their powers
Faith, humility, obedience, patience, and love
(Thomesen: 1569, 81v).[8]

The text continues with a thorough description of the qualities of each of the 'precious gems' and how they each serve to protect the pious soul. The concluding remarks state: "Write this cross in the root of your heart, so that it may know that the Lord is good." (Thomesen: 1569, 82r).[9] This main function of the image is to illustrate and aid the internalization and memory of the most important deeds of Christian life. Faith is at the center, the root, as the foundation of daily practice. Humility, obedience, patience, and love are the principles of faith that stems from the center as branches of faith that should be present in any human activity. In this way, the small image in Thomesen's book illustrates the devotional practice of the pious Lutheran; by beholding the image and internalizing it into the heart, it was possible to remember the fundamental articles of faith (Bach-Nielsen: 2000).[10]

As mentioned above, the Lutheran books and material objects did not enter a void, but grew out of and responded to a long tradition of theology, iconography, rhetoric, and practice (Jørgensen/Laugerud/Skinnebach: 2015).[11] As art historian Erwin Panofsky once stated in an essay on the genesis of early modern tomb sculpture: "the intrusion of the new upon the old took place in innumerable different ways and with extremely varying intensity, from almost imperceptible changes of detail to a complete reversal of attitude." (Panofsky: 1964, 67). This heterogeneous practice of change was a general and even focal aspect of the Lutheran Reformation. Luther himself favored a gradual transition.[12] In Denmark, "[…] pre-Reformation forms of decoration and fittings […]" were accepted and retained to a wide degree (Isaiaz: 2012, 18). However, this "preserving power of Lutheranism" (Kaufmann: 2006, 157 ff) was paralleled by both violent

8 "Huo som Christi Kaarss vil pryde / Oc der aff euig salighed nyde / Fem ædele Stene han der i sette / Oc deris kraffter aldrig forgætte / Tro Ydmyghed, Lydactighed, Taalmodighed og Kiærlighed."

9 "Scriff dette Kaarss udi hierte rod / Saa kant det kiende huad HERren er god."

10 The description of the five virtues of the cross from Hemmingsen's hymn is written in golden letters around a crucifix as part of the altarpiece in Rud church in the eastern part of Jutland, Denmark.

11 Concerning questions of instruments and instrumentality I am greatly inspired by and indepted to Hans Henrik Lohfert Jørgensen, who has developed and refined the concept and applied it to historical material.

12 Luther wrote in favor of a reformation of the "old" prayer books: "das sie woll wirdig weren eyner starchen, gutter reformacion order gar vertilget weren." (LW 43:3/WA 10 II: 375,10f).

rupture – as the destruction of side-altars described in the Danish visitations reports illustrate – the *re*-formation of old objects and the introduction of new material object and practices (Skinnebach: 2016; Skinnebach: 2017).[13] In Denmark, a national synod of 1555 stated that the images of the churches should first and foremost be removed from the hearts of folk and then gently eradicated by the church wardens. According to Peder Palladius eradication was necessary if kneeling before the images or other forms of superstitious practices were observed (Rørdam I, 461). The Danish Lutheran practice of transformation was characterized by contingency: a polysemous practice of transformation and cultural selection.[14]

This tendency towards preservation also characterized other cultural products and practices such as church inventory, devotional objects, rituals, and devotions, etc. (Marshall: 2015, 25–43). Old and new material often co-existed, as an excavation of a house in Mühlenstrasse in the Hanseatic town, Stralsund has revealed. Between 1525–1555, the old stove of the house with its images of, among others, the Virgin Mary and St Olaf was removed and a new stove installed complete with tiles of protestant leaders. This iconographic modernization was, however, not extended to the painted glass windows that contained an image of St Anne, the Virgin Mary and Child, a typical *Annaselbdritte* motif (Gaimster: 2010, 140). But we should be careful not to judge this as a sign of inconsistency. Often the attempt to make distinction between what is medieval and what is early Lutheran make little or no sense when applied to a period in which material culture was undergoing a dynamic practice of selection and development. Continuity, cultural memory, accommodation and appropriation played a prominent role in the Danish Reformation. The formation of the spiritual Lutheran household was a complex process, but a detailed examination of *how* the devout family was imagined in a small selection of images and texts circulating at the time, illuminates the gradual incorporation of Lutheran ideals.

3. The Fundamental Presence of Christ

This materially-instrumentalized formation of a social imaginary, the lived world of belief and reinvigoration of domestic devotion, was not only confined to the domestic sphere. Another important aspect of Luther's theology, was the concurrent attempt to redefine the concept of sacred space. The early Lutheran period

13 On visual reformation in Germany see Koerner (2003). On visual transformations in England see Hamling/Williams (2007). On the practice of material appropriation in Denmark see Skinnebach (2016).

14 The new reformed ideas materialized parallel to and palimpsestuously upon earlier objects, images, texts and music, as sensory contrafacts.

saw the fluid and constantly debated boundaries between the sacred and the profane newly negotiated and drawn (Spicer/Hamilton: 2005; Spicer/Coster: 2011; Isaiaz: 2012, 37). From a theoretical point of view, Luther and other leading reformers of the sixteenth-century questioned the holy preeminence of the church-space. Luther's 1520 treatise on *Good Works* (1520) emphasizes the importance of faith and devotion instead of space, faith alone is the service of God, and: "What matters is not the places and buildings where we assemble, but this unconquerable prayer alone, and our really praying it together and offering it to God" (LW 44: 66/ WA 6: 239,17ff). The presence of the faithful, Luther argued, was an indispensable component of the sacredness of the church (LW 51: 348–353/WA 49: 588–614, see also Isaiaz: 2012, 23). The distinction between church and domestic space was blurred – if it had ever been sharp. Commemorative material culture, such as epitaphs and new liturgical practices concerning death and burial, helped construct new forms of identities that linked the public and private virtues. Often epitaphs depicted families praying, grieving, and hoping together and in doing so, the material culture drew the domestic sphere into the sacred (Finch: 2007, 195; Isaiaz: 2012, 20). Domestication of devotion was a public matter as much as it was private.

This blurring of the spatial distinction between household and church was also – according to Ronald F. Thiemann – extant in Luther's Christology and Eucharistic theology, or what Thiemann (2013, 29) has termed "sacramental realism." Luther argues that God is present in even the simplest matter such as a stone or a leaf, but this presence is not a gracious or saving presence. Sacramental and thus saving presence is only found through faith in the confidence that God's promises are trustworthy. Faith preconditions that the general divine presence can also be a saving presence. Thiemann summarizes:

> In formulating this theology in which flesh and blood, bread and wine, words and water truly save, Luther believes he has provided a theology that has the pastoral power to reassure, console, and comfort those who long for salvation. For the only God whom we can truly love and trust is the God clothed in the familiar, ordinary, and everyday. (Thiemann: 2013, 31).

Through faith the believer is given new sight, a sight restored to see everything, the everyday, ordinary, and commonplace in the light of Christ. Thiemann makes the point that faith simply makes it possible to understand the general and fundamental presence of God as a sacramental presence. Luther's sacramental realism was not connected to a specific place or space, but simply to faith and the practice of works of love for ones neighbour. This practice of faith and love was, according to Luther, supposed to permeate the domestic sphere. In this respect the household was indeed regarded as the "little church" (Finch: 2007, 201; Hill: 1964). The spiritual household was, thus, present in an all-encompassing manner: it was communicated in theology, in devotional books and religious images, present in church and household and new forms of matter. Religious motives were present in the household in the guise of completely ordinary everyday objects, mugs, house ware etc. A popular feature in domestic settings became tiles, ceramics, textiles and furniture decorated with religious subject matter (David: 2010, 137). For example, tiles were decorated with images of biblical figures, allegories or important Reformation spokespersons. Initially, it was mainly a phenomenon characteristic in the towns and amongst the nobility, but later it spread to rural settings. In a subtle manner they kindled faith and referred thoughts and actions to Christ as a matrix for making sense of the world. The household was saturated by the ideal of the saving presence of Christ constituted by faith. The following examples illustrate how the devout family was construed and communicated in devotional books and epitaphs.

4. The Social Imaginary of the Devout Household: The Case of Devotional Books

During the sixteenth- and seventeenth-centuries printed vernacular devotional books, typically illustrated, were gradually integrated into domestic life. So too were broadside prints and pictures (Appel/Fink-Jensen: 2011, 3). The cornerstone of domestic devotional reading was Luther's *Small Catechism*, which in its original form consisted of a fixed selection of texts that, according to Luther's prologue, every Christian should know.[15] The catechism was translated into Danish in the year of the Reformation, 1536, and published in numerous copies the following year. In the course of the sixteenth century the catechism – or elements hereof – was absorbed into devotional literature such as, for example, Reravius *Table of Duties (Hus Taffle)* mentioned above.

These new devotional books generally express a fundamental focus on domestic affairs and behaviors. The *Table of Duties* organized the relation and interaction between the different family members. Whereas daily actions, such as eating, going to sleep, or getting dressed surfaced only occasionally in the medieval prayer books, the early Lutheran devotional books display an explosive growth of this kind of material that framed and reinforced the ideal image of devout domestic life.

En Liden Vandrebog, a prayer book published by the Danish pastor Hans Christensen Sthen (1544–1610) delineate in an exemplary way how devotional practice was integrated into and served to organise domestic life. The first prayer in the book is supposed to be said first thing in the morning when getting up. When

15 As stated by Luther in the prologue to the *Small Catechism* (BC 347–351).

the reader is dressed, he/she is advised to go to church or the private chamber and pray. The book is, just as Luther's *Small Catechism*, organized chronologically so that the reader will find appropriate prayers for different times of the day. Compared to Luther's original, Sthen's *Vandrebog* is quite comprehensive. It includes prayers for joining the table at meals and after having eaten, for praying at noon, going to bed, and when laying down in order to fall asleep. Furthermore, the book includes prayers to be used in church (before confession, before and after taking the Eucharist) for the dying, for the sick, for children in the house, for poor prisoners, prayers to be said while travelling, and for friends (Sthen: 1994).

A section of hymns included in the book focus on themes such as morning and evening, the estate of marriage (modeled on Adam and Eve), and different sentiments, feelings, and circumstances that might affect married life (among others sorrow, affect, fear, neglect, adultery). The hymns comment on, regulate, instruct, and inspire the wellbeing of marriage and household values. The book then continues with the *Regula pietatis* (the first paragraph focuses on love of God and neighbor) that frames and instructs the devotional life.

The prayer book reflects the (ideal) life of a devout Christian. It illustrates and instrumentalizes a Christian life in which pious conduct is firmly interweaved with and incorporated into the patterns of daily domestic life and practice. Furthermore a collective aspect of devotional practice shines through. Some prayers are written in the plural, suggesting a communal situation:

> The Lord Jesus who suffered and died on the Cross/ He blesses us and multiplies our Beer and Bread [...] God comforts all the sad in their sorrow/ and frees us from eternal death/ God grant us to enjoy and use his gifts in such a way/ that we all may rejoice in Heaven [...]. (Sthen: 1994, xyz).[16]

The "image" of the godly family gathered around the table was a common topic in the devotional books. One version can be found in Reravius' translation of *Oeconomia* mentioned above. The first hymn in the book is an exposition of Ps 128: "Thy wife shall be as a fruitful vine by the sides of thine house: thy children like olive plants round about thy table." (Mathesius: 1571, D1r).[17] It comes as no surprise that the thirteenth rule in Reravius' *Hus Taffle* directed at Christians in general begins by stressing the exact same two passages (Weber: 1572, K4v).[18] The

16 "Et kort *Benedicite*, naar du gaar til Bords. DEn HErre IEsus som tolde paa Korset død,/ Hand velsigne oc mangfoldig giøre vor Øl oc Brød,/ Oc oplad oss sin runde oc milde Haand,/ Met huilken hand spjser baade quind oc Mand/ Gud trøste alle Bedrøffuede i deris Nød,/ Oc frj oss fra den euige død,/ Gud vnde oss at nyde oc bruge hans gafuer saa, At wi alle Himmerigis glæde kunde faa, Amen."

17 "Din Hustru om dit Huss skal være / Som it Vintræ god fruct mon bære. Oc dine Børn skulle side i kor / Som Olie quiste omkring dit Bord."

18 "Hør til du Christen/ oc merck nu mig / Almindelig Lærdom gifue ieg dig. For all ting frycte oc

ideal family was led by a collective heartfelt faith and love of one's neighbor, both of which were core Lutheran values.

Ill. 2

elske skal du/ Din HERRE oc Gud aff hierte oc hu. Din Næste elsk du oc retttelig / Lige som du elsker selffuer dig."

5. The "Image" of the Godly Household: The Case of Epitaphs

The image of family members praying together and expressing their communal faith and love is a recurring topic in epitaphs from the sixteenth-century. A simple epitaph from Kerteminde in Denmark over the unknown couple C.P and K.D from around 1600 shows the family members kneeling below a Crucifix (Ill. 2). Husband and wife are positioned on each side at the foot of the cross, right below the cross-arm as if protected and embraced by the outstretched arms of Christ. Their children, one son and two daughters, are kneeling right behind their parents. Foregrounded in the middle of the painting is a small deceased child on a pillow, its face positioned right below the foot of the cross and the scull of Adam – as an extended *memento mori* motif – and the crucified savior above. The act of family devotion includes all members, dead and alive. A reference to Psalm 90:1 above the image emphasizes the biblical allegory for Christ as a dwelling. Thus, it stresses the metaphorical connection between the household and Christ: "Lord, thou hast been our dwelling place in all generations."[19] The epitaph displays the family as a devout household who lives in Christ, but it also accentuates that to live in Christ is a family matter.

In 1584, Peder Pedersen (1517–1595), major in Køge in Denmark, commissioned an epitaph for his family chapel in Køge Church (Ill. 3). The epigraphy on the epitaph states:

> Peder Pedersen, Major in Køge, with both his wives and both of their kids. Bodil, his first wife [...] lived with him for 16 year and gave birth to three sons [...] and four daughters [...]. Alhed, his second wife [...] gave birth to six sons [...] and two daughters [...] AND two children without a name...and they lived together for 35 years (Danmarks Kirker, http://danmarkskirker.natmus.dk/uploads/tx_tcchurchsearch/kob_amt_166-271.pdf, seen 10.03.2017).[20]

All members of the family are mentioned and all are depicted in the image. Peder and his sons to the left; wives and daughters to the right: all depicted kneeling with hands piously clasped in front of their bodies. As a common feature in epitaphs not only from the second half of the sixteenth-century, but also from the pre-reformation

19 "Psalm 90,1, Herre du, du har været vor Bolig fra slægt til slægt," below the image stands a reference to verse 3 of the same Psalm;" vers 3 "Du omvender eet menniske at hand bliuer knust, siden siger du, Kommer Igen I menniskens Børn." (Thou turnest man to destruction; and sayest, Return, ye children of men.)

20 The full text reads: "Peder Pedersen, Borgmester i Kiøge met sine tvende Hustruer oc beggis deris Børn. Bodil, hans ørste hustru, som wor Siger Lauritsen Borgmesters Daater i Kiøge, lefde met hannem paa sext(n)de Aar og fødde tre Sønner: Laurits, Siger, Peder oc fire Døther: Bodil, karine, Anne og Marine. Alhed, hans anden hustru, som wor Povil Fectels Myntermesters Daather i Kiøbenhafn, fødde sex Sønner: Povil, Simen, Didrick, Laurits, Rasmus, David oc tho Døther: Bodil og Anne OC and tvende Børn foruden Naffn...oc leffde de sam(m)en 35 Aar."

Ill. 3

period, the family members do not interact, but pray individually and with concentration. At the same time, however, it is not their subjective characteristics that stand out, but the family as one organism, underlined by their similar clothing, bodily posture and severe faces, bound together across time and space, death and life, in the faith of Christ. The *paterfamilias* is positioned in the center, visually foregrounded, as the organizing principle of the devout household just below the heavenly father in the shape of the resurrected Christ, the organizing principle of the Christian life. The family members present themselves as partakers in the life of Christ; the father of the household as the earthly equivalent and mirror of God the father; the household as the earthly framework for the practice of faith in Christ. The connection is emphasized by the inscription on the wooden and carved frame around the painting. Below the painting a reference to John 11: "I am the resurrection and life: he that believeth in me, though he were dead, yet shall he live: And whosoever liveth and believeth in me shall never die. John 11." And above the image a wish is expressed that the resurrection of Christ will be paralleled by the members of the family: "Oh, mildest Christ, resurrected from the dead, let our resurrection be god."[21]

21 Above the image is written: "O milde Christ af døde opstod/ Lad wor opstandelse bliffve God." Below the image is quoted from John 11:25 and 26: "Ieg er opstandelsen oc Liffvet, hvo som tror paa

A life in Christ, constituted by shared values of faith and prayer, may ultimately lead to resurrection. The final salvation of the family members is ultimately a family matter.

Ill. 4

mig han hand/ skal leffve alligevel at hand dør. Oc hvo som/ leffver oc tror paa mig hand skal aldrig dø. Iohan.11."

The devotional values of family life itself was also the subject matter of an epitaph for Oluf Bagers (baker) commissioned for St Johns Church in Odense in 1576 (Ill. 4). The lower part of the epitaph depicts Oluf Bager and his wife, Margrete, with their twelve children, all kneeling on a dark green mat. The upper section – depicted as a visual background – shows Christ at the Last Judgment, joined in heaven by holy men and women (among others Virgin Mary and John the Baptist). The relation between the two scenes is ambiguous: the distinction between the biblical scene and the praying family members is clearly marked by the difference in color-tone from the dark green in the lower part to the light green foundation under the horde of humans awaiting their assessment. At the same time, however, the family members are included in the scene, awaiting their appraisal with the others. The family members are placed in the breach between here-and-now and eternal afterlife.

Below the image, a (rhymed) inscription gives a hint at how the family members imagined their devotional status:

> I, Oluf Bagher and my wife Margrete/We have commissioned this altarpiece/In order to teach all pious/What good deeds and great honour/God by his grace granted us/Healed friends with life's necessities/And with the fruit of life our twelve dear children/Who are depicted with us here/For your gifts, God and father bold/We pay thee thousandfold praise and thanks /Your holy name, us and our kin/Let us use your gifts for the best/ Hence to live, grant us all/That we may obtain eternal life/Anno 1576.[22]

In light of the inscription, the pious prayers performed by the family members depicted, should be understood as an expression of praise and gratitude as well as a hope for future salvation for *all* members of the family. The fact that Bager's family regarded salvation as a family matter is demonstrated even more firmly in the inscription above the painting. The inscription informs us that Oluf Bagher himself died in 1602 and his wife in 1581. A daughter, Ane, died earlier in 1562 at the age of one, fourteen years prior to the production of the epitaph. When the death year of Oluf Bager was added to the epitaph, little Ane had been dead for forty years. This illustrates the importance of keeping the memory of deceased family members intact for the sake of their salvation. Furthermore, the Bager family regarded themselves as a pious model: "We have commissioned this altarpiece/In order to teach all pious/What good deeds and great honor/God by his grace granted us." They are indeed depicted as a the ideal of virtuous family

22 "Jeg ollvff Bagher och min hvstrv Margrete / Wii hafver ladet denne taffle opsette / Alle frome der med at lere / Hvad welgierningeer ock stor ære / Gud aff sin naade oss betide / Med lijfs nødtørfft wenner helbrede / Och med liffsfrvct vore tolff børn kiære / Som her met oss affmalit ere / For dine gaffver Gvd fader bold / Ske dig loff og tack i tvssindfold / Dit hellige naffn, os, og vor neste / Dine gaver lad oss brve til beste / Her saa at leffve oss alle giff /At wii maa faa det evige liff / Anno 1576."

conduct: a family that prays together under the guidance of a strong father (the earthly equivalent of the just Father in heaven), that cares for the afterlife of others, and are blessed with the grace of God for their life in Christ.

The epitaphs illustrate that by the end of the sixteenth-century the social imaginary of the spiritual household was firmly integrated in the self-fashioning of families and had materialized in images and object. These images also display a fundamental appreciation for biblical quotes that support and consolidate the 'image' of the family as an organic body that prays together, tends to the devotion of the children, carries the memory of the dead, and cares for the salvation of all members.

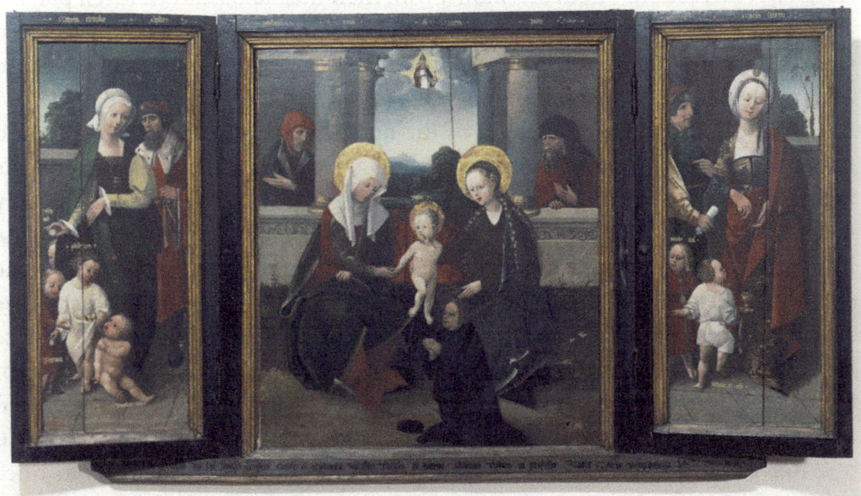

Ill. 5

6. Concluding Remarks

The early Lutheran emphasis on the devotional values of the household may also explain the fate of a small alter piece produced for an unknown church in 1522 by a priest, Bo Madsen (Ill. 5).[23] Sometime after the Reformation, in 1578, it was transferred to the completely newly built church on the island, Omø.[24] It might have been used as altarpiece until 1601 when the church was replaced by a new structure. A new altarpiece depicting Christ with the little children is first

23 According to a Latin inscription on the footstall.

24 Omø had an old medieval church and chapel, and the altarpiece could have been transferred from here.

mentioned around 1605 (Danmarks Kirker, http://danmarkskirker.natmus.dk/uploads/tx_tcchurchsearch/Soroe_0958-0961.pdf, seen 10.03.2017).

The main motif of the altarpiece is the holy family. The central panel display the Virgin Mary and her Mother Anna with the Christ Child (*Anna selbstdritt*). In the background, behind a low ornate wall, Anna's husband Joachim and Joseph behold the scene. Above the holy family, God the Father is visible from a lit opening in the clouds and the Holy Spirit in the shape of a dove hovers between Father and Son, thus underlining the mystery of the Incarnation. The paintings on the inside of the wings depict two of the three Marias who were, according to Mark 16:1–8, present at the grave and thus the first to receive the message of Christ's resurrection.[25] Both are shown with their husbands and children playing at their feet: Maria (sister of the Virgin Mary) and Kleofas with their four children (Jacob, Simon, Phillip and Josef, according the inscriptions) and Zebedee and Maria Salome with two children (John the Evangelist and Jacob the Elder).

Before the Reformation, images of the holy family were widely popular and served as models for a devout life. The altarpiece from Omø is merely one example, but its layout corresponded well with the Lutheran ideal of the holy family: God as the ultimate Father in the most holy of families, served, within the iconography of the altarpiece, as the fundamental model for the families in the side wings, just as the holy family, from a perspective of the beholder, served as model for a pious family life. When the noble couple Herluf Trolle and Birgitte Gøye commissioned a private winged altarpiece in 1560, they chose the motif of the holy family for the alabaster corpus (Ill. 6). A family living in faith and according to the devout model of the holy family was a family living in Christ.

After the Reformation, a new system of belief developed that was at once informed by the cultural memory of pre-Reformation material and devotional culture. At the same time, new Lutheran ideals, practices, and cultural products were gradually incorporated and appropriated into daily devotional practice, giving shape to a transformed system of belief. The ideal household, to some extent inherent in medieval culture, further prompted in the writing of Luther, and disseminated, communicated, and consolidated through texts and images in domestic and ecclesiastical spaces alike, became the new central locus of devotion. Gradually *oeconomia* became completely permeated with devotional ideals and matter.

25 The third Mary, Mary Magdalen, is mentioned in the dedication below the image.

Ill. 6

Bibliography

APPADURAI, ARJUN (Ed.) (1986), The Social Life of Things: Commodities in Cultural Perspective, Cambridge: Cambridge University Press.

APPEL, CHARLOTTE (2001), Læsning og bogmarked i 1600-tallets Danmark, Copenhagen: Museum Tusculanums Forlag.

APPEL, CHARLOTTE/FINK-JENSEN, MORTEN (2011), Introduction: Literacy, and Religious Reading in the Lutheran North, in: Charlotte Appel/Morten Fink (ed.), Religious Reading in the Lutheran North: Studies in Early Modern Scandinavian Book Culture, Newcastle upon Tyne: Cambridge Scholars Publishing, 1–14.

BACH-NIELSEN, CARSTEN (2000), Kors, krucifix og krumspring: Lidt om 1500-tallets varsomhed med billeder, ICO 3, 20–30.

BLATT, CATHERINE/RENEVEY, DENIS/ WHITEHEAD, CHRISTIANIA, (2005), Domesticity and Medieval Devotional Literature, Leeds Studies in English 36, 195–250.

DANMARKS KIRKER, http://danmarkskirker.natmus.dk/ (seen 10.03.2017).

Davis, Kathleen (2008), Perdiodization and Sovereignty: How Ideas of Feudalism and Secularization Govern the Politics of Time. Philadelphia: University of Pennsylvania Press.

Feike Dietz/Adam Morton et al. (2014), Illustrated Religious Texts in the North of Europe, 1500–1800, Farnham/Burlington, VT: Ashgate.

Finch, Jonathan (2007), Sacred and Secular Spheres: Commemoration and the "Practice of Privacy" in Reformation England, in: Carola Jäggi/Jörn Staecker (ed.), Archäologie der Reformation: Studien zu den Auswirkungen des Konfessionswechsels auf die materielle Kultur (AKG 104), Berlin/New York, NY: de Gruyter, 195–210.

Findlen, Paula (2013), Early Modern Things: Objects in Motion 1500–1800, in: Paula Findlen (ed.), Early Modern Things: Objects and their Histories 1500–1800, London/New York, NY: Routledge, 3–27.

Fink-Jensen, Morten (2011), Printing and Preaching after the Reformation: A Danish Pastor and his Audience, in: Charlotte Appel/Morten Fink (ed.), Religious Reading in the Lutheran North: Studies in Early Modern Scandinavian Book Culture, Newcastle upon Tyne: Cambridge Scholars Publishing, 15–47.

Gaimster, David/Gilchrist, Roberta (ed.) (2003), The Archaeology of Reformation 1480–1580, Leeds: Maney Publishing.

Gaimster, David (2010), Archaeology of an Age of Print? Everyday Objects in and Age of Transition, in: Tara Hamling/Catherine Richardson (ed.), Everyday Objects. Medieval and Early Modern Material Culture and its Meanings, Farnham/Burlington, VT: Ashgate, 133–144.

Hamling, Tara/Richardson, Catherine (2010), Introduction, in: Tara Hamling/Catherine Richardson (ed.), Everyday Objects: Medieval and Early Modern Material Culture and its Meanings, Farnham/Burlingon, VT: Ashgate, 1–23.

Hamling, Tara/Williams, Richard (2007) (ed.), Art Re-Formed: Re-Assessing the Impact of the Reformation on the Visual Arts, Newcastle upon Tyne: Cambridge Scholars Publishing.

Hanawalt, Barbara A./Kobialka, Michal (ed.), Medieval Practices of Space, Minneapolis, MN: University of Minnesota Press.

Hill, Christopher (1964), Society and Puritanism in Pre-Revolutionary England. London: Secker and Warburg.

Isaiaz, Vera (2012), Early Modern Lutheran Churches: Redefining the Boundaries of the Holy and the Profane, in: Andrew Spicer (ed.), Lutheran Churches in Early Modern Europe, Farnham/Burlington, VT: Ashgate, 17–37.

Joby, Christopher Richard (2007), Calvinism and the Arts, Leuven: Peeters.

Joseph, Leo (2003), The Reformation of the Image, Chicago, IL: University of Chicago Press.

Jones, Caroline A. (2006), The Mediated Sensorium, in: Caroline A. Jones (ed.) Sensorium: Embodied Experience, Technology, and Contemporary Art, Cambridge, MA: MIT Press.

Jørgensen, Hans Henrik Lohfert (2015), Prostheses of pious perception: on the instrumentalization and mediation of the medieval sensorium, in: Henning Laugerud, Salvador Ryan and Laura Katrine Skinnebach (eds.), The Materiality of Devotion in Late Medieval Northern Europe, Dublin: Four Courts Press.

Jørgensen, Hans Henrik Lohfert/Henning Laugerud/Laura Katrine Skinnebach (ed.) (2015), The Saturated Sensorium: Principles of Perception and Mediation in the Middle Ages, Aarhus: Aarhus Universitetsforlag.

KAUFMANN, THOMAS (2006), Konfession und Kultur: Lutherischer Protestantismus in der zweiten Hälfte des Reformationsjahrhunderts (SuR.NR 29), Tübingen: Mohr Siebeck.

LAUGERUD, HENNING (forthcoming 2017), En reformation av blikket? Skrift, bilder og synskultur i det etter-reformatoriske Danmark-Norge, in: Bente Lavold & John Ødemark (eds.), Reformationstidens religiøse bokkultur 1400–1700, tekst – materialitet – visualitet, Oslo.

LUTHER, MARTIN (1520), On Good Works (LW 44: 21–114/WA 6: 202–276)

LUTHER, MARTIN (1522), The Estate of Marriage (LW 45: 17–49/WA 10 II: 275–304).

LUTHER, MARTIN (1522), Personal Prayer Book (LW 43: 3–45/WA 10 II: 375–428).

LUTHER, MARTIN (1528), Confession Concerning Christ's Supper (LW 37: 161–372/WA 26: 261–509).

LUTHER, MARTIN (1935–45), Lectures on Genesis (LW 1–8/WA 42–44).

LUTHER, MARTIN (1539), On the Councils and the Church (LW 41: 9–178 /WA 50: 509–653).

LUTHER, MARTIN (1544), *Sermon at the Dedication of the Castle Church* in Torgau (LW 51: 348–353/WA 49: 588–614).

MARSHALL, PETER (2002), Beliefs and the Dead in Reformation England, New York: Oxford University Press.

MARSHALL, PETER (2015), After Purgatory: Death and Remembrance in the Reformation World, in: Tarald Rasmussen/Jon Øygarden Flaeten, Preparing for Death, Remembering the Dead (R5AS 22), Göttingen: Vandenhoeck & Ruprecht, 25–44.

MATHESIUS, JOHANNES (1571), Oeconomia eller Underuisning Huorledis en Husfader skal skicke sig, trans. Rasmus Hansen Reravius, Copenhagen: Laurentz Benedicht (LN 1150).

MORGAN, DAVID (2010), Introduction: The Matter of Belief, in: David Morgen (ed.), Religion and Material Culture: The Matter of Belief, London: Routledge/New York, NY, 1–18.

PANOFSKY, ERWIN (1964), Tomb Sculpture: Its Changing Aspects from Ancient Egypt to Bernini, London: Thames and Hudson.

PEDERSEN, CHRISTIERN (1531), Om vaar Herris Død oc Pine, Antwerpen: Willem Voesterman. (LN 158).

PLEIJEL, HILDING (1970), Hustavlans Värld, Stockholm: Verbum.

SCRIBNER, R.W. (2001), Religion and Culture in Germany,1400–1800, Leiden/Boston, MA: Brill.

SKINNEBACH, LAURA KATRINE (2016), "Dhetta er Oret": Materielle Forandringer som Praksis og Instrument, Kunst og Kultur 3, 154–162.

SKINNEBACH, LAURA KATRINE (2017), Visuel Forandringspraksis. Appropriering af billeder efter reformationen, in Kari G. Hempel/Poul Duedahl/Bo Poulsen (eds), Efter Reformationen. Beyond the Reformation, Aalborg: Aalborg Universitetsforlag 2017, 49–87.

SPICER, ANDREW/HAMILTON, SARAH (2005) (ed.), Defining the Holy: Sacred Space in Medieval and Early Modern Europe, Aldershot: Ashgate.

SPICER, ANDREW/COSTER, WILL (2011), Sacred Space in Early Modern Europe, New York: Cambrigde University Press.

STHEN, HANS CHRISTENSEN (1994), En liden Vandrebog, in: Jens Lyster (ed.), Hans Christensen Sthens Skrifter, vol. I, Copenhagen: C.A. Reitzels Forlag.

STROHL, JANE E. (2014), Luther on Marriage, Sexuality and the Family, in: Robert Kolb/Irene Dingel/L'ubomir Batka (ed.), The Oxford Handbook of Martin Luthe's Theology, Oxford: Oxford University Press, 370–382.

TAYLOR, CHARLES (2001), A Secular Age, Cambridge, MA: The Belknap Press of Harvard University Press.

Thiemann, Ronald F. (2013), The Humble Sublime. Secularity and the Politics of Belief, New York, NY: I.B. Tauris.

Thomesen, Hans (1569), Den Danske Psalmebog met mange Christelige Psalmer, Copenhagen: Lauentz Benedicht (LN 1426).

Walsham, Alexandra (2014a), Idols in the Frontispiece? Illustration Religious Books in the Age of Ionoclasm, in: Feike Dietz/Adam Morton/Lien Roggen/Els Stronks/Marc Van Vaeck (ed.), Illustrated Religious Texts in the North of Europe, 1500–1800, Farnham/Burlington, VT: Ashgate, 21–52.

Walsham, Alexandra (2014b), Holy Families: The Spiritualisation of the Early Modern Household, in: John Doran/Alexandra Walsham/Charlotte Methuen (ed.), Religion and the Household: Studies in Church History vol. 50, Martlesham/Rochester, NY: Boydell & Brewer, 122–160.

Walsham, Alexandra (2016), Domesticating the Reformation: Material Culture, Memory, and Confessional Identity in Early Modern England, in Renaissance Quarterly 69, 566–616.

Wartofsky, Marx (1979), Picturing and Representing, in: Calvin Nodine/Dennis FisheR (ed.), Perception and Pictoral Representation, New York: Praeger Publishers.

Webb, Diana (2005), Domestic Space and Devotion in the Middle Ages, in: Spicer/Hamilton: 2005, 27–49.

Weber, Matthias (1572), Hus Taffle / huvorledis huert Menniske udi sit Kald oc stat skal skicke sig / baade mod GUD oc Mennisken. Oc der hos gudelige Bøner for alle Stater. Vdsæt på Danske af Rasmus Hanssøn trans. Rasmus Hansen Reravius, Copenhagen: Vingaard (LN 1608).

Wolgast, Eike (2014), Luther's Treatment of Political and Societal Life, in: Robert Kolb/Irene Dingel/L'ubomir Batka, The Oxford Handbook of Martin Luthers Theology, Oxford: Oxford University Press, 397–413.

Ørnbjerg, Jakob (2011), Mod en ny tid? Studier over det aalborgensiske rådaristokratis økonomiske, politiske, sociale og kulturelle udvikling 1600–1660, unpublished PhD Thesis, Aalborg University.

Agnes Arnórsdóttir

Marriage Regulations in Denmark and Iceland 1550–1650

With a Special Focus on Change in the Practice of Marital Gift Giving and the Ideal of Motherhood

1. Introduction

How did Reformation ideas shape social practices in the Nordic countries? The present chapter seeks to answer this question by examining changes to marital regulations in the Danish and Icelandic territories of the Danish Kingdom after the Reformation. Changes in jurisdiction produced new sources, which can throw light on how the Reformation affected the community on a daily level. Historical research has shown that, compared to previous centuries, the relatively large number of sources on marriage and sexual customs from the last part of the sixteenth century is in part the result of a stronger system of sexual control (Arnórsdóttir: 2010, 206–212). This chapter will investigate the changing regulation of marriage after the Reformation. First, I will discuss the direct impact of the Protestant Reformation on marriage legislation and legal practice in Denmark and Iceland. The existing sources on marriage practices in Iceland in the Late Middle Ages and early modern periods is also part of Danish history – the Danish Church Ordinance from 1537/1539 was ratified in Iceland in 1541/1551 and published in Icelandic translation in 1541. The ratification of the Ordinance subjected the Icelandic church-court relationship to the Danish King in 1541, after which the Danish royals actively interfered in Icelandic social conditions through a variety of directives. One of those directives, the Danish Marriage Ordinance of 1582, became law in Iceland in 1587 with minor revisions adapted to Icelandic cultural practices and customs, such as the absence of any town and cities in Iceland.

In the Middle Ages, marriage was a sacrament and the only acceptable context for having sexual relations. Those who chose to have a sexual relationship outside of marriage were required to confess their sins, show regret through penitential practice, and pay fines for their offenses. These practices changed after the Reformation when marriage lost its sacramental status. At the same time, the sacrament of the Holy Communion came to play an increasingly important role in sexual control. Therefore, I will discuss the role of Communion in controlling undesirable behavior as the second point of inquiry. Third, I will examine the meaning of marriage regulations and sexual control for succession practices and the custom of marital gift giving in Iceland. The final section will discuss the symbolic role of the household for establishing a new importance of the earthly family in Lutheran society. The chapter concludes by discussing the implications of these changes for larger social questions. For instance, how might we better understand the principles of social organization in the Reformation by examining the special status of childbirth and motherhood in the Danish Church Ordinance from 1537/1539? More generally, what does this focus suggest about the changing notions of gender after the Reformation? Throughout the chapter, data will be derived from sources such as legal regulations, court decisions, and marriage contracts (Arnórsdóttir: 2010; 2014) as well as ongoing studies on the Reformation's impact on gift-giving practices, both in relation to the status of the illegitimate children and in marital gift exchange (Arnórsdóttir: 2017a; 2017b; 2017c).

2. Lutheran Understanding of Marriage: From Sacred Contract to Social Institution

Historical documentation of marriage contracts and related court material reveal how Lutheran theology influenced a new non-sacramental understanding of marriage in Denmark and Iceland. It is important to note, however, that the desacramentalization of marriage altered, but did not entirely remove, the theological importance of marriage as a model or as a social institution. The role of the priest in guiding married couples expanded as the significance of marriage as a universal ideal for all members of society increased. The only exception to this marital goal pertained to those select few who possessed a special grace for the celibate life. At the same time, the sexual contract intensified and standardized harsh punishments for sexual deviance. Historical sources also show the introduction of a strong educational element into the marriage contract that increased control within the family to discipline children, servants, and so on (Witte: 2002, 231 ff).

John Witte Jr. has shown that Lutheran criticisms of canon law on the topic of marriage required a new theological foundation. New theological grounds for marriage were especially necessary to support clerical marriage. Witte argues that the new foundation elevated marriage as a social contract over the sacramental view of marriage in canon law (Witte: 2012, 121). This contract contained three specific benefits for human societies. The social contract more strongly stressed mutual love and support between spouses; it ensured procreation and upbringing of children; and it provided protection against sexual sin. The notion of a social contract was not new in the sixteenth century; it was inspired by the ancient Roman and early Christian thought. The innovation during the Reformation came via the rejection of the sacramental understanding (Witte: 2002, 17ff).

In order to ascertain changes to marital practice in the Reformation, it is necessary to contextualize these changes against medieval marital practices. Generally, the most significant change after the Reformation was the relocation of responsibility for marriage and welfare to the political authority. As a result, marriage became a public matter and jurisdiction over marriage moved gradually from church to state. As the ideal of celibacy was abolished, priests were increasingly permitted to marry. Marriage was no longer understood as a sacrament. Moreover, traditional barriers to marriage were adapted. For example, the so-called spiritual relatedness (cognatio spiritualis) no longer prevented marriage; the doctrine of consent was modified so that children under a certain age could no longer enter into binding agreements of marriage – parental consent was required. Increasingly, wedding ceremonies were required, and modern notions of divorce were introduced. This meant, for example, that if one spouse had committed adultery, the innocent spouse could divorce and remarry (Witte: 2002, 202).

The reformed social marriage contract lacked gender equality. The husband's role was to rule and protect all members of the household. It was his duty to represent the household to the world, to protect his wife, and to help her to fulfill her duties, which were closely linked to child rearing. That said, it is also important to emphasize that mutual respect governed the relationship between spouses. The wife's role was to help and support her husband, to be his religious mentor, and to stand by his side as the mother of their children. The background for this new role can be located in canonical marriage contracts from the 1200s. Here, the doctrine of consent introduced the woman's own will as a necessary component of the contract (Sigh: 2012, 40–44). The Reformation further formalized the mutuality of this medieval gender contract. As we will see, by the time of the Reformation, the marital bond between man and woman became more than just a mutual contract between the parents of the spouses and the spouses themselves. It also became an ideal for organizing the entire society.

Before we turn to discussing marriage as a social ideal, it is necessary to clarify the changes that occurred in Danish and Icelandic marriage legislation after the Reformation.

3. New Marriage Legislation and Legal Practices in the Danish Church Ordinance

King Christian III (1503–1559) promulgated the Danish Church Ordinance for "Denmark and Norway and their northern realms, including Iceland, as well as the Duchy of Schleswig and Holstein" in Copenhagen on September 2, 1537. It was translated into Danish in 1539. The ordinance applied to the entire Danish kingdom, but regional differences arose in its adoption. In Iceland, it was accepted for the See of Skálholt in 1541, but it was not adopted in the bishopric of Hólar until 1551 (DI X, 117). Norway did not accept the Church Ordinance until 1607. The Church Ordinance declared that people should be married in the church, and it set parameters for determining incestuous relationships and formulated the marriage ceremony according to Martin Luther's Small Catechism. The ritual of marriage in Luther's Enchiridion was translated into Danish by Peder Palladius in 1538 (KiO, 187, and Stephensen et al.: 1853, 45).

In Denmark, jurisdiction over marriage was handed back to the church in 1542, according to royal legislation, the so-called Ribeartikler. The name of this legislation is related to the fact that it was accepted in the town of Ribe. After the Reformation in Denmark, it was customary to treat marriage cases in mixed courts made up of both secular authorities and church clergy (Tamm: 2008, 173 f). In Iceland, however, marriage cases were already addressed by mixed courts consisting of royal officials and clerics before the Reformation (Arnórsdóttir: 2010, 132 ff). Nonetheless, both Danish and Icelandic sources indicate increased regulation of marriage and sexuality after the Reformation. Numerous sources speak directly to the start of the marriage. Several regulations and rulings on marriage cases also refer directly to the paragraphs on marriage in the Church Ordinance. Helle Møller Sigh has investigated some of these sources on Danish marriage in her doctoral dissertation on the Christianization of marriage and the legal effect in Denmark from 1200 to 1600. She concentrates in particular on the demand for public engagement and the forbidding of private vows, the so-called "clandestine marriages," which began toward the end of the sixteenth century (Sigh: 2012, 262–267, and Rørdam II, 14f, 38f, 341 and 401). The amount of written sources regulating marriage increased dramatically in the seventeenth century (Arnórsdóttir: 2017a). One very important new regulation was the requirement that marriage take place in the church (Rørdam III, 50, 166). At the practical level, however, it appears that medieval customs of betrothal and contracting marriage continued to exist. The contract was made as an agreement between families where the exchange of marriage gifts, as well as the mutual consent of the spouses and their parents, were the main criteria for a legal marriage. New research on the Danish sources suggests that the older custom of the betrothal gift, or dowry, continued to some extent after the Reformation. In these situations, it seems that gift giving functioned as proof that a marriage had been contracted (Knudsen: 2015, 29, 58). This practice violated the ordinance that marriage must occur only in the church under the watchful eye of the parish priest. This discovery could explain why the 1621 Royal Decree prohibited wedding gifts in Iceland (Arnórsdóttir: 2017c) and the prohibition of the bridal dowry in the Danish regulation from 1672 (Rørdam III, 38ff).

Another important issue in the Danish Church Ordinance was the charge to parish priests to either live in celibacy, "which very few could live up to," or get married (KiO, 216). The abolition of celibacy had an immediate impact throughout the kingdom. If the clergy did not follow the injunction to celibacy or marriage, they risked the sudden loss of their posts (KiO, 216, and Stephensen et al.: 1853, 49f). Sources from this period depict the creation of new practical solutions to the problem of illicit clerical relationships. These solutions included regulations requiring the surviving widow and her children to be excluded from the church for a year after the priest's death (KiO, 215, and Rørdam II, 11f). The abolition of the ideal of celibacy was probably the most radical change that came through the Danish Church Ordinance 1537/1539 in the wake of the Reformation. However, the abolition of celibacy also spurred heightened interest in the households of parish priests as the quintessential model for organizing family life.

Legal dictates defining who was permitted to marry within different kinds and degrees of spiritual or biological relations also saw immediate change under the new Danish Church Ordinances. According to the Danish superintendent Peder Palladius (1503–1560), "no spiritual relationship [...] should [...] prevent a marriage, as the wicked pope's public gardens learned and lied to us: Two god-parents may well have each other in marriage" (Palladius: 1543/1925, 35). Prior to the Danish Church Ordinance, marriage within the degree of one-fourth was forbidden. This changed by the Reformation to the degree of one-third. This change very soon became practice, as an Icelandic lawsuit from 1557 indicates. Here, it is declared that marriage within the forbidden degree of one-fourth was from now on actually lawfully permitted (DI XIII, 226–233). A 1559 case defending a similar judgment also referred to the Danish Church Ordinance (DI XIII, 399f). In comparison to medieval marriage laws, a more detailed judgment from 1558 states that those who were related within the fourth degree were now allowed to marry under the king's new rules promulgated in the Church Ordinance (DI XIII, 332–338). New injunctions did not replace the older ones; rather, they justified court judgments.

Another case mentioned the Church Ordinance provision requiring parental permission for marriage. Otherwise, the case suggested, the marriage might be declared in violation of the king's and the church's legal mandates (DI XIII, 382–

386). The Icelandic superintendent Gisli Jónsson (ca. 1515–1587) issued a judgment over an Icelandic marriage prohibiting all marriages that did not follow the Church Ordinance or other ancient Icelandic laws (DI XIII, 430–433). The judgment, preserved in its original form, gives insight into the basic problems created by changes to the legal parameters surrounding marriage. The Jónsson ruling reflects that the problems were not only related to new religious foundations but were also rooted in the secular legal basis for the right of inheritance. As this judgment reveals, after the Reformation, some men married women with whom they had previously lived in adultery. Others made marriage contracts with their wives in the morning, were engaged to them in the evening, and were in bed together that same night! The judgment also mentioned other problems, including that people married with full knowledge that the marriage was unlawful, and incestuous marriages – marriages within the forbidden degree. Another significant problem had to do with marriages to individuals from outside the immediate legal district who, it was later discovered, were already married. The Jónsson judgment makes clear that such behavior goes against God's order. Interestingly, Jónsson refers to both the Bible and secular medieval marriage laws and the Church Ordinance (DI XIII, 431 f). Many of the lawsuits discussed here refer to both the medieval laws and the new Church Ordinance, but direct references to the Bible do not appear until after the Reformation. The Old Testament, in particular, was considered an exemplary source of law for these cases (Tamm: 2008, 165, 173, 175). In this sense, the Protestant view of marriage and elevation of the scriptures came to have a direct impact on the trials.

New, reformed perspectives on marriage began to affect court despite the fact that new marriage laws did not arise until the end of the sixteenth century. A 1565 Icelandic case declared that "the marriage bed shall be without sin" (Arnórsdóttir: 2010, 285, and DI XIV, 365–368). Even in the Church Ordinance, we find provisions for those living sinfully, those who enjoyed "flagrant vice and debauchery." The ordinance required that they be excluded from communion until they confessed their sins. They were also seen to be guilty of public crimes and could be punished by secular law in the form of monetary fines. Within the church, however, they were required to confess their sins in public confession. The most serious cases were punishable by death (KiO, 1989, 68 f, and DI X, 148).

Court cases like the one from Iceland in 1565 reveal how a new notion of valid cohabitation was shaped by legal practices. The reason why I have chosen to treat the marriage cases in the Icelandic courts prior to the Reformation so thoroughly has to do with the impressive preservation of the sources. This gives us the unique opportunity to identify how new marriage ideals were quickly transformed through practice and then used as documentary evidence for finding solutions at a more widespread level. For example, Icelanders contacted King Frederik II in 1561 asking how to deal with the problem of incest. This led the King to consult some theological experts and gave rise to a new moral court of Stóridómur (Arnórsdóttir: 2010, 128). Therefore, Lutheran marriage practices were shaped not only from above, as, for instance, by learned theologians or law teachers, but also at a more practical level through legal judgments.

In 1572, theologian Niels Hemmingsen published a Latin guide for marital matters. His work was included in preparations for the first Lutheran marriage legislation in Denmark. The ordinance on marital matters of Denmark and Norway was published on June 19, 1582 (Sigh: 2012, 11). Five years later, on June 2, 1587, the marriage ordinance was published in Iceland (Arnórsdóttir: 2010, 129). In particular, it required that betrothal be made in the presence of witnesses, and the marriage ceremony was required before the couple was permitted to have intercourse. It also included provisions for the dissolution of marriage in cases of adultery. The foundation for these ideas in the secular Marriage Act 1582/1587 was the Church Ordinance published in 1537/1539, but it is important to remember that from the Reformation until the Marriage Act of 1582/1587, there had been a constant effort to increase public control over marriage at the judicial level. This first secular Marriage Act in the Nordic countries was issued to resolve a number of questions as the new Protestant views of marriage gained ground. But this effort alone did not alter the rituals and everyday married life after the Reformation; rather, the major changes were promulgated via judicial judgments. I turn now to examine further changes after the Reformation reflected in other types of source material.

4. The Role of the Lord's Supper and Sexual Control

The Church Ordinance already stressed Sunday as a public holiday when it emphasized that people "once a week must rest from work, listen to the Word of God, and receive together the Sacrament" (Stephensen et al.: 1853, 44, and KiO, 180). Whereas the marriage came increasingly under the control of secular jurisprudence, the marriage ceremony itself was incorporated into the ecclesiastical liturgy to a higher degree. As Martin Schwarz Lausten has explained, Luther considered marriage to be a secular matter and thought that the laws concerning marriage should be shaped by the secular authorities. But Luther also wanted a church ceremony to commence a couple's entry into married life (KiO, 187). This had an influence on the architectural furniture of the churches. Thus, we see a rise in new church furnishings like the bridal bench in the church at Skarð on the West coast of Iceland after the Reformation (Arnórsdóttir: 2010, figure 29). This piece of furniture was used as part of the liturgical entrance of marriage in the church.

As previously mentioned, marriage required the blessing of a priest, but not everyone could get married. Criminals, including those who had lived in adultery, were excluded from the church liturgies until they publically confessed their sins. Going to public communion on Sundays was, thus, part of the penitential practice, just as it was in medieval Catholicism prior to the Reformation. After the Reformation, however, exclusion from communion was made more stringent (Ólafsson: 2014).

The Skálholt superintendent in Iceland Gísli Jónsson issued a declaration in 1560 that exemplifies a more stringent regulation of sacramental participation. Jónsson issued a regulation that forbade the admission of unrepentant adulterers to the sacrament (DI XII, 466–468). The 1537/1539 Church Ordinance outlines clear parameters for how the sacrament was to take place. Prior to receiving the sacrament, people were required to know Christian doctrine and to go to confession (DI X, 148). Although Luther had rejected mandatory private confession in medieval Catholicism, he replaced it with an "examination of faith." Individuals who had been publicly excommunicated, those who "were glorified by heresy," "demented people and foolish children," and, notably, people who publicly maintained lives of adultery were all excluded from the ritual of communion (KiO, 183–186). This meant that those who were found guilty of sex outside of marriage lacked access to the sacrament apart from public confession. This law is important for assessing the impact of Luther's view of marriage. Luther himself rejected marriage as a sacrament but simultaneously retained its inviolability as a divine order. Reflecting Luther's influence, the 1582/1587 Marriage Law made virginity a prerequisite for marriage. Violations of the new sexual legislation, such as loss of virginity or adultery, had serious consequences for the life of the soul. Sex crimes barred an individual from one of only two sacraments in the Christian life. The Icelandic source material from the late 1500s examined here reveals that this new theological orientation toward the importance of the sacrament of communion after the Reformation directly impacted marital practices in society and judicial control of sexuality (Arnórsdóttir: 2010, 141–150, and see, for example, DI X, 119).

5. The Status of Legitimate and Illegitimate Children

Luther understood marriage as a divine gift intended to rescue individuals from sexual sin. We have seen that those unrepentantly living in adultery were excluded from the sacrament of the Lord's Supper. Several studies have shown that exclusion from sacramental practices for controlling deviant sexual behavior also coincided with harsher punishments for sexual sins by the secular authorities

(Riisøy: 2009; Sigh: 2012).[1] Some studies have also examined the impact of new marriage ideals on gender relations in the Nordic countries, though from a more legal perspective than from a social or religious one (Korpiola: 2009; Riisøy: 2009; Sigh: 2012; Knudsen: 2015). The question of how the stronger sexual control influenced inheritance practices remains unanswered, however. In particular, the social implications for the rights of illegitimate children to inheritance have not been fully explored in relation to changes to the practice of marital gift giving.

Changes in the regulation of marriage after the Reformation did not affect marriage partners alone. These innovations also altered the right of illegitimate children to an inheritance from their unmarried parents. Typically, the division of property was regulated through the institution of marriage by means of the transfer of property to legitimate children. In Iceland, written marriage contracts became important documentation for the widowed partner's property rights as well as her legitimate children. The typical heirs both before and after the Reformation were children born within lawful wedlock (Jónsbók, 80). However, property was not only left to legitimately-born heirs or adopted children. It was also possible to transfer property to illegitimate children or other non-relatives. As we shall discuss here, strategies for leaving property to non-traditional heirs also grew in frequency after the Reformation. Strategies for leaving wealth to illegitimate children became increasingly common (Arnórsdóttir: 2017b). The custom, used both by priests and lay people, was a holdover from the Middle Ages (DI XIII, 517ff; DI XIII, 233f, 369f; DI IX, 450f). Abundant sources that address the question of succession have been preserved from the Late Middle Ages and early modern periods in Iceland. Some of the Icelandic lawsuits contain statements attesting to a child's rightful birth. For instance, in a witness letter from 1558/1562, a father declares that his son was of legitimate birth (DI XIII, 360f). As the 1500s progressed, however, many of these cases were concerned not only with determinations about the legality of a marital union but also with the inheritance rights of the resulting children. Many cases came, instead, to deal with parental adoption of illegitimate children. By adopting their illegitimate children, parents assured that their children became legitimate and retained their inheritance rights. The tradition of adopting illegitimate children began well before the Reformation. But after the Reformation, the frequency of cases increased.

Adoption in late-medieval Iceland took the form of a ritual resembling a christening rather than a purely legal case. The ritual took place in the church where a form was read, and the child was adopted with the consent and in the presence of their closest heirs and a priest. Finally, the parents swore an oath on a holy book to procure the adoption (Arnórsdóttir: 2010, 400–405). Some existing

1 It is important to note that scholars underline that this control existed already before the Reformation, but indeed more documents exist for the later period.

documents indicate that both men and women made efforts to adopt their illegitimate children or to leave them wealth through the institution of legal gifts. Legal gifts constituted one-tenth, tíundargjöf, of one's inherited property, and this percentage could be given away to a non-legitimate heir to the disadvantage of the legal heirs. Another quarter, fjórðungsgjöf, of property that had been acquired by other means, could also be legally gifted to parties other than the legal heir. The latter could be given either as property or as a leasehold on a plot of land (Arnórsdóttir: 2010, 400–405).

The use of legal gifts and adoption of illegitimate children seem to have increased at the same time as practices of leaving inheritances to the church declined after the Reformation. Gifts could be given either as legal gifts (DI XIII, 485f) or by adopting illegitimately born children (DI XIII, 517ff; DI XV, 233f) or both (DI XI, 150f; DI XIII, 200f). Interestingly, this strategy seems to have been most commonly used by priests (DI XV, 233f; DI XV, 369ff). These practices arose at the same time as donations of land stopped being handed over to church institutions. Instead, Iceland saw an increase in gifts of land to close relatives.

Sometimes, the inheritance of land followed particular names. For example, toward the end of the sixteenth century, Ragnheiður Eggertsdóttir declared in her will that the daughter of her brother should receive her land at Breiðdalur. Were Eggertsdóttir's niece to have a daughter and name her Katrín, the land should follow that name (Þorkelsson: 1912, 25f). Similarly, the mother of Jón Magnússon declared just before 1561 that the property at Hvammur in Höfðahverfi should go to Magnússon's son who was to be named Magnús. And in 1598, Elen Magnúsdóttir declared that the land at Þórustaðir should be given to a girl with the baptized name Elen and that, in the future, this land should continue to follow persons with that name (Arnórsdóttir: 2010, 416, note 190).

These examples can be understood as a shift from the donation of property to holy institutions in the name of a saint to the distribution of property amongst close, living relatives. This was also a part of the change in the gift culture in Iceland after the Reformation. The non-sacramental view of marriage after the Reformation strengthened the focus on the earthly family at the same time as the Holy Family lost its meaning as a locus of adoration and comfort. In short, this development can be described as a shift from a focus on the afterlife of the members of the family to the earthly life. Before the Reformation, wealth was donated to church institutions, but after the Reformation, the transfer of property to illegitimate children and other close relatives became more common. The existence of saints continued to be widely accepted, but they were no longer seen as the recipients of gifts. Property was no longer given to church institutions in the name of saints, nor were they any longer part of the votive culture (Arnórsdóttir: 2017c).

Shortly after the Reformation, the tradition of adoption was still widespread as was the custom of giving legal gifts. As time passed, however, authorities increasingly began to regulate the practice of giving legal gifts not only to illegitimate children but also within marital gift giving.

6. Change in Marital Property Agreements in Iceland

In the Middle Ages, marriage was more than just a financial matter. It also involved religious beliefs about the close union of spouses. These beliefs influenced the way marital property was transferred as women became partners in the actual marriage contract (Arnórsdóttir: 2010). After the Reformation, this idea of the "union of the spouses" gained potency. Luther saw conjugal love as the highest of all forms of love. Prior to the Reformation, love was increasingly a condition for a happy marriage, but Luther's ideas elevated the mutual love between spouses as a condition for a good family life. Like Augustine, Luther praised marital faithfulness. Both partners were to honor marriage and be faithful and loyal to each other, he said. Unlike Augustine, the Lutheran reformers based their ideas about marriage on Aristotle (384–322 BCE) and also on Thomas Aquinas (ca. 1225–1274). In Luther's view, spouses were spiritual, intellectual, and emotional partners with a strong need for each other (Witte: 2012, 123f). There is some evidence that Luther's new views of marriage also affected marital property understanding.

New rules for the exchange of legal gifts indicate an equalizing of the inheritance rights of illegitimate and legitimate children. Research on gift-giving practices also supplies a better understanding of changes in the marital economy, as we have seen in discussing the transfer of wealth to illegitimate children (Arnórsdóttir: 2017c). Legal gifts were not only used for giving illegitimate children property but also within marriages themselves. The one-quarter land gift was especially common in relation to the exchange of marriage gifts in late-medieval Iceland. Normally, these gifts are mentioned in marriage contracts in cases where each partner promised to leave the other a quarter of their possessions (Arnórsdóttir: 2010, 400–405). Throughout the married life of a couple and during the widower period following the death of one partner, it was possible to maintain the household through the use of joint ownership or even through the use of the wife's independent ownership, bolstered by a portion of the marital gift (Arnórsdóttir: 2010, 333–336, 400–405, 424f).

The gifts given from husband to wife or wife to husband were often intended to keep the household together in the case of the death of one of the spouses. The problem was the protection of the widow. Many court cases reflect the challenges that women or their heirs faced if the husband died. Women struggled to actually claim their property after their husband's death (DI XIII, 308 ff).[2] An Icelandic judgment from 1626 declared that those legal gifts that were given against the dowry at marriage could no longer exist. No matter how this had been legally defined in the past, going forward any wealth taken into the marriage became part of the husband's estate, even the bride's dowry (Stephensen et al.: 1853, 212). But what did this mean for the transfer of property?

In my ongoing research on gift cultures and marital exchange after the Reformation, 1550–1650, I have found no evidence of the one-quarter property gift in seventeenth-century marriage contracts. It seems that the so-called tilgjöf was the only gift given at the start of a marriage.[3] A contract from 1633, for example, mentioned that the husband gave a tilgjöf to the wife, but the wife could only receive this gift after his death and only if they had children. The amount of the gift, then, was meant for the support of the child but never for the wife specifically (AM dipl. Isl. Fasc. LXX, 24). In two contracts from 1648 and 1649, the tilgjöf was again given as property, but the transfer of property was conditioned by the couple's marriage in accord with Church Ordinances.[4] Another contract from 1649 highlights that the property contract was established after the couple had received a church blessing according to the new rule, the "Ordínantsíunni og hávirðulegs ríkisráðs" – the Ordinance and highly prominent Council of the State (AM dipl. Isl. Fasc. LXX, 31). This rule is from The Act of Marriage, given to Icelanders in 1587 by the Danish King, Frederik II.

The rising frequency of remarriage after the Reformation was also immensely consequential for succession practices. In fitting with the Lutheran ideal of marriage, remarriage after the death of a spouse was preferred over the life of a widow or widower. The opportunity to live as a widow was no longer idealized, but changing opinions held that a widow or widower should remarry as protection against sin (Witte: 2012, 128 f). Marriage protected against the sinful life that celibacy could not. Celibacy was not something that people could settle for; it was only possible as a gift from God. Likewise, monasteries were shut down

2 A judgment from 1558 concerns the efforts of Þórunn Einarsdóttir to claim her property after she was widowed. The court decided to grant her the husband's property. This judgement was based on the following principles: First, if a man took a wife according to the law of the country, gave her *tilgjöf*, and then subsequently died, then she should receive all her things, *þing*, and her dowry from his property so long as his estate retained sufficient funds to pay this. Second, neither of the spouses should waste the other's wealth. Third, she had a written testimony from her husband that he had lost her fortune. Because the household was in debt, the husband's heirs were obliged to pay this back to his wife, and the case ended with her receiving all her property as well as her personal possessions.

3 The husband, though, brought wealth to marriage as *kvánarmundr*, and the wife had her dowry from her parents. This wealth was not defined as marriage gifts but as payment, *gjald*, for marriage.

4 The word "samtenging" is found in the contract, but this is a direct reference to what is said in the Church Ordinance from 1537/1539 about entering marriage.

because their existence lacked any biblical warrant. One consequence, however, was the rising frequency of remarriage over and above life as a widow or widower (Witte: 2012, 121).

Inheritance customs evolved as a result of the rise in remarriage and new rules about marital gifts. Legal gifts had made it possible for the surviving partner to retain a great deal of their property after the death of the other spouse. From the start of the seventeenth century onward, however, these customs were no longer widely accepted. The tilgjöf was not given to the childless widow, but rather it was handed over to her dead husband's heirs. The legal custom of granting the widow one-fourth of the couple's property was nullified even though this custom had been a common part of marital gift exchange in late-medieval Iceland. Typically, these gifts were mentioned in marriage contracts where both partners promised to give the surviving spouse one-quarter of their possessions (Arnórsdóttir: 2010, 400–405). What does this mean? First, a childless widow could easily remarry, taking only her dowry to her new marriage. Second, these strict rules of marital economy underline the importance of the succession through a legitimate heir, i.e. the child born in a marriage as the sole heir of its parents.

This section has shown that at the same time as the saints were disappearing as "legal persons" (*Rechtssubjekte*),[5] marital property arrangements also underwent notable renovations. The rules governing legal gifts were originally part of larger ordinances concerning donations to church institutions. The custom of donating property to the church in the name of a particular saint did not survive the Reformation; neither did the custom of giving legal gifts in marriage. When the custom of legal gifts fell out of use in marriage contracts, the inheritance rights of legitimate children overpowered the right of the surviving spouse and other illegitimate children through the new customary gift of tilgjöf. Future research on this topic could explore the changing inheritance customs pertaining to illegitimate children's parents after the start of the seventeenth century. However, I have also shown that common ownership of property between spouses became more prevalent. Common ownership, then, diminished the rights of distant relatives, granting the surviving spouse a greater claim to the inheritance than was the case prior to the Reformation (Arnórsdóttir: 2010). The spouses' status was elevated over that of other heirs. Meanwhile, the husband's right to dispose of the total possessions increased. This strengthened the power of his position within the household and in society. Engagement came to partially replace the old betrothal contract, which in its most antiquated form had been signed by both families of the couple. This change was essential for both spouses' personal and property relationships. Not only was it forbidden to give gifts to the church

5 See a discussion about this in Bueren et al. (2011, 186), with references to Oexle (1976; 1983).

for the benefit of the soul after the Reformation, but gifting practices in marriage itself were also influenced (Arnórsdóttir: 2017c).

7. The Earthly Family and New Understandings of Motherhood

I have been discussing how the non-sacramental view on marriage after the Reformation strengthened the focus on the earthly family just as the Holy Family was losing its meaning as a locus of worship and comfort. The argument in this chapter is that this change also affected inheritance rights within earthly families due to a focal shift from the eternal to the earthly life. In practical terms, the wealth that had been given to church institutions prior to the Reformation was increasingly transferred to living relatives and heirs after the Reformation.

Unsurprisingly, the Church Ordinance of 1537/1539 included a chapter dealing specifically with midwives, mothers, and childbirth. The Church Ordinance emphasized the role of midwives in childbirth, thereby diminishing the traditional place of the saint in helping and procuring the safe delivery of a baby. Several paragraphs discuss broad themes, such as the pregnant woman, the midwife, and the baptism of newborns. Special attention is given to the dangers of fetal death before birth, during birth, or after the baby was born, how pregnant women are to seek help from the midwife, and how midwives are to prepare pregnant women for birth (DI X, 153–154). Despite the new emphasis on the midwife's role in facilitating childbirth, the mother bore central responsibility for her child's birth and protection from the Devil. Most importantly, the baby was to be baptized as soon as possible after birth, preferably in a church.

The topic of motherhood and childbirth also appeared in litigation and legal regulations in the late 1500s. Pregnant women were to be educated about childbirth "because mothers are God's instrument in the lives of their children" (KiO, 200). Presumably, women were God's instrument not only during their maternity leave but also later in the child's life by virtue of their status as mothers and wives who would continue to bear children as long as possible. Therefore, "preachers" should teach pregnant mothers to dedicate their child, their "fruit of life," to God in prayer during childbirth: "We thank you almighty, eternal God, for your blessing. And we ask you, O Lord Jesus Christ, that you will let this child's life bear the fruit you have always commanded" (ibid.).

What is perhaps most important in connection to the new understanding of motherhood exemplified here is that, during the Late Middle Ages, women's piety was expressed through various types of pious deeds in hospitals and through care of the sick and dying. After the Reformation, these deeds continued to be part of the image of a good wife, but the sphere of a woman's pious work turned inward toward the family, not to institutionalized work in hospitals. As

Witte shows, this privatization of the female role did not only have a practical implication but also wider social consequences because "the organization of the state" came from "the way the household was organized." This pious wife's concern for her family was significant given the demonstrative role of the household oeconomia for the organization of society and the secular government (Witte: 2002, 231). Keeping that in mind, it is interesting to examine the way the new doctrine constructed an ideal status for motherhood.

A prevailing view during the Middle Ages was that women became increasingly unclean during pregnancy. "The closer to birth, the farther from God." The medieval period celebrated virginity as an expression of an unmarried woman's holiness. However, this view changed sharply after the Reformation when family life became the ideal life for all men and women. As the ideal of married life was disseminated at the popular level through sermons and books, the unmarried became increasingly suspect (Wiesner-Hanks: 2001, 130). The Danish Church Ordinance can be understood to play a role in this transformation. Turning the medieval view of female pollution on its head, the Church Ordinance stated instead that mothers were "the proper tools of God, and therefore closer to God, the closer they came to birth" (KiO, 200).

Midwives received new roles in the life of expectant mothers as a result of these evolving views. According to the historian Grethe Jackobsen, midwives had to be honest and God-fearing because midwives were to comfort and instruct pregnant woman without recourse to Catholic prayers, and they had to be able to properly baptize children in case of emergency. However, a 1555 synod underscored that midwives should not baptize unborn fetuses in the womb (Jakobsen: 1995, 236). This special focus on childbirth also appeared in the literature in the so-called "midwives' books." These books were first written in German and Latin but were also gradually written in Danish, which helped to disseminate midwives' books throughout the Nordic region. Doctors and theologians alike were particularly interested in the question of the origins of birth defects. Doctors borrowed their moral considerations from the theologians; inversely, theologians used medical examples as the basis for their doctrinal considerations (Weiser-Aall: 1968, 35f). Similarly, priests taught midwives, and the first medical book was published in Danish in 1557 in a translation by a citizen in Malmo, Henrik Smed. Noting a great shortage of good doctors and midwives in Denmark in the preface to his book, Smed's aim was to teach women "how so easily, by God's help, they could give birth to their children into the world" (Møller: 1940, 100).

The strong emphases that priests were to educate midwives and that midwives were to teach pregnant women prayers and comforting words for childbirth reflect the new understanding of mothers as God's instruments extending from Luther's Reformation. Pastoral literature illustrates how this important role was introduced to women. According to Peder Palladius, women often reported fearing the Devil while they were in childbirth (Palladius: 1543/1925, 107). Later on, Palladius wrote that a woman could be saved by giving birth even if she died during labor or her baby died before it could be baptized. She should not fear, he said, "because [God] is mighty enough to save a child's soul even during pregnancy" (Palladius: 1543/1925, 108f). In a previous work, I discussed the importance of saints' culture for the ideals and practices of motherhood in the Late Middle Ages (Arnórsdóttir: 2014). There, I argued that the saints' culture not only affected the practice of motherhood but also the mothers' social identity. Lutheran pastoral care aimed at altering the Catholic practice of using the saints as helpers for mothers during birth. Instead, Lutheran pastoral care manifested another ideal for mothers' identities. As time passed, motherhood gained another meaning in the earthly life of the Lutheran families as a source of piety and even salvation.

8. Conclusion

The Reformation inculcated new social attitudes toward marriage that increased its strength as a social institution. As time passed, marriage even became the model for regulating sexual life. John Witte Jr. has shown that Luther himself saw marriage as part of the divine plan for human life on earth. Marriage came to fulfill the role that the church had occupied before the Reformation; that is, as the site for the responsibility of loving care. In this chapter, I have examined transformations in marital customs in parts of the Danish Kingdom, primarily in Denmark and Iceland.

Marriage laws and practices offer unique material for understanding the possible incorporation of Reformation ideas into everyday life. I have shown how ideals and ideas were conceived in relation to the social formation of marriage. Marriage was no longer a sacrament but a social institution of the secular order that took the place of the monastic life. The divine was located in the three goods – conjugal love, procreation, and child rearing – and in marital care and protection against sin. The normalization of these ideals was critical for the abolition of the ideal of celibacy. As a result, the monastic vow was no longer seen to possess a higher religious status than the married life. Additionally, public marriage in which the parish priests married each couple was elevated, and problematic secret marriages were abolished. Exceptions to these new rules could only be granted by the Prince, indicating the movement of power from the Pope to secular authority. But how important was the Reformation for the formation of new ideals of femininity and masculinity within gender relations and in parental roles over legitimate children?

The Church Ordinance from 1537/1539 and the Marriage Ordinance issued by King Frederik II in Denmark 1582 and in Iceland in 1587 directly influenced new views toward deviant sexual behavior, rejecting these behaviors not only as a sin but also as a crime. The widely documented increase in secular control of marriage demonstrates the way these views greatly impacted sexual control. For instance, these changes are reflected in the legal regulations, court cases, and in the new Eucharistic practices for the control of sexual conduct discussed throughout this chapter.

The tradition of adopting illegitimate children into the family was part of a certain ad hoc inheritance strategy before the Reformation, especially amongst the clergy in Iceland. More stringent control over marriage and non-married sexual lives was also part of the new moral code after the Reformation. The glaring absence of the one-fourth gift in marriage contracts from the seventeenth and eighteenth centuries indicates that this regulation influenced the inheritance strategy of the elite in Iceland. This might also suggest that the possibilities for leaving the surviving spouse the gift of one-fourth, an incredibly popular strategy during the late fifteenth and early sixteenth centuries, was no longer available.

Interestingly, the Holy Family also lost its meaning as a locus of worship and comfort in this same period. The Holy Family was replaced by a focus on the earthly family as the model for all other social institutions. The saints continued to exist, of course, but practices like leaving gifts of land or property to the church in the name of a saint fell into disuse. The votive culture surrounding the saints also went out of vogue. These changes coincided with changes in inheritance strategies that can be described as a shift in focus from eternal life to earthly life. Whereas wealth had previously been given to church institutions in the memory of family members and the good of their souls, after the Reformation, property was transferred to illegitimate children and other close relatives. Those transfers are also interesting in relation to the culture of Remembering after the Reformation.

The social marriage contract established as an ideal after the Reformation was crucial to sexual relationships. The status of the married woman eclipsed the status of the unmarried virgin. Similarly, married men were given authority over entire households, their wife, children, and servants. A husband's role was to chastise and serve, to guide his wife, giving care and service. Those who repeatedly violated this ideal risked not only the death penalty but also the salvation of their souls. How this practice came to affect other community issues such as the relationship between community organization and state development, charity, childrearing, and education are not addressed here. It is important to emphasize that the external community development must also be viewed in light of Luther's teachings on marriage as an ideal model for organizing the entire community. The claim that the "marriage bed should be free from all sin" points to the essential role marriage had after the Reformation.

Bibliography

Arnórsdóttir, Agnes S. (2010), Property and Virginity: The Christianization of Marriage in Medieval Iceland 1200–1600, Aarhus: Arhus Universitetsforlag.

Arnórsdóttir, Agnes S. (2014), Motherhood as Emotion and Social Practice: Mary and Anne as Maternal Models in Medieval Iceland, in: Kerstin Hundahl/Lars Kjær/Niels Lund (ed.), Denmark and Europe in the Middle Ages, c. 1000–1525: Essays in Honour of Professor Michael H. Gelting, Surrey: Ashgate, 43–58.

Arnórsdóttir, Agnes S. (2017a), "Ægtesængen kal være uden synd": Reformationens betydning for ægteskabets idealer og sociale praksisser i Island og Danmark, in: Ole Høiris/Per Ingesman (ed.), Reformationen: 1500-tallets kulturrevolution, Aarhus: Aarhus University Press, 303–325.

Arnórsdóttir, Agnes S. (2017b), Gender and Donation Culture in Icelandic from 1300–1600, in: Ole-Albert Rønning/Helle Møller Sigh/Helle Vogt (ed.), Donations, Strategies and Relations in the Latin West/Nordic Countries from the Late Roman Period until Today, Oxford: Routledge, 165–178.

Arnórsdóttir, Agnes S. (2017c, forthcoming), Marital Property and Change in the Donations Culture of Late 16th and Early 17th Century, in: Auður Magnúsdóttir/Lars Ivar Hansen/Bodil Selmer/Marianne Holdgaard (ed.), Space of Action and Legal strategies, Leiden/Boston, MA: Brill.

Bueren, Truus van et al. (2011), Researching Medieval Memoria: Prospects and Possibilities: With an Introduction to Medieval Memoria Online (MeMO), Jaarboek voor Middeleeuwse Geschiedenis 14, 183–234.

Jakobsen, Grethe (1995), Kvinder, køn og købstadslovgivning 1400–1600: Lovfaste mænd og ærlige kvinder, Copenhagen: Museum Tusculanum.

Knudsen, Nina Dahl (2015), "Saa længe Mennesker er til, bliver Leiermaale til …": En undersøgelse af seksualnormer i retsmateriale fra 1500-tallet, unpublished MA Thesis, Aarhus University.

Korpiola, Mia (2009), Between Betrothal and Bedding: Marriage Formation in Sweden 1200–1600 (The Northern World 43), Leiden/Boston, MA: Brill.

Møller, Jens Schou Christensen (1940), Moder og barn i dansk folkeoverlevering: Fra svangerskab til daab og kirkegang, Copenhagen: Munksgaard.

Oexle, Otto Gerhard (1976), Memoria und Memorialüberlieferung im frühen Mittelalter, FMSt 10, 70–95.

Oexle, Otto Gerhard (1983), Die Gegenwart der Toten, in: Herman Braet/Werner Verbeke (ed.), Death in the Middle Ages, ML.St. Series 1: Studia 9, Leuven: Leuven University Press, 19–77.

Ólafsson, Skúli S. (2014), Altarisganga á Íslan di 1570–1720, Fyrirkomulag og áhrif, Reykjavík: Háskólaútgáfan.

Palladius, Peder (1543/1925), Visitatsbogen, in: Lis Jacobsen (ed.), Peder Palladius' Danske Skrifter, vol. 5, Copenhagen: H. H. Thieles Bogtrykkeri, 1–240.

RIISØY, ANNE IRENE (2009), Sexuality, Law and Legal Practice and the Reformation in Norway (The Northern World 44), Leiden/Boston, MA: Brill.

SIGH, HELLE (2012), Samtykke og samfund: Kristningen af ægteskabet og retsvirkninger i Danmark c. 1200–1600, unpublished PhD Thesis, Aarhus University.

STEPHENSEN, ODDGEIR et al. (ed.) (1853), Lovsamling for Island, vol. 1, Copenhagen: A. F. Høst.

TAMM, DITLEV (2008), Retshistorie: Danmark - Europa - globale perspektiver, Copenhagen: Jurist- og Økonomforbundets Forlag.

TROELS-LUND, TROELS FREDERIK (1969), Dagligt liv i norden i det sekstende århundrede, vol. 4: Årlige fester, fødsel og dåb, Copenhagen: Nordisk Forlag.

WEISER-AALL, LILY (1968), Svangerskap og fødsel i nyere norsk tradisjon: En kildekritisk studie, Oslo: Norsk Folkemuseum.

WIESNER-HANKS, MERRY (2001), Gender in History, Oxford: Wiley-Blackwell.

WITTE JR., JOHN (2002), Law and Protestantism: The Legal Teaching of the Lutheran Reformation, Cambridge: Cambridge University Press.

WITTE JR., JOHN (2012), From Sacrament to Contract: Marriage, Religion and Law in Western Tradition, Louisville, KY: Westminster John Knox Press.

ÞORKELSSON, JÓN (ed.) (1912–1914), Alþingisbækur Íslands, vol. 1: 1570–1581, Reykjavík: Sögufélag.

Archival sources

AM Den Arnamagnæanske Håndskriftsamling: Det Arnamagnæanske Institut, Copenhagen/Stofnun Árna Magnússonar á Íslandi, Reykjavík.

Søren Feldtfos Thomsen

Marital Love, Marital Obedience

Gender and Emotion in Danish Lutheran Marriage and Household Books, 1571–1653

1. Introduction

Scholars have discussed whether the Protestant Reformation had a detrimental or a beneficial impact on early modern women since at least the 1980s. Some have argued that Protestantism negatively impacted women's lives, identities, and means of self-expression by abolishing devotion to the Virgin Mary and the (female) saints, by barring women from the communal life of the monastery, and by idealizing marriage and homemaking as the only legitimate occupation for women (e.g. Wiesner: 1987; Roper: 1989; Karant-Nunn: 1998). Others have maintained that Protestantism empowered women by granting them new authority and independence as housemothers and by emphasizing the priesthood of all believers and the spiritual equality of the sexes (e.g. Ozment: 1983; Wunder: 1992).

As Kirsi Stjerna (2009, 39) has pointed out, the diverging opinions of Reformation scholars on questions of gender reflect an inherent ambiguity in Reformation attitudes toward early modern women. The Reformation encompassed both an egalitarian critique of medieval misogyny as well as a hierarchical insistence on female subordination to male authority. The purpose of this chapter is to elucidate this ambiguity specifically with regard to the Lutheran tradition in Denmark. I will do so by looking at the way in which the Lutheran theology of marriage was articulated in sixteenth and seventeenth century marriage and household books. My question is how the authors of such books balanced an understanding of marriage as a partnership between husband and wife with a traditional, patriarchal conception of gender order. This question prompts many other lines of inquiry, including how Lutheran moralists constructed marital intimacy and the role of the Christian housewife.[1] In attempting to answer these

1 I am dealing here strictly with a prescriptive level of description. The texts that will be discussed

questions, I will focus on the affective dimension of gender prescription, i. e. the relationship between prescribed gender roles and the emotional norms that Lutheran moralists (implicitly or explicitly) tried to establish.

I draw on recent insights gained in the study of the history and sociology of emotion, where a number of scholars have pointed to the gendered nature of emotional norms and roles.[2] Far from universal, human emotional responses are both culturally and socially specific, varying with class, ethnicity, and gender. As Arlie Hochschild (1983, 162–184), Stephanie A. Shields (2002), and Ute Frevert (2011, 87–147) have pointed out, expectations about male and female displays of emotions, for instance anger and grief, often diverge, and are tied to culturally variable norms governing social interaction and the (often unequal) distribution of power between men and women. Stephanie A. Shields argues: "Whether explicitly represented in statements of beliefs about emotion or subtly transmitted via judgments about the appropriateness of others' emotions and emotional display, gender limits are clearly delineated by emotional standards." (Shields: 2002, 63). Gender norms and emotional norms are, from this perspective, closely related: to perform gender is often also to perform certain emotions consonant with culturally and socially prescribed gender expectations.[3]

As Susan C. Karant-Nunn (2010, 63–99) has convincingly shown in her study of the emotional cultures of Catholicism and Protestantism in early modern Germany, Lutheran authorities not only sought to alter people's religious beliefs and practices but also to (re)shape the emotional lives of their readers and parishioners. Sermons, for example, were not simply mediums of rational argumentation. Sermons also appealed to the feelings and spiritual experiences of their hearers, conveying moods and idealizing certain emotional states as expressive of true Christian piety above others. Confessionalization and the consolidation of confessional cultures, in other words, was not only a matter of realigning the institutional framework of church and state, of implementing changes in religious education and introducing liturgical reforms. Con-

in what follows cannot tell us to what extent husbands and wives in early modern Denmark actually adhered to a Lutheran ideal of marital life. They can, however, tell us something about the attempt by Lutheran moralists to translate theological ideas into precepts for social practice and how they constructed female identity in the process. At the same time, the fact that such literature enjoyed considerable popular success in the early modern book market suggests that the Lutheran marriage ideal resonated with many in the Danish reading public, whether they actively sought to conform to it or not.

2 On the field of history of emotion and what has variously been termed the "emotional turn" and the "affective turn" in humanities and social sciences, see e. g. Lemmings/Brooks: 2014 and Matt/Stearns: 2014.

3 See also McNamer (2010, 13ff.)

fessionalization also shaped religious emotions and experiences (ibid., 250).[4] Confessional culture and emotional culture are, in other words, closely intertwined. A comprehensive understanding of Danish Lutheranism and its impact on social structures and relations must not lose sight of the affective dimension of confessionalization.

2. Love and Obedience in Martin Luther's Understanding of Marriage

In his *A Sermon on the Estate of Marriage* from 1519, Martin Luther (1483–1546) set out a distinction between three kinds of love: false, natural, and marital. He elaborated:

> False love is that which seeks its own, as a man loves money, possessions, honor, and women taken outside of marriage and against God's command. Natural love is that between father and child, brother and sister, friend and relative, and similar relationships. But over and above all these is married love, that is, a bride's love, which glows like a fire and desires nothing but the husband. She says, "It is you I want, not what is yours: I want neither your silver nor your gold; I want neither. I want only you. I want you in your entirety, or not at all." All other kinds of love seeks something other than the loved one: this kind wants only to have the beloved's own self completely. If Adam had not fallen, the love of bride and groom would have been the loveliest thing. (LW 44: 9/WA 2: 167,26–35).

Though tainted by carnal lust because of the fall of mankind, marital love, according to Luther, is "the greatest and purest love of all loves." In a marriage sermon from 1531, the reformer wrote:

> ...W]hen you look at your wife as if she were the only woman on earth, and when you look at your husband as if he were the only man on earth; if no king, yes, nor even the sun itself shines more brightly and lights up your eyes more than your husband or wife, then right there you are in possession of God's Word [...] (WA 34 I: 52,13–17, translation by me).

Such passages indicate Luther's emphasis on the importance of intimacy and affection in marriage and his ideal of the marital union as a spiritual and emotional companionship between husband and wife. Indeed, Luther regarded women as indispensable companions for men not just within the domestic sphere but also throughout all social life, asserting that society would virtually collapse without them (LW 54: 160f/WA TR 2: 166, no. 1658).

4 Karant-Nunn is among the first scholars to integrate Reformation studies and the emerging field of the history of emotion; see also Scheer (2012).

Following Luther's lead, many Lutheran reformers stressed conjugal love as one of the three essential "marital goods" (along with mutual protection from sexual sin and procreation). There is, therefore, a strong emphasis on intimacy and emotional parity between husband and wife in the Lutheran understanding of marriage, as Hans-Martin Gutmann (1991; 2013), John Witte Jr (2002, 119ff), and most recently Elisabeth Gerle (2015) have pointed out. This emphasis appears in particular in the concept of marital love as a unique emotional bond between husband and wife.[5]

Equally strong, however, is the Lutheran insistence on the necessity of female subordination to male authority in marriage. This is readily apparent in Martin Luther's several commentaries on Genesis, where Eve's role in the fall is ascribed to her simplemindedness and weakness in comparison with Adam. Commenting on Gen 3:16 in a 1527 marriage sermon, Luther argued:

> [...S]he does not live according to her own free will. It would have been such that they [Adam and Eve] might have gone their separate ways, one here, the other somewhere else, though in moderation. But now the wife can undertake nothing without the husband. Wherever he is, she has to be with him, and humble herself before him. (Karant-Nunn/Wiesner-Hanks: 2003, 23/WA 24: 102,27–30).

Because of their intellectual and physical inferiority, it is necessary for wives to submit to the authority and guidance of their husbands. Luther underlined this repeatedly – for example in his 1529 *A Marriage Booklet for Simple Pastors*, where he instructed pastors to remind bridal couples that just "as now the church is subject to Christ, so also are the women subject to their husbands in all things." (BC 370/WA 30 I: 79,11f).

This hierarchical view of social relations was perhaps most clearly articulated in Luther's so-called doctrine of the three estates, formulated piecemeal in several writings, ranging from *Confession Concerning the Lord's Supper* from 1528 to *On the Councils of the Church* of 1539. Here, Luther spoke variously of three divinely instituted orders or hierarchies – state, church, and household – through which God governs the earthly realm (cf. Saarinen: 2005). Commenting on the fourth commandment in his *Large Catechism* (1529), Luther argued that the source of all authority is parental authority and asserted that God had established the authority of three fathers "of blood, house, and country" in addition to the "spiritual fathers" of the church (BC 408/WA 30 I: 155). Luther expanded paternal authority beyond the realm of the family to include civil and ecclesiastical

5 Lutheranism did not represent a complete *novum* in this regard: The Lutheran understanding of companionate marriage and emphasis on mutual love was foreshadowed by the ideology of domesticity that emerged among the European urban middle classes from the fourteenth century onwards. On this topic, see e.g. Wunder (1992) and contributions in Kowaleski/Goldberg (2008).

offices when he maintained that all Christians are obliged to honor and obey not only their biological parentage but also the "fathers" of state and church.

On the one hand, Luther's understanding of the three estates or orders is clearly egalitarian. The state, the church, and the household are not conceived as separate social classes, as in the medieval distinctions between, for example, nobility and peasantry, but as equally important and God-given social spheres in which every Christian takes part, regardless of class or position. On the other hand, each sphere is governed by a hierarchical relation between superiors – those whose duty is to command – and subordinates – those whose duty is to obey. Within the household, the male head is granted authority over his wife, children, and servants, but he must provide for them in exchange for their obedience. Luther outlined the duties that befall each Christian depending on their position within each estate in the *Table of Duties* of the *Small Catechism* (1529). He cited 1 Pet 3 and admonished wives to be "subjected to their husband as to the Lord." Husbands should "live reasonably with [their] wives and, as co-heirs of the grace of life, give honor to wives as the [weakest] instrument." (BC 366/WA 30 I: 333f). Given his emphasis on paternal authority, it is worth noting that Luther described the wife as a "half-child" in a 1524 sermon on the same scriptural passage. He also reminded his male listeners that "the man who marries a wife should know that he cares for a child." (WA 15: 420,15f, my translation). Here, Luther was quite explicit in equating women with children, at least in so far as both wife and child must be subject to paternal supervision and discipline.

3. Social Order and Emotional Order in the Marital Household

Martin Luther's egalitarian understanding of conjugal love was offset by a decidedly hierarchical, patriarchal conception of social order in which male dominance over women was taken for granted as part of the natural order of postlapsarian creation (cf. Gerle: 2015, 137). In this context, we should remember that the reformer's statements on the nature and role of women were often part of more comprehensive discussions on marriage, sexuality, and sin and could serve various argumentative purposes. Thus, Luther's emphasis on the spiritual and emotional equity between husbands and wives on the one hand, and his strongly hierarchical understanding of social and gender order on the other, were never systematically resolved. They represented different aspects of married life that the reformer could emphasize in different contexts to serve specific arguments about marriage, the nature of women, and the duties of husbands and wives.

Subsequent Lutherans would echo this ambiguity. They both praised women as spiritual equals to men, who share fully in the numerous household responsibilities, while also often retaining a strong belief in female inferiority and obedience.[6] Lutheran marriage and household books from the period after the Reformation show that this was not simply a social ideal but also an emotional ideal of female deference to male authority. The majority of such literature in Denmark was made up of translated German works, as second generation reformers sought a quick and efficient means to promote the Lutheran understanding of marriage and to provide the reading public with moral guidelines for everyday married life.[7]

Rasmus Hansen Reravius (d. 1582), a pastor and former student of Niels Hemmingsen (1513–1600), was among the most prolific of Danish translators. He published a series of translations of German evangelical books on the household and marriage during the 1570s.[8] One such title was a 1571 translation of the *Oeconomia Oder Bericht vom Christlichen Hauswesen* (Wittenberg, 1564), written by German Lutheran pastor Johannes Mathesius (1504–1565).[9] The intended reader (the male head of the household) was instructed to regard the woman as God's gift to man. She is his chief means of warding off sexual sin, and her main responsibility is to bear children and run the household (Mathesius: 1571, B1vff). Indeed, said Mathesius, without her the latter is simply impossible because the wife is the one who rules the household, maintains order, and supervises the servants. She is, as Mathesius metaphorically put it, "the wall surrounding the house" (ibid.). Just as she protects her husband against fornication, a good wife also guards the household against the dangers of a sinful world. In so doing, however, she must be obedient and faithful to her husband as well as industrious and frugal (B2v). Although the wife is granted authority within the domestic sphere, Mathesius left no doubt as to the superiority of male authority, emphasizing that female obedience is inscribed in the very order of creation (B4r).

Similar notes resounded in the *Haustaffel: Wie sich ein jglich Mensch in seinem beruff vnd stande […] halten sol* (Magdeburg, 1561) by the otherwise unknown author Matthias Weber, published in Reravius' Danish translation in 1572. Structuring his exposition according to Luther's *Table of Duties*, Weber echoed Luther in admonishing wives to fear and love God and husband alike. Chastity, subservience, and obedience are expected of the good wife, whose duty it is to

6 See the discussion on women, marriage, and sexuality in the context of Lutheran marriage sermons in Crowther (2010, esp. 104–117).

7 On early modern German household and marriage literature, see Lemmer (1991) and Classen (2005, 108–261). Charlotte Appel (2001) offers a comprehensive study of the Danish book market in the seventeenth century and the various genres of devotional and catechetical vernacular literature available to Danish readers.

8 See Fink-Jensen (2011).

9 On Mathesius, see in particular Karant-Nunn (1992).

support her husband in all things and to manage the household economy (Weber: 1572, F4vf). An ideology of separate spheres of labor emerges here: a woman's natural place is assumed to be within the domestic sphere while men are thought to manage external household affairs. Mathesius was more explicit in this regard. He described the ideal wife as someone who stays at home and does not go about town. He also emphasized that young girls belong at home and should be taught above all to perform their proper household duties (such as baking, brewing, preparing meals, etc.) (Mathesius: 1571, C1r). Since both authors agree that female inferiority is part of the natural order of creation, for a woman to challenge the authority of her husband is a violation of divine order (Weber: 1572, F2v).

Mathesius' and Weber's guidelines were not merely of a social character but also had a clear emotional dimension. Husbands and wives were admonished not only to act in certain ways towards each other but also – as a prerequisite – to cultivate certain feelings towards each other consonant with their social responsibilities. Since the wife is supposed to heed her husband in all things, a good wife should never succumb to pride or vanity, according to Mathesius (1571: B2v). These are feelings characteristic of the bad housewife who, "like a bitter herb," annoys and provokes her husband, causing emotional discord within the household (B2r). For the husband's part, the obligation of conjugal love entails that he should always be patient and kind toward his wife and be a strong leader over her (the weaker vessel) (B4r). The social and gender hierarchy of the marital household here implies an emotional order, or what may perhaps be termed a division of emotional labor[10] that reinforces the authority of husband over wife. The husband is admonished to cultivate feelings of love, kindness, and patience towards his wife while suppressing feelings of anger and resentment. The wife, on the other hand, is to cultivate feelings of love, humility, patience, submissiveness, and reverence for her husband while eschewing feelings of pride, anger, and entitlement.

This marital balance was most radically set out in German pastor and playwright Paul Rebhun's *Hausfried. Was fur ursachen den Christlichen eheleuten zubedencken den lieben hausfried in der ehe zuerhalten* (Wittenberg, 1546), published in Reravius' Danish translation in 1575. According to Rebhun, the harmonious marital household depends upon the proper relation between a loving husband and an obedient wife (Rebhun: 1575, B5rff). Only through the right balance between love and obedience can marital strife be avoided for the good of the household and society at large. The primary marital duty of a husband is, therefore, to love his wife in accordance with biblical injunctions, while a wife, similarly, is to obey her husband and submit to his will. These obligations

10 See also Hochschild (1979; 1983) and below.

are all but unconditional. They are grounded in the order of creation and reinforced by the fall of Adam and Eve (C2vff; L2vff; L5rff). To neglect one's calling as husband or wife is not only a sin against one's spouse but also against God and the divine order of creation. A disobedient wife not only challenges the authority of her husband but also God's authority (C8v; L6v).

The emotion of anger was of particular concern to Rebhun who believed that it poses a threat, especially to the pious husband. The inability to control feelings of anger towards one's wife is the hallmark of the tyrant (F7rff; P2r; V4rf). A good husband must learn to control and suppress such emotions. Even when using corporeal punishment to discipline his wife – which Rebhun allowed as a final means of correction – a good husband should never be motivated by anger and vengefulness, "but in the same way as when a friend punishes a friend, or a father punishes his dear child." (V4r). In return, Rebhun stressed the responsibility of the wife not to provoke her husband by giving in to pride and boastfulness and so increase his anger and force him to act tyrannically (N3rf; R7vff). Instead, she must make an effort to comfort and please her husband and prove herself to be industrious, pious, and obedient to him (H7r). Although both parties share the responsibility of preserving marital peace, Rebhun unequivocally regarded wifely obedience as a prerequisite for the cultivation of conjugal love. A wife cannot demand nor expect her husband to love her without having first submitted to his rule. This must be so, argues Rebhun, since female obedience was imposed as a punishment for Eve's role in the fall of mankind while a husband's obligation to love his wife was issued as a reward, rather than a punishment (V8v). Rebhun thus emphasizes the wife's duty of caring for the emotional economy of the household: to cultivate and receive love from her husband she must first offer him her obedience.

4. Cultivating Emotion: Domestic Prayer

Household and marriage books of the sort translated and published by Rasmus Hansen Reravius can be seen as manuals for "emotion management' or "emotion work." They contain what Arlie Hochschild has called "feeling rules," defined as "social guidelines that direct how we want to try to feel" and "guidelines to the assessment of fits and misfits between feeling and situation." (Hochschild: 1979, 563.565; see also Hochschild: 1983, 56–75). Hochschild (1983: 37–48) argues that human social relations are governed by latent and implicit rules that individuals must follow in order to conform to the emotional norms of their community. This encompasses not only expressive rules for the display of emotion ("surface acting") but also rules for what we should be feeling "inside" ("deep acting"). More recently, in a study of Middle English Passion meditations, Sarah McNamer

(2010, 11ff) has shown how devotional texts may contain "intimate scripts" for the cultivation and expression of emotions proper to social and gender roles. For example, by scripting first-person utterances and emotion claims or by addressing the reader directly and providing instructions for affective response, such texts not only describe how their readers should feel but become tools for the cultivation of emotions.

In Lutheran marriage and household books, such intimate scripts were often provided by various prayers, which became increasingly tied (in both form and content) to the domestic sphere and its members during the latter half of the sixteenth century. Once again, Martin Luther's *Table of Duties* from the *Kleine Katechismus* provided a structuring principle. Thus, we find prayers intended for the members of the household, including marital prayers such as "A Husband's Prayer" from Matthesius' *Oeconomia.* Here, the male reader is supposed to petition God for the protection of his household and the wisdom to rule over his wife, children, and servants (Matthesius: 1571, D3r). In the corresponding "A Wife's Prayer," on the other hand, a female reader must ask God for the ability to humble herself before her husband, to manage the household economy well, to raise and instruct her children, and to live in harmony and love with everyone (D4vf). In a similar vein, Weber's *Haustaffel* includes prayers for each estate, including household prayers for husbands and wives. A husband is to ask God for the ability to "love my wife, just as Christ has loved, and still loves, us poor human beings, his congregation, and church" and for his wife "to be obedient and subservient to me in all proper things, as the congregation is obedient to Christ." (Weber: 1572, F3r). A wife should ask for God's help "that I might follow your command and be obedient to my husband, love and obey him, remain steadfast in my faith, in love, and lead a holy, chaste life." (G1v).

Prayer texts such as these articulated social and emotional roles for the marital couple and explicated which expectations husbands and wives might legitimately have for each other. Paul Rebhun's *Hausfried* included prayers for husbands and wives plagued by "wicked" spouses. A passage from the husband's prayer reads:

> Give my wife the grace of your holy spirit, that she might change her ways and mind through your mercy and help; that she make an effort to learn from your word in what way she is to live as a wife and to act accordingly, that she, firstly, recognizes me as her husband and head and so shows me the proper obedience and subservience, faithfulness, kindness and good will […]. That she would, secondly, prove herself pleasingly quiet and meek, not to quarrel with me nor murmur tauntingly and with wicked words […] that I might have better cause to love her. (Rebhun: 1575, X6rf).

The book offered a similar prayer text for the wife who suffers under a tyrannical husband. The wife must petition God for the husband to mend his ways and to treat the wife properly as the weaker vessel, "[...] that I might in all proper things be obedient, kind, polite, faithful, and courteous toward him, that he might not be moved to greater unkindness and cruelty toward me on account of my impropriety, but that we should both, every day, give each other cause for domestic peace and harmonious love [...]" (X8vf).

Gender-specific prayers such as these made it into other popular prayer books and household manuals of the time (most famously, perhaps, Johann Habermann's *Christliche Gebet für alle Not vnd Stende* (1567), which appeared in a Danish translation in 1571). These prayers were expressive of a hierarchical piety, suggesting a division of emotional labor between husband and wife that was clearly intended to have social repercussions. Though voicing the hope for salvation and the religious ideals for which their authors believed every earnest Christian should strive, they clearly set divergent social standards for how men and women were to realize those ideals within the marital union. While it is tempting to regard such prayers – written as they are for each member of the marital household – as vehicles of individualized piety, there is also a strong element of social control. The act of prayer is frequently constructed as one in which the wife is intended to enact and sustain feelings of love, obedience, and humility toward God and husband. In this way, clearly gendered emotional roles for the marital couple are articulated, reinforcing a social hierarchy modeled on paternal authority congruent with Martin Luther's understanding of the household as a divine order. To pray properly as a wife is to adopt the proper emotional stance of humility and obedience toward both God and husband. Meanwhile, the role offered to a male reader generally emphasizes forbearance, wisdom, and authority in relation to his wife. The prayer texts themselves reveal that these are not emotional ideals circumscribed by the act of praying itself but should be carried over into everyday life and should inform the intimate sphere of the household.

5. Managing Emotion: Devotional Literature for Women

Devotional literature specifically for women illustrates that the cultivation of emotion through domestic prayer and devotion was seen as a means of disciplining the Danish reading public and promoting Lutheran social and gender ideals. Flourishing particularly from the late sixteenth century onwards, such easily accessible literature (predominantly written by men) offered female readers advice and moral guidelines for proper behavior both within and prior to entering marriage (cf. Appel: 2001, 618–627). The latter was of particular concern to Lutheran pastor and superintendent Lukas Martini (1548–1599) whose popular *Der christlichen Jungfrawen Ehrenkränzlein* (Prague, 1580) was published in a Danish translation by Lorentz Benedicht in 1594, going through five editions by 1660 (Appel: 2001, 620). It belongs to the subgenre of devotional literature termed *hortulus animæ* ('Little Garden of the Soul'), characterized by the use of horticultural and botanical symbolism, making use of the garden and its plants as objects of reflection on Christian truths and virtues (cf. Arvidsson: 1991). Martini listed twenty virtues (likened to individual plants), which young maidens are admonished to cultivate in their 'spiritual garden,' including humility, industriousness, chastity, modesty, kindness, fidelity, and silence (Martini: 1594, C1r).

Martini's exposition is based on Martin Luther's vocational ethics with its emphasis on paternal authority. Martini defines the virtue of true humility as "when a truly god-fearing human being understands his own weakness and earnestly subjects himself to God, both when it comes to the obligations of his calling and [...] in showing other people the honor they are owed." (D5r). By listing the honoring of one's parents as a virtue in itself (F4vff), Martini implicitly took his cue from Luther's generalization of the fourth commandment to include all figures of authority: "What honor demands is that they [children] regard parents and others, who are in their stead, as God's order and means, whom God himself has appointed and ordained [...]" (F6v). To Martini, Christian virtue is realized by submitting oneself to the authority of superiors – God, parents, the church, one's husband – and fulfilling the obligations of one's divine calling. This takes place not only on a social level but also on an emotional level.

Christian maidens must not only learn how to behave in accordance with their position in the social hierarchy but must also strive to cultivate certain emotions as the basis for and fulfillment of a truly Christian way of life. Allegorizing the medicinal quality of various plants and herbs, Martini repeatedly stresses that fulfilling social obligations serves to drive away improper feelings and replace them with proper feelings. Regular church attendance, he asserted, along with education, confession, and prayer help to alleviate despair and impede carnal desire (C2rff). Indeed, continual prayer and daily invocation of God and the Holy Spirit are not only means to alleviate fear; they also shield against sin and help to drive away pride (E2rff). Discussing the virtue of industriousness (G4rff), Martini emphasizes the importance of young girls getting used to manual labor from an early age, first in the kitchen, then the stables and fields, etc.: "Through manual labor and the observance of God's law those worms are killed and removed which are the passions and improper desires and the wicked appetite for fornication, in addition to laziness, which obstruct those gifts which God gives us in our calling" (G6vf).

Studying the text, most early modern readers (and hearers) – whether male or female, young or old – could hardly have failed to notice that Martini's virtuous Christian maiden was, above all, characterized by the ability to exert spiritual and emotional self-discipline. To be chaste and honest, for example, is to be able to "rule one's desires, appetites, and inclinations." (H2r). Martini correlated this ability to humility such that to be truly chaste and honest "one must consider oneself inferior to others and humble oneself before them in thought, speech, and deed." (H3r). Modesty, likewise, meant being able to keep desire and lewdness at bay, while eschewing vulgarity both in outward dress and also inwardly by shunting feelings of pride and vanity (J7r).

The role envisioned for young women by Martini and other Lutheran moralists who sought out female audiences was unequivocally that of the dutiful wife. It was a role often articulated in terms of emotional ideals and expectations, though the authors' didactic means varied. While Martini explicitly addressed the issue of human passions, others were more indirect in their approach. A 1619 translation of Lutheran poet Erasmus Alberus' *Ehebüchlin* from 1534 (itself a reworking of part of Erasmus of Rotterdam's *Colloquia familiaria*, first published in 1518)[11] presented Danish readers with a dialogue set in verse between two women, Karine and Dorothe, on the topic of marriage and women's marital duties. Karine complains to Dorothe of her husband's neglect in spending all their income on drinking, gaming, and whoring, leaving her to dress in tattered and worn-out clothes (Alberus: 1619, A4vff). Dorothe admonishes Karine to suffer these burdens in silence because she dishonors herself by openly chastising her husband (A5v). However, Karine admits to scolding her husband and defiantly declares that any attempt at a corporeal retort on his part will be repaid (A6v). Attempting to correct her friend, Dorothe refers to Paul's Epistle to the Ephesians to remind Karine of her duty to be humble and loving toward her husband. Dorothe asserts that women should be submissive and silent in order to avoid the anger of their husbands (A6r). She opines that a good wife must learn to bear with her husband and asserts that women often have themselves to blame for the abuse they suffer (B1vff). Dorothe says of her own husband: "If I do not want to quarrel with him, I must reconcile my mind to his." (B2v). She admonishes Karine to restrain her pride and obey her husband (B4r), adding that her own mother taught her always to heed the mood of her husband and do his bidding

11 The question of Erasmian influence on Lutheran ideas about marriage and family is too broad to consider in any detail here. However, I note that Erasmus' writings on marriage are characterized by an ambiguity towards women that is no less striking than Luther's, which should remind us that Lutheran marriage ideology did not emerge in a vacuum. Thus, while Erasmus regarded men as naturally superior to women and argued in favor of female subordination to male authority, he also emphasized the equality of the sexes before Christ and stressed the importance of mutual love between spouses, see Christ-von Wedel (2013, esp. chapter 18). Given such similarities, Alberus would likely have had little difficulty in adapting Erasmus' dialogue for his own purposes. Furthermore, Sommer's chapter in the present volume briefly discusses the possible influence of Erasmus' *Adages* on Hemmingsen's thought.

unconditionally: "Yes, were he to bid me run through fire, I would do so quite willingly, rather than offend him" (B5v), she declares. Later, she compares the relationship between husband and wife to the relationship between a mirror and that which it reflects: "When her husband laughs and is merry she should not cry and be sad. Nor go dancing and feasting when her husband is ill and mournful. Thus he knows that she is devoted to him." (B6r).

The exchange between the two women implicitly addresses the emotional economy of the marital household. It articulates limits of female displays of emotion and emphasizes female emotional deference as a means of establishing and maintaining marital harmony. In this context, Karine appears as the prototypical bad wife or "shrew" of late medieval and early modern satirical literature, so closely related to the stereotypical witch or "old hag" of popular imagination (cf. Brauner: 1995, 72ff). Unable to restrain her feelings and unwilling to bear the burdens placed on her, she is vociferous, crass, and potentially violent. She threatens to invert traditional gender hierarchies and usurp the husband as ruler of the household. In short, she is everything that an obedient and humble wife should not be.

If Karine of Alberus' dialogue gave dissatisfied and unhappy wives of early modern Denmark a voice – raging, as she did, against tyrannical husbands and lamenting women's fate as harnessed animals (B7v) – it was an act of literary ventriloquism by Alberus. He ultimately silenced his boisterous creation. In the end, Karine accepts the admonitions of her friend and declares that she will follow Dorothe's advice (C8rf).

The 1653 translation of German Pastor Johann Holtzmann's (d. 1657) marriage and conduct manual entitled *Fromme Quinders Speyel* by prominent Danish publicist Joachim Moltke (d. 1664) illustrates that such ideals of female deference and submissiveness were persistent in devotional books for women well into the seventeenth century.[12] It is worth briefly noting that Moltke's preface to the book echoes the characteristically ambiguous Lutheran understanding of the female sex: On the one hand, he blames Eve for "letting herself be deceived" by the Devil and so causing the fall of mankind (Holtzmann: 1653, 4vf). On the other hand, he emphasizes Christ's incarnation through 'woman's seed' and praises the excellence of women "not only because we are [...] brought into the world by them, but also because from them spring [...] the bodies that are necessary and useful in all offices in churches and schools in both the order of the household and the state." (5vf). For this reason, marriage has a central role in upholding Christian society, just as wives act as bulwarks against fornication and protect their husbands and society against the ravages of sin (6vf).

12 I have been unable to track down a copy of the German original.

Holtzmann's manual outlines the duties of the wife on the basis of an allegorical comparison with the characteristics of the female deer. In so doing, it summarizes much of what we have come to appreciate as central themes in Lutheran marriage and household books in terms of ideal feminine behavior. Obedience, submissiveness, humility, and chastity are keywords in Holtzmann's recurring admonitions for wives to mind their duties within the household. He enumerates such duties as managing the kitchen and yard, cleaning, sowing, supervising the servants, and raising the children (Holtzmann: 1653, 13.59.84). Here, too, the good wife is described as someone who knows not only how she should act but also how she should feel.

This ideal is articulated in terms of the contrast between anger and pride on the one hand, and humility and submissiveness on the other. A virtuous Christian wife "should be careful to guard against such shameful and improper anger and hatred, [should] not act as an image of the Devil, but strive for humility and restraint, and be kind and gentle with her dear husband; comfort, please, and delight him and not agitate him, nor drive him into quarrels or cause him grief." (15f). She must, Holtzmann maintained, continually strive to alleviate her husband's concerns and drive away negative emotions (17.49.78.90). Echoing Dorothe, the good wife of Alberus' *Ehebüchlin*, Holtzmann asserted that a wife must continually adjust her own emotional needs to those of her husband: "If the Husband is sad, she should not be happy; if he is happy, she should not be sad." (58). The bad wife, on the other hand, is portrayed by Holtzmann as an emotional deviant, much the same way as Karine in Alberus' dialogue:

> When the woman is defiant and angry and does not speak a kind word to her husband, but instead growls, rages and snarls without end, like a chained dog or a grim bear / Then one should rather live among lions and dragons than with such a bitter herb; nor are these Christian but ungodly women who wish to rule over their husbands. (45).

Intimately linked to anger is pride, the original sin of the female sex. According to Holtzmann, Eve's pride, her desire to raise herself up to equality with God, was the catalyst for mankind's fall (43). For a wife to rebel against the authority of her husband is deemed a repetition of that original transgression and a cause of divine anger (44). The implication is clear: A proud and domineering wife is not only a cause of marital disharmony but also an affront to God. In challenging her husband's authority, the wife rebels against divine and social order. Apparently, this was (still) an acute problem in Holtzmann's eyes since he noted the widespread frustration caused by women's desire to dominate and rule over men (41).

The remedy, he argued, was to ensure greater marital harmony: for spouses to be more forgiving of each other's faults and for women in particular to act toward their husbands "no differently than a female deer or a pleasing and humble roe deer, to submit and surrender in subservience and humility to the husband [...]"

(48). Towards the end of the manual, he once more drove home the point to his readers: Pious wives "should not be presumptuous nor arrogant and proud but rather modest, small, and humble; should always be demure and unassuming in their relationship with their husbands, follow and obey them in all just and proper things, and honor them appropriately." (95). Clearly, Holtzmann's concern was both with the wider social order as well as the emotional relationship between spouses. We must note the correlation that he and many of his fellow Lutherans assumed between emotional, social, and gender order: a wife who does not respect the emotional order of the marital union potentially undermines the entire fabric of hierarchical relations that sustains social harmony.

6. Conclusion

The current study indicates that when male and female readers in sixteenth- and seventeenth-century Denmark consulted the many marriage and household books available to them, they were very often met not only by a particular vision of the marital household as a social and religious unit but also by a set of emotional norms and "scripts" that were closely related to ideals of masculine and feminine behavior. Martin Luther's characteristically ambivalent attitude towards the status and the role of women carried over into Lutheran conduct literature. Along with it came his double-sided understanding of marriage as both an emotional partnership based on conjugal love and a hierarchical relation between husband and wife. As we have seen, when Lutheran moralists converted the Lutheran theology of marriage into guidelines and instructions concerning married life in the household, ideas of spiritual and emotional equality between the sexes tended to lose out to a traditional, hierarchical understanding of gender order. Luther's notion of conjugal love was not, in other words, translated into an understanding of marital intimacy as constituting a sphere of emotional equality, far less one of social equality. Rather, social inequality was reinforced by ideals of female emotional subjugation. Thus, emotional reciprocity between husband and wife tended to become marginalized by the concern for maintaining a social hierarchy. Emotional reciprocity was subsumed under the perceived need for female obedience to male (paternal) authority. Female obedience was conceived not merely as a social relation but as an emotional ideal tied to the role of the housewife vis-à-vis her husband. For all of our authors, a Christian housewife should not merely project the outward appearance of obedient behavior but should, more fundamentally, assume an "inward" emotional disposition of obedience.

Far from subverting traditional notions of female inferiority, the texts we have investigated predominantly cast women as objects of male control by promoting emotional norms that encouraged female readers to act and *feel* subservient to their husbands, while male readers were taught to expect and require subservience from their wives. This is not to say that ideals of emotional parity and companionship in marriage were completely eclipsed. Rather, Lutheran moralists writing about marriage as the foundation of Christian society in the post-Reformation era were, perhaps unsurprisingly, more preoccupied with articulating a vision of social order than with exploring the realm of marital intimacy. In the end, it was precisely the importance they ascribed to the marital union as the source of social cohesion that legitimized their attempt to extend the reach and depth of social control to the intimate sphere of the household and the emotional lives of their readers.

Bibliography

ALBERUS, ERASMUS (1619), Ecteskabs Samtale / Eller Dialogus, imellem Tuende Quinder / lystig oc nyttelig / alle dem som ere indgange / eller indgaa ville / det hellige Ecteskab / etc., trans. H.V., Copenhagen: s.n.

APPEL, CHARLOTTE (2001), Læsning og bogmarked i 1600-tallets Danmark, Copenhagen: Museum Tusculanum.

ARVIDSSON, BENGT (1991), Själens örtagård: Trädgårdskonstens betydelse för bildspråket i uppbyggelseslitteraturen omkring år 1600, Lund: Lund University Press.

BRAUNER, SIGRID (1995), Fearless Wives and Frightened Shrews: The Construction of the Witch in Early Modern Germany, Amherst, MA: University of Massachusetts Press.

CLASSEN, ALBRECHT (2005), Der Liebes- und Ehediskurs vom Hohen Mittelalter bis zum frühen 17. Jahrhundert, Münster/New York, NY/München/Berlin: Waxman.

CHRIST-VON WEDEL, CHRISTINE (2013), Erasmus of Rotterdam: Advocate of a New Christianity, Toronto/Buffalo, NY/London: University of Toronto Press.

CROWTHER, KATHLEEN M. (2010), Adam and Eve in the Protestant Reformation, Cambridge: Cambridge University Press.

FINK-JENSEN, MORTEN (2011), Printing and Preaching after the Reformation: A Danish Pastor and his Audiences, in: Charlotte Appel/Morten Fink-Jensen (ed.), Religious Reading in the Lutheran North: Studies in Early Modern Scandinavian Book Culture, Newcastle: Cambridge Scholars Publishing, 13–47.

FREVERT, UTE (2011), Emotions in History: Lost and Found, New York, NY/Budapest: Central European University Press.

GERLE, ELISABETH (2015), Sinnlighetens närvaro: Luther mellen kroppskult och kroppsförakt, Stockholm: Verbum.

GUTMANN, HANS-MARTIN (1991), Über Liebe und Herrschaft: Luthers Verständnis von Intimität und Autorität im Kontext des Zivilisationsprozesses (GTA 47), Göttingen: Vandenhoeck & Ruprecht.

GUTMANN, HANS-MARTIN (2013), Martin Luthers „christliche Freiheit" in zentralen Lebenskonflikten: Intimität gestalten, Verantwortlich leben, Freiheit realisieren, Berlin: EB-Verlag.

HOCHSCHILD, ARLIE (1979), Emotion Work, Feelings Rules, and Social Structure, AJS 85/3, 551–575.

HOCHSCHILD, ARLIE (1983), The Managed Heart: Commercialization of Human Feeling, Berkeley, CA: University of California Press.

HOLTZMANN, JOHANN (1653), Fromme Quinders Speyel / Eller Alle gudfryctige Matroners Plict oc Skyld imod Gud / deris Ecte=Mænd / Saa oc alle Mennisker / oc dem /selff, trans. Joachim Moltke, Copenhagen: Georg Lamprecht.

KARANT-NUNN, SUSAN (1992), Kinder, Küche, Kirche: Social Ideology in the Sermons of Johannes Mathesius, in: Andrew Fix/Susan Karant-Nunn (ed.), Germania Illustrata: Essays on Early Modern Germany Presented to Gerald Strauss (Sixteenth Century Essays & Studies 18), Kirksville, MO: Truman State University Press, 121–140.

KARANT-NUNN, SUSAN C. (1998), The Reformation of Women, in: Renate Bridenthal et al. (ed.), Becoming Visible: Women in European History, 3rd ed., Boston, MA: Houghton Mifflin, 174–201.

KARANT-NUNN, SUSAN C. (2010), The Reformation of Feeling: Shaping Religious Emotion in Early Modern Germany, Oxford: Oxford University Press.

KARANT-NUNN, SUSAN C./WIESNER-HANKS, MERRY E. (2003), Luther on Women, Cambridge: Cambridge University Press.

KOWALESKI, MARYANNE/GOLDBERG, P.J.P. (2008), Medieval Domesticity: Home, Housing and Household in Medieval England, Cambridge: Cambridge University Press.

LEMMER, MANFRED (1991), Haushalt und Familie aus der Sicht der Hausväterlitteratur, in: Trude Ehlert (ed.), Haushalt und Familie in Mittelalter und Früher Neuzeit, Sigmaringen: Jan Thorbecke, 181–191.

LEMMINGS, DAVID/BROOKS, ANN (2014), The Emotional Turn in the Humanities and Social Sciences, in: David Lemmings/Ann Brooks (ed.), Emotions and Social Change: Historical and Sociological Perspectives, New York, NY/London: Routledge, 3–18.

LUTHER, MARTIN (1519), A Sermon on the Estate of Marriage (LW 44: 7–14/WA 2: 166–171).

LUTHER, MARTIN (1524), Sermon at the Second Sunday After Epiphany (WA 15: 417–421).

LUTHER, MARTIN (1527), Sermons on Genesis (Karant-Nunn/Wiesner-Hanks: 2003, 16–25/WA 24: 1–710).

LUTHER, MARTIN (1529), The Small Catechism (BC 347–375/WA 30 I: 243–425).

LUTHER, MARTIN (1529), The Large Catechism (BC: 379–480/WA 30 I: 125–238).

LUTHER, MARTIN (1531), Eine Hochzeitpredigt (WA 34 I: 50–75).

LUTHER, MARTIN (1532), Men Cannot Get Along Without Women (LW 54: 160f/WA TR 2: 166, no. 1658).

MARTINI, LUKAS (1594), Alle Christelige oc dydelige Jomfruers ærekrantz. Udi huilcken alle deris Dyder / formedelst de almindelige Krantzeblomster oc Urter / affmalis oc forklaris, Copenhagen: Laurentz Benedicht (LN 1149).

MATHESIUS, JOHANNES (1571), Oeconomia eller Underuisning Huorledis en Husfader skal skicke sig, trans. Rasmus Hansen Reravius, Copenhagen: Laurentz Benedicht (LN 1150).

MATT, SUSAN J./STEARNS, PETER N. (2014), Doing Emotions History, Urbana, IL/Chicago, IL/Springfield, IL: University of Illinois Press.

MCNAMER, SARAH (2010), Affective Meditation and the Invention of Medieval Compassion, Philadelphia, PA: University of Pennsylvania Press.

Ozment, Steven E. (1983), When Fathers Ruled: Family Life in Reformation Europe, Cambridge, MA: Harvard University Press.

Rebhun, Paul (1575), Husfred. Det er Aarsager aff den hellige Scrifft, som skulle beuege alle Christelige Ectefolck, til at holde Fred oc Endrectighed i deris Husholdning, trans. Rasmus Hansen Reravius, Copenhagen: Heirs of Andrea Gutterwitz & Hans Stockelmann (LN 1366).

Roper, Lyndal (1989), The Holy Household: Women and Morals in Reformation, Augsburg, Oxford: Clarendon Press.

Saarinen, Risto (2005), Ethics in Luther's Theology: The Three Orders, in: Jill Kraye/Risto Saarinen (ed.), Moral Philosophy on the Threshold of Modernity, Dordrecht: Springer, 195–215.

Scheer, Monique (2012), Protestantisch fühlen lernen: Überlegungen zur emotionalen Praxis der Innerlichkeit, Zeitschrift für Erziehungswissenschaft 15, 179–193.

Shields, Stephanie A. (2002), Speaking from the Heart: Gender and the Social Meaning of Emotion, Cambridge: Cambridge University Press.

Stjerna, Kirsi (2009), Women and the Reformation, Oxford: Blackwell Publishing.

Weber, Matthias (1572), Hus Taffle / huvorledis huert Menniske udi sit Kald oc stat skal skicke sig / baade mod GUD oc Mennisken, trans. Rasmus Hansen Reravius, Copenhagen: Vingaard (LN 1608).

Wiesner, Merry E. (1987), Luther and Women: The Death of Two Marys, in: Jim Obelkevich et al. (ed.), Disciplines of Faith: Studies in Religion, Politics and Patriarchy, London: Routledge, 295–308.

Witte Jr., John (2002), Law and Protestantism: The Legal Teachings of the Lutheran Reformation, Cambridge: Cambridge University Press.

Wunder, Heide (1992), "Er ist die Sonn', sie ist der Mond": Frauen in der Frühen Neuzeit, Munich: C.H. Beck.

Nina Javette Koefoed

The Lutheran Household as Part of Danish Confessional Culture

> God has given this walk of life, fatherhood and motherhood, a special position of honor, higher than that of any other walk of life under it. Not only has he commanded us to love parents but to honor them. (BC 400f//WA 30 I: 147,22ff)

1. Introduction

Luther elevated the relation to parents above all other secular relations when he explained the fourth commandment in his *Large Catechism.* Other hierarchical relations extended from this primary relation; all authorities in household, church, and state were to be honored as parents. In this way, Luther placed the household at the center of the secular world. He emphasized the household, the work done within it, and its social relations as the main path for a pious life. This innovation must be understood both as part of his critique of celibacy and indulgences within the Catholic Church as well as a consequence of his theology of creation. However, neither of these contextual dimensions will be the focus of this chapter. Instead, the aim is, first, to analyze Luther's understanding of the social and emotional relations and responsibilities within the household as a social teaching; and then, to investigate the influence of this social teaching on the social developments in seventeenth and eighteenth-century Denmark.

Luther's *Small* and *Large Catechisms* are important sources for transmitting Luther's understanding of the social and emotional relations within the household. These two texts were translated into Danish soon after the Reformation and were quickly known to a Danish audience. By focusing on the influence of these texts, this chapter will examine how the understanding of responsibilities within the social relations of the household developed in the Danish tradition through a central explanation of the *Small Catechism* printed in the early eighteenth century. The chapter will also probe how the Lutheran social teaching on the family influenced government legislation in the seventeenth century, culminating in early absolutism after 1660. Finally, the chapter will briefly discuss day-to-day practices in correspondence with religious and legislative understandings of social responsibilities within the household as popular interpretations of these practices emerge from court- and prison records and petitions in the eighteenth century. Court cases help to determine widespread norms by identifying incursions against those norms. By studying these seventeenth- and eighteenth-century sources, it becomes possible to determine the influence of Luther's ideas on culture and popular perceptions.

Thomas Kaufmann's understanding of "confessional culture" supplies an important interpretive frame for this chapter. Kaufmann attends to specific developments within a given political and geographical setting through the intersection of confession and culture; that is between the structures, symbols, metaphors, and discourses of the confession and the mentality, emotions, and thoughts behind everyday practices of ordinary people (Kaufmann: 2006, 3–26).[1] Drawing on this perspective, I will argue that the confessional influence over everyday life can be found through a combination of confessional influence on the content and emphases of childhood education[2] and legislative developments.[3] The time period of interest, the seventeenth- and eighteenth-centuries, is central to my argument since the mono-confessional situation in Denmark was uninterrupted from the Reformation until the 1849 Constitution. The 1849 Constitution legislatively transformed the Lutheran state church into a national church, still regulated by the state and financed through taxes. This situation offers a unique long timespan for confessional influence on society, and I will argue that this influence did not culminate before the rise of absolutism in 1660 and became especially clear in the 1683 law code, *Danish Code.*

2. Confessional and Legal Background

After the Danish Reformation in 1536, a Church Ordinance in 1537 (translated from Latin into Danish in 1539) described the new church order and the relation between the king and the Church by drawing on the Lutheran understanding of the two kingdoms. The Ordinance focused on the king's obligation to ensure that the words of God regulated the earthly kingdom. The Ordinance regulated church services and ceremonies, election of the clergy, clerical work and payment, care of the poor, and education. Childhood education was structured according to Luther's *Small Catechism* (Rørdam I, 119; Appel: 2001, 139). An

1 See also the introduction in this volume.

2 This co-existed with various other kinds of influence through written culture already shown by research (cf. Appel: 2001).

3 For the legislative process in the eighteenth-century as an interaction between state, church and state, see Koefoed (2008).

ordinance in 1629 mandated that content knowledge of Luther's *Small Catechism* be a prerequisite for receiving communion, establishing a kind of confirmation (Secher IV, 470; Appel: 2001, 145). Further, a treaty from 1643 again emphasized the duty of the pastor to teach the catechism from the pulpit as part of the sermon (Secher V, 148). I will return to the content of the catechism below, the point here is its central position in the development of a confessional culture through childhood education.

One duty of the Lutheran king was to organize the church and make sure his people were raised in the right belief (Ingesman: 2000, 82). Another duty was legislation, a tool to ensure proper Christian behavior amongst the subjects. In 1643, King Christian IV dispersed a general treaty that included legislation to regulate social relations and responsibilities within the household. The treaty is structured in two books: one on the clergy and its office and another on secular order (Secher V, 140–354).[4] In this way, the treaty reflects the church ordinance and its description of the relation between king and God. But by including regulation of the church and the secular society in one law, it also points forward towards the law code promulgated by the absolute king in 1683, the *Danish Code* (DL). The first three books of the *Danish Code* were formatted according to the three estates: government, church, and household. Furthermore, the sixth book on criminal law followed the structure of the Ten Commandments. Between the treaty of Christian IV and the *Danish Code*, the 1665 *King's Code* (KL) underscored the King's obligation to rule according to the Augsburg Confession.

3. Social Relations Built on the Fourth Commandment

Both the *Small* and the *Large Catechism* were translated into Danish immediately following the Reformation. The *Small Catechism* was central to childhood education and it can be assumed that knowledge of the catechism was widespread as a result of education both at home and at school. Most people were able to read it themselves. Also, the *Large Catechism* was widely disseminated, known by all local pastors and by the elite. Likely, masters of large households were familiar with it too (Appel: 2001, 131; contribution by Jakobsen in this volume). Both catechisms consisted of the Ten Commandments, the Creed, the Lord's Prayer, the sacrament of the altar, and the sacrament of the baptism. The table of duties occurred only in the *Small Catechism*. It is discussed when the table of duties entered the Danish translations of the *Small Catechism*, but it was at least part of it from the beginning of the seventeenth century (Appel: 2001, 143–148).

4 There is a third book on Norway, not included in this study.

The table of duties introduced the doctrine of the three estates. Quoting scripture, the table of duties explained how to fulfill the will of God in daily life and relations. According to Luther, the three estates – government, church, and the household – regulate social order in the earthly kingdom. All members of society belong to all three domains, either commanding those below or obeying those above oneself. According to Luther, these hierarchical structures between individuals consisted of mutual obligations. In the household, in particular, these obligations were both social and emotional (see also Koefoed: 2017). Through childhood education and the table of duties, the household along with the socio-emotional obligations within it became an important tool in the king's attempt to ensure the pious Christian life of his subjects. As research has shown, pastors commonly referenced the table of duties in their sermons without further clarification or explanation until the mid-eighteenth century (Bregnsbo: 1997, 103–125). This suggests a shared cultural context having to do with popular familiarity with the table.[5] It is important to stress that this was not only a question of disciplining the subjects, but also of ensuring religious instruction and salvation for the subject and the country as a whole.

The fourth commandment, "to honor your father and your mother," was the foundation of the table of duties.[6] Luther explained in the *Small Catechism* that to "honor your father and your mother" meant to "fear and love God; so that we neither despise nor anger our parents and others in authority, but instead honor, serve, obey, love, and respect them" (BC 352/WA 30 I: 244,12–19). The obligation to obey both biological parents and all authorities also becomes clear in the *Large Catechism.* The fourth commandment was to be understood as God's model for all social relations; within each of the three estates, authorities were to be obeyed as if they were parents. The table of duties balanced the obligation to obey with the authority's duties (rather than rights) towards the obedient person.[7] The household contained three possible social relations: between husband and wife,

5 The cultural influence from the table of duties has not been subject to much research in Scandinavia, but Swedish research has, to a greater extent than Danish, discussed the concept of the Lutheran household and the extent to which the table of duties had more than ideological influence (Pleijel: 1970; Ahlberger/Malmstedt: 1993). The main conclusion of this research has been that the catechism and the table of duties might have been widely spread, also that its ideology did not lead to the existing of a strong household ideology in the early modern period. Later legal, cultural studies in Sweden have suggested a much stronger element of household culture (See Jansson: 2002; Marklund: 2004; Hansen: 2006; Brilkman: 2013). This chapter builds on the latest part of this research into the cultural expectations of household members.

6 Luther's understanding of authority in his explanation of the fourth commandment is also discussed by Vercruysse (1974). His focus is on the obligation to honor and not on the obligations embedded in authority.

7 Danish research has often focused on the right of the head of the household to castigate (cf. Henningsen: 2006; Jacobsen: 2008).

between parent and children and between master and servant. Although each type of relation could be reduced to a relation between commanding and obeying, the table of duties explained the social and emotional obligations within each relation differently. The *Large Catechism* explained the mutual obligations between parents and children and between masters and servants in more details through the explanation of the fourth commandment rather than the table of duties.

The *Large Catechism* went into more detail regarding the obligations of children than the table of duties. The table of duties did not go into further detail than the explanation of the fourth commandment in the *Small Catechism* mentioned above. The *Large Catechism* had a more extended explanation of the fourth commandment in which Luther explained the hierarchical relations of the household as the will of God. Even though we are all equal to God, Luther thought that inequality between humans is necessary. Parents function as God's representatives, and because the hierarchical order of the household reflects the order of God, the most pious deed was to honor one's parents (BC 401/WA 30 I: 147,23–148,6). Luther defined honor using numerous attitudes and behaviors. To honor one's parents is to "esteem them above all things," but also to behave respectfully in words and actions, that is "serving them, helping them, and caring for them when they are old, sick, feeble, or poor." This should be done "with humility and reverence, doing it as if for God" (BC 401/WA 30 I: 148,7–15). Obedience to the fourth commandment was the best way to do good and holy works, and these works of honor would be rewarded in the temporal life (BC 401 ff/WA 30 I: 147 ff). Those who honored their parents would live a long life in peace and harmony with "health, spouse and child, sustenance, peace, good government, etc." (BC 404f/WA 30 I: 151,28f). Here, Luther explained human obligations in social relations and also the good earthly life. Although common people may not have read the *Large Catechism* themselves, parish pastors had access and familiarity with this text and likely disseminated its contents to their parishioners through teaching.

Luther not only discussed the obligation to obey in his treatment of the fourth commandment. The relationship between parents and children built on mutual obligations. In the table of duties, Luther reminded parents of their duty to raise their children through discipline and the words of God. But he also warned parents not to anger their children (BC 366/WA 30 I: 400,13 ff). Parents' obligations towards their children were described in more detail in other parts of the *Small Catechism.* In the guidelines for confession, Luther told every subject to confess according to the Ten Commandments and their position within the household. Confession was mandated if "you had been disobedient, unfaithful, lazy, whether you have harmed anyone by words or deed; whether you have stolen, neglected, wasted or injured anything" (BC 360/WA 30 I: 384,10–13).

Confession was based on one's fulfillment of the duties connected to one's position in the world. More specifically, parents would have to confess if they did not raise their children to honor God, but rather, had been bad examples through evil words and deeds (BC 361/WA 30 I: 386,1 f).

Luther offered more specifics about parental obligations in the *Large Catechism*. In order to raise obedient children for "happiness, love and peace" in the household, parents needed to set good examples for their children. Obedient children learned pious living in households characterized by good and loving feelings. Therefore, parents had to live pious with a Christian lifestyle themselves. They were not to be tyrants, but "earnestly and faithfully discharge the duties of their office" (BC 409/WA 30 I: 156,12). Moreover, parents should raise their children and servants "to serve God and the world," that is to be both good Christian people and good citizens of the state in both the heavenly and the earthly kingdoms (BC 410/WA 39 I: 156,27 f). Luther talked about obedience towards both parents, but only of the authority of the father, indirectly pointing to the wife as equal to her husband in honor, but part of a hierarchical system in which only the husband possessed authority. All authority was to be regarded as father and to have a father's heart. The social relations and the obligations outside the household were thus similar to those inside: "through civil rulers, as through our own parents, God gives us food, house and home, protection and security, and he preserves us through them." (BC 407/WA 30 I: 153,32 ff).

In the table of duties, servants were commanded to obey their masters "with fear and trembling," not because they should want to please any human being, but in order to "do the will of God from the heart with a good will." Both the servants and masters were reminded that good deeds would be rewarded by the Lord, no matter if they were free or servants (BC 366/WA 30 I: 401,1–7). Masters should not use threats, but remember that all are equal to God (BC 367/WA 30 I: 401,8–11). The table of duties indicated that God would reward those who fulfilled their position in this world, whether master or servant. The *Large Catechism* further developed this idea. The most direct way for a servant to live a pious life was to fulfil her servant's obligations: "a servant girl would dance for joy and praise and thank God; and with her careful work, for which she receives sustenance and wages, she would obtain a treasure such as those who are regarded as the greatest saints do not have." (BC 406/WA 30 I: 153,11–14). All work, even work within the household, became the will of God and doing this work constituted the pious life.

In the *Large Catechism*, Luther complained that people did not regard the fourth commandment with enough esteem and underlined that God wants human beings to be punished for breaking the commandments. He addressed the punitive task assigned to authorities, saying: "Now, if you are unwilling to answer your father and mother or to take direction from them, then answer to the executioner; and if you will not answer to him, then answer to the grim reaper, death!" (BC 405/WA 30 I: 151,30 ff). It was the obligation of political authorities to enforce the commandments. The fourth commandment took on special weight in this regard because parental authority was delegated from God to ensure social order in the earthly kingdom. This both legitimized and obligated the intervention of the state in what could be regarded as household affairs. In the doctrine of the three estates, the *Large Catechism* specifies that all authorities were to be honored like parents. Parents were to be regarded as fathers of the house, fathers of the country, and spiritual fathers, that is in the household, in government, and in church (BC 405 f/WA 30 I: 152,19–35).

The obligations Luther placed on the different positions within the household were not only social obligations, but they were also emotional as well. The husband was to be gentle towards his wife; it was important not to make her bitter (BC 366/WA 30 I: 400,1–6). And even though parents were obliged to discipline their children in order to give them a good, Christian upbringing, it was important not to make them angry (BC 366/WA 30 I: 400,13 ff). Likewise, servants were not to be threatened (BC 367/WA 30 I: 401,8–11). The duty to obey was also connected with emotions. The wife should not fear her husband; children were not to feel anger towards their parents. They should not only honor, but also respect their parents, like servants were reminded to do their duty from the heart.

Taken together, the socio-emotional obligations defined the social relations between individuals and the identity associated with one's position within the household. The master of the house was commanding, but also had an obligation to be reasonable and fair. He had an obligation to ensure the right emotions within the household, to create an atmosphere in which anger, bitterness, and threats were prohibited emotions, and to raise his children as good Christians and citizens. The obedient members of the household should obey not only as an earthly duty but also as a divine calling. By attending to household emotions, it becomes clear that Luther did not understand the authoritative side of a social relation as an unrestrained right to power, but as an obligation to establish a certain ethos within the household (See also Koefoed: 2017).

4. Development of the Theological Frame in the Eighteenth Century

In 1736, the pietistic king, Christian VI requested confirmation. The following year, the king approved the printing of an official explanation of the *Small Catechism*, written by Erik Pontoppidan, thus distributing an official teaching of Luther. Researchers have explained this as a pietistic break with seventeenth-century orthodox Lutheranism, pointing to the exclusion of the table of duties from the explanation as a marker of this text's declining social influence (Horstbøll: 2003). I argue contrary to this that the ongoing social influence of the table of duties has to do with the way the table's social structures built on the fourth commandment. The table's socio-emotional obligations did not disappear with the table's explanation. Instead, they were integrated into the specific explanation of the fourth and the sixth commandment and, thus, relocated from a tangential position in the appendix to a central part of the Catechism. I will further argue that this move was inspired by the *Large Catechism*, establishing a close relationship between the explanation and Luther's understanding of social relations and identities within the household. Pontoppidan did not just establish a new explanation for the commandment. Rather, he widely dispersed Luther's understanding in the *Large Catechism* to all who formerly were only acquainted with the *Small Catechism* and the table of duties. He did so in a more structured way, focusing more on the obligations themselves that the society their fulfillment would create.

The explanation explicitly likened all authorities in their respective estates to parents. The document concretized the reference to the doctrine of the three estates by mentioning parents in government, church,[8] and household (Pontoppidan: 1737, § 161–162). The table of duties and the understanding of social relations comprised of mutual obligation emerged in the explanations for obligations within each estate. The obligation to obey parents was highlighted in all three estates as the order of God for the welfare of the individual. Unlike Luther in the *Large Catechism*, Pontoppidan did not go on to develop ideas about the kind of household that would result from this parental obedience. This left his reader with a good understanding of how to behave as a good Christian and citizen, but lacking a theological grasp of why.

Within the estate of the government, subjects had to obey and honor the authorities, to pray for them, and to pay their taxes (Pontoppidan: 1737, §163, 165). Inversely, in a concretization of the obligations Luther described in the *Large Catechism*, the government was responsible for tending to its subjects' eternal and earthly welfare, to maintain peace and good order, to punish evil and reward goodness (Pontoppidan: 1737, §169). Similarly, subjects in the estate of the church were obligated to love, honor, obey, reward, and to pray for their teachers. Teachers were obligated to teach, admonish, and punish their listeners with a loving and tender heart, to pray for them and to be a good example (Pontoppidan: 1737, §173–174). This definition of setting a good example was vaguer than the description found in the table of duties for the example of

8 The function of teaching is underlined rather than the service as a church.

pastors. In Pontoppidan, the focus was more concentrated on the teaching role of ministers than the role as an example.

Finally, in the estate of the household, Pontoppidan began with parents' obligations to their children. First of all, parents had to pray for their children and tend to their earthly, spiritual, and eternal well-being (Pontoppidan: 1737, §177). Parents were obligated to provide for and educate their children, to raise them as good Christians and citizens. Pontoppidan also mentioned discipline. Parents should discipline disobedient children, but in a sensible and loving way, not out of anger but for the child's betterment (Pontoppidan: 1737, §178). Discipline should not be avoided, but this was not license to unlimited violence towards one's child. Balance was required in the discipline of children. Pontoppidan maintained children's traditional obligations to their parents. Children were required to honor, love, serve, and obey in heart, thoughts, words, behavior, and deeds. These obligations never ended, but actually continued into adulthood, even when children gained wealth and power. Finally, children were to pray for their parents (Pontoppidan: 1737, §181).

Pontoppidan then turned to describe the relations between masters and servants using the parental language. Masters, as fathers and mothers of their households, were obligated to provide their servants with sufficient food and to pay them on a timely basis. Like parents, masters were to rule and govern servants with loving patience and to take care of their bodily needs, especially in cases of illness, and their spiritual needs through education and admonition (Pontoppidan: 1737, §184). For their part, servants were to love, honor, and obey their masters, always to do their best, to be hard-working, and to pray for their master (Pontoppidan: 1737, §185). In addition to the mutual duty to pray for one other, Pontoppidan placed greater emphasis on the working relationship between master and servant.

Pontoppidan carefully explained obligations within each of the three estates. In doing so, he cultivated the social order of the kingdom. In particular, Pontoppidan gave greater specificity to earthly obligations, clarifying it is a direct application of the larger structure of society than is found in Luther. However, Pontoppidan abandoned some of the religious understanding and commentary on the fourth commandment that Luther included in the *Large Catechism.* Additionally, Pontoppidan added gender specificity to the obligations, pointing towards a more gendered understanding of the obligation not necessary indicated in Luther's *Catechism* (See also Koefoed: 2017). Through Pontoppidan, Luther's doctrine of the three estates clearly became a social teaching and a concrete model for society.

5. Regulating the Household: The Responsible Parent and Master

Childhood education and catechisms were not the only means by which new understandings of the household and the socio-emotional relations within it were disseminated. Legislative developments between during the seventeenth century also dispersed these new social models.

In 1643, during the late years of his orthodox Lutheran regime, Christian IV ratified a treaty that legislated certain duties also seen in Luther's Catechism: the parental duty to raise good, Christian children, the general duty to go to school, and the duty to work honestly. The treaty required every town to establish a board of guardians. This was not in itself a new phenomenon. Previously, a board of guardians supervised the economic interests of children placed under guardians. But now, the board of guardians was given new responsibilities to supervise the Christian behavior of young people and their parents more generally, in addition to the board's past monitoring of economic concerns for children and guardians (Secher V, 232f). The treaty also specifies that every child must have an occupation. If parents did not take responsibility for the proper upbringing of their children, then the board of guardians was responsible (Secher V, 234f; also in Secher III, 678ff). The paragraph specifically addresses parents, not guardians. Therefore, we must assume it is the Christian upbringing done in ordinary households in the towns that are in focus here.

This legislation was integrated into the *Danish Code* in 1683. Part of the third book that regulated the household had to do with marriage, guardians, children, and servants. Here, the general requirement that each town establish a board of guardians was reiterated. As in the 1643 treaty, the board was to monitor all guardians in the town and the children in their care (DL 3–18–1). But they also had to have "surveillance with how the youth was raised, as well as with how the parents kept their children" (DL 3–18–2). The board of guardians was to maintain records of possible violations by parent or child and, then, to pass these records onto their successors to make them aware of possible parental neglect (DL 3–18–5). The *Danish Code* listed the kinds of activities the board was to monitor, including: "parents keeping their children, boys or girls, to school, honest service, trade or craftsmanship." Even if parents did not require their children to work for economic reasons, parents were nevertheless required to prepare their children for a particular occupation. If parents failed to do this, the board of guardians was required to do so at the parents' cost (DL 3–18–7). Here, we see an echo of the emphasis on work, childhood education, and the parental duty to raise good Christians and citizens that Luther developed in his *Large Catechism.*

Boards of guardians were only established in towns. In the countryside, we must assume that most of this obligation was placed on the estate owner. But not exclusively; the parish pastor also had a role to play. The *Danish Code* stated that pastors were obligated to monitor their parishes and to visit homes in order to ensure that parents educated their children and taught them a craft (DL 2–7–1).[9]

The *Danish Code* also carefully regulated the relationship between master and servants. Among other things, it specified when servants were personally culpable for their actions or when culpability fell to their masters. Much of the regulation had to do with the terms of service, specifying conditions under which a servant could enter or leave a contract, which was only possible twice a year (DL 3–18). Thus, an obligation to work, to be in someone's service, and to belong to someone's household was actually built into this legislation. Every individual was part of a household; it was not possible to be without a household or without work.

6. Creating the Good Christian Household in Practice

The seventeenth and, especially, the eighteenth centuries saw the development of new poor- and workhouses, which functioned to carry out the obligations assigned to parents and masters. As early as 1620, Christian IV built a 'child-house' connected to an existing workhouse. This child-house was intended to teach orphaned and poor children the *Small Catechism* and a decent trade (Olsen: 1978). In 1738, a prison and workhouse (manufacturing facility) was built in Viborg, a central town on the Jutland. The workhouse had a clear, religious motivation (Allernaadigste Fundatz: 1745, 2–3). It took in people who could not pay their fines for a variety of crimes and needed to work their fines off instead. This included people convicted for sexual relations outside marriage, "unfaithful and obstinate servants, vagrants and beggars who were not permitted to beg" (Allernaadigste Fundatz: 1745, cap. 2, art. 1–3). While the last group had to be convicted of a crime before they were imprisoned, the other two already were so, but unable to pay their fine.[10] Disobedient children and married couples who were living together in conflict or behaving in other ways unbecoming of Christians were also relegated to the prison and workhouse in Viborg. It fell to local pastors to call attention to unchristian marital life. A clerical court then

9 As other parts of this legislation, this obligation on the pastor was developed in legislation during the seventeenth century and integrated into DL in 1683.

10 As pointed out by Lis/Soly (1996) the workhouses in Holland was also used to correct and discipline, but the behavior needed not necessarily to be criminalized. In Denmark, deeds against the ten commandments were criminalized and the workhouse used for correction in relation to criminal behavior convicted in court.

heard two or three witnesses before sending married couples to the workhouse for a certain amount of time (Allernaadigste Fundatz: 1745, cap. 2, art. 4). The prison and workhouse was meant for people who did not obey the command to work and be part of a household, and for those who threatened the household by violating the fourth or sixth commandments. The workhouse was also used to provide work for the poor in exchange for welfare resources from the town. The poor, however, were not considered to be imprisoned. Thus, the people who ended up in the poor- and workhouses had not just broken the law but were those who had publically behaved in an unchristian way and violated the moral norms of local societies.

A new prison and workhouse was also built in the central town of Funen, Odense in 1749. The religious dimension in the founding deed was less obvious here. The first chapter of the deed did not address the religious aspect of the workhouse, but potential inmates. Additionally, one paragraph states that this workhouse was for beggars who could work, pointing specifically to their laziness (Fundation: 1752, art. 1). The next paragraph addresses another class of the poor: namely, those who were too weak to work, but still lived as vagrants and beggars despite the availability of poor relief in their home parish. They were also to be arrested and placed in the workhouse for a certain period of time after conviction (Fundation: 1752: art. 2). Thus, the workhouse and prison in Odense placed more emphasis on correcting attitudes to work and lifestyles of the poor more generally.

The Odense workhouse also functioned as a destination for disobedient children, servants, and married people living an unchristian life together. However, these groups could be sent to the workhouse after a trial at the lowest court, not through a special church court as was the case in Viborg (Fundation: 1752, art. 2). And as a special condition, if parents or masters could prove that an offense was serious enough to demand formal correction and pay the cost of correction themselves, they could place disobedient children and servants in the workhouse for correction without any formal convict (Fundation: 1752, art. 4). It was underscored that the persons had to be released from the workhouse when their behavior improved and that the stay should not influence their honor. Although the particular religious frame for the prison and workhouse disappeared in the founding deed for the Odense prison and workhouse, focus was more concentrated on correcting the immoral life of vagrancy, drinking and begging, and on correcting disobedience within the hierarchical relations of the household, though not quite as clearly between spouses.[11]

11 Even though the workhouse here could be used as a house of correction on the initiative of the master of the house, the legal regulation and demand for a convict seem to be stronger than in the Calvinist houses of Corrections in Holland at the time (Lis/Soly: 1996).

Like the child-house in Copenhagen, the prison and workhouse in Odense accepted children as young as 12 and 14. As the founding deed clarified, these kids could be placed in the workhouse at the prerogative of their master. Often this was the result of disobedience, but also so the children could work and learn a trade. This reflects the parental obligation specified in the law to ensure the education and honest work of their children, but local authorities also used the workhouse to rear children in their care. In 1753, Peder from Nyborg, for example, was sent to the workhouse by his local authorities at age 15. His guardians determined that the workhouse would be the best place for him to learn to work and to have his Christian childhood education. Peter was described as having both neglected his Christian upbringing and as being unstable at work, drifting around even though he was not exactly begging (Prison record Odense, no. 78). It is not absolutely clear that disobedience was the problem at the time when Petten Høbsheman, aged 12, was placed in the workhouse. Rather, it seems he was there to sufficiently learn a trade so that he might earn his own living (Prison record Odense, no. 79). He was placed there by a Councilor of State, who had taken the education of the boy upon himself and fulfilled the obligation through the workhouse.

Children of inmates were also placed in the prison and workhouse together with their parents (Prison record Odense, no. 61–64). Anne Sophie Jørgensdatter was 13 years old when she was sent to the workhouse by the local authorities because her father (and apparently only parent) was there. She had been begging with him her whole life, learned no occupation other than begging, and could not earn her living (Prison record Odense, no. 71). Karen Lauritzdatter was 20 when her local pastor sent her to the prison and workhouse in Odense. Because of her frivolous and loose lifestyle, she had not received the Eucharist for two years and showed no respect for either the pastor's attempt or her parents' to correct her. (Prison record Odense, no. 70). As it turns out, the workhouse was used, not only to create discipline within the household when the parents' or master's authority proved insufficient, the workhouse was used to ensure a Christian upbringing in childhood education and to provide decent work for poor children who were, for one reason or another, outside a household.[12]

A petition to the absolute king displayed the understanding of parents' and masters' responsibility to ensure children's proper behavior and education. As late as 1775, a county governor complained to the King because the young people of the town were making noise in the street day and night instead of going to school. He suggested that they should be arrested if they were found in

12 These and other examples are chosen to indicate the overall picture and the kind of argumentation.

the streets without legal reason and business. Moreover, important in this context, their parents or master should be kept responsible. The King agreed with him, and it was decided that younger children who caused a public nuisance should be punished with the rod. Older children were to be imprisoned for 24 hours on bread and water. In addition to this, parents and masters of the house were to be fined and, in the event they were unable to pay, to serve time in prison (Petition, 24.05.1775). Parental obligation did not end at the walls of the house. Rather, the way young people behaved outside the household was the responsibility of the parents and master of the house. These obligations were created and implemented by the absolute king, the government, through law, but also infused by local authorities.

7. Regulating the Household: Disobedient Children and Servants

Luther thought that parents were obligated to both keep children in school and also to discipline them. In the *Small Catechism*, parental discipline was limited so as not to evoke the child's anger. The sixth book of *Danish Code* expanded discipline as a right to chastise with the cane, but not weapons. Discipline was further limited by a prohibition from harming the child's health (DL 6–5–5). If the line of just discipline was crossed, the parent was to be punished as if he (or she) had harmed a stranger. When it came to masters and servants, masters were prohibited from illegal or unjustifiable treatment of their servants. In cases where this standard was violated, servants were able to bring a case against the master as though he were a stranger (DL 6–5–10). Then, if the line of legal violence, of expected discipline, was transgressed, the violence moved from within the household relations into society.

The parental obligation to keep their children in school and proper work was instituted indirectly through the board of guardians, part of the third book on the household. The way in which children were to honor and obey was formulated through the criminal law in book six as part of a chapter dealing with violence within the household. Jonas Liliequest has pointed to the fact that special legislation for children's violence against parents did not develop until after the Reformation in Sweden in 1536 (Liliequist: 2014). In Denmark, this kind of legislation first emerged with *Danish Code.*

The first three paragraphs of chapter five in the sixth book of *Danish Code* focused on crimes committed by children against their parents, a direct violation of the fourth commandment and the duties written into the table of duties. The first paragraph stated that:

> Anyone proven to be disobedient towards their parents, of contempt for their Christian admonition to fear God, to honesty, to soberness, to peacefulness, to hard work and to be provident and the like, loses their inheritance after them. (DL 6–5–1).[13]

This paragraph shows that the violation of the obligation to obey and honor was punishable by a symbolic cancellation of the parent-child relationship. Inheritance rights were built on kinship, to lose this right was to lose the sign of familial bond – and probably to abrogate the parental responsibility. At the same time, the paragraph also defines the ways in which children were expected to obey. In doing so, it outlines the content of the Christian life that was to be inculcated in children by their parents.

While the first paragraph punished violation of the fourth commandment understood as disobedience and lifestyle, the second paragraph moved to regulation of verbal assault of parents:

> If anyone swears at their parents or talks shamelessly to them or speaks against their honor and welfare, they lose their inheritance, and are to be punished with work and iron on Bremmerholm, that is if it is a male person, and Spindehuset, that is if it is a female person, for their lifetime. (DL 6–5–2).[14]

This paragraph defines verbal assault as a means of dishonoring. Through this, it clarifies how the forbidden anger and lack of respect, underlined in the table of duties, is expressed and regulated. Thus, the legislation defines what it means "to honor and obey," and draws the lines around it. The punishment for a verbal violation of the fourth commandment is both the symbolic abatement of the parent-child relationship seen in the first paragraph and exclusion from society by means of a life sentence. This is only exceeded by the death penalty, which is connected to a child's physical violence against its parents, as stated in the third paragraph: "If anyone hits their parents, then they are to lose their neck." (DL 6–5–3).[15]

Together the three paragraphs regulating the behavior of children towards their parents displayed an understanding of the obligation to honor and obey as a way of life, words, and physical behavior.

---

13 "Findes nogen at være sine Forældre ulydige, og foragte deres christelige Formaninger til Guds Frygt, Ærlighed, Ædruelighed, Fredsommelighed, Flittighed, Sparsommelighed og deslige, og det skielligen bevises, miste Arv efter dennem." Translated by author.

14 "Bander nogen sine Forældre, eller dennem ubluelig tiltaler, eller paataler paa Ære og Lempe, miste Arv, og straffes med Jern og Arbeid paa Bremmerholm, om det er Mands-Person, eller i Spindehuset, om det er Qvindfolk, deres Livs-Tid." Translated by author.

15 "Slår nogen sine Forældre, da er det halsløs Gierning." Translated by author.

8. Disobedience in Practice

Among other places, the limits of masters' right to use violence were negotiated in petitions. When subjects felt that their master had crossed the line between legitimate and illegitimate violence, they turned to their king for help. The law granted them the right to bring cases against their master, but it could be a difficult ordeal to undertake. In 1715, Jens Knudsen asked for help to bring a case against his master (who happened to be the local pastor) because the pastor had used violence against him. Knudsen was granted help because he had not been treated fairly (Petition, 24.09.1715, Book OO, no. 171). But in the same year, when Niels Nielsen asked for help because he had been physically assaulted by the master of his house, it was not granted. Nielsen had even unsuccessfully brought a court case against his master. But when he asked the King for support, it was argued that he had not been crippled by the assault (as required by the law). On the contrary, the chancellery judged that he had been disobedient and, on this basis, the discipline was fair. He had even been offered an out-of-court settlement but rejected it (Petition, 18.06. 1715, book NN, no. 586). Several factors distinguish the two cases. In the first, the man asking for help was a master of the house himself, just the smaller household of a serf. Moreover, he did not ask the King to intervene directly, only to let him bring the case to court. Thus, he moved across estates – from one in which he was commanding to one in which he was obedient. In the other case, the applicant was apparently a servant who asked the King to correct a court judgment, a quite different matter.

Just as the prison and workhouse in Odense helped parents and masters fulfill their duty to provide education and work for their children, the prisons and workhouses also served a more direct disciplinary or punitive purpose for violations of the fourth commandment. Several people were imprisoned for disobeying their parents or master. Even the prison in Viborg, which primarily took in adult populations, took adults on the basis of disobedience. This indicates that the obligation to honor and obey parents and master went unchanged as 'children' grew into adulthood.

The length of prison sentence varied as did, we can safely assume, the concrete cause and conflict behind the sentence. Poul Nielsen from Aarhus, for example, was imprisoned indefinitely in 1759 for disobedience against his parents. It is difficult to say from the prison record which kind of disobedience brought with it a sentence of indefinite confinement. Nielsen was thirty years old at the time of his prison sentence and died in prison six years later in 1765. He would have served time together with the 36-year-old, Mette Knudsdatter, who, in 1764, was imprisoned for two years because of disobedience against her parents and insubordination to her master. However, she was released after serving only one year, indicating the purpose of her sentence was to re-discipline or correct her.

Erich Kristensen seems to have been a problem in general when he was imprisoned for three years in 1764 for disobeying his parents as well as for adultery and drunkenness. He was released after only serving half a year of his sentence, which could suggest that he himself had a family to provide for.[16] Likewise, a woman of unknown age was prisoned for one year in 1768 due to insubordination of her parents. She served the whole year. Elisabeth Hansdatter also served her full sentence when she was imprisoned for two years for disobeying and being insubordinate to her parents in 1769 (Prison record Viborg).

People were also imprisoned for disobeying their masters. In 1767, Poul Pedersen Søbye was sentenced to a one-year imprisonment for willful insubordination of his master. He was released after only half a year. The following year, in 1768, a woman of unknown age was imprisoned for three weeks for disobeying her master (Prison record Viborg). It is not possible to derive many details of these cases from the prison records, but they do tell us about a commonplace and practical criminalization of unchristian behavior in social relations within the household. Thus, these records reveal the attempts by legislators, local authorities, and common people themselves to uphold and create Christian households.

9. In Conclusion

After the Reformation, the household changed position. Marriage shifted from being a sacrament under clerical jurisdiction to a secular institution under secular jurisdiction. The household also became a central feature of the social order of society. Moreover, the household became the locus of the pious life, giving a central meaning to the fourth commandment. Both the work done within the household and obedience towards parents and masters was appointed a central role in the pious life by Luther. This chapter has argued that Luther's doctrine of the three estates and his elevation of the fourth commandment as a model for all social relations was an influential social model in the development of a Danish confessional culture. Through childhood education and legislation, the household was placed as a central social unit and the obligations within it as important features of a pious life. Social relations within the household were hierarchical, but at the same time structured by mutual obligations. The duties in the social relations had both an emotional and a social quality.

The *Small Catechism*, the table of duties, and childhood education laid the foundation for the understanding of the obligations in the social relation of the

16 See Koefoed (2008; 214f) for the implication of the obligation to provide the punishment of fathers and husbands (see Koefoed: 2008, 214f).

household. The understanding of the doctrine of the three estates as a social model and social relations as build on the fourth commandment was strengthened through Pontoppidan's explanation of the catechism and the legislation of the absolute king. By drawing on the three estates and by making the obligations connected to work and household more specific and concrete, while removing part of the religious explanation of the obligations, Pontoppidan helped to turn the religiously-motivated understanding of the socio-emotional obligations within the household into a secular social model.

In the *Large Catechism*, Luther emphasized the importance of parental obligations to raise their children as both good Christians and good citizens. Later, this emphasis found its way into the legal history, which underscored parents' duty to raise their children in the right Christian faith and for honest work. The role of the board of guardians along with the use of workhouses to teach children a trade and catechesis both indicate the development and integration of this obligation into everyday practice during the seventeenth century.

The further specification of the obligation to honor and obey in the *Danish Code* points towards the central position of the fourth commandment in the development of a confessional culture in Denmark. Inherent to this was the description of violence against parents in the *Danish Code* as lifestyle, words, and deeds. This reflects Luther's own definition of the obligation to obey in heart, thoughts, words, and deeds. The practice of the prison and workhouses reflect this social obligation. Here, both children and servants were punished for disobedience. Finally, petitions to the king reflect certain forms of negotiation between superiors and subordinates in relation to the parental obligation. Petitions to the king both functioned to enforce the parental duty of parents and masters to keep young people in school and work, but also to negotiate and limit their power.

The understanding of authority within the household, reflected in the state, should be seen as part of a Danish confessional culture. This culture develops out of an understanding of the fourth commandment as made up of mutual socio-emotional obligations. Through the concept of the three estates, these mutual obligations were made concrete in legislation and in the explanation of the *Small Catechism*. The prison records indicate cultural reflection on these obligations within the household as well as an understanding of the Christian household, but this requires further study.

Bibliography

AHLBERGER, CHRISTER / MALMSTEDT, GÖRAN (1993), Västsvensk fromhed: Jämförande studier av västsvensk religiositet under fyra sekler, Gothenburg: Göteborg Universitet.

Allernaadigste Fundatz Og Reglement For Det Viborgske Manufactur- og Tugthuus (1745), Viborg: Johan Peters Holtkberg.

APPEL, CHARLOTTE (2001), Læsning og bogmarked i 1600-tallets Danmark, vol. 1–2, Copenhagen: Museum Tusculanum Press.

BREGNSBO, MICHAEL (1997), Samfundsorden og statsmagt set fra prædikestolen, Copenhagen: Museum Tusculanum Press.

BRILKMAN, KAJSA (2013), Undersåten som förstod: Den svenska reformatoriska samtalsordning och den tidligmoderne integrationsprocessen, Skellefteå: Artos.

Fundation Til Det med Kongl. Allernaadigst Approbation oprettede Tugt- og Manufactuurhuus, udi Odense, For Fyen og Langeland Med underliggende Øer (1752), Odense: s.n.

HANSEN, ANNA (2006), Ordnade hushåll: Genus och kontroll i Jämtland under 1600-talet, Uppsala: Studia Historica Upsaliensia.

HENNINGSEN, PETER (2006), I sansernes vold: Bondekultur og kultursammenstød i enevældens Danmark, Copenhagen: Landbohistorisk Selskab.

HORSTBØLL, HENRIK (2003), Læsning til salighed, oplysning og velfærd: Om Pontoppidan, pietisme og lærebøger i Danmark og Norge i 17- og 1800-tallet, Fortid og Nutid, 83–108.

INGESMAN, PER (2000), Kirke, stat og samfund i historisk perspektiv, in: Tim Knudsen (ed), Den nordiske protestantisme og velfærdsstaten, Aarhus: Aarhus Universitetsforlag, 65–86.

JACOBSEN, ANETTE FAYE (2008), Husbondret: Rettighedskulturer i Danmark 1750–1920, Copenhagen: Museum Tusculanum Press.

JANSSON, KARIN HASSAN (2002), Kvinnofrid: Synen på Våldtäkt och konstruktionen af kön 1600–1800, Uppsala: Studia Historica Upsaliensia.

KAUFMANN, THOMAS (2006), Konfession und Kultur: Lutherischer Protestantismus in der zweiten Hälfte des Reformationsjahrhunderts (SuR.NR 29), Tübingen: Mohr Siebeck.

KOEFOED, NINA (2008), Besovede kvindfolk og ukærlige barnefædre: Køn, ret og ægteskab i 1700-tallets Danmark, Copenhagen, Museum Tusculanum Press.

KOEFOED, NINA (2017), Emotions, Obligations and Identities within the Lutheran Household: From Luther's Small Catechism to Cultural and Social Responsibilities in the 18th Century Household in Denmark, in: H. Assel/J.A. Steiger/A. Walter (ed), Reformatio Baltica: Kulturwirkungen der Reformation in den Metropolen des Ostseeraums, Berlin/Boston, MA: Walter de Gruyter, 751–768.

MARKLUND, ANDREAS (2004), I hans hus: Svensk manlighet i historisk belysning, Umeå: Boréa.

LILIEQUIST, JONAS (2014), "The Child Who Strikes His Own Father or Mother Shall Be Put to Death": Assault and Verbal Abuse of Parents in Swedish and Finnish Countries 1745–1754, in: Olli Matikainen/Satu Lidman, Morality, Crime and Social Control in Europe 1500–1900, Helsinki: Finnish Literature Society, 19–42.

Lis, Catharina/Soly, Hugo (1996), Disordered Lives: Eighteenth-Century Families and their Unruly Relatives, Cambridge: Polity Press.
Luther, Martin (1529), The Large Catechism (BC: 379–480/WA 30 I: 125–238).
Luther, Martin (1529), The Small Catechism (BC 347–375/WA 30 I: 243–425).
Olsen, Olaf (1978), Christian 4.s tugt- og børnehus, Holstebro: Wormianum.
Pleijel, Hilding (1970), Hustavlens värld: Kyrkligt folkliv i äldre tiders Sverige, Stockholm: Verbum.
Pontoppidan, Erik (1737/1902), Sandhed til Gudsfrygtighed udi en enfoldig og efter Mulighed kort, dog tilstrækkelig Forklaring over Sal. Doct. Mort. Luthers liden Katekismus indeholdende alt det, som den, der vil blive salig har behov at vide og gøre, Copenhagen: N.B. Kongsgaards Forlag.
Vercruysse, Jos E. (1974), Conscience and Authority in Luther's Explanation of the Fourth Commandment, in: Heiko A. Oberman (ed), Luther and the Dawn of the Modern Era: Papers for the Fourth International Congress for Luther Research, Leiden: Brill, 184–194.

Petitions

Danske Kancellis Supplikprotokoller, Copenhagen: Selskabet for udgivelse af kilder til Dansk Historie (2005).

Archival sources

Prison records in the Danish National Archives:
Viborg: Viborg Tugthus, Fortegnelse over fanger 1763–1779, B-204, pakke nr. 57–58.
Odense: Odense Tugthus, Bog over tugthusfanger (1752–1865).

List of Abbreviations

AES Archives européennes de sociologie/European Journal of Sociology, Cambridge: Cambridge University Press, 1960–.

AJS American Journal of Sociology, Chicago, IL: University of Chicago Press, 1895–.

AKG Arbeiten zur Kirchengeschichte, Berlin/Boston, MA: Walter de Gruyter, 1915.

AKThG Arbeiten zur Kirchen- und Theologiegeschichte, Leipzig: Evangelische Verlagsanstalt, 1996–.

ARG Archiv für Reformationsgeschichte/Archive for Reformation History, Berlin/Boston, MA: Walter de Gruyter, 1904–.

ASD *Opera omnia Desiderii Erasmi Roterodami, Amsterdam/Oxford/Leiden/Boston, MA: North-Holland Publishing Company/Brill, 1969–.*

BC Robert Kolb/Timothy J. Wengert (ed.) (2000), The Book of Concord: The Confessions of the Evangelical Lutheran Church, Minneapolis, MN: Fortress Press.

BHTh Beiträge zur historischen Theologie, Tübingen: Mohr Siebeck, 1929–.

BSELK Irene Dingel (ed.) (2014), Die Bekenntnisschriften der Evangelisch-Lutherischen Kirche: Vollständige Neuedition, Göttingen: Vandenhoeck & Ruprecht.

CChr.SL Corpus Christianorum, Series Latina, Turnhout: Brepols, 1953–.

CR Karl Gottlieb Bretschneider/Heinrich Ernst Bindseil (ed.) (1834–1860), Corpus Reformatorum, vol. 1–26: Philippi Melanthonis Opera Quae Supersunt Omnia, Halle/Braunschweig: Schwetschke.

DBL Dansk Biografisk Leksikon, http://denstoredanske.dk/Dansk_Biografisk_Leksikon.

DI Diplomatarium Islandicum: Jón Sigurðsson/Jón Þorkelsson/Páll Eggert Ólason/Björn Þorsteinsson (ed.), Íslenzkt fornbréfasafn, sem hefir inni að halda bréf og gjörninga, dóma og máldaga, og aðrar skrár, er snerta Ísland eða íslenzka men, vol. 1–16, Copenhagen/Reykjavík: S.L. Møller, 1857–1972.

DL: Danske Lov (Danish Code): KONG CHRISTIAN den FEMTEs Danske Lov af 1683, Copenhagen: Casper Peter Rothe, 1753.

DM Danske Magazin, Copenhagen: Det Kongelige Danske Selskab for Fædrelandets Historie, 1745–.

FKDG Forschungen zur Kirchen- und Dogmengeschichte, Göttingen: Vandenhoeck & Ruprecht, 1952–.

FMSt Frühmittelalterliche Studien, Berlin/Boston, MA: Walter de Gruyter, 1967–.
FSÖTh Forschungen zur systematischen und ökumenischen Theologie, Göttingen: Vandenhoeck & Ruprecht, 1962–.
GTA Göttinger Theologische Arbeiten, Göttingen: Vandenhoeck & Ruprecht, 1975–.
HST Handbuch systematischer Theologie, Gütersloh: Gütersloher Verlagshaus, 1979–.
HT Historisk Tidsskrift, Copenhagen: Den danske historiske Forening, 1840–.
HZ Historische Zeitschrift, Munich: Oldenbourg, 1859–.
JBTh Jahrbuch für Biblische Theologie, Göttingen: Vandenhoeck & Ruprecht, 1986–.
JEMC Journal of Early Modern Christianity, Berlin/Boston, MA: Walter de Gruyter, 2014–.
Jónsbók Ólafur Halldórsson (ed.), Jónsbók: Kong Magnus Hakonssons Lovbog for Island vedtaget paa Altinget 1281 og Réttarbætur, de for Island givne retterbøder af 1294, 1305 og 1314, Copenhagen: S. L. Møller, 1904.
JusEcc Jus ecclesiasticum: Beiträge zum evangelischen Kirchenrecht und zum Staatskirchentum, Tübingen: Mohr Siebeck, 1965–.
KHS Kirkehistoriske Samlinger, Copenhagen: Selskabet for Danmarks Kirkehistorie, 1849–1913.1933–.
KiO Martin Schwarz Lausten (1537/1989) (ed.), Kirkeordinansen: Ordinatio Ecclesiastica Regnorum Daniae et Norwegiae et Ducatuum Sleswicensis Holtsatiae etcet., Copenhagen: Akademisk Forlag.
KL *Kongeloven* (*King's Code*): KONGELOVEN af 14. november 1665, http://danmarkshistorien.dk/leksikon-og-kilder/vis/materiale/kongeloven-1665/
LC Large Catechism, BC 379–480/WA 30 I: 125–238.
LN Lauritz Nielsen (1996), Dansk Bibliografi 1482–1600: Med særligt hensyn til dansk bogtrykkerkunsts historie, vol. I–IV, Copenhagen: C. A. Reitzel.
LStRLO Leucorea-Studien zur Geschichte der Reformation und der Lutherischen Orthodoxie, Leipzig: Evangelische Verlagsanstalt, 2002–.
LuJ Luther Jahrbuch, Göttingen: Vandenhoeck & Ruprecht, 1919–.
LuthQ Lutheran Quarterly, Baltimore, MD: Johns Hopkins University Press, 1949–.
LW Martin Luther (1955–1986.2009–), Luther's Works: American Edition, St Louis, MO/Philadelphia, PA: Concordia Publishing House/Fortress Press.
ML.St Mediaevalia Lovaniensia, Leuven: Leuven University Press, 1972–.
MSA Philipp Melanchthon, Werke in Auswahl [Studienausgabe], Gütersloh: Bertelsmann, 1951–1975.
NZSTh Neue Zeitschrift für systematische Theologie und Religionsphilosophie, Berlin/Boston, MA: Walter de Gruyter, 1959–.
PL Patrologiae cursus completus, Series Latina, ed. Jacques Paul Migne, Paris: Impremerie Catholique, 1841–1855.
QFRG Quellen und Forschungen zur Reformationsgeschichte, Gütersloh: Gütersloher Verlagshaus, 1923–.
R5AS Refo500 Academic Studies, Göttingen: Vandenhoeck & Ruprecht, 2011–.
RGG[4] Die Religion in Geschichte und Gegenwart, 4th ed., Tübingen: Mohr Siebeck, 1998–2005.

Rørdam	Holger Frederik Rørdam (ed.) (1883–1889), Danske Kirkelove samt Udvalg af andre Bestemmelser vedrørende Kirken, Skolen og de Fattiges Forsørgelse, 1536–1683, vol. I–III, Copenhagen: Selskabet for Danmarks Kirkehistorie.
SC	Small Catechism, BC 347–375/ WA 30 I: 243–425.
Secher	V.A. Secher (ed.), Corpus Constitutionum Daniæ: Forordninger, Recesser og andre kongelige Breve, Danmarks Lovgivning vedrørende, 1558–1660, vol. I–IV, Copenhagen: Rudolph Klein.
SMHR	Spätmittelalter, Humanismus, Reformation, Tübingen: Mohr Siebeck, 2007–.
SMRT	Studies in Medieval and Reformation Thought, Leiden/Boston, MA: Brill, 1966–.
STC	A Short-Title Catalogue of Books Printed in England, Scotland, & Ireland and of English Books Printed Abroad, 1475–1640, 2nd ed., London: The Bibliographical Society, 1976–1991.
SuR.NR	Spätmittelalter und Reformation. Neue Reihe, Tübingen: Mohr Siebeck, 1990–2007.
SVRG	Schriften des Vereins für Reformationsgeschichte, Gütersloh: Gütersloher Verlagshaus, 1883–.
TBT	Theologische Bibliothek Töpelmann, Berlin/Boston, MA: Walter de Gruyter, 1952–.
TRE	Theologische Realenzyklopädie, Berlin/Boston, MA: Walter de Gruyter, 1976–2004.
VD 16	Verzeichnis der im deutschen Sprachbereich erschienenen Drucke des XVI. Jahrhunderts, http://www.vd16.de.
VIEG	Veröffentlichungen des Institut für Europäische Geschichte Mainz, Göttingen: Vandenhoeck & Ruprecht, 1952–.
WA	Martin Luther (1883–2009), D. Martin Luthers Werke: Kritische Gesamtausgabe, Abteilung Schriften, Weimar: Böhlau.
WA DB	Martin Luther (1906–1961), D. Martin Luthers Werke: Kritische Gesamtausgabe, Abteilung Deutsche Bibel, Weimar: Böhlau.
WA TR	Martin Luther (1912–1921), D. Martin Luthers Werke: Kritische Gesamtausgabe, Abteilung Tischreden, Weimar: Böhlau.
ZEvKR	Zeitschrift für Evangelisches Kirchenrecht, Tübingen: Mohr Siebeck, 1951–.
ZHF	Zeitschrift für historische Forschung, Berlin: Duncker & Humblot, 1974–.
ZKG	Zeitschrift für Kirchengeschichte, Stuttgart: Kohlhammer, 1877–.

List of Authors

Svend Andersen, dr. theol., Professor in Systematic Theology, Department of Theology, Aarhus University.

Agnes Arnórsdóttir, dr. phil, Associate Professor in Medieval and Early Modern history, Department of History and Classical Studies, Aarhus University.

Theodor Dieter, Prof. Dr., Director of the Institute for Ecumenical Research, Strasbourg.

Hans-Martin Gutmann, Dr., Professor in Practical Theology, Department of Practical Theology, University of Hamburg.

Gorm Harste, dr. scient. pol. Associate Professor in Political Sociology, Department of Political Science and Government, Aarhus University.

Bo Kristian Holm, PhD, Associate Professor in Systematic Theology, Department of Theology and Center Director for LUMEN: Center for the Study of Lutheran Theology and Confessional Socities, Aarhus University.

Rasmus Skovgaard Jakobsen, PhD-student, Department of History and Classical Studies, Aarhus University and The Danish Research Centre for Manorial Studies.

Thomas Kaufmann, Dr., Professor in Church History, Faculty of Theology, University of Göttingen.

Nina Javette Koefoed, PhD, Associate Professor in Eighteenth and Nineteenth Century history, Department of History and Classical Studies, Aarhus University.

Candace L. Kohli, PhD, Visiting Assistant Professor, Department of Religious Studies, Northwestern University.

Laura Katrine Skinnebach, PhD, post-doc., Department of Art History, Aarhus University.

Mattias Skat Sommer, PhD-student, Department of Theology, Aarhus University.

Sasja Emilie Mathiasen Stopa, PhD, post-doc., Department of Theology, Aarhus University.

Søren Feldtfos Thomsen, PhD, Independent researcher.

Vítor Westhelle, PhD, Professor in Systematic Theology, Lutheran School of Theology at Chicago.

List of Illustrations

Index of Names

Index of Subjects